THE CONSISTORY AND SOCIAL DISCIPLINE
IN CALVIN'S GENEVA

The Consistory and Social Discipline in Calvin's Geneva

Jeffrey R. Watt

UNIVERSITY OF ROCHESTER PRESS

First published 2020
University of Rochester Press
668 Mt. Hope Avenue, Rochester, NY 14620, USA
www.urpress.com
and Boydell & Brewer Limited
PO Box 9, Woodbridge, Suffolk IP12 3DF, UK
www.boydellandbrewer.com

ISBN-13: 978-1-64825-004-0
ISSN: 1542-3905; vol. 22
Cataloging-in-Publication data available from the Library of Congress.

Cover illustration: *John Calvin Presiding over the Company of Pastors of Geneva in 1549* from *Harmsworth History of the World: Western Europe from the Middle Ages to the Close of the Napoleonic Era* (London: Educational Book Company, 1914). Lithograph based on a painting from ca. 1852 by Pierre-Antoine Labouchère.

For Isabella, again and always

CONTENTS

ABBREVIATIONS

AEG	Archives d'État de Genève
C.O.	*Ioannis Calvini Opera Quae Supersunt Omnia*, edited by Gulielmus Baum, Eduardus Cunitz, and Eduardus Reus. Brunswick: C.A. Schwetschke and Sons, 1834–1968.
Jur. Pen. A1	"Livre des informations prises contre ceulx de la faction de Perrin, Vandel et complices"
Jur. Pen. A2	Juridictions Pénales A2, "Livre des Criminelz," i.e., sentences passed by the Conseil, 1559–1561.
Jur. Pen. A3	Juridictions Pénales A3, "Livre des Criminelz," i.e., sentences passed by the Conseil, 1562–1564.
Jur. Pen. K1	Juridictions Pénales K1, "Rapports et Renvois du Consistoire, 1559–1797"
PC	Procès Criminels, 1ère et 2e Séries
RC	Registres du Conseil de Genève (du Petit Conseil, Conseil des LX, Conseil des CC, et du Conseil Général, 1409–1792)
R.Consist.	*Registres du Consistoire de Genève à l'époque de Calvin* (published editions)
R.Consist.	Registres du Consistoire de Genève (archival manuscripts)
RC Part.	Registres du Conseil pour les affaires des Particuliers

ILLUSTRATION

ACKNOWLEDGMENTS

Although I was unaware of it at the time, I began work on this book way back in 1987. Having just defended my dissertation, under strong encouragement from my mentor, Robert Kingdon, I agreed to take part in the initial stage of the ambitious project to transcribe and publish scholarly editions of the registers of the Consistory during the time of John Calvin. I accordingly spent several weeks that summer at the Meeter Center at Calvin Seminary in Grand Rapids, Michigan, transcribing the minutes of the first volume. In the decades that followed, I have pursued research projects that had nothing to do with the Consistory, but I have always maintained an interest in this morals court, which finally became the principal focus of my research in the early 2000s. Given how long it has taken to bring this book to fruition, the list of people I need to thank is obviously lengthy.

Without the project to publish the volumes, fourteen of which have now appeared in print, I would never have undertaken this monograph. I of course owe a huge debt to Bob Kingdon. Aware of how rich these sources are, he assembled a team of scholars and secured many years of funding to pursue this ambitious project. He deserves heartfelt thanks from all scholars interested in the Reformation in Geneva. Tom Lambert dedicated many years to the project and served as coeditor for the first several volumes. His superb paleographical skills and incredible attention to detail have left a lasting positive imprint on the editions, and he remains most generous in sharing his knowledge of this institution. He graciously agreed to set aside time to read parts of this manuscript, and I am most grateful for his advice. Many thanks also to Wallace McDonald, another former member of the team who made very important contributions to many of the volumes. My profound appreciation goes to my good friend Max Engammare, director of Droz, for his steadfast support for the project. His erudition and attentive reading of the volumes have been invaluable, and collaborating with him since the 1990s has been a wonderful experience. Many kind thanks also to Christophe Chazalon, who, starting with volume 7, has assiduously read all the annotations and has made numerous suggestions for improvements in them. I am also quite grateful to Lee Palmer Wandel, Bob Kingdon's successor at the University of Wisconsin, for the financial support we continued to receive for several years after Bob's passing.

I also want to express my deep appreciation to the superb staff of Geneva's Archives d'État, one of the richest and almost certainly the best organized archive in all of Europe. My sincere thanks therefore to Catherine Santschi and Pierre Flückiger, the past and present Archiviste d'État, and I am especially much obliged to Sandra Coram-Mekkey, Anouk Dunant Gonzenbach, and Barbara Roth-Lochner for their most generous assistance. Over the years I have benefited enormously from the exchange of ideas with numerous scholars who share an interest in early modern Geneva. These include Christian Grosse, Liliane Mottu-Weber, Philip Benedict, Cristina Pitassi, Daniela Solfaroli Camillocci, Nicolas Fornerod, Sonia Vernhes Rappaz, Karen Spierling, Scott Manetsch, Elsie McKee, Michel Grandjean, Bernard Lescaze, Michel Porret, Antoinette Emch-Dériaz, and William Naphy. I have also profited greatly from the exchange of ideas with Raymond Mentzer, the dean of historians of consistories, as well as with other esteemed scholars, such as Merry Wiesner-Hanks, James Farr, Barbara Diefendorf, Joel Harrington, David Whitford, Hal Parker, Ward Holder, Bruce Gordon, Michèle Robert, Jon Balserak, Danièle Tosato-Rigo, and Paul Thayer.

Work on this book has been facilitated by extended stays as a guest scholar in various venues. Many thanks to the Meeter Center and to its former and current directors, Rick Gamble and Karin Maag, for providing funding for the Consistory project at its inception. I spent a delightful semester as a guest fellow at the University of St. Andrews in the spring of 2009, and I thank Bridget Heal and Andrew Pettegree for affording me that great opportunity. In the fall of 2010, thanks to friend and colleague Philippe Chareyre, I was honored to be a Professeur invité at the University of Pau. Sharing ideas about consistories with Philippe was and continues to be most fruitful, and I deeply appreciate his warm hospitality. More recently, I had the pleasure of being a guest professor at the University of Geneva's Maison de l'histoire and Institut d'histoire de la Réformation, and I thank in particular Daniela Solfaroli Camillocci for her efforts behind that appointment, which allowed me to complete the last details of archival research.

Here at the University of Mississippi, I thank my three successive chairs—Robert Haws, Joseph Ward, and Noell Wilson—for their strong support of my scholarly pursuits. I have truly benefited from the rich exchange of ideas with a number of colleagues, especially Les Field, Kees Gispen, Marc Lerner, Nicolas Trépanier, Theresa Levitt, and Isaac Stephens. My sincere gratitude goes also to

Lee Cohen, dean of the College of Liberal Arts, as well as his predecessor, Glenn Hopkins, for the generous research support they provided. I am also indebted to Ron Wilson, director of development, for his genuine interest in the Consistory project and his tireless efforts to find funding for it, and to Frank and Judith Mitchener for their generous support.

I am quite happy to be publishing again with the University of Rochester Press. Sonia Kane, editorial director, expressed an interest in this book several years ago, and I appreciate her patience in waiting for the manuscript. Working with her and her colleagues at the Press, most notably Rio Hartwell and production manager Tracey Engel, has been a distinct pleasure. My appreciation also to Mack Holt and James Collins, editors of the series Changing Perspectives on Early Modern Europe for their guidance and support. I am indebted to the two anonymous readers for their constructive criticism, and special thanks to Amy Burnett, John Thompson, Mack Holt, and Tom Lambert for sharing their ideas about how best to answer a provocative question raised by one of the readers. I am quite pleased that this book is part of the Sustainable History Monograph Pilot program funded by the Mellon Foundation and administered by Longleaf Services. I thank Longleaf's Ihsan Taylor for diligently overseeing the production process of this book. Through her meticulous copyediting, Elsa Dixler improved the prose and showed the need to clarify some imprecisions.

Far and away my greatest debt is to my much better half, Isabella Watt. A few months after our marriage, she came upon me sitting in front of a microfilm reader trying to decipher the notoriously bad handwriting of the Consistory records. When she told me that looked like fun, I suggested she have a seat to get a closer look. Thus began her uninterrupted work—thirty-three years and counting!—on the Consistory project. Though trained as a geologist, Isabella has become a superb paleographer and has done far more work on the project than anyone else. Without her contributions, only a small fraction of the volumes would have appeared in print, and without those editions, this and a host of other studies would have never been possible. In addition to serving as my IT specialist, she pored over the manuscript and made some very good recommendations for changes. What I owe her professionally, however, pales compared to what I owe her personally. Finally, many thanks to Julia and Plicca for continuing to make two happy people even happier.

Introduction

THROUGHOUT HISTORY, THERE HAVE been a few city-states whose cultural influence far surpassed their political, military, or economic power. Ancient Athens may have suffered a humiliating defeat in the Peloponnesian War, but its impact on philosophy, theater, and history far eclipsed that of any other ancient *polis*. Renaissance Florence was not a great political power but the literary, artistic, and cultural flowering unleashed by native sons such as Petrarch, Boccaccio, Michelangelo, and Leonardo extended throughout Italy and beyond. And in the sixteenth century, the small independent city of Geneva had an enormous influence in the area of religion, and perhaps no other city-state has been so closely identified with one historical figure. For better or for worse, ever since the Reformation, Geneva has been associated with the French reformer John Calvin, who transformed his adopted city into the so-called Protestant Rome. This study examines the Consistory, a type of morals court that was created by Calvin himself and was a key instrument for implementing the Reformation in Geneva. This institution had jurisdiction over a wide range of "sins" such as blasphemy, illicit sexuality, Catholic practices, drunkenness, and simply quarrels, to name just a few. Its registers are a gold mine of information concerning popular culture and the reception of the Reformation in the city and the surrounding countryside. Geneva's Consistory also served as a model for disciplinary institutions wherever Reformed Protestantism or Calvinism took hold.

Nestled below the Jura Mountains at the site where the Rhône River flows out of Lac Léman, Geneva was the episcopal seat of a large diocese, and in the late Middle Ages the bishop wielded temporal power over the city and the surrounding territory. The bishop of Geneva, however, was increasingly coming under the influence of the Duke of Savoy; indeed, starting in the fifteenth century, all bishops were either members of the House of Savoy or close supporters of the duke. Not surprisingly, religious and political motivations were tightly intertwined in the Reformation in Geneva. In the early sixteenth century, many Genevan citizens chafed under Savoyard influence and dreamed of throwing off the bishop and the duke and forming an independent republic. A key development

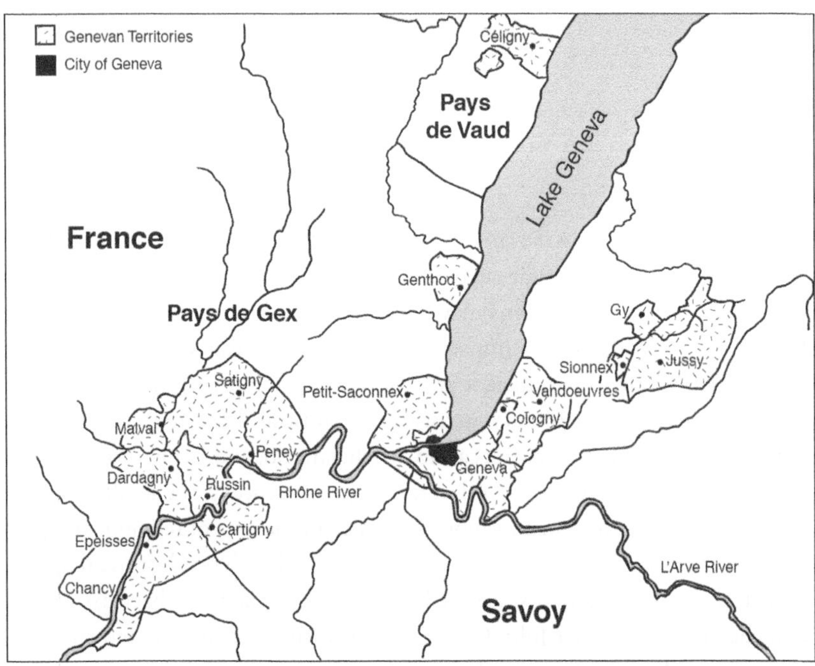

FIGURE I. Map of Early Modern Geneva and Its Territories. From Jeffrey R. Watt, *Choosing Death: Suicide and Calvinism in Early Modern Geneva*. Sixteenth Century Essays & Studies Series. Kirksville: Truman State University Press, 2001. Based on map in Paul Guichonnet, ed., *Histoire de Genève* (Toulouse: Privat, 1974), 237. Reproduced with permission from Penn State University Press.

toward independence was an alliance made in 1526 between Genevan citizens and the Swiss cantons of Fribourg and Bern, both enemies of Savoy. In 1532 the French reformer William Farel started proselytizing in the city with strong support from Bern, which had converted to Protestantism in 1528 and was the most powerful member of the Swiss Confederation. After the bishop and the duke attacked Geneva militarily in 1534, the city's magistrates declared that the office of bishop was vacant. After a series of iconoclastic attacks, in August 1535 the celebration of the Mass was prohibited in Geneva, and on May 21, 1536, the General Council of Geneva, composed of all male citizens over twenty, voted unanimously to embrace Protestantism.[1]

At this time, Farel was the most prominent religious leader in the city, but he recognized the talent of his younger compatriot, John Calvin, a native of Noyon in Picardy, who happened to be passing through Geneva on his way to Strasbourg in the summer of 1536. Farel met with the twenty-seven-year-old Calvin and warned him that he would incur God's judgment if he did not stay to assist the Reformation there. Calvin reluctantly agreed to do so, a decision that would have a profound effect on both Geneva and the Reformation.[2] As William Monter aptly noted, "No other [European] city won its independence in the sixteenth century and then succeeded in preserving it for over two hundred and fifty years." This "new and tiny urban republic provided Calvin with the ideal political base for his experiments, and probably colored Calvin's interpretation of economic and social issues."[3]

Among the changes brought by the Reformation was the reduction in the number of churches (or temples) in the city from seven to three: Saint-Gervais, La Madeleine, and the cathedral of Saint-Pierre.[4] Moreover, four of the five male religious houses were razed, part of the Franciscan house was converted into a school, and the house of the Poor Clares, Geneva's only nunnery, became the city's hospital or poorhouse. The reduction in the number of Genevan clergy was even more remarkable. On the eve of the Reformation, a good estimate suggests that Geneva, with a total population (including its faubourgs) of about 12,000, was probably home to approximately five hundred priests, monks, friars, and nuns. With the Reformation, by contrast, pastors numbered no more than a half dozen in the city, even though the population eventually doubled during Calvin's ministry because of the flood of refugees into Geneva. Including the ministers serving the various churches in the countryside brought the total number of pastors to around fifteen.[5]

Shortly after the break with Rome, Farel wrote a confession of faith, perhaps with some assistance from Calvin, which the Small Council—consisting of twenty-five members in whom political and judicial power was concentrated—approved in November 1536. This confession included aggressive attacks on a range of Catholic beliefs and practices, most obvious in its denunciation of the Mass as "diabolical."[6] While Genevan authorities accepted this confession, only with considerable reluctance did they agree in 1538 to Calvin and Farel's wishes to oblige all citizens to swear fealty to it. Immediately thereafter the two reformers overplayed their hand by firmly resisting efforts to conform to the liturgical practices of the powerful ally Bern.[7] What most upset the reformers, however, was the Council's refusal to allow the church the authority to excommunicate those deemed unworthy of taking communion. Calvin and Farel showed their displeasure by refusing to administer communion—or as Reformed Protestants preferred to call it, the Holy Supper—on Easter and defending their decision from the pulpit even though they had been expressly forbidden to do so. This act of rebellion promptly led to the expulsion of Calvin and Farel from the Republic on April 23, 1538.[8] Calvin left for Strasbourg, expecting never to return to the shores of Lac Léman.

After an exile of three years, Genevan authorities, recognizing his considerable talents, invited Calvin to return to lead the church there. He agreed to do so on two conditions: that Geneva have a catechism to educate all residents in basic Christian doctrine and that it implement a form of discipline to ensure that all residents behaved in a Christian manner. Magistrates acceded to these requests, and Calvin accordingly did return and drew up ecclesiastical ordinances, approved by the General Council in November 1541. These provided a blueprint for the organization of the church in Geneva, including the creation of an institution called the Consistory for the enforcement of discipline.[9] In order to address a wide range of moral infractions committed by residents of Geneva, the Consistory, comprising the city's pastors and elders, met every Thursday morning and, if the quantity of business required it, sometimes reconvened after lunch and, later, occasionally also met on Tuesdays. Far from being an ivory-tower scholar, Calvin faithfully attended the meetings of the Consistory, missing only when impeded by poor health or travel. From the creation of the Consistory in late 1541 until his death in 1564, he and his colleagues essentially dedicated at least one day a week to listening to the serious sins and peccadilloes of Genevans and to exhort them to forswear their wayward behavior.[10]

Reformed Protestants, including Calvin, placed a great deal of emphasis on discipline, considerably more than did Lutherans. And among the Reformed, Calvin and Calvinists put more emphasis on discipline than Zwinglians.[11] In this era of intense religious conflict, theologians and competing confessional groups issued statements concerning the marks of the true church. While Lutherans recognized only two marks of the true church—the pure preaching of the Gospels and the proper administration of the sacraments—some Reformed leaders, such as Martin Bucer, claimed that discipline was the third. As we shall see throughout this study, Calvin gave enormous importance to discipline in practice, but he never explicitly recognized it as a third mark of the church, perhaps in order to avoid offending Reformed leaders in Zurich who insisted that magistrates, not an ecclesiastical institution like the Consistory, had the right to discipline. Other Calvinist confessions, such as those adopted by the Scottish and Dutch churches, later overtly recognized ecclesiastical discipline as the third mark of the church.[12]

Reformed Protestantism and Discipline

In his magisterial *Institutes of the Christian Religion*, Calvin mentioned in the chapter on discipline three goals in correcting sinners and, if all else failed, in excommunicating them. First, he believed it would dishonor God if people who were guilty of moral turpitude were allowed to remain in the Church; doing so could also result in profaning the Holy Supper. Second, he warned that not excluding such people could corrupt the good through their "constant association with the wicked." The third goal was to lead those who had been corrected or excommunicated to repentance and readmission to the community of Christians.[13] Significantly, Calvin warned against being too harsh in implementing discipline. He repeatedly called for moderation, stressing the need for discipline to be tempered by gentleness; the ultimate goal was repentance, and discipline must in no case go beyond what the specific sin warranted: "when the sinner gives the Church a testimony of his repentance, . . . he is by no means to be pressed any further."[14] He specifically opined that one should rarely if ever oblige Christians to ostracize people because of their sins; such severity, he believed was counterproductive to the reintegration of sinners into the Christian community.[15]

Though they generally agreed on the importance of discipline, Reformed thinkers offered different opinions on how discipline was to be carried out.[16] The biblical basis for church discipline was Matthew 18:15–17: "If your brother sins against you, go and tell him his fault, between you and him alone. If he listens to you, you have gained your brother. But if he does not listen, take one or two others along with you, that every word may be confirmed by the evidence of two or three witnesses. If he refuses to listen to them, tell it to the church; and if he refuses to listen even to the church, let him be to you as a Gentile and tax collector." There was disagreement, however, as to what it meant to "tell it to the church." The term for the church in the original Greek was *ekklesia*, which in Classical Athens referred to the assembly of all adult male citizens. Catholic thinkers generally agreed that in the Gospel, *ekklesia* meant to tell it to the bishops, and bishops accordingly established courts that had jurisdiction over matters such as marriage. Rejecting this interpretation, Ulrich Zwingli asserted that "the church" referred to the Christian magistrates, who had the exclusive authority to discipline the faithful, including the right to excommunicate. By contrast, Johannes Oecolampadius of Basel and Martin Bucer of Strasbourg maintained that *ekklesia* referred to the local Christian community and that magistrates did not have the exclusive right to discipline. Bucer insisted that discipline actually should be under the purview of the pastors who were to be assisted by elders.[17] John Calvin, who became well acquainted with Bucer during his stay in Strasbourg, reflected the older reformer's ideas on discipline. Robert Kingdon persuasively argued that when private admonitions did not suffice to put sinners back on the straight and narrow path, Calvin interpreted "tell it to the church" as meaning "tell it to the consistory."[18]

The Consistory was not the first Reformed disciplinary institution in what is now Switzerland; that distinction went to Zurich's Ehegericht, which was founded in 1525 and had jurisdiction over issues concerning marriage and sexuality.[19] Three years later, inspired by the Zwinglian Reformation, Bern, Switzerland's most powerful state, embraced Protestantism, and it played an enormous role in spreading the Reformed movement in what would become Romandy (the French-speaking part of Switzerland), through conquest in the case of the Pays de Vaud and through political pressure and energetic proselytizing in Geneva and Neuchâtel.[20] In 1528 Bern established a morals court known as the Chorgericht, and starting in 1529, a consistory was established in each parish in Bernese territory, consisting of the pastor and at least two "honest, pious men," who served as elders. The local consistories had the power to impose fines, brief jail terms, and certain forms of public humiliation; serious cases, such as suits for divorce, could be appealed to the Chorgericht in Bern.[21] After being conquered by Bern in 1536, Vaud converted to Protestantism and consistories were eventually established in its territory.[22] With support from Bern, Farel also led the conversion of Neuchâtel in 1530, and *consistoires seigneuriaux* were established there too. The best example was the consistory for Valangin, a seigniory within the principality of Neuchâtel, which could condemn miscreants to censures, excommunications, fines, brief prison sentences, the pillory, and even banishment.[23]

The Genevan Consistory consisted of twelve laymen, elders who were drawn from the city's three smaller councils—the Small Council (of twenty-five), the Council of Sixty, and the Council of Two Hundred[24]—and the city pastors, who usually numbered about five or six. One of the four syndics, the highest executive official in the Genevan city-state, presided over the Consistory. In a typical meeting only about half the lay members attended, so that there were roughly equal numbers of pastors and elders in attendance. The Consistory was assisted by an *officier* or bailiff, who summoned people to appear, and a scribe who wrote down the proceedings. In spite of Zwingli's and Calvin's differences concerning the authority to discipline, the Swiss institutions and Geneva's Consistory had much in common, especially in regard to structure. The members of both were mixed; the Swiss courts consisted of four lay officials (later six for Bern's Chorgericht) and two pastors. The Consistory, the Ehegericht, and the Chorgericht were all subordinate to their respective city councils.[25] So as far as structure is concerned, the key difference among these institutions is that pastors were more numerous and played a more prominent role in Geneva's Consistory, which was dominated by Calvin during his ministry.[26]

When it first started functioning, the presiding syndic was entrusted with questioning all those who appeared before the morals court.[27] Other members (or assistants, as they were known) could interject questions, and the records make clear that, as the years passed, the questioning of defendants and witnesses did not necessarily pass through the syndic. One thing that one cannot know from reading the registers of the Consistory is differences of opinion among its members. Undoubtedly there were disagreements among the various assistants, but the records never indicate what the vote was on a particular case, which was a general policy of most consistories. The decision rendered tends to give the impression that the pastors and elders were in lockstep and easily reached a consensus. That surely was not always the case.[28] One can find some cases, especially starting in the late 1550s, in which the Consistory immediately reversed a decision. The registers do not give an explanation for any such about-face, but one can easily surmise that it reflected strongly divergent opinions among the assistants. Despite disagreements, members of consistories endeavored to show the public that they spoke with one voice.[29]

A most crucial distinction between Geneva's Consistory, on the one hand, and the Chorgericht and *consistoires seigneuriaux*, on the other, is that while the latter were actual tribunals that had the power to impose a range of secular punishments, the Consistory was an ecclesiastical institution that could not impose any secular penalties; if it deemed miscreants worthy of a secular penalty, such as a fine or a jail sentence, it referred them to Geneva's Small Council, which did have that authority. Calvin and his associates definitely did not consider the Consistory to be an actual court, an attitude that was clearly shown in October 1547 when they told Pierre Tissot, an important official in Genevan government, that he could not appear before them in support of his father-in-law, François Favre, himself a fierce opponent of Calvin and the Consistory. Rather, everyone had to appear personally before the Consistory without legal counsel.[30] If this were truly a court, legal counsel would of course have been allowed.[31] To be sure, residents of Geneva absolutely had to appear when convoked. Failing to respect a summons from the Consistory could result in being jailed.[32]

Though Geneva's Consistory could not impose secular penalties, it did have one vitally important power that most Swiss consistories generally did not have: the right to excommunicate. True, as we will see in chapter 1, some Genevans questioned this power, and the Consistory did not start claiming to have the *exclusive* right to excommunicate until 1551;[33] this issue was not definitively resolved in the Consistory's favor until 1555. Nonetheless, from the moment it started functioning in 1541, the Consistory passed three types of sentences against sinners: it could admonish them; it could exclude them from the Supper; and it could refer them to the city council for criminal sentencing. Admonitions, the most common sentences, were usually spoken by one of the pastors, a large percentage of them delivered by Calvin himself.[34] In theory, there were two different levels of excommunication: simple suspension or exclusion from the Supper and full excommunication, which included cutting off all social contacts with the excommunicants. [35] In practice, the Consistory used only the former, and one finds no explicit sentence of full excommunication in Calvin's Geneva. By the later 1540s, Calvin's Consistory could also oblige people to do *réparation publique*, a confession of their sin before the entire congregation whereby they got on their knees and asked forgiveness from God and from the state. Similar public expressions of repentance for notorious sins were mandatory in some other Calvinist areas.[36]

The Consistory's power over admission to and exclusion from the Supper differed drastically from practices in Zurich and other Swiss polities. Zwingli and Heinrich Bullinger, his successor in Zurich, insisted that all disciplinary powers resided with magistrates alone, and both demonstrated a strong distaste for excommunication. As Bullinger noted, if Jesus allowed Judas to participate in the Last Supper, why should people who were guilty of much lesser sins be excluded from the sacrament?[37] Since the Consistory eventually had the exclusive right to excommunicate in Geneva, a right that was quite frequently employed and was unchallenged after 1555, the pastors of Geneva enjoyed a power over the Supper and a degree of independence from secular authorities that their counterparts in Zurich, Bern, and Basel did not have.[38]

Consistories were established in France and the Netherlands, which both resembled and differed from Geneva's. French and Dutch consistories did not have even indirect judicial power because in both countries, political authorities tended to be wary of these institutions. In the Netherlands, membership in the Reformed church was strictly voluntary, and in France authorities were often outright hostile to Protestants, who were a religious minority. Accordingly, in France a pastor, not a magistrate, presided over a consistory, which included deacons in addition to elders; and consistories had many administrative duties, including matters pertaining to finances and social welfare, which Geneva's Consistory did not. In the Netherlands, the consistories comprised pastors and elders and summoned people for many of the same issues (fornication, dancing, quarrels, drunkenness, etc.) for which people in Geneva were convoked. Moreover, both Dutch and French consistories, like Geneva's, had the right to excommunicate and tended to do so freely, unimpeded by local magistrates. Since consistories lacked the support of political authorities, their reprimands and excommunications lacked teeth. In France and the Netherlands, unlike in Geneva, excommunicants could simply leave the church and return to Catholicism.[39]

Like Swiss consistories but unlike Geneva's, consistories in Scotland—known there as kirk sessions—were tribunals that could impose mundane penalties (even corporal punishments) on miscreants. Elders and deacons served on the sessions, which were dominated by lay members, who easily outnumbered the ministers. Like French consistories, kirk sessions had administrative in addition to disciplinary functions, and also had the power to exclude people from communion (though they did not appear to exercise that right as often as Geneva's Consistory did).[40]

Scholarship on Social Discipline

Social discipline was arguably one of the most important developments of the early modern period, and this subject has been of considerable interest not just to historians but also to scholars from many branches of learning. The sociologist Norbert Elias argued that in the early modern era, Western societies underwent a process of the "civilization" of manners, which promoted self-control and discouraged violence against others. Elias and the historian Gerhard Oestreich both discussed the civilizing process of social discipline. They both emphasized the police actions of the increasingly powerful state, which imposed social discipline on unruly populations, and saw decisive change taking place in the seventeenth and especially eighteenth centuries. While Oestreich accentuated the role of laws, Elias stressed manners, whereby external norms governing behavior eventually led to their internalization and, consequently, to civility. They both viewed this as a top-down process and found that discipline and civility contributed to the development of absolutism.[41] The philosopher Michel Foucault asserted that in France social discipline was a product of the absolutist state. As the idea that humans could be readily manipulated and reformed gained prominence, the state reputedly introduced, beginning in the mid-eighteenth century, the pervasive surveillance of individuals and the institutions of discipline or modern policing (e.g., prisons, schools, workhouses, barracks).[42] The works of these thinkers have been most thought-provoking, but all three paid scant attention to the role of religion and the Reformation in effecting change and stimulating social discipline.

By contrast, though he did not discuss social discipline per se, the sociologist Max Weber stressed the importance of religion in general and the Calvinist Reformation in particular in bringing about social change. In his very provocative thesis, *The Protestant Ethic*, he argued that Calvinism nurtured the spirit of capitalism.[43] In addition to this thesis, which will be discussed in greater detail in chapter 6, Weber argued more broadly that Calvinism promoted a disciplined society, which was evident in the creation of a rational system of poor relief and the promotion of social order in general.[44]

More recently, the sociologist Philip Gorski asserted that the Reformation "unleashed a profound and far-reaching process of disciplining—a disciplinary revolution—that greatly enhanced the power of early modern states and that the effects of this revolution were deepest and most dramatic in the Calvinist parts of Europe."[45] Emphasizing the role of discipline in the formation of the modern state, he declared:

> Calvin and his followers helped created an infrastructure of religious governance and social control that served as a model for the rest of Europe—and the world. . . . [L]ike the industrial revolution, the disciplinary revolution was driven by a key technology: the technology of observation—self-observation, mutual observation, hierarchical observation. For it was observation—surveillance—that made it possible to unleash the energies of the human soul . . . and harness them for the purposes of political power and domination. What steam did for the modern economy, I claim, discipline did for the modern polity: by creating more obedient and industrious subjects with less coercion and violence, discipline dramatically increased, not only the regulatory power of the state, but its extractive and coercive capacities as well.[46]

Gorski further maintained that the impetus for this disciplinary revolution was not top-down but rather bottom-up, arguing that the principal movers and shakers were not centralizing princes but rather "Protestant clerics and reformist magistrates."[47]

Among historians, proponents of the "confessionalization" paradigm have addressed the subject of discipline. Conceived by German scholars, most notably

Heinz Schilling and Wolfgang Reinhard, and first applied to the German Reformation, the theory of "confessionalization" has served since the 1970s as a useful framework for very fruitful historical research on the Protestant and Catholic Reformations throughout Europe. The theory gets its name from the different "confessions," detailed and rigid statements about proper Christian beliefs and practices, that were written for the Lutheran, Catholic, and Reformed faiths in the sixteenth century. The term "confessionalism" is commonly used to refer to the division of Christians into these three competing well-defined groups, while the theory of confessionalization stresses the role of the state in effecting social and religious change, be they in Lutheran, Calvinist, or Catholic regions. While acknowledging the important theological differences among these three groups, supporters of this theory stress their structural similarities as all three aggressively sought to enforce popular adherence to their respective confessions, especially after 1550. Into the eighteenth century, the three groups employed similar methods, including mandatory schooling and catechism lessons, to inculcate appropriate Christian beliefs and practices among common folk. The confessionalization paradigm is very much top-down, as the state assumed the central role in bringing about confessional uniformity within its borders, imposing strict social discipline through close scrutiny of religious and moral behavior by morals courts, consistories, or inquisitions. Reformed consistories and Catholic inquisitions were of course all-male institutions that were important instruments of social discipline that sought, among other things, to effect religious uniformity.[48] Becoming essentially a branch of the state, the church was assuming unprecedented power over society, while the state was appearing more "sacral" than ever before, as enforcement of religious behavior was becoming an increasingly important function. Because the state was acquiring increased centralized authority replete with ever more intrusive powers, confessionalization reputedly represented an important phase in the development of the modern state.[49] Taking issue with proponents of the confessionalization paradigm, Gorski acknowledges that social discipline was also developing in Catholic and Lutheran areas but insists that the process "went further and faster in Calvinist polities."[50]

The Consistory and the Laity

This book endeavors to study not only the Consistory itself but also the people who appeared before it. Court records are among the few sources from the early modern period that can reveal much about common folk and popular culture.[51] Critics, however, have avowed that the records of inquisitions, consistories, and other courts cannot be used as if they are the field notes of anthropologists. Criminal records of any sort, it has been argued, cannot provide a simple window to popular culture, since they are closely shaped by contemporary laws, legal procedures, power structures, and the like.[52] Conducting research on Utrecht, Judith Pollman noted discrepancies between the actual consistory records and the personal journal kept by an elder who served on the consistory, thereby sowing doubts about the reliability of consistorial registers.[53] For Calvin's Geneva, no such source external to the Consistory exists for comparison, but there are some lists of excommunicants for certain years in the 1550s and 1560s. The numbers found in these lists correspond closely, but not perfectly, to the numbers that can be extrapolated from the actual Consistory records.[54] The corrective role that pastors and elders played in the lives of parishioners extended well beyond the meetings of consistories, which means that some of their activities left no trace or, at most, appear only indirectly in the records. Moreover, all court records reveal only what the scribe has written down, and clearly some scribes were more thorough in recording than others. For many consistories, the minutes that the scribe wrote down in haste during the meetings were later rewritten to provide a clean copy. This could mean that the scribe omitted or modified some information in the final draft. In the specific case of Geneva, it does not appear that minutes were rewritten for a clean copy. Although one can find some corrections—including a few instances in which Calvin himself clearly read and corrected the registers[55]—the partial sentences and omitted words strongly indicate that we are reading the minutes that were actually written down during the Consistory meetings. Ultimately, there is no escaping the fact that everything we read is through the lens of the educated men who recorded the minutes.

Although one should not accept at face value everything found in these records, the registers of consistories—and for that matter of inquisitions and of other tribunals—are far too important to ignore. They are absolutely necessary to understand the history of Reformed churches in sixteenth-century Europe.[56] The records of the Consistory are, bar none, the most valuable sources available for the history of religious practices in Geneva. They provide a front-row seat to the reception of Calvinism in Geneva and reveal Calvin's attitudes toward and treatment of the common laity. The people appearing before the Consistory came from a wide range of social backgrounds: bourgeois men and women, artisans, day laborers, and peasants from neighboring villages all appeared before this morals court. As we will see, members of prominent Genevan families were liable to be called before Calvin and his colleagues. Although this was obviously true if they criticized the reformer, a good number of men and women from the

Genevan elite, including some lay members of the Consistory itself, were subpoenaed for various transgressions.[57] The testimony of witnesses and defendants provides unique access to early modern popular culture, replete with details about daily life that were often only tangential to the actual proceedings. These records shed valuable light on women, providing insight to how they responded to and participated in the Reformation and what impact it had on their lives. Moreover, although, excluding witnesses, the majority of people appearing had to answer to allegations of misbehavior, some people were plaintiffs and were trying to use the Consistory as an instrument for redress of grievances, such as filing suit for defamation of character or enforcement of a marriage contract. Since the Consistory's activities were entirely free of charge, even the poorest of residents could make such petitions.[58]

The Registers of the Consistory

The Consistory of Geneva was the disciplinary institution par excellence of the sixteenth century, and its records provide a unique window into the introduction of social discipline as the Reformation took root. Though the Consistory has long been recognized as the essential instrument for promoting Calvinist religiosity and discipline among the laity, its registers until fairly recently have scarcely been studied because the original documents are extremely difficult to read. Sixteenth-century French handwriting is generally hard to decipher, and the minutes of the Consistory of Geneva are exceptionally challenging. A long-term project, initiated in the 1980s, to publish the twenty-one extant volumes that date from Calvin's ministry has enormously expanded access to the records of the Consistory for scholars. The driving force behind that project was Robert Kingdon, one of the premier historians of the Reformation who, recognizing the inestimable value of these records, assembled a team of scholars to transcribe, edit, and publish them. Two key former members of the team were Thomas M. Lambert, co-editor of volumes 1–5, and Wallace McDonald, who made valuable contributions to volumes 2–9. Having participated in the publication of volume 1 (1996), I rejoined the project several years later and became the de facto leader of the project after Professor Kingdon was incapacitated by a stroke in 2008 and the official leader after he passed away in 2010. The person who has by far performed the most work on this project is Isabella M. Watt, who has been fully engaged with the project since its inception in 1987; she has been an editor of all fourteen volumes published so far and continues work on the remaining seven volumes from Calvin's time.

Thanks to this project—first the transcriptions, then the published editions—several works on Reformation Geneva have appeared in the past three decades that were based at least in part on the records of the Consistory. To name just a few, William Naphy wrote a provocative work on the consolidation of Calvin's Reformation in Geneva, and Kingdon published a most useful study of adultery and divorce in Geneva during the time of Calvin.[59] Christian Grosse and Karen Spierling offered superb studies on, respectively, the Holy Supper and baptism, the two sacraments that Protestants kept in Reformation Geneva (and elsewhere).[60] Combining social history with historical theology, Scott Manetsch has provided an outstanding study of the ministry in Geneva during the time of Calvin and his successor, Theodore Beza. He dedicates a chapter to the ministers' role in moral oversight, based to a considerable extent on the records of the Consistory.[61]

While the registers of the Consistory have thus been quite effectively used to examine a range of issues, relatively few studies have concentrated on the institution itself. In 1972, Robert Kingdon published his first article on the subject. After reading selected passages in different volumes, he issued a clarion call for scholars to study the records of the Genevan Consistory, declaring that he was convinced that "the essential source of modern moral puritanism" was to be found in these rich volumes.[62] In 1976, William Monter offered a good study of the Consistory based on selected records for the years 1559–1569.[63] Kingdon would go on to publish a number of other works based on the Consistory records, the most important being *Reforming Geneva: Discipline, Faith and Anger in Calvin's Geneva*, which was based on the Levi Stone Lectures he delivered at Princeton Theological Seminary in February 1999. Nine years later, he intended to revisit and expand those lectures, which by then were quite outdated, in order to publish a book that would include new research on the morals court. Unfortunately, a stroke left him visually impaired and unable to read, but Tom Lambert, his former student and at that time coeditor of the Consistory volumes, graciously agreed to collaborate with Professor Kingdon in order to expand and correct the original. Kingdon passed away two days after approving the last change in the text.[64] *Reforming Geneva* is an excellent brief introduction to the Consistory in Calvin's Geneva, but it is definitely not the last word. Benefiting from much subsequent research—most important, the publication of several more volumes of the Consistory registers—this study will expand on a number of issues Kingdon addressed, introduce some that he did not consider, and include extensive comparisons with other disciplinary institutions, both Protestant and Catholic.

CHAPTER I

The Consistory Encounters Resistance

IN ITS EFFORTS TO change the behavior and piety of Genevans, the Consistory attacked certain misdeeds, such as fornication and blasphemy, that were universally viewed as sins in sixteenth-century Europe and could have resulted in prosecution in Catholic areas as well. The Consistory, however, had jurisdiction over a much broader range of behavior than did Catholic institutions such as the Inquisition and episcopal courts. As we shall see, the Consistory frequently summoned people because of quarrels, whereas Catholics never ran the risk of being called before the Inquisition solely because they were angry with others. Reformed leaders in Geneva also tried to root out certain diversions, such as dancing, games of chance, and secular songs, which, to varying degrees, Catholic leaders had long tolerated. Moreover, Calvin and his colleagues aggressively sought the elimination of practices that had become an important part of Catholic piety, such as saying prayers for the dead and to the Virgin Mary and celebrating saints' days. Genevans were forbidden to attend Mass in neighboring Catholic communities but were required to attend regularly services at one of the city's three (later four) churches. Given the ambitious goals of reforming the behavior of the rank and file, it is not at all surprising that the pastors and the Consistory encountered some opposition, both active and passive, to their efforts.

Opposition to the Clergy

Some Genevans clearly resented the introduction of major disciplinary changes by clergymen who were virtually all French and new arrivals in Geneva.[1] Some locals insisted that they had not fought a war to free themselves from a bishop only to be dominated now by a bunch of foreign pastors. They derisively said that while they had risked their lives fighting for independence, Calvin and the other ministers arrived in the city and "found the table laid and the soup made."[2]

An important case of early resistance to the Consistory involved François Favre, a wealthy Genevan citizen who had played a key role in Geneva's struggles for independence and had served on the Small Council during the decisive years of 1526–1537. In 1546 the Consistory summoned Favre because his wife was living apart from him outside Geneva and because he was suspected of having an adulterous affair with one of his domestic servants. Flatly denying the authority of the Consistory, Favre refused to appear and remained on lands his family owned outside Genevan territory. His son Gaspard was equally hostile to the Consistory and, after he refused to appear to account for scandalous words attributed to him, the Council ordered Gaspard jailed in March 1546, releasing him after three days provided that he appear before the Consistory. He did so, but when the presiding syndic urged Calvin to admonish Gaspard, the latter responded that he would answer to the syndic but no one else. When the reformer asked why he would not address the ministers, the younger Favre replied that the syndic and the other lay members (and members of the Council), unlike the ministers, were citizens of Geneva. Following the example of his father, Gaspard avowed that, according to the Republic's Franchises, a type of charter of rights, citizens of Geneva had the right to be judged solely by the Council and by their fellow citizens. This would preclude the pastors from passing judgment on them since they were all French and not citizens of Geneva.[3] When in June Gaspard again appeared and spoke in a "rebellious" manner to Calvin, the reformer angrily stormed out of the chamber, and the Council had Favre jailed for ten days; he left Geneva shortly thereafter.[4]

In January 1547 François, the elder Favre, returned to the city with the permission of the Council, provided he submit to the punishments for his previous sins. He admitted to the Council that he had indeed had sexual relations with two servants during his wife's absence, and he was accordingly sentenced to jail for three days, which appeared to be the default jail sentence for relatively minor offenses in Calvin's Geneva. Upon his release, the Council ordered him to go before the Consistory but when he did so, on February 3, 1547, Favre was defiant. Pressed by Pastor Abel Poupin, Favre, like his son before him, declared that he would answer no one but the syndic because the ministers had all come from France. When asked if he had been jailed for fornication, Favre replied that might be the case but that the sole purpose for calling him before the Consistory was to torment him. Calvin and his associates were most upset with his "rebellion" of refusing to receive their admonitions.[5]

Clearly other Genevan citizens shared the Favres' belief that the Consistory violated their fundamental rights as established by the Franchises,[6] because on February 8, just five days after this acrimonious appearance, François Favre was elected to the Council of Sixty (an institution that convened much less frequently than the Small Council and the Council of Two Hundred), an election that showed unabashed support for his resistance. Later that month, all members of the Consistory and Favre himself appeared before the Small Council. Favre declared that he was quite willing to conform to the orders of the Republic but categorically refused to admit his errors to the Consistory. Moreover, he expressed the desire to leave Geneva, with permission to come and go freely, and offered to pay the fee for residency as if he were a foreigner. At this point, the Council ruled that he had to reappear before the Consistory with the threat of being sent back to jail if he failed to do so. Some Council members, though, were obviously impatient with the actions of the Consistory and exhorted its members not to summon people lightly and to admonish sinners "kindly" (*gracieusement*), not aggressively.[7] Members of the Council indicated that they, not the Consistory, would decide whether a person who had already appeared before them should also be sent to the Consistory to receive its admonitions and to show repentance. Insisting that while he in no way wanted to undercut their authority, Calvin told *Messieurs* of the Council that this was unacceptable because he and his colleagues needed to distinguish the repentant from impenitent sinners in order to determine who should have access to the Supper.[8]

For the next several weeks, François Favre continued to be defiant, and the conflicts with the Consistory extended to yet another member of the family, his daughter, Françoise. She was the wife of Ami Perrin, who, though a key early supporter of Farel and Calvin, would become Calvin's fiercest adversary. In late September, the Council ordered the detention of François, Françoise, and Perrin for outbursts they had made. They all remained jailed for several days, and François proclaimed that he was ready to renounce his citizenship and leave Geneva. At one point he averred that Calvin had "tormented" him more than the four bishops he had lived under and that he wanted to leave because he could not recognize Calvin as his "prince."[9]

Officials of Bern, who had long had a favorable opinion of Favre, intervened on his behalf and asked Genevan magistrates to release him. In response to this pressure from its powerful ally, the Council agreed to do so. The sentence, passed on October 5, 1547, indicated, however, that he would still have to confess his errors to the Consistory. He indeed appeared the next day and was far less adversarial than he had been in previous months. Favre proclaimed that he recognized all the pastors as having been approved by the Council and wanted to go hear each of them preach the Gospel. He received their admonitions but added that if Calvin had always been as gentle in his reproaches as he was at that moment, these matters would have been resolved much more easily. He concluded

by shaking hands with each minister.[10] Notwithstanding this apparent reconciliation, the Favres continued to have a fraught relationship with Calvin, the other
pastors, and the Consistory. This exemplified the conflict involving certain Genevans, including some from very influential families, who resented the power
of the foreign ministers and the strong disciplinary regime that was based upon
the power of the Consistory.

Perhaps the most famous (or infamous) case of resistance to the clergy during
Calvin's ministry involved Jacques Gruet. The son of a Genevan notary, Gruet
resented the influence and strict discipline that Calvin promoted. In April 1546
the Consistory summoned him, along with many others, for dancing. After
spending time in jail for lying to the Consistory about what he saw, Gruet told
Calvin and his associates that he was sorry he had lied but that he did not think
that dancing was particularly scandalous. When reproached for his lack of repentance, Gruet affirmed that Jesus had instructed that if one had to admonish
one's brother, it should be done in private (Matthew 18:15), implying that he
should have received a pastoral visit rather than a summons to appear before
the Consistory. Not pleased with this suggestion, the Consistory issued still
stronger reprimands.[11] Over a year later, on June 27, 1547, someone attached to
the pulpit in the church of Saint-Pierre an anonymous message, written in the
local patois, which threatened the pastors with death and ended with the words,
"We don't want to have so many masters."[12] Although no one saw Gruet enter
or leave the church on that day, suspicions were immediately directed toward
him, and authorities raided Gruet's abode and seized some writings they found
there. In a letter to the reformer Pierre Viret, Calvin conceded that the note in
Saint-Pierre was not in Gruet's handwriting.[13] He and some authorities were
nonetheless alarmed at some things in his writings. These included drafts of
letters and various thoughts he had jotted down, in which Gruet aggressively
criticized Calvin, whom he decried as arrogant, sneering, overly ambitious, and
eager to be revered as a pope. Also found was a rough outline of a speech that
Gruet reputedly hoped to read to all citizens of Geneva in the General Council, defending individual liberty and proclaiming that magistrates should not
prevent people from dancing and taking part in similar distractions that did no
harm to others. Perhaps the most damning evidence was in the form of max-
ims that, according to Calvin, Gruet had copied from texts written by others.[14]
These sayings included that there is no heaven or hell; that the human soul dies
with the body; that the Christian religion is "a fable"; and that "All laws, both
human and divine, have been made according to the good pleasure of men."[15]
Such ideas smacked of atheism and, to be sure, would have been anathema to all

major sixteenth-century Christian theologians, both Protestant and Catholic. Under interrogation, Gruet persistently asserted that he knew nothing about the menacing note left in Saint-Pierre and that he never seriously thought about speaking before the General Council; rather, he was just expressing some concerns. As for speaking ill of the reformer, he now asserted that Calvin was a true preacher but that pastors should limit themselves to preaching the Gospel and not get involved in mundane affairs.[16] Calvin complained that the syndics were too slow in coming to a judgment, but after he was subjected three times to torture by means of the *strappado*, Gruet confessed to all accusations made against him, including writing the threatening note in the church. Concluding that Gruet merited capital punishment, authorities sentenced him to death on July 25, 1547, and the execution took place the next day, less than one month after the discovery of the note.[17] In light of the flimsy grounds on which Gruet was convicted, this incident certainly put Calvin and secular authorities in a very bad light to modern observers. Though this was an extreme case, it vividly shows that resisting or denigrating pastors, especially Calvin, could be dangerous in Reformation Geneva.

Ministers, too, got in trouble if they were caught criticizing Calvin, even in private. In 1546, Henri de La Mare, pastor in the village of Jussy, got on the wrong side of the reformer because he privately said that Calvin was an inflexible hothead. He also showed some sympathy toward Pierre Ameaux, a prominent citizen who had a bitter conflict with Calvin that exacerbated tensions between the pastors and members of certain influential Genevan families. One night after dinner and a few glasses of wine, Ameaux apparently made some disparaging remarks about Calvin to the others at the table, most importantly that the reformer preached "false doctrine."[18] When he later defended (at least somewhat) Ameaux and criticized Calvin for his temper, de La Mare was briefly jailed, made the subject of a criminal investigation, and eventually expelled from the ministry. The investigation detailed, among other things, a conversation between de La Mare and the physician Benoît Tixier about the words that Ameaux uttered against Calvin. When Tixier asked him if Ameaux had spoken "against God or only against men," de La Mare replied, "I think that he said something against Calvin. . . . [A]nd if [Ameaux] was wrong, this was done after having drunk [alcohol]. I have always known him as a good man, virtuous, and of a great spirit. Calvin is a bit subject to his tempers, [he's an] impatient man, hateful, and vindictive." To prove that he was not a vindictive man, Calvin ensured that de La Mare would never again serve as a minister in Genevan territory.[19]

Starting in the later 1540s, some Genevans viewed the Consistory with great suspicion. In his magisterial work on the Supper, Christian Grosse rightly observes that some people viewed it as a type of Trojan horse, created by the ministers, which amounted to an ecclesiastical plot against the Republic. The fact that the Consistory was a mixed institution and included elders who were members of the city councils in no way assuaged this fear.[20]

The Increase in Resistance

The registers of the Consistory show that resistance to the pastors continued and even intensified during the 1550s. Apart from a few exceptions, this opposition did not stem from people who were clandestine Catholics. Genevans had accepted Protestantism in 1536, and the large majority of those who preferred Catholicism had already left the city and its dependent territory well before 1550. Rather than opposing the Reformation per se, some Genevans simply resented the growing power of the foreign clergy. In May 1550, for example, Jeanne, the wife of Pierre Bon, was interrogated because she allegedly said, "the preachers do not have all their ears and are all banished."[21] In saying this, she implied that they had been banished from France as heretics or criminals, who at times were sentenced to have an ear amputated as a sign of their misdeed.

Many also thought that the ministers were being too severe and inflexible in their efforts to root out "immoral" behavior among the laity. In May 1553 a certain Jeanne Bochut condemned the pastors and wished that "the great devil would carry off all the ministers because they have not brought any benefit to the country." For these harsh words, the Council condemned her to be whipped through the streets and banished for life from Geneva.[22] In March 1554, a man was heard saying that "he would rather return to the papacy to have a joyous life because people don't laugh at all here [anymore]."[23] Raymond Chauvet was almost certainly the most judgmental of all pastors in Geneva, regularly castigating people both inside and outside of church. A former Franciscan who was zealous in his pursuit of "sinners," Chauvet on one occasion in 1546 cursed from the pulpit some parishioners who were leaving before he had completed his sermon: "May evil, plague, war, and famine fall upon you!"[24] The feeling was mutual for many Genevans, who derisively nicknamed Chauvet *Torticol* ("Crooked Neck") because his neck was literally askew.[25] In May 1552, the cutler Louis Curlet told the Consistory that one day, while admittedly slightly drunk, he kissed his wife in public in the presence of Chauvet. When the pastor reproached him for the kiss, Curlet took offense and blasphemed. The Consistory obliged Curlet to get on his knees and beg mercy from God, an action that blasphemers usually had to perform, but no doubt Curlet was not the only person in Geneva who felt that kissing one's spouse in public did not merit a reprimand.[26] In August of the same year, Guillaume Rougement was summoned for a quarrel with a neighbor. When asked why he had not taken communion, Rougemont explained that he was not in a good state of mind since appearing before the Small Council, where Pastor Chauvet had called him "an evil heretic" and "made a greater scandal than I [had]."[27] Over the years on several occasions, the Council and even the Company of Pastors rebuked Chauvet for his intemperate verbal attacks, but he nonetheless would serve as a pastor in the city for twenty-five years until his death in 1570.[28]

A sermon delivered by William Farel exacerbated tensions between pastors and lay authorities in 1553. By that time, Farel had been pastor in Neuchâtel for many years; as a guest preacher in Geneva that day, he managed to infuriate a large number of people. Farel gave a sermon in which he excoriated the youth of Geneva, declaring that they were "worse than bandits, murderers, thieves, fornicators, and others, to the great insult of the children of the city." Two days later, on November 3, several people, including Jacques-Nicolas Vulliet, an elder and lay member of the Consistory, went to the Council to protest and demand justice for Farel's slanderous denunciation of the Genevan youth. They asked to press charges against him in Geneva if he were still present or elsewhere if he had left town.[29] Ten days later, Calvin and Farel appeared before the Council along with other ministers to complain about the criticism, protesting that such complaints would contribute to "scandal and the dishonor" of the church. Facing his accusers, Farel tried to contain his anger and claimed that his criticism had been directed only toward some and not all the youth in Geneva. He asserted that his sermon should be understood as a form of paternal correction and admonition so that those youths would mend their ways and forswear their vices. Farel's explanations sufficed to assuage the ire of his critics, who now assured him that they viewed him as a "good minister and spiritual father." For its part, the Council informed Farel that he was always welcome to preach in the city.[30] At its next meeting, the Consistory admonished Vulliet by telling him that as a member of the Consistory, he did not have the right to participate in such protests.[31] This brief incident shows that Geneva's clergy and Consistory did not want to hear any criticism of ministers, but the pastors almost certainly also concluded that using such intemperate language from the pulpit could be counter-productive.

During the first half of the 1550s, as conflicts intensified, criticism of the clergy became more and more concentrated on the person of John Calvin. In August

1554, several people testified that the laborer Bernard Mognet, also known as
Patavel, had denounced Calvin, saying, "there are two devils in hell, and Calvin is one of them." Patavel denied saying these words, but the Consistory was
convinced of his guilt and sent him to the Council, which eventually banished
Patavel from the city.[32] In January 1555, three anonymous love letters were left
at Calvin's seat in the chamber where the Consistory met. We cannot know if
the intention behind the letters was humor, defamation, or both, but members
of the Consistory were not amused and viewed them as an attempt to discredit
the reformer.[33]

The Influx of Refugees

Few other cities at this time welcomed religious refugees to the same degree as
Geneva, which received a huge number of religious refugees in the 1540s and
1550s. Calvin was adamant that the city be open to all people who sought the
gospel, regardless of where they were from.[34] In his sermons, Calvin declared
that Geneva must be "a bright lamp to illuminate those who are still far from
the Gospel" and "a nest and shelter for his poor faithful, who are like chicks
who are frightened by birds of prey." Demanding that such religious refugees be
admitted, Calvin blasted, "Those who cry out against foreigners, and consider
this word an insult, could not show more clearly that they are not worthy to be
numbered among the children of God, and no more belong in His Church than
do dogs or pigs."[35]

The refugees included a good number of Italians who in 1551 petitioned the
Council, with the full support of Calvin, to hire at their own expense a minister
to preach in Italian at the church of La Madeleine.[36] The large majority of the
refugees, however, came from France, the native land of Calvin and almost all
the other ministers in Geneva. The number of French people who were admitted
to the bourgeoisie, i.e., who became naturalized citizens in Geneva, began to
increase starting in 1549, when 122 received citizenship. As a result, authorities
created in September 1550 the Bourse française, a system of poor relief dedicated
exclusively to those coming from France.[37]

The influx of Frenchmen, combined with the power of Calvin and the other
pastors, caused resentment among a fair number of Genevans, who proposed an
edict in 1551 that would oblige the new naturalized citizens to wait twenty-five
years after admission before they would have the right to participate in any of
the city councils, including the General Council to which all male citizens be-
longed.[38] The Small Council accepted this proposition, though the Council of

Two Hundred, which had the power to vote up or down on matters brought to it by the Small Council, later rejected it. The fact that it was even proposed reflected the growing unrest caused by the increasing numbers of refugees into the city.[39]

Two years later, it was the Council of Two Hundred, which represented a wider range of social statuses than did the Small Council, that showed concern about the increasing number of foreigners.[40] On April 11, 1553, the Council of Two Hundred issued various rules concerning new arrivals in Geneva. Landlords were not allowed to rent rooms to foreigners unless they notified authorities, and only people who were citizens or bourgeois were allowed to run taverns or inns or even to put up a sign for a business. This council also mandated that innkeepers must notify the authorities of who was staying with them within three days of their arrival, and that no foreigners were allowed to serve as watchmen. All foreigners were also obliged to give up their arms, and anyone suspected of heresy was to be expelled from the city. Two syndics in conjunction with a number of other officials, including the captains serving the lieutenant (the official in charge of civil litigation and of lesser criminal offenses) and the *dizeniers* (officers who each oversaw one of twenty-five *dizaines* or districts in the city) were to conduct a visitation to identify all foreigners in Geneva.[41] This desire to disarm the foreigners and to oversee their movements closely shows that many Genevans feared that the new arrivals might be prone to violence or even sedition.

The registers of the Consistory provide abundant proof of the animosity of some residents toward the French and their growing influence in Geneva. In October 1551, Calvin and the other assistants convoked Pernette Bertet for allegedly speaking ill of the French, proclaiming that they were causing a rise in the cost of living—a common complaint that was entirely justified, as the influx of refugees from France resulted in higher prices, especially for housing[42]—and that "there was not one good man among them whatsoever."[43] A month later, Jean Grasset was accused of insulting a French knight and of blaspheming when he declared, "May God curse so many Frenchmen."[44] The Consistory reprimanded Monet Burnet for having said to a foreigner who was going to church on Christmas Day in 1553, "Are you going to the sermons? Look, here is the preacher," whereupon he bared his buttocks to that man. Two men who were with him were accused of saying, "These damned French don't come here for the gospel but to cause others to get into fights."[45]

Various individuals continued to be cited for showing disrespect to pastors. Boniface Conte was a longtime critic of the pastors, especially Calvin, and of the Consistory. In 1549 *Messieurs* of the Council indignantly reproached Conte for allegedly naming his dog "Calvin," an accusation he denied.[46] When Conte appeared before the Consistory in January 1551 to answer charges of fornication, insults, truancy from church, and his previous refusal to appear before the Consistory, Calvin reproached and exhorted him to show repentance for his actions. Conte, however, refused to respond to Calvin's admonishments, repeating the defiant declaration that we encountered above that "Mr. Calvin is not his prince."[47]

The Power of the Consistory and Jurisdiction over the Supper

Communion and baptism were the only sacraments Protestants retained from the seven practiced by Roman Catholicism, and the manner in which the Supper was administered differed greatly from Catholic practice. As in most Reformed areas, in Geneva the Supper was celebrated only four times a year, whereas the Eucharist was the central part of every Mass. The Supper, like the entire church service, was now celebrated in the vernacular rather than in Latin. The laity now received communion in both kinds, partaking of the bread and the wine, whereas only the clergy received the cup among Catholics. And in Geneva it was the elders or deacons, not the pastors, who administered the cup.[48]

The pastors and the Consistory gave great importance to the Supper and insisted, at least after 1551, on having the exclusive authority to determine who had permission to participate in this sacrament. The first reference in the records to excluding someone from the Supper occurred on March 30, 1542, when Calvin and his associates informed Jacques Emin that he would not be allowed to take communion on Easter unless he learned the basics of the faith.[49] In its early days, however, the Consistory's right over the Supper definitely did not go uncontested. In March 1543, the Council of Sixty concluded that the Consistory did not have the right to exclude people from the Supper, declaring that it could only issue admonitions and make recommendations to magistrates who could pass judgment on delinquents. Notwithstanding that ruling, the Consistory continued to exclude people from the Supper, though at a rate far below that which it would reach in the 1560s, and Genevan political authorities for the time being tacitly allowed the pastors and elders to continue wielding that authority.[50]

Starting in 1550, the pastors, accompanied by a *dizenier* and/or by an elder, went to meet with all parishioners in the weeks preceding the Supper, especially but not exclusively that of Easter,[51] in order to determine if they were spiritually in the proper frame of mind to take communion.[52] Those conducting the visitation made appointments in advance with families and individuals to conduct their interrogations; they were not randomly, unexpectedly knocking on people's doors.[53] Through the visitations, the ministers wanted to ascertain if people knew the rudimentary tenets of the faith. The rank and file were expected to be able to recite the Lord's Prayer and the Apostles' Creed, and they were sometimes also queried about the Ten Commandments.[54] As we will see in greater detail in chapter 7, the ministers also wanted to know if parishioners had committed any serious sins or were feeling rancor toward others, which would render them unfit to take communion. In that regard, these visitations can be viewed as an alternative, non-sacramental form of auricular confession.[55]

The evidence we find in the Consistory registers about these visitations is almost entirely negative. That is, the records mention the visits almost exclusively when people failed to meet with the pastor, got angry over the questions they were asked, or demonstrated ignorance in matters of the faith. At the meeting that preceded the Supper of Pentecost in 1551, a woman had to appear because she had told others, when she was about to be subject to the visitation, that she "was going to the confessors."[56] Shortly before Easter in 1557, Pierre Duchesne and Pierre Des Estuves were "accused of having said to those who had been examined by [Pastor] Enoch, 'Have you confessed?'" They admitted having said those words but did not think that they had done anything wrong. For their "contempt for the visitation," the Consistory sent the two men to the Council, which gave them "good and bitter remonstrances."[57] The following week, the Consistory rebuked three men and a woman for having compared the admonitions of the Consistory to the Catholic sacramental confession.[58] The pastors were most unhappy with this analogy, but, as noted, the methods they employed during the visitation—and, as we shall see, in the Consistory meetings themselves—had much in common with those of Catholic confessors.

Starting especially in 1551, the question of the power to admit or exclude people from the Supper became the most important source of disagreements in Geneva. Calvin insisted that the Consistory had the exclusive right to determine who could partake of the sacrament, a stand that, as mentioned in the introduction, differed drastically from practices in most Swiss Reformed states. Upset by the growing authority of Calvin, the pastors, and the Consistory, a significant number of Genevans argued that the power to excommunicate should be under the purview of the Council.[59] In March 1551, for example, the coppersmith Hudri Langin confessed to blasphemy but defiantly insisted that the Consistory did not have the right to excommunicate. Those comments notwithstanding, the Consistory denied him access to the Supper and referred him to the Council, which sentenced him to three days in jail.[60] Initially, even François Chabod, the *châtelain* of the village of Céligny, sided with Langin and declared that only the Small Council had the right to exclude someone from communion. Chosen by the Council, a *châtelain* was a citizen and resident of the city but was the highest official in rural districts. As such, he investigated possible crimes in the Genevan countryside and sent people to the Consistory in the city either at the request of the local pastor or at his own initiative.[61] When he appeared on April 16, Chabod at first continued to argue that the Council alone had the power to exclude and admit people to the Supper. After persistent questioning, the *châtelain* finally accepted the admonitions of the Consistory, thereby recognizing, at least in theory, its power to excommunicate.[62]

Other *châtelains* also did not share the Consistory's zeal for the reformation of morals. On April 6, 1553, Jacques Bernard, pastor in the village of Peney, complained bitterly of the incompetence of officers who were supposed to bring people who were convoked by the Consistory. Since certain *châtelains* clearly did not want to respect the subpoenas of the Consistory, Calvin again went to the Council to oblige the *châtelains* and other officers "to follow the ordinances."[63] After listening to his protests, the Council ruled that all officials must indeed bring to the Consistory all people who were accused of misbehavior.[64] At the very same time that the Council gave this support to the Consistory, however, it also expressed its displeasure with the aggressive actions of some pastors toward miscreants. The Council declared that, as outlined in the edicts, the proper manner in which pastors should deal with those who fell short of their goals was first to admonish them privately rather than immediately summoning them to the Consistory.[65]

In 1551 even a member of the Consistory itself rebelled and tried to restrict the authority of that institution and of the pastors. Jean-Philibert Bonna was a member of an influential family and the younger brother of Pierre Bonna, himself a close ally of Calvin. Jean-Philibert was elected an assistant on the Consistory in February 1551. Bonna had a very combative character and appeared many times before the Consistory for quarrels with others, including with his brother Pierre. On March 5, 1551, just two weeks after his first meeting as a member, Jean-Philibert Bonna was reprimanded by the other members—they complained, among other things, about the way he was attired, taking offense at the "bouquet in his hat"—but Bonna rejected their authority and avowed that if he were accused of some error, he should be called before the Small Council. The other assistants subsequently refused to let him participate in the meetings of the Consistory, which caused a conflict with the Council. Even though Calvin and the other pastors at one point proclaimed that they "would rather die" than have Bonna as a fellow assistant, the Council decided that if he came to the Consistory, made a confession of faith, and showed contrition for his previous actions, Bonna should be readmitted as a member. Notwithstanding that decision, Jean-Philibert Bonna's name never appeared on the list of assistants in the Consistory minutes after June 18 of that year.[66]

Bonna was a member of the self-proclaimed Enfants de Genève also known as the Perrinistes, named after Ami Perrin, the leader of Geneva's militia (*capitaine général*) for the period 1544–1555 and a fierce opponent of Calvin and the other pastors.[67] Another leader of the Perrinistes, derisively called the Libertins by Calvin and his supporters, was Philibert Berthelier, a member of another prominent Genevan family. On a number of occasions, Berthelier refused to recognize the Consistory's authority to discipline him or exclude him from the Supper.[68] From the perspective of local power dynamics, the following year, 1552, did not start well for Calvin. On February 7, four new syndics were elected, only one of whom, Jean-Ami Curtet, could be considered a supporter of the reformer. Three of Calvin's allies were ousted in those elections, and a few days later the Council appointed Jean-Philibert Bonna and Jean-Baptiste Sept, both strong opponents of Calvin, to the Court of Last Appeals.[69] In September the Small Council appointed Calvin's archnemesis Perrin to serve as envoy to Lyon to try to negotiate the release of a naturalized Genevan citizen,[70] and in November the General Council named Pierre Tissot, Perrin's brother-in-law, lieutenant, an election that showed strong support among the citizenry for the Enfants de Genève.[71]

Opponents of Calvin's disciplinary agenda were understandably feeling emboldened. In October 1552, members of the Consistory became most upset when Berthelier and two other members of well-established Genevan families, Balthasar Sept and the former member of the Consistory, Jean-Philibert Bonna, verbally attacked Pastor Chauvet, even following him into the church of Saint-Pierre and insulting him and the other ministers. Apparently Chauvet had reproached Bonna for having touched a married woman in an inappropriate manner. Berthelier and Sept aggressively defended Bonna, who was also accused of saying to Chauvet and to Pastor Abel Poupin that he would gladly give up his coat if the ministers were truly better than he was. Even though this was the first case discussed that day, Calvin and his colleagues considered it so important that they suspended all other activity for that meeting and decided that the members would go en masse to the Council the next day to demand an investigation of this rebellion.[72] The Council agreed to investigate and eventually condemned the three men to three days in jail for their insolence, and the

Consistory excluded them from the Supper. Be that as it may, all three continued to argue that the Consistory did not have the right to excommunicate and
refused to admit their errors in front of Calvin and his colleagues.[73]

Various opponents of Calvin continued to wield considerable influence in
Geneva in the following two years. In February 1553 Ami Perrin was elected a
syndic, and he became first syndic (*président des syndics*) when another man,
Étienne de Chapeaurouge, asked to be relieved of those duties because of poor
health.[74] Even though the Consistory had not readmitted him to communion,
Philibert Berthelier played a very active role in the trial of Michael Servetus,
who was burned for heresy in Geneva on October 27, 1553.[75] And in November
1554, Jean-Philibert Bonna was named an *auditeur*, a type of police officer who
investigated crimes.[76]

The conflict with Philibert Berthelier would continue for well over a year
as he repeatedly tried to bypass the Consistory entirely by asking the Council
to be readmitted to the Supper. Despite vehement objections from Calvin and
the other pastors, more than once the Council acceded to his request, though
officiating pastors refused to let Berthelier partake of the bread and the wine.
At one point, all the pastors of the city and the dependent countryside went to
the Council to argue against admitting Berthelier to the Supper "until he had
reconciled" with the pastors (i.e., apologized for his errors). The ministers even
proclaimed that they all would rather die, be exiled, or suffer other torments
than allow Berthelier to receive the sacrament. Most upset by this declaration,
the Council admonished the clergymen and stated that "the magistracy is faithful and had given no reason" for them to speak thus, warning them that they
must never again address the Council in this manner.[77] This dissension between
the pastors and the Council was quite remarkable, and Berthelier appeared before the Consistory again in 1554 and 1555 but steadfastly refused to confess his
errors and to ask forgiveness of its members.[78] In short, through the mid-1550s,
the ultimate success of Calvin and the Consistory looked far from certain.

The Riot of 1555 and the Defeat of the Perrinistes

The year 1555 marked the definitive turning point in favor of Calvin and his disciplinary regime. The results of the city's election, held every February, were quite
favorable to Calvin in that year. On February 3, the General Council elected the
new syndics, all four of whom were supporters of Calvin, and the Councils of
Twenty-Five, Sixty, and Two Hundred also witnessed increases in the number of
Calvin supporters.[79] To consolidate further their power, Calvin's partisans also

decided to grant citizenship in April to forty-three French residents in Geneva—compared to only seven for the entire previous year—knowing that the admission of these refugees would diminish the influence of the Enfants de Genève. As citizens, they became members of the General Council and were eligible for various public offices.[80] On May 6, the Perrinistes expressed their concern to the Council about this large number of new admissions to the bourgeoisie, but far from backing down, the Council granted citizenship to sixteen more people on May 9. This resulted in more protests from certain Genevans, including Hudriod Du Molard, then lieutenant and previously five times a syndic, and Nicolas Gentil, Balthasar Sept, and Jean-Philibert Bonna.[81]

On the evening of May 16, 1555, several prominent opponents of Calvin dined together, including Ami Perrin and his fellow member of the Small Council, Pierre Vandel. There is no evidence that this group was drawing up plans to attack their adversaries, much less to orchestrate a coup d'état. After supper, Vandel and Perrin parted company with the others, who went for a stroll in the lower part of town. Some members of this group, no doubt under the influence of alcohol, got into a fight with Claude Dumont, a native of Savoy, and tumult ensued, with a large number of people from both sides, many of them armed, taking to the streets. This fracas appears to have lasted no more than an hour, was quelled with relative ease, and resulted in one minor injury. In short, this incident was clearly a spontaneous ruckus, not an attempted insurrection. That said, as Genevan historian Amédée Roget rightly asserted, "it is certain that there is no other event in the internal history of our city which had more serious and extensive consequences."[82] Evidence indicates that some prominent Perrinistes were trying to act as peacemakers during the disturbance. For example, in an attempt to restore order, Perrin himself at one point seized the baton of justice from the hands of a syndic. The majority in the government, which supported Calvin and his partisans, used this incident as a pretext to destroy the opposition.[83]

On May 24, 1555, the Small Council ordered the arrest of seven men, including Ami Perrin, but he and several others decided to flee Geneva on the same day. Although the evidence against them was meager, their decision to leave was wise considering the fates of those who remained. Bern sent a long letter on May 31, asking Genevan authorities to grant a safe-conduct pass to the accused so that they could return to defend themselves in court. The Genevans, however, paid absolutely no attention to that request and on June 3, just two weeks after their flight, passed sentence that Perrin, for having seized the syndic's baton—only a syndic was supposed to wield the baton—was to have his hand cut off. Then he, Sept, and four others were to be decapitated; then they were to be quartered; their heads and Perrin's hand were to be nailed to the gallows and their bodies left in four different sites in the city.[84]

Those, like Perrin, who had fled were able to avoid execution, but others who remained in the city were not so fortunate. Two brothers named Comparet had taken part in the melee and, under torture, confessed to sedition and implicated others.[85] On June 27, the two brothers were condemned to be decapitated and their bodies quartered.[86] Philibert Berthelier, Calvin's long-time adversary, was among those who fled, but his brother François-Daniel remained, mistakenly believing he had nothing to fear. In July François-Daniel and others were jailed and interrogated, about which Calvin declared in a letter to Farel, "I hope that we will see in two days what torture will draw from their mouths."[87] On September 11, François-Daniel Berthelier was condemned to be decapitated, and this verdict marked the end of judicial actions related to the riot of May 1555.[88]

All told, the skirmish resulted in the executions of four men, and about twenty others fled Geneva to avoid capital punishment. Others were banished, forced to pay fines, or obliged to abdicate public offices. The historian Roget argued convincingly that this violent purging of the Perrinistes was probably entirely avoidable, as their defeat had already been assured by the elections of 1555 and the admission of many new bourgeois. Far from putting a brake on the passions that had been unleashed in Geneva, Calvin was blatantly stirring them up. This affair also bred animosity among the Swiss Reformed toward Calvin and his church in Geneva; it especially ran the risk of provoking a definitive rupture with Bern.[89] From the point of view of Genevan politics, however, this incident undeniably enabled Calvin and his supporters to consolidate their power. Following the tumult of 1555, the disciplinary power of the Consistory and of the church, especially in regard to the right to admit and exclude people from the Supper, was no longer seriously questioned, even well after the reformer's death.[90]

The Consistory's Expanding Power
and the Persistence of Distrust

After the disturbances of 1555, the Consistory's position was quite secure and it became bolder, increasing its activity and expanding the types of actions pursued.[91] The number of people excluded from the Supper increased dramatically after the defeat of the Perrinistes. Christian Grosse found that the average number of cases heard per meeting went from eleven in 1555 (compared to under ten in the 1540s) to 14.5 in 1556, reaching a peak of 20.5 in 1559.[92] Moreover, according to Scott Manetsch, the number of people appearing before the Consistory, either as defendants or as witnesses, increased from about sixteen per week through 1555 to thirty-four per week for the years 1556–1569.[93] He also found that the numbers of people excluded from the Supper increased in the years after 1555, reaching their peak in the late 1560s. Suspensions from the Supper averaged less than one per Consistory meeting prior to 1555 and then rose steadily until reaching a peak of twelve per session in 1568.[94] Predictably, the increase in the number of suspensions was accompanied by unprecedented numbers of requests for readmission in the weeks preceding the celebration of the Supper.[95] As we will see in later chapters, the Consistory prosecuted certain sins with unprecedented vigor and expanded the number of misdeeds that were under its purview.

The increase in the Consistory's activity was part and parcel of its expanding power. In July 1556, it received for the first time the authority to administer an oath to those testifying before it. In that regard, the Consistory was beginning to function more like a tribunal, as thereafter people who lied before it could be prosecuted for perjury.[96] In and of itself, lying was generally not a reason for being called before the morals court. Bearing false witness of course violated one of the Ten Commandments, but Genevan pastors realized that it was virtually impossible to prosecute this sin, unless it involved slander directed at others. It was much more practical to attack lying through moralizing sermons than through consistorial actions.[97] Calvin and his colleagues, however, did not tolerate lying to the Consistory, most obviously when such a lie resulted in summoning witnesses to a subsequent meeting. This was true well before the events of 1555. A good example involved Pierre de Vella, who, when he first appeared before the Consistory in December 1550, emphatically denied criticizing Genevan leaders for the abolition of holidays. Witnesses contradicted his claim, however, and two weeks later, with the full support of the Council, Vella was required to get on his knees before Calvin and company and beg for mercy from God for having lied to the Consistory.[98] By the early 1560s, the Consistory was even requesting that the Council inflict corporal punishment on those who had lied to the assembly of pastors and elders. Appearing before the Consistory at the end of April 1562, Claude Clemensat of the village of Peissy was accused of cursing her pregnant aunt in the vilest way: "Cursed be that sow. May the bad chancre eat away at her. May the big devil go into her womb."[99] Since she denied the accusations, the Consistory called witnesses who the following week affirmed that Clemensat had uttered those curses. The Consistory excluded her from the Supper and ordered that she do *réparation* after the church service, asking for mercy from her aunt, the justice system, and God. It also sent her to the Council and asked *Messieurs* to make her drink some water (*de luy faire boyre d'eau*).[100] Drinking water referred to the forced ingestion of water, a common form of torture in early modern Europe. In this case, the Consistory was recommending it as a punishment for slander and lying to the morals court.[101]

Though its power was enhanced and its harshest critics had been eliminated, one could still find signs of animosity toward Calvin and the Consistory after 1555. In May 1556, a woman reported hearing the niece of Jean Chapelle of the village of Vandœuvres complaining that "the devil and the Consistory never sleep."[102] Moreover, while the ministers' concern about the control of the Supper was understandable, it is hard to escape the conclusion that Calvin and his colleagues were hypersensitive to criticism and at times took offense over frankly trivial matters, a trend that did not end with the fall of the Enfants de Genève. For example, in October 1556 the mason Guigo Rey and his wife, Pernette, were called because of their marital discord and because they had not willingly accepted the admonitions given to them by a pastor. When notified that they were to appear before the Consistory, Pernette supposedly said, "May God give good life to *Messieurs* [of the Council]."[103] Calvin and the other pastors became quite angry over this and interpreted the good wishes for the members of the Council as a thinly veiled attack on the Consistory. The laborer Claude Vuillerme was questioned for reputedly saying that he would rather listen to a dog barking than Calvin preaching. Vuillerme denied the charge and claimed that he simply said that one might as well sit at home by the fire if one was not going to take the sermon to heart. That claim, however, was undercut by witnesses. Subjected to a criminal investigation in March 1557, Vuillerme continued to deny the charges until he was tortured, after which he conceded that he had uttered those unflattering words about the reformer eight years earlier. He was required to ask forgiveness and to go to the Consistory to express his remorse.[104] Similarly, on August 31, 1557, the Consistory interrogated Pierre Bron for having criticized a sermon Calvin delivered. Several people maintained that, referring to that sermon, Bron said that Calvin preached that never had there been a greater problem with theft than what Geneva was experiencing at that moment. Under questioning, Bron, who apparently had not been present at that sermon, maintained that if Calvin had indeed said such a thing, he was not following the biblical text upon which the sermon was supposedly based.[105] Clearly if Calvin did in fact say such words, he was not explicating Scripture. Nonetheless the Council condemned Bron to six days in jail on bread and water and then he was "to be brought here with the torch in his hand and must confess to have done badly and evilly and to make reparation on his knees and great remonstrances are to be made to him."[106] Summoned to testify about Bron's words concerning Calvin's sermon, André Peronet was caught lying under oath to the Consistory and, after arguing with its members, asked the presiding syndic for permission to go earn his living elsewhere. For Peronet's lies and outburst, the Consistory excluded him from the Supper and sent him to the Council, which condemned him to six days in jail and to do reparation before the Council and the Consistory, and forbade him to leave the city for a year and a day.[107] Always sensitive to criticism, the pastors were now showing absolutely no tolerance whatsoever to those who in any way disparaged the clergy, even if the offenses were several years old. Although Calvin had complained in 1555 that the Council did not support him against the "insolences and contempt" suffered by the Consistory,[108] these incidents show that two years later the Small Council was in lockstep with the reformer and his morals court.

Magistrates were quite severe in dealing with anyone who showed any sign of support or just sympathy for the Enfants de Genève even years after their defeat. The Consistory's secretary, Pierre Alliod, got into trouble in 1558 merely for not contradicting another man who had said in his presence that Pierre Vandel, a fugitive who had been sentenced to death in absentia, was a good man. For this, Alliod was expelled from the Council of Two Hundred, fired from his position of scribe, and fined ten écus.[109] In the same year, the widow Clauda Bonna had to pay a hefty fine of a hundred écus just to get out of jail for having associated with and provided drinks to some of the condemned,[110] and Jean Philippin, a former Council member, was fined the enormous sum of five hundred écus for having contacts with some of the Perriniste exiles and for having spoken against the ministers ten years earlier.[111]

In 1562, at which time the position of the Consistory and the pastors was quite secure, the Consistory still would brook no criticism of ministers, even when the pastors' actions might offend most modern sensibilities. In November of that year, Nicolas Poutrier appeared because he was critical of a sermon delivered by Raymond Chauvet. Poutrier was accused of telling two other men that Chauvet had been wrong to refer by name to three Genevan men in a recent sermon. Facing the members of the Consistory, including Chauvet, Poutrier affirmed that he felt that the pastor had no business naming names from the pulpit.[112] A week later, the two men who had heard Poutrier's criticism were questioned. One of these, Pierre Phillippon, reported that Poutrier had said that it was wrong for Chauvet to have named individual Genevans from the pulpit and that the names of those men most definitely were not in the Scriptural text. Poutrier reputedly further said that "Saint John had not acted thus when he rebuked Herod of

Herodias," a reference to John the Baptist's criticism of the tetrarch Herod for having married Herodias, who was both his niece and his brother's wife (Luke 3:18–20). Poutrier now regretted this criticism of the minister, and the Consistory excluded him from communion until he could demonstrate sufficient knowledge of the faith. The Consistory also admonished the second witness, Pierre Dufour, for simply stating that he had not heard Poutrier say anything about Chauvet.[113] It seems ironic for the Consistory to say that Poutrier had to learn the basics about the Reformed faith, since his reference to Herod suggests a pretty good knowledge of Scripture (though contrary to Poutrier's implication, there is no evidence from Scripture that John the Baptist's denunciation of Herod was not made in public). Most modern readers would recoil at singling out individuals for criticism from the pulpit, a rather common practice in Reformation Geneva,[114] and Poutrier most definitely was right that Pastor Chauvet was deviating from the explication of the text when he did so. For the Consistory, however, even Dufour's claim that he had not heard the disparagement of the sermon was unacceptable.

The Consistory appeared very heavy-handed in dealing with Jeanne Essautier, whose only error was defending her own brother, Sebastian Castellio, the champion of religious toleration who had aggressively attacked the execution in 1553 of Michael Servetus.[115] She and her son appeared in March and April 1561 because they had defended the character (and perhaps obliquely, the ideas) of Castellio. Facing Calvin, who had denied Castellio's request to become a minister back in 1544, Jeanne claimed that her brother was a good man (*homme de bien*). She added that her husband, Matthieu Essautier, himself pastor in the village of Grand-Saconnex, had not told her that Sebastian was "a heretic and an evil man" and she asked rather provocatively to be shown how her brother had erred. At this point, the Consistory decided that Jeanne and her son should be examined about their faith by Pastors d'Agnon and Beza and by the lay assistant, the Marquis Galeazzo Caracciolo.[116] Five days later, Jeanne and her son again faced the Consistory because of certain words that they had used that tended to "magnify" Castellio. When Calvin and company asked mother and son if they still believed that Sebastian was a good man, Jeanne and her son meekly replied that they did not know. The Consistory then sharply rebuked them and declared that her husband, Matthieu, had erred in hiding from them the fact that "Castellio was repugnant to the doctrine and discipline administered in this city and . . . had even attacked the books of Mister Calvin." At this, Jeanne had nothing to say other than that her husband was indeed a good man, and she reacted angrily when Pastor Chauvet contradicted her and said that her husband had not behaved as he should have. Beza, however, reported that when he questioned them in private, they did not persist in their previous opinions. On the basis of Beza's rather favorable impression, the Consistory decided to limit itself to admonishing Castellio's sister and nephew, especially Jeanne, whom the Consistory found very proud and arrogant.[117]

This case shows the Consistory at its worst in terms of human relations. Jeanne Essautier and her son were not defending free will and attacking predestination, as her brother had. Just saying, in response to a very pointed question, that they did not know whether Castellio was a good man sufficed to draw the ire of Calvin and his colleagues. Was her angry reaction to Chauvet's criticism of her husband, whose "error" was failing to convince Jeanne that her brother was a despicable person, really so hard to foresee? In short, Jeanne Essautier's "sin" amounted to nothing more than defending in mild terms the character of her brother, whom Calvin excoriated as a heretic.

Like his wife, Matthieu Essautier also had bitter conflicts with the Consistory, especially with Calvin. When Essautier appeared before Calvin and his colleagues in November 1562, he was no longer pastor in Grand-Sacconex but had recently served as a minister in Provence. Back in Geneva, Essautier admitted that he had said to others participating in France at a synod, a regional meeting of church leaders, that Geneva must not be considered a Rome for Protestants that had the power to reject anyone from serving as a pastor in any Reformed church. It was not right, he felt, that potential pastors would have to seek letters of approval or to "kiss the boots" of Calvin or others in Geneva in order to be recognized as ministers. The Consistory decided on December 3, 1562, that Essautier should be excluded from the Supper since he did not recognize that he was causing a schism in the church.[118] The following month, when the Consistory repeatedly asked if he did not realize that his brother-in-law was a heretic, Essautier reaffirmed that he did not want to condemn Castellio, though he did not agree with some of his ideas. He also complained that members of the Consistory, especially Chauvet, had treated his wife and children quite rudely when he was away in Provence. This did not sit well with the Consistory, which declared that he should be thankful for the "great lenience" it had shown them since both his wife and his son deserved to be punished for having defended Castellio "to the dishonor of the Word of God and its ministers." Given his "lies and contradictions" and his rebellion against the Consistory, Calvin and his colleagues declared that Essautier was to be excommunicated and asked that *Messieurs* proceed to prosecute him for having said that Castellio harbored opinions and "minor errors" that were not heretical.[119] Three months later, in March 1563, the Consistory admonished Essautier for having said that he would not appear before the morals court if Calvin were present. To this, Essautier replied that Calvin acted as if he were the "governor" of the Consistory and could decide by himself how to prosecute his former colleague. The Consistory again reproached Essautier, especially for his "arrogance" for refusing to address Calvin and directing his words to the syndic instead.[120]

In August of the same year, the Consistory questioned Michel Castellio, the nephew of Essautier's wife, for having two copies of *Advice to a Desolate France*, written by his uncle Sebastian and published in Basel in 1562. This was a pacifist work in which Castellio deplored the religious war that had recently broken out in France, and the champion of religious toleration argued that the principal source of the turmoil was the religious persecution perpetrated by both Catholics and Protestants. Religious persecution in turn stemmed from the forcing of consciences, and Castellio asserted that the Golden Rule should be applied to matters of conscience.[121] Examining the book, the Consistory concluded that the author charged "the ministers of this church with having raised the sword in France and that they should leave everyone in peace and not force consciences." The Consistory decided that the nephew should be sent to the Small Council and the book condemned as "evil" and full of errors. It also alerted *Messieurs* that Essautier, though excommunicated, was still preaching in Lancy, a nearby village that was under the suzerainty of Bern but included residents who were subject to Geneva.[122] Appearing before the Consistory for the last time on September 9, 1563, Essautier conceded that he had asked his nephew to procure copies of *Advice to a Desolate France* but did not recall if he told him that it was a good book. The Consistory concluded that since there was no proof, it would leave Essautier to the judgment of God but again strongly rebuked him for claiming to be a minister even though he was currently excommunicated and that he had been declared a schismatic by the synod of Provence, where he caused many troubles.[123]

The case of Matthieu Essautier reveals a number of things. First, it shows unequivocally that in 1563 Geneva had not in fact become a Protestant Rome with the power to depose clergymen wherever the Reformed faith was practiced. Calvinists in Provence clearly deferred to Geneva, as shown by the fact that several pastors denounced Essautier for his unflattering comments about Calvin. Nonetheless, even after eleven months of locking horns with Calvin, Essautier was still preaching in Lancy, located just outside Genevan territory, even though he was excommunicated in Geneva itself. Essautier mentioned that he was residing in Bern, and this Reformed neighbor had already showed on numerous occasions that it would not be pushed around by Geneva, which politically was by far the weaker of the two allies. His support from Bern no doubt explained why he was still serving the small church in Lancy. Viewed as a whole, Calvin and the Consistory's dispute with Essautier was really a clash of personalities rather than divergent theological stands. Essautier did not want to repudiate his brother-in-law even though he rejected some of his ideas; his desire to obtain a copy of *Advice to a Desolate France* probably meant that he accepted Castellio's call for toleration and liberty of conscience, but there is nothing to suggest that Essautier embraced Castellio's belief in free will and rejection of predestination.

As these various cases demonstrated, the Consistory certainly enjoyed the full support of the Small Council by 1560. Indeed, in 1561 the Council even notified the Consistory that if someone appearing before it seemed to be a flight risk, the Consistory itself had the right to put that person in jail, provided that it notified one of the syndics of this action.[124] By this time the Consistory was also asserting itself in some unprecedented ways. In 1560, one can even find a few cases of the Consistory convoking people for theft, a crime that was not under the purview of this institution. Moreover, the Small Council often deferred to the Consistory on matters that were actually under its own jurisdiction, such as granting people who had been banished permission to return to the Republic.[125] By this time, the Council and Consistory were clearly in lockstep as far as discipline was concerned, and the civil authorities gave considerable importance to the opinion of the pastors and elders.[126]

All told, the registers of the Consistory show that, especially from the early 1550s, there was considerable resistance to the French pastors, but this animosity in general was not based on theological differences. Many Genevans were upset by the large number of foreigners, most of them from France, who had arrived in the city, and were angry about the growing power of the pastors in the area of discipline. Part of this animosity was directed against specific ministers, such as Raymond Chauvet, who were especially aggressive in rebuking sinners. But it was John Calvin who was by far the most controversial figure among the clergy. As we have seen, the question of the power to excommunicate was central to the various disputes in Geneva at this time. Calvin relentlessly defended the Consistory's exclusive right to admit or exclude people from the Supper. Some of his critics were members of the Small Council and one was even a member of the Consistory itself. Hypersensitive to criticism, Calvin was absolutely inflexible whenever his own authority or that of the Consistory was in any way questioned. After the riot and the defeat of the Perrinistes in 1555, Calvin was successful in assuring the important role of the pastors and of the Consistory in the matter of discipline.[127]

It is also important to emphasize that those who resisted the pastors and the Consistory represented a minority of Geneva. Without the support of influential citizens in the Small Council, Calvin and the Consistory would not have had the power to implement Reformed morality. More broadly, the Consistory depended on the residents of Geneva for information on those who were deviating from Calvinist mores. The fact that so many people were summoned to appear before Calvin and his colleagues bears witness to the general support that they enjoyed in Geneva.

CHAPTER 2

The Push for Religious Uniformity

CALVIN AND OTHER AUTHORITIES desired to bring about uniformity in worship and beliefs among the residents of Geneva and the dependent countryside. The Reformation unleashed a veritable revolution in worship as the sermon replaced the Mass as the core of the service, and Genevans had to become accustomed to an entirely different form of worship. Each Mass included the celebration of the Eucharist, and the highlight of each service was when the priest, praying in Latin in an undertone and facing the altar with his back to the congregation, elevated the host, which, according to Catholic theology, was transformed into the body of Jesus. This moment, often popularly referred to as the miracle of the Mass, was accompanied by the ringing of bells and might elicit shouts of joy and awe from the parishioners. With the conversion to Reformed Protestantism, the sermon replaced communion, which was celebrated only four times a year, as the core of the service.

After Geneva's break with Rome, one spoke not of going to church but rather of going to the sermons. While the Mass had involved all the senses, worship now became almost exclusively an aural experience.[1] The altars were removed from all three of Geneva's churches and were replaced by a simple pulpit which had a sounding board overhead to help the preacher project his voice. Benches were brought into the churches and when people attended services, they were expected to sit and listen attentively to the sermon from beginning to end. The Consistory exhorted people not to come late, leave early, or murmur during sermons (directed at people, mostly women, who prayed in an undertone, a vestige of the Mass).[2] Although sermons had been known in Geneva prior to the Reformation, they were given by members of the mendicant orders, the Dominicans and the Franciscans, not by parish priests.[3] As he stood in the pulpit, the pastor was dressed in a plain black robe rather than in the colorful vestments of priests, and delivered the sermon in the vernacular.

Sermons were supposed to be strictly based on Scripture, and Calvin and the other pastors followed the practice of *lectio continua*, whereby the preacher would read just a few verses from the Bible and then expound on them at length. Calvin himself usually preached on books from the New Testament or the Psalms on Sundays and books from the Old Testament on weekdays.[4] A sermon typically lasted about an hour, and the pastor would continue delivering sermons on a selected book of the Bible until he had preached on it in its entirety. Collectively Genevan pastors typically offered two dozen or more sermons a week. On Sundays there were usually eight services and three catechism services in the city's three churches combined, and, apart from the sermon, the services included only the recitation of the Lord's Prayer and perhaps the singing of some Psalms. Sermons were delivered every day of the week, though weekday services were usually shorter than the Sunday services and did not include the singing of Psalms. During the week the earliest sermon began at 4:00 a.m. (5:00 a.m. in winter), which was aimed primarily at servants to allow them to listen to a sermon before beginning the day's work. Wednesday was a special day of prayer in which the service, as on Sunday, included the singing of Psalms. No one attended all these services—several were contemporaneous—but everyone was expected to go to church at least once on Sunday (the principal service was at 8:00 a.m.), and ideally more often.[5]

In addition to getting people to go to church, Genevan authorities sought to educate residents in the Reformed faith and to wean them of a wide range of Catholic and popular practices they deemed unacceptable. Although Calvin was leading a religious movement, most of the issues heard by the Consistory were not directly related to religious beliefs and practices. As we shall see, among the most common reasons for which women and men were subpoenaed were illicit sexuality, domestic discord, and quarrels. The Consistory, however, also summoned a not insignificant number of men and women specifically for religious noncompliance, and this was especially true during the first years of its existence.

Heresy

Calvin's Consistory was most interested in the regulation of morals and behavior and, with respect to religion, like similar Reformed institutions, was much more concerned with rituals and worship than with theology per se. Serious cases of heresy, which were rare in Calvin's Geneva, were generally not even under the purview of the Consistory. By far the most famous case of "heresy" in Calvin's Geneva was that involving Michael Servetus, the Spanish physician who was executed for his non-trinitarian views in Geneva in 1553.[6] His execution set off a very important controversy over toleration, as Sebastian Castellio excoriated religious intolerance and promoted liberty of conscience, though he did not share Servetus's views on the trinity.[7] There is no evidence, however, that Servetus's unconventional beliefs resonated with anyone in Geneva.

The same cannot be said of the second most important theological controversy in Reformation Geneva: Calvin's conflict over predestination with Jerome Bolsec. A native of Paris, Bolsec (d. 1585) was a physician and a former Carmelite friar who was living in Veigy, a village in Bernese territory but quite close to Geneva. In March 1551, Bolsec attended a congregation, a meeting held every Friday in Geneva at which a pastor would explain a biblical text and then invite all present to take part in a discussion of the passage. Bolsec took that opportunity to take a stand against the doctrine of predestination, and he further developed his ideas on this subject in a letter to Pastor Abel Poupin. After this, Geneva's Company of Pastors summoned Bolsec, and Calvin and other ministers tried to persuade him to accept the doctrine of eternal election. Bolsec, however, was not convinced and attended another congregation in October at which he proclaimed that the belief that God preordained some people to damnation makes God a tyrant. He condemned such a doctrine as "heretical" and "scandalous." Shortly thereafter Bolsec was arrested, but he remained steady in his beliefs. Though disapproving of his ideas, church officials in Bern and Zurich urged the Genevans to show moderation in handling Bolsec's case. In spite of that request, on December 22, Geneva's Small Council condemned Bolsec to be banished for life. This sentence was carried out the next day, but Bolsec was again able to take up residence in nearby Bernese territory.[8] This remained a point of contention between Bern and Geneva, and this bad blood was exacerbated when the Council of Bern actually prohibited the teaching of predestination in Bernese territory to avoid further conflicts.[9]

Predestination has often been portrayed as representing the very essence of Calvinism. The first volumes of Consistory records, however, contain no reference whatsoever to this doctrine. Calvin and his associates wanted to impress on Genevans that hearing sermons, reciting the Lord's Prayer, and participating in the Supper were good whereas attending Mass, praying to the Madonna, and fasting during Lent were bad. It was rare for people to be summoned for purely theological reasons, such as rejecting the belief in salvation by faith alone. During Calvin's ministry, no one was accused of defending the Catholic belief in transubstantiation, and no reference to the doctrine of predestination is found during the first several years of extant consistorial records. That would change, at least briefly, with Calvin's conflict with Bolsec.[10]

Some residents of Geneva closely followed this debate, and the Consistory convoked several people in the wake of this dispute for reputedly supporting the ex-Carmelite. One woman was called simply because she had protested that Bolsec was a good man and did not deserve to be punished.[11] More numerous were those who were accused of actually defending his theology. In this regard, these actions differ from the large majority of the Consistory's investigations. The fact that formal heresy, which was so central to the concerns of the Roman and Spanish Inquisitions, was not a primary focus of the Consistory is most evident from the fact that neither Bolsec nor Servetus ever appeared before Geneva's Consistory; their cases went directly to the Small Council. In 1551, though, discussions about the polemic over predestination and free will clearly resounded in the streets and households of Geneva. Three men—Simon de Saint-Paul, Jean de Cortean, and Jacques Goudard—appeared before the Consistory on Christmas Day 1551 because they were suspected of being supporters of Bolsec who had been exiled the previous day. All three were rather circumspect when facing the Consistory and refused to acknowledge supporting Bolsec's ideas, notwithstanding others' testimony to the contrary. Goudard and de Cortean were excluded from the Supper. The following week Goudard had to get on his knees before the Consistory and ask forgiveness for his faults.[12] Far less docile was the dyer François Des Cassines, who was the subject of a long investigation by both the Consistory and the Small Council. In January 1552, Des Cassines underwent a trial and was jailed and obliged to renounce his previous statements and to beg for mercy. The Consistory excluded him from the Supper and ordered him to see a pastor once or twice a week until the next celebration of communion (at Easter) to ensure that he was sufficiently grounded in the Reformed faith to participate. All this did not suffice to silence Des Cassines, who was summoned again in March for having said that he was imprisoned because he did not "want to believe that if we do something evil or sin, [then] God is half the cause of this."[13] Unlike the others accused, Des Cassines kept expressing his disgust with the Calvinist belief in predestination. Calvin was so irritated that he declared before *Messieurs* of the Council that "if they did not kick the dyer out of the city, they would have to look for other ministers."[14]

Occasionally one finds instances of people objecting to predestination even a few years after the Bolsec affair. The schoolteacher Toussaint Mesquin was banished in July 1558 for strongly denouncing this doctrine.[15] In November 1561 Geneva's Council of Two Hundred gave him permission to return to the city in order to appear before the Consistory to apologize for his previous stand. Mesquin admitted that he had previously said that "God had not created anyone to be damned" and avowed that he had come to this opinion by being "corrupted" by Pierre Moussard, another former schoolteacher in Geneva whose wife, Étiennette, was the sister of the radical reformer Castellio, who strongly defended the belief in free will.[16] Mesquin now declared that he totally detested his former views. When asked if he hoped to return to Geneva, Mesquin replied that he planned to remain in Morges where he was already employed as a teacher. Calvin and his collaborators accepted this apology but said that he needed to apologize publicly since he had caused a public "scandal" and thus had to do *réparation* in Saint-Pierre on a Sunday.[17] In this case, it appears that Mesquin was genuinely motivated by a change of heart on the issue of free will versus predestination. He had no intention of returning to Geneva and had already secured employment in Morges, a city in the neighboring Pays de Vaud, which was under the control of Bern. In short, while doctrinal differences were not common grounds for being called before the Consistory in Calvin's Geneva, a few people did get in trouble for explicitly condemning predestination.[18]

False Prophecy

In the 1560s, Calvin and other authorities confronted a most unusual case involving two women whose claims of divine visions raised serious suspicions of heresy. In December 1560 the Consistory summoned for the first time Marie, a native of Picardy and the widow of the goldsmith Louis de La Pierre, who had held Genevan citizenship. Facing Calvin and his associates, Marie openly proclaimed that she received divine revelations and had the ability to prophesy, claiming that the Lord regularly answered her prayers and revealed to her everything she wanted to know. God informed her in advance, for example, about how her husband was going to die. In itself, this testimony resembled cases of pretense of sanctity heard by the Inquisition in Italy and Spain. Scholars have found that most of those accused by the Inquisitions of false sanctity, which quite often included apparitions of saints or other visions that were supposedly divinely inspired, were women. Roman Catholic leaders since the later Middle Ages had expressed concern about pretense of holiness and visions, and in the 1520s the Inquisition in Spain started taking action for false sanctity against so-called *beatas*, women who made informal vows of chastity and poverty without joining convents, many of whom claimed to have divine visions. Italian Inquisitions began prosecuting people, mostly women, for this alleged sin in the 1630s.[19]

Marie de La Pierre's testimony took a very odd turn when she further avowed that "the Spirit revealed to her that [John Calvin] was her husband."[20] According to witnesses, she also warned Marguerite Gannerel, the wife of Simon Brouet, that she was among the reprobate. In spite of or perhaps because of that warning, Gannerel became a close associate of de La Pierre, began to experience similar visions, and reputedly declared that the devils were in league with the Genevan ministers. Under interrogation, de La Pierre admitted that she had told others of a dream in which Calvin defecated in her mouth, though she now attributed that dream to an "assault by Satan." The Consistory asked the Small Council to arrest Marie and Marguerite lest they flee.[21] Gannerel was indeed incarcerated, but Marie de La Pierre somehow managed to avoid arrest by moving just outside Genevan territory, taking her son, who was a citizen, with her.[22] The Consistory thereupon advised the Council to release Gannerel with the expectation that upon learning of her release, de La Pierre would return to Geneva and that both could then be seized and questioned about their beliefs.[23]

This strategy apparently worked because the two women were interrogated on January 2, 1561. Gannerel was all too willing to discuss her visions with members of the Consistory. She related that one day while Calvin was preaching, she took a look at the second chapter of Revelations. Suddenly she felt a cold wind that enveloped her face and found that her New Testament was open even though she had just closed it. Overwhelmed, she went to ask Pastor Theodore Beza what could have caused this, and he said that this was "a vision of Satan," whereupon she closed her book again. Gannerel reported that Marie told her that one day while in Saint-Pierre she saw the devil who was wearing "a cap with ear flaps and a beautiful feather and bouquet" and that the devil was Marie's master because she had abandoned herself to him. She further recalled that de La Pierre described a dream in which Calvin "put his milk in her mouth."[24] When questioned later that day, de La Pierre now insisted that she was not a "prophetess." The Consistory rebutted, however, that she had even claimed she had prayed to God to give her a husband, and that He had granted this wish and Calvin himself was her spouse. She denied making this and other claims, though Beza asserted that she once sought him out and announced that "she knew for a fact that Mister Calvin was her husband."[25] Marie and others avowed that Marguerite Gannerel had once applied Jesus's words (John 14:6) to herself by saying that *she* was "the way, the truth, and the life." And Marguerite confessed that she told others that Satan was living among them in the person of Calvin. For their scandalous and blasphemous bantering, the Consistory sent the two women back to prison and referred them again to the Small Council.[26] For the most part, Marie and Marguerite were not reluctant to discuss their visions and even took the initiative to describe them to Beza and others.

Civil authorities began a criminal investigation of the two on the same day, and both of them provided further details, much of which involved putting each other in a very bad light. Marguerite, for example, reported that Marie had proclaimed that Calvin, her husband, sometimes came to her at night and that she had seen him in the pulpit in Saint-Pierre sporting a feather and bouquet in his hat, which would definitely have been a most unusual sight in Reformation Geneva. For her part, Marguerite asserted that Marie, not she herself, had said that all the devils were with the ministers, who devoured the goods of the poor. When she was then questioned on the same issues, de La Pierre initially denied all accusations, apart from admitting to saying that Gannerel was among the damned because she had done Marie many wrongs. When confronted with Beza, de La Pierre backed down on whether she claimed that Calvin was her husband and that she could prophesy. In the presence of Marie, Marguerite now admitted that she had claimed that the devils were allied with the ministers and said that this was because René Gassin, who oversaw poor relief, had refused to provide her with any money for sustenance.[27]

Questioned again two days later, Marie de La Pierre admitted that she had prayed to God for the gift of prophecy but tried to shift attention away from herself onto Marguerite. She maintained, for example, that she told Gannerel that she was damned only because of her claim to be the way, the truth, and the life. Moreover, Gannerel had related that she sometimes saw the stars, the sun, and the sky beating against and playing with each other at the top of her bed. De La Pierre further averred that about three weeks ago, she encountered Marguerite who was returning from making complaints about Marie to Pastor François Bourgoin, sieur d'Agnon. On that occasion, Marguerite reputedly told Marie that she must no longer be angry with her for siding with the devil one day and God the next because the devil was definitely with the ministers. Immediately after saying this, Marguerite supposedly picked up a Bible and read the following passage: "Then a great and mysterious sight appeared in the sky. There was a woman, whose dress was the sun and who had the moon under her feet and a crown of twelve stars on her head" (Revelation 12:1). Marguerite purportedly explained to Marie: "Behold how I adhere to the word of God; the woman is me, the twelve stars are my children, and the sky is Jesus."[28] Moreover, de La Pierre now denied having said that she saw Calvin wearing a hat with a bouquet or that Satan came to her in the form of the reformer. She also disavowed having claimed that she could prophesy, even though she admitted having said as much to the Consistory. Interrogated again on January 6, Marie referred to a complaint made by both women that the poor were not being treated well in Geneva;

she admitted telling Marguerite that Calvin was not like a father because he gave nothing to some people while giving huge quantities of meat (*grosse viande*) to others. De La Pierre added that one day while heading toward the vineyards, Marguerite proclaimed that she saw the heavens opening up, whereupon Marie warned that she must be on guard because this was likely a diabolical illusion. She conceded, though, that the faithful, when suffering persecution for the word of God, sometimes received consolation by seeing the heavens open up. When authorities questioned her three days later, Marie admitted that she had accused Marguerite of praying to Satan as her father. She also admitted telling Beza that Calvin was her husband and confessing to the Consistory that she could prophesy, but now claimed that she was so troubled when she appeared before the pastors and elders that she did not know what she was saying. De La Pierre emphatically denied all the other accusations, such as saying that Calvin came to her at night, appeared in the pulpit wearing a feather and bouquet, or gave her his "milk."[29]

A few days later, magistrates passed sentence against these two would-be prophets. Marguerite Gannerel was condemned to be whipped in the presence of Marie de La Pierre. For her scandalous words, including her declaration that Calvin was her husband, de La Pierre was considered the guiltier of the two and was sentenced to be banished under pain of the whip.[30] The sentence did not specify how long this banishment was to last, but already on February 6, 1561, just three weeks after the verdict, magistrates asked the Consistory for its opinion concerning de La Pierre's request for permission to return to Geneva. Calvin and the other assistants recommended that she stay away a bit longer in light of the gravity of her offense and the very short length of time since she had been banished.[31] In early April, however, the Consistory advised the Small Council to readmit de La Pierre, who seemed to repent fully of her "errors" and begged forgiveness from God and the Council; members of the Consistory did warn her that she would be punished more severely if she fell back into her errors.[32] When Marie de La Pierre petitioned on May 22, 1561 to be readmitted to the Supper, the Consistory determined that she was truly repentant and granted her request.[33] In light of her claims of receiving divine revelations, her bizarre dreams, and her assertion that Calvin was her husband, the Consistory was surprisingly lenient, lifting her exclusion from the Supper less than five months after her expulsion. The key to this clemency was de La Pierre's admission of guilt and her repentance. Calvin and his colleagues routinely readmitted to communion those who were genuinely sorry for having strayed from the straight and narrow Reformed path.

Notwithstanding her renunciation of her previous ideas, Marie de La Pierre would again show an unusual interest in Calvin shortly after her return to Geneva. In July 1561, she was arrested for having gone to Calvin's home in order to tell the reformer that she wanted to be either his wife or his chambermaid. Rebuffing her efforts to put her arms around him, the reformer bade Marie to follow him and proceeded to lead her to city hall to have her arrested. This time when questioned, de La Pierre freely described her first divine vision, which she claimed had taken place in September 1557. She asserted that the Lord showed himself to her in all his glory and that she heard a voice enjoining her to pray for the faithful and that she "must pray with her brother, John Calvin." The voice told her further that she was being prepared for a mission, and the next day she discovered that she had received the "mark of the children of God so that her duty was to pray to God according to the doctrine of John Calvin." Marie added that she drew inspiration to announce the word of God not from men but directly from God, who spoke through her mouth, leaving her at times unable to eat or drink. Her direct spiritual union with God sometimes left her "surprised by joy," but she also experienced the torments of the devil who presented her with a "horrible vision," a vision from which God released her. For her scandalous words, Marie de La Pierre was to be whipped and then banished a second time, with the threat of another whipping should she return.[34]

The experiences and treatment of de La Pierre and Gannerel can be viewed as both positive and negative for women as a whole. These women not only were literate but also had a fairly good knowledge of scripture, though their interpretations of certain passages were unusual, to put it mildly. The two of them could easily have been accused of witchcraft, especially given their numerous references to the devil or devils. In particular, Marie de La Pierre's bizarre claims that Calvin was her husband or the devil might have resulted in her being tried and perhaps convicted and executed for witchcraft in other jurisdictions. For their reputed visions, both de La Pierre and Gannerel might have been suspected of being possessed by demons. Alternatively, they might have been aggressively investigated for pretense of sanctity in Italy or Spain. Whenever a person claimed to experience mystical visions, the Inquisitions virtually always raised the concern that the vision might be of diabolical rather than divine origin. The fact that Marie de La Pierre was readmitted to communion in Geneva just five months after being banished shows Calvin and the Consistory's strong interest in reintegrating into the community people who had gone astray.

This lenience definitely came at a price. Neither de La Pierre nor Gannerel was taken seriously by members of the Consistory. By contrast, in rare instances, women called before the Inquisitions were able to persuade their interrogators that they had indeed received divine visions. Inquisition records can generally allow scholars to study in much greater detail the beliefs of people who were summoned than do consistory registers. Inquisitors' probing questions often allowed, for example, suspects to expound at length about their religious beliefs or practices, thereby preserving the voices of some early modern women.[35] By comparison, no consistory heard any case even remotely resembling that of Teresa of Avila, who effectively used the Inquisition as a forum to defend her spirituality and female independence and eventually became a very significant actor in the Reformation. While people who appeared before consistories were often asked to recite the Lord's Prayer and the credo, perhaps even the Ten Commandments, they were almost never subjected to lengthy interrogations concerning theological or spiritual nonconformity. In Geneva, as in all Reformed areas, women had no hope of ever being revered as mystics, and they could not reform a religious order or even pursue a religious calling if they felt so inclined. Both de La Pierre and Gannerel were essentially laughed at and considered crazy.[36] Indeed on the same day that both women admitted saying that Satan was in their midst in the form of Calvin, following the advice of the Consistory, authorities ordered that the two be returned to prison to be prosecuted, as the Council deemed prudent, since there were "many illusions in their brains."[37] Some of their claims, such as de La Pierre's dream that Calvin had defecated in her mouth, might seem to justify questioning their mental stability; and, to be sure, for every Catholic woman, such as Teresa of Avila, who became widely revered, there were countless would-be mystics who were rejected, rebuked, and silenced by the Inquisitions. Nonetheless, Genevan authorities' casual dismissal of these women's "illusions" can be viewed as a mixed blessing.

Vestiges of Catholicism

Much more common than cases that smacked of formal heresy were those involving the continuation of various Catholic practices that Calvinists deemed unacceptable. Such cases were most frequent in the first years of the Consistory's existence in the 1540s. Throughout Calvin's ministry, men comprised the sizable majority of those who were summoned to appear before the Consistory. Calvin and his associates, however, appeared especially concerned about the religious behavior of women, apparently in part out of fear that women were more likely than men to remain tied to various Catholic beliefs and practices. Evidence suggests that there was basis in fact for this concern.[38] In the first two years of extant records (February 1542–May 1544), the Consistory of Geneva convoked twice as many women as men for attending Mass in neighboring states, saying prayers for the dead or to the saints or to the Virgin Mary, fasting during Lent, or observing other similar vestiges of "popery." Some of the discrepancies for specific offenses are quite remarkable. During those two years, the Consistory convoked twenty-four women but only two men for possessing a rosary or Catholic literature, twenty-three women and three men for celebrating Catholic holidays, and twenty-nine women and thirteen men for saying prayers to the Virgin Mary.[39] The Consistory was wholly intolerant of anything that obliquely resembled the invocation of the Madonna even in the most trying circumstances. In January 1547, a Mister Pechod and his wife and daughter had to appear because of the "rancor" they felt toward Pastor Raymond Chauvet. Pechod affirmed that at the moment when his son-in-law passed away, his wife cried out, "Jesus Maria!" Chauvet—who was apparently present to give "consolation" to the dying man and the family—readily admitted that he immediately called her an "evil idolater," though he denied the Pechods' claims that he called her an "evil woman" and that he chased her out of the room. When Pechod declared that he wanted to prove these charges against Chauvet, the Consistory strongly rebuked him for his slanderous words but did not in any way reproach the pastor for aggressively attacking a grieving woman for merely uttering the name of Mary at the moment her son-in-law died.[40]

Even years after the conversion to the Reformed faith, some women, especially those living in the surrounding countryside, resisted giving up saying prayers to the Virgin Mary, the veneration of whom appeared much more deeply rooted than that of local saints.[41] Jeanne, the wife of Jean Favre, and Claude, the wife of Pierre Voutier, both from the village of Chancy appeared in August 1560, having been excluded from the Supper in part because of saying prayers to the Madonna. In response to a question, Claude proclaimed that the Virgin Mary had been saved by her works and that she herself would likewise be saved by her own works, an opinion that of course would have been anathema to Calvin.[42] When she reappeared in September 1561 requesting to be readmitted to the Supper, Voutier denied any wrongdoing and claimed that she had merely spoken of the Virgin Mary, not prayed to her. The Consistory rebuked her for defending her actions rather than confessing her sins and accordingly rejected her request.[43] The Consistory was equally concerned when in February 1558, Pernette Baud of the village of Peissy reputedly said that a recently deceased woman had appeared to her in a dream and informed her that souls were in purgatory—belief in which all Protestants rejected—because people no longer recited the Ave

Maria. Though at first denying the charges, she relented and promised to confess her error to her pastor and to all those with whom she had discussed the dream.[44]

Far less compliant was Clauda Blanc, summoned by the Consistory because of a conflict with her pastor in March 1562, eleven years after she was first accused of saying Catholic prayers. This latest encounter with the Consistory stemmed from a rebellion during a pastoral visitation preceding the celebration of the Supper at Easter. Pastor Nicolas Colladon reported that when he asked Blanc if she still put her trust in the Virgin Mary, she angrily responded that she did indeed because the Virgin was "her advocate to her blessed son." Blanc conceded that she had responded thus and the Consistory accordingly denied her access to the Supper and referred her to the Small Council, advising that she be sent to jail and obliged to do reparation in church.[45] Lay authorities actually went beyond this recommendation and banished Blanc for three months, after which she would be able to return if she proved to be "better instructed" in religion.[46] Protestantism prohibited saying prayers to any female figure, and Genevan women were clearly more reluctant than men to give up the veneration of Mary.

The records also reveal examples of people, again mostly women, who sought solace in certain other Catholic practices that were forbidden by Reformed leaders. Early in its existence, in November 1543, the Consistory convoked Tevene Peronet for having made a wax votive offering to Saint Claude for her husband, Marquet, who had been seriously ill and had, indeed, since died. The grieving widow told Calvin and his colleagues that she now realized that such rituals did no good and she begged mercy from God, the Republic, and the Company of Pastors. Convinced that she was repentant, the Consistory limited itself to admonitions and gave her two weeks to learn to recite the Lord's Prayer and the Apostles' Creed.[47] In a similar manner, in November 1559, Antoine, the widow of Monet Pernin of the village of Onex, admitted that she said prayers for her late husband. Concluding that she was still a "papist," the Consistory ordered that she return before Christmas to show that she was better instructed.[48] In the following month, Charles Manuel, originally from the Dauphiné in France, was admonished and excluded from the Supper because he had been caught singing some Psalms in a cemetery—perhaps the only place where Reformed authorities would have looked askance at the singing of Psalms, as they assumed that he was doing this for the benefit of the souls of those buried there.[49] In 1557 Jacquème Villette and her sister, Antoine Ballard, had to appear because they had gone to a cemetery in order to pray for the deceased on November 2, the Day of the Dead on the Catholic calendar. The two admitted that they had gone to this location but claimed that they had recited only the Lord's Prayer and that they were not kneeling, as Catholics were wont to do, while they prayed. Concluding that the two had made this trip out of "superstition," the Consistory referred them to the Small Council and required them to meet with a pastor before the next Supper to show they had sufficient knowledge of their faith.[50] Calvin and other Reformed leaders were opposed to formal funerals and were even inclined to do away with all prayers, singing, and readings at burials; if people are saved by faith alone, then prayers for the deceased can have no impact on their fate. There is no evidence of graveside sermons in Geneva, and any prayers that were pronounced were for the consolation of the bereaved, not for the benefit of the deceased. All Reformed theologians strongly rejected the belief in purgatory, upon which prayers for the dead were based.[51] The above cases indicate, however, that prayers and votive offerings for the dead provided comfort for some people. It is important to note that by the late 1550s, such examples were rather rare, which suggests that most Genevans had accepted the Reformed ban on these practices.

In January 1554, three women appeared before the Consistory accusing Pernette Chicand of defending the Mass and Catholic feast days. Pernette's family had wielded considerable power in the Republic of Geneva; her late husband, Antoine Chicand, had served as syndic six times during the period 1531–1551.[52] Having already appeared several times for her "papist" sympathies, Pernette was now accused by the other women of having complained that Catholic feast days were celebrated everywhere except in Geneva. When her companions objected to her praising the Mass and criticizing the pastors, Pernette continued to deride the ministers and proclaimed that she would prefer being taken by the devils to eating meat on Fridays.[53] The Consistory rebuked her and sent her to the Small Council.[54]

Unlike Protestants in neighboring Bern, Reformed Genevans put an end to the celebration of Christmas, which Calvin viewed as a papist innovation. Starting in 1550, in Geneva the Supper was celebrated on the Sunday nearest Christmas Day, but the twenty-fifth itself was to be a regular workday.[55] The Consistory set an example by always convening on Christmas Day if it fell on a Thursday, its usual day for meetings. The registers of the Consistory reveal that far more women than men resisted this change and remained committed to the celebration of Christmas. Three women appeared in January 1554 for having celebrated Christmas. When Pastor Chauvet reproached them on the twenty-fifth for celebrating the now banned feast, one of the women, Michée, the wife of Antoine Amied, reacted quite angrily and declared that such festivals had been observed before the arrival of the pastors and would continue to be celebrated.

Facing Calvin and his colleagues, however, Michée and the others were all contrite and asked forgiveness for their actions.[56] Eight years later the Consistory convoked twenty-one women but only one man for observing Christmas. Testimony revealed that they were celebrating the holiday in a very passive manner—they were all simply not working on Christmas Day. The innkeeper Guillaume Costel, the husband of one of these women, reported that on December 25, he found "several" women in his domicile with his wife and reproached them all for doing nothing, warning that they would be sent to the Consistory. His wife, Antoine, told him that he could go ahead and work himself but that he must not force her and her friends to do so. Since she had already been reprimanded several times and since she lied and was disrespectful on this occasion, Antoine was sent to the Small Council, which sentenced her to three days in jail. The Consistory also mandated that she and the twenty others attend church services and the catechism every Sunday until Easter. To ensure their faithful attendance, they were all obliged to make their presence known to the pastor as they left the catechism services each Sunday.[57] Obviously women appeared much more reluctant than men to give up Christmas even if their rebellion was limited to not working on Christmas Day.

Quite interestingly, while the Consistory aggressively attacked taking off Christmas Day in 1561, it was far less rigid two years later. In early December 1563 Antoine Cadran was summoned after having a conversation with four other men. The other four testified that they had been sitting around recently when one asked what day Christmas would be on this year, and Cadran responded that it would be on a Saturday. Another man noted that this meant that there would be no market on that Saturday because people from Catholic and Bernese territories would not be coming on that day—clearly the market in question depended to a considerable extent on buyers and sellers from outside Geneva. At this point, Cadran said that it had been right to celebrate this holiday and that there is scriptural justification for doing so, though he admitted that he could not cite the passage. Two men later asked Cadran where the celebration of Christmas is mentioned in Scripture since they had read the Bible and could not recall such a passage. Cadran replied that Christmas was the "feast of the Deluge [!]." More important, Cadran declared that the leaders of Bern were just as wise as Geneva's, and if celebrating Christmas was not good, Bern would not have kept it.[58] Members of the Consistory excluded Cadran from the Supper because he lied to them and sent him to the Council to be punished for sowing divisions.[59] Unexpectedly, though, Calvin, who was definitely present, and his colleagues also rebuked the four men who testified against him. They proclaimed that those men should not put too much emphasis on indifferent things, which included the celebration of Christmas. The Consistory avowed, "We do not at all condemn those who observe such a day [as Christmas], provided that they do so without superstition." Citing a Biblical example, members of the Consistory noted that while King David tolerated the bronze serpent which Moses had created (i.e., the Nehushtan), Hezekiah later destroyed it because it had become the object of idolatry.[60] How do we explain the fact that in January 1562 the Consistory appeared quite concerned about two dozen women simply not working on Christmas but specifically said in December 1563 that, barring "superstition," celebrating Christmas was acceptable? This is one of many examples of Calvin and the Consistory picking their fights one at a time. Apparently the fear they harbored two years earlier that the celebration of Christmas lent itself to Catholic superstition was waning; just as the fear of giving children the names of non-biblical saints would disappear by the 1560s (see chapter 3), so Genevan religious leaders were showing greater flexibility on Christmas toward the end of Calvin's life. This limited flexibility reflected the Consistory's growing confidence in the success of the reformation of morals in Geneva.[61]

As this case indicates, though women comprised the majority of those allegedly continuing "papist" practices, the Consistory did take action against men who attended Mass, said prayers to Mary, or took part in other "papist" rituals. In December 1550 a man was summoned for having recently been seen kneeling in Lyon as the communion host was being carried before him. He denied the charge, but a witness affirmed that he had indeed "knelt before the God of dough and then made the sign of the cross," both actions that Calvin and his associates considered idolatrous.[62] Genevan authorities also pursued native artisans who manufactured objects that were intended for use in Catholic worship services. In July 1550 the Consistory summoned a goldsmith by the name of Mallard who had recently made a chalice, which was denounced as an object of "idolatry" because it was intended for use in the Mass. Although Mallard protested that he simply needed to earn a living, the Consistory told him to stop making such objects and referred him to the Council, which ordered him to destroy the chalice.[63]

In spite of a few examples to the contrary, the unavoidable impression from the records of the Consistory, especially from the earliest registers, is that Genevan women remained more closely tied than men to certain Roman Catholic practices. During Calvin's ministry, such cases declined in number as residents learned to distinguish acceptable from unacceptable rituals for Reformed Protestants.

Attendance at Mass

Quite common were cases of both men and women who were immigrants to Geneva but returned temporarily to their native land where they attended Mass, even though they had, in theory, come to Geneva to practice the Reformed faith. In March 1554, for example, the Frenchmen Charles Marchepoin and Jean de Serre were summoned because after living in Geneva where they had partaken of the Supper, they returned to France for a year during which time they attended Mass. The Consistory ordered them to confess their error and excluded them from the sacrament.[64] In the same manner, Jacques De Lyon from Blois in central France appeared voluntarily in April 1557 and confessed that "having lived in this state and having received the Supper [here], he went back to his country at the instigation of his parents . . . and was constrained to go to Mass, of which he repents and requests to be readmitted to the Supper." The Consistory ordered him "to approach one of the ministers to hear his confession before taking and receiving the Supper."[65] One may of course question if De Lyon was really forced to attend Mass, but since he approached the Consistory at his own initiative, he almost certainly felt guilty for his actions. This highlights the fact that the Consistory was playing a role similar to that of the Catholic confessor. In this case, the records do not speak of any punishment and the "sentence" consisted of going to a pastor to confess the error. In April 1561, Michel Ivon also appeared voluntarily and confessed that he had received the Supper in Geneva nine years ago, but then returned to his native land where he regularly attended Mass, of which he now greatly repented. The Consistory accepted his expression of contrition and noted that he had never actually established residency in Geneva, which helps explain why he was not excluded from the Supper even once.[66]

In dealing with cases of attending Mass, members of the Consistory at times expressed a certain sympathy toward women that they probably would not have shown toward men in similar circumstances. In November 1559, for example, the widow Estiennette Boistier voluntarily appeared before the Consistory to confess that, after her husband's death, she was burdened with six children and had to seek assistance from relatives in a Catholic area. While there, family members obliged her to attend Mass, and Boistier now expressed remorse for having thus committed "idolatry." Referring her to the Small Council, members of the Consistory were convinced that her remorse was genuine because she had appeared at her own initiative. They recommended that the Council take her poverty into consideration and show her mercy. Though she was suspended from the Supper, Boistier clearly received sympathetic treatment from the Consistory. Calvin and his colleagues surely would have been less inclined to believe that a man could have been similarly "forced" to attend Mass, and they no doubt rightly believed that a man would have had more professional opportunities to avoid the poverty that pushed her to leave Geneva in the first place.[67] It must be noted, however, that on this occasion the Consistory and lay authorities were not entirely on the same page, as the latter sentenced Boistier to one day in jail and to do *réparation* before them.[68] Calvin was no doubt most upset when his own stepson, Jacob Stordeur, was summoned in 1556 for leading a life of debauchery instead of learning a trade. Worse still, from the reformer's perspective, he had taken the "god of dough" (*dieu de paste*) while in Germany. Far from cutting him any slack, the Consistory excluded him from the Supper and the Council sent him to jail.[69]

Many people seemed to move quite freely between Protestantism and Catholicism, attending the sermons in Geneva but going to Mass in Savoy or France. Many undoubtedly had attitudes similar to those of Pierre Gallatin even if most would not have been so bold as to state them publicly. In 1559 witnesses declared that Gallatin, a carpenter from the village of Peney now living in Geneva, had said that "if he were in Chambery or Annecy [in nearby Catholic Savoy], he would go to Mass and would do as his prince does, and if *Messieurs* [of the Small Council of Geneva] ordered us to go to Mass, he would go."[70] Previously banished and put in the stocks for blasphemy, Gallatin called his accusers a bunch of liars.[71] The impression one gets is that many people had little problem switching between the Mass and the sermons and between the Eucharist and the Supper, depending on where they happened to be. For many people, going to Mass while visiting relatives in Savoy was not a form of "idolatry," as Calvin and other Reformed leaders believed. It simply amounted to going along with the prevailing religious practices in a given area.

Blasphemy

Blasphemy, viewed as a sin by Catholics and Protestants alike, was among the most common infractions heard by the Consistory, a sin for which far more men than women were convoked. This latter trend almost certainly was not just a reflection of the gendered expectations of the male authorities in Geneva. Men probably did commit blasphemy more often than women, or at least they were more likely to do so in public and thus draw the attention of authorities.[72] In some Reformed areas, laws were passed that obliged those who took God's name in vain to immediately get on the ground and kiss the earth as a sign of repentance, and anyone who observed a blasphemy was enjoined to command the blasphemer to perform this act of contrition.[73]

The Consistory was initially not particularly harsh in dealing with most cases of blasphemy. For example, it summoned the carpenter Pierre Gentil for blasphemy in August 1553. Gentil confessed that he lost control and blasphemed when he saw another man brutally strike Gentil's nephew. Before Calvin and his colleagues, he got on his knees and asked forgiveness from God, and the Consistory limited itself to admonishments.[74] Gentil was atypical insofar as he was supoenaed exclusively for blasphemy. Perhaps more than any other sin under the purview of the Consistory, blasphemy rarely appeared as the only indiscretion committed by an individual. A person accused of blasphemy was often charged at the same time with drunkenness, quarreling, marital discord, fornication, or other possible offenses. The sentence he received, however, was fairly typical. More often than not the Consistory did not go beyond rebuking the blasphemers, exhorting them to mend their ways, and having them get on their knees to ask forgiveness for taking God's name in vain.

Several cases also show clearly that many Genevans embraced the notion that it was everyone's duty to reproach anyone who blasphemed, an attitude that dovetailed with the scriptural command to confront privately someone who sinned. In November 1546 Jacques-Nicolas Vulliet was in the baths with some other men and, noticing some sores on the legs of one man, said, "By the body of God, this pox is finer than mine." Another man immediately rebuked him, and Vulliet's friend Claude Serex put his hand on his shoulder and told him to kiss the earth, which he did. The Consistory limited itself to censuring Vulliet.[75] Summoned in July 1557 for his marital quarrels, Humbert Trolliet of the village of Vandœuvres denied his wife's charge that he often swore and blasphemed. Witnesses, however, contradicted this assertion. One man reported that one day while working in a vineyard, Trolliet blasphemed by crying out, "the body of God" (*corps Dieu*). He rebuked Trolliet, who immediately prostrated himself and kissed the ground and begged God for mercy. Two other men asserted that Trolliet yelled at another, "Goddamn you" (*Maulgré Dieu soys tu*), and kissed the earth right after they reproved his words.[76] Clearly these other rural laborers considered it their duty to scold anyone who blasphemed, and Trolliet's reaction of immediately dropping to his knees to kiss the ground and ask forgiveness from God indicates that he, too, recognized this as a serious sin. Secular authorities sentenced him to make amends by carrying a torch in his hand as a sign of contrition.[77] When someone reproached another for swearing, there was of course the risk that the blasphemer might react violently, as was the case with the miller Aimé Reymond, who struck with a club a man who had rebuked him for blasphemy. Confronted by witnesses, Reymond admitted his error and was sent to the Small Council, which admonished him for the scandal and his violence.[78] These cases show that discipline in Geneva was not just top down. The norms promoted by the Consistory were shared by many residents who did not hesitate to reprove their neighbors for their sins, especially, but not exclusively, blasphemy.[79]

At times, the Consistory and Genevan authorities could be quite severe in handling cases involving particularly egregious cases of blasphemy or habitual blasphemers who refused to mend their ways. Over a period of years Calvin himself repeatedly called for more rigorous discipline in several areas. In 1551, with the support of the Consistory, the reformer several times called for increased penalties for adultery, fornication, and blasphemy, since he found that the ordinances that had been passed the previous year were too lax on those sins.[80] Those attempts failed, but Calvin renewed these efforts five years later.[81] Concerning blasphemy, in February 1556 the Consistory asked Calvin to propose appropriate penalties in consultation with Michel de L'Arche, secretary of law, and that they request the Council to take suitable action, noting how often such sacrilegious language was heard in Geneva and how frequent recidivism was among blasphemers.[82] In that year it appeared as if Calvin and the Consistory had truly declared war on blasphemy as the number of actions against that sin were quite numerous. In November 1556 the Small Council passed edicts concerning the legal treatment of fornication, adultery, and blasphemy, and the next day, with Calvin's assistance, these edicts were approved by the Council of Two Hundred.[83] When, however, the General Council debated these edicts, there was quite an uproar as certain members protested that the punishments were too severe. To Calvin's chagrin, these edicts were rejected.[84]

Nevertheless, records show that in practice blasphemy was punished more severely starting in 1556. Early that year, the servant Clauda Fichet from Savoy was convicted of singing profane songs and of pronouncing numerous blasphemous words. Civil authorities condemned her to three hours in the stocks and then banishment for life.[85] On Christmas Eve of the same year, four men appeared before the Consistory denouncing the young carpenter Guyot Veyturier for having blasphemed in a most scandalous way, having sworn on the blood, wounds, and body of God. When they protested and told Veyturier to get on his knees and kiss the earth for this affront, the young man continued with his curses and blasphemy, yelling that "they should go screw their old mother." Veyturier and his father appeared and both acknowledged that they had blasphemed. The

Consistory admonished the father and dismissed him but referred Guyot to the Small Council.[86] Four days later the Council ordered that Guyot be jailed and brought to justice for having "grossly blasphemed against God and uttered most heinous words."[87] Under interrogation, Guyot Veyturier confessed in part but denied having sworn on the blood, wounds, and body of Christ. The evidence was overwhelming, however, and the Council sentenced him to be put in the stocks for three hours, then to do *réparation* at the site of the blasphemy, and finally to be banished for three years under pain of the whip.[88] The pin-maker Claude Rime, originally from France, was definitely most imprudent in his choice of places to blaspheme. Subpoenaed in July 1556 on suspicion of adultery, Rime swore to the Consistory on the "wounds of God" that he was innocent of the charges.[89] For uttering these blasphemous words to Calvin and his associates, Rime was excluded from the Supper and referred to the Small Council, which jailed him for three days and condemned him to the stocks for three hours.[90]

The Consistory and the Council predictably could be harsher still when dealing with recidivist blasphemers. In November 1561 Jacques Chapelle appeared before the Consistory accused of blasphemy and threatening to beat up a man who reproached him for his sacrilegious language. Though he denied the accusations, the Consistory excluded Chapelle from the Supper and sent him to the Council for punishment, persuaded by the testimony of witnesses that he had used God's name in vain and had declared that "he had eaten the devil but could not swallow his horns."[91] When questioned by lay authorities, Chapelle confessed to all the accusations and to having already been rebuked for blasphemy. Pointing out that they had shown him lenience a few years earlier by obliging him merely to do *réparation* at the location where he had blasphemed,[92] magistrates now sentenced him—claiming to show "mercy rather than rigor"—to be taken bound to the public square of Bourg-de-Four, where he was to have his tongue pierced by a hot iron for being an incorrigible blasphemer.[93] Though seldom employed in Geneva, piercing the tongues of blasphemers was a well-known punishment in early modern Europe.[94]

Attending Church and Learning the Tenets

Also of great concern to Calvin and his colleagues were truancy from church and simple ignorance about the faith. The Consistory of Geneva, unlike certain other consistories, had a pedagogical in addition to a disciplinary role.[95] In the early days of its existence, the Consistory paid special attention to the church attendance of Genevans and regularly questioned people about their knowledge of prayers and the credo even if they were appearing for something with no obvious connection to religious instruction, such as quarrels or drinking. Evidence from the registers also suggests, perhaps not surprisingly, that ignorance and truancy from church were an even greater problem among the residents of the rural communities surrounding Geneva than among the city dwellers. In November 1550 the Consistory summoned "a dozen" heads of family from the village of Saconnex because the entire village was causing "a great scandal" by not attending church and by continuing to celebrate certain feasts. The people of Saconnex had caught the attention of the Consistory in May of the same year when Pastors Chauvet and Fabri reported that only three people in the whole village could recite the creed. In the later appearance, the Consistory warned the family heads that if the villagers did not mend their ways the Council would be asked to take action.[96] These two related incidents underscore the extra challenges that Geneva's pastors and elders encountered in trying to promote attendance at sermons and knowledge of the faith in the Genevan countryside.[97]

As the years passed, questions about one's knowledge of prayers and such became less common, probably because the pastors and elders believed that most residents of Geneva had assimilated the most fundamental tenets of the Reformed faith. Yet even more than a quarter century after Geneva's conversion to Protestantism, many adults were still required to attend catechism because of their ignorance. Ordinarily it was not the Consistory but rather the pastors, probably through their visitations preceding the Supper, who ordered parishioners to attend catechism.

As we have seen, in Geneva the pastoral visitations preceding the Supper could be the source of conflicts. There were several cases of people trying to avoid these meetings either because they did not know the basics of Reformed doctrine or because they did not want to confess certain sins that they had committed. In April 1560, a female servant had to appear before the Consistory because she had fled when the pastor Nicolas Des Gallars was conducting the visitation. The Consistory mandated that she go to catechism lessons to show that she knew her faith.[98] More surprising was the case of another maidservant, Claude Pralet, referred to the Consistory in April 1562 by Pastor Jean-Raymond Merlin, who found that she was quite ignorant in matters of faith. Significantly, Pralet had recently spent a year working for Jean Chenu, who served as a *dizenier*, the officer who usually accompanied a pastor when making the visitations in the weeks prior to communion. Chenu rather sheepishly apologized and indicated that he did not realize that it was his responsibility to see that his servant be instructed in religion, a claim that seemed to be contradicted by Pralet's assertion that he sent her out of the house whenever the visitation was taking place. The Consistory issued admonitions to both Pralet and Chenu: the former to learn the basic tenets of the faith before the next celebration of the sacrament, the latter to take his charge more seriously.[99] Still more striking was the "rebellion" in April 1562 of a "large number of people—men, women, and children—of the *dizaine* . . . of Bourg-de-Four," who did not want "to present themselves before Mr. Raymond [Chauvet], minister, and other assistants for the most recent visitation." On three successive meetings, individuals who were part of this "rebellion" received admonitions and were obliged "to appear together before the minister and some of the assistants of the Consistory" to prove that they had learned the basics of the faith.[100]

Various cases show that in the 1560s, members of the Consistory could still be dumbfounded by the degree of religious ignorance of some of those appearing before them. In April 1564, the Consistory complained that the tailor Jean Malchamp was "so ignorant that he said that Our Lord Jesus Christ sent . . . his son to death for us."[101] In October 1560, the fisherman Claude Pascard appeared because he was not attending the catechism as required. When asked how many commandments there are, Pascard replied that there are three, which he identified as, "Our Father is in heaven"; "I believe in God"; and "I believe in the Holy Ghost." When asked if he was violating any commandments by fornicating or stealing, Pascard replied in the negative. When he was strongly rebuked for his error and "silliness," the fisherman protested that he could not know everything. The Consistory sent him to the Council to order Pascard to attend catechism every Sunday for a year. Excluded from the Supper, he also had to see his minister every week to show proof of his attendance at catechism.[102]

The case of Tivent Bastard of the village of Bourdigny shows how far pastors were willing to go to try to impress upon parishioners the need to learn the basics of the Reformed faith. When he appeared before the Consistory in May 1561 asking permission to take communion, Bastard's answers to two very simple questions left the members of the Consistory flabbergasted: he answered that the son of God was God and that he did not know who suffered and died for the salvation of humanity. Concluding that Bastard was a "monster" as far as his salvation was concerned, the Consistory mandated that he go to church every Sunday and that he meet with Pastor Jean Trembley after each service to become better informed.[103] A month later, he was back because he had not been diligent in either attending church or becoming better instructed. Clearly he did meet with his pastor occasionally, because Trembley reported warning

Bastard that while his wife would go to heaven because she was well instructed, Bastard himself was still ignorant about religion (which implies that he would not go to heaven because of his ignorance, an idea that is not in accord with the Calvinist doctrine of predestination). At this, Bastard replied, "If I knew that she were [going to heaven] and I wasn't, I would go beat her so much that it would be a famous case." The Consistory continued to exclude him from the Supper because of "his ignorance and stupidity, also his mockery. He is enjoined to become instructed on the path to his salvation, and for this he must go often to find his minister."[104]

The number of times that pastors questioned parishioners to see if they were knowledgeable enough to participate in the Supper could be quite impressive. On April 17, 1561, eleven days after Easter, a servant named Thomasse appeared because her minister had questioned her three weeks before Easter and four times after (in eleven days!), and he complained that "she knew nothing" and was still incapable of reciting entirely the Lord's Prayer and the Apostles' Creed. The Consistory excluded Thomasse from the Supper and told her to continue meeting with the pastor to become better instructed.[105] Pastors also regularly made reports to the Consistory on the progress (or lack thereof) that people were making through their one-on-one meetings with ministers in learning the basics of Reformed Protestantism. In May 1561, for example, Pastor Chauvet reported that the boatman Guillaume Bachelard, who had appeared twice recently for his ignorance, had learned the Lord's Prayer and the confession of faith but still did not know how to answer other questions. As a result, the Consistory decided that he should continue to abstain from the Supper.[106]

In spite of these examples, overall the evidence indicates that Genevan leaders enjoyed considerable success in getting residents to learn the basics of the faith. The large majority of cases in which the Consistory asked people to recite the Lord's Prayer and the Apostles' Creed occurred during the very first years of its existence. It is possible that this simply meant that in later years the scribe did not bother recording such queries. It is also possible that such questions were regularly asked during the visitations preceding the Supper starting in 1550, thus obviating such inquiries before the Consistory. But the most persuasive explanation for the drop in such questions is that most people were now capable of reciting both the Lord's Prayer and the Apostles' Creed.[107]

As previously noted all residents of Geneva were required to attend church, and this did not mean just going to the main service (at 8:00 a.m.) on Sunday. Jean Soutier, who had been reproached for truancy from church as early as 1542,[108] was summoned again in December 1560 for the same issue. Soutier admitted that the previous Sunday he let some people get warm in his home during the sermon of 2:00 p.m. He claimed, rather implausibly, that he did not hear the lieutenant's assistant banging on his door to notify them that they had to go to church. Convinced that Soutier just did not want to face the official, the Consistory rejected his story and sent him to the lieutenant to be punished.[109]

Although Genevan authorities encouraged a very strong work ethic, people might be censured for working during the principal church services on Sundays and on Wednesdays—a prayer service, which included the singing of Psalms, was held every Wednesday in Saint-Pierre at 7:00 a.m., 8:00 a.m. in the winter.[110] For Calvin and the other pastors, the commandment to remember the Sabbath and keep it holy meant that everyone was to dedicate one day a week to worship and rest. To a certain extent, Calvin viewed the fourth commandment as a vestige of Jewish ceremonial law and therefore no longer mandatory for Christians. For Calvin, there was nothing inherently sacred about any particular day of the week, but he nonetheless deemed it wise to continue to follow tradition and recognize Sunday as the day dedicated to worship and repose.[111]

In Calvin's time the Consistory did not appear especially zealous in forbidding work on Sundays; in that regard, he and his colleagues did not take as hard a line on Sabbath observance as some Reformed leaders did in the centuries that followed. Shops and boutiques were to stay closed during the services, and in December 1559 the Consistory specifically asked the Council to forbid tavern keepers to serve food or drink during the sermons on Sundays and Wednesdays to anyone, including foreigners—taverns were supposed to cater primarily to foreigners, whereas the locals were supposed to eat and drink at home.[112] There were relatively few actions taken against working on Sundays, however, unless it coincided with the sermons. The infrequency of such actions means either that residents had already conformed and did not work on Sundays or that the Consistory did not consider this a sin worth pursuing. Two cases from June 1561 are telling. Two cobblers, Vidal Gibellin from Languedoc and Jacques Livon from Provence, were questioned about working the previous Sunday. The two men confessed that they made a leather collar for a man who wanted to leave the city quickly. They proclaimed that they had not done this out of greed and asked for forgiveness. Asked at what time they did this work, they replied that it was in the afternoon after dinner and that they had been at the 8:00 a.m. church service. Witnesses confirmed their account, and the Consistory concluded that this was "not a major crime" and noted the work was performed for someone who was just passing through; it accordingly limited itself to admonitions.[113] The very next entry in the register involved Michel de Loges, who was charged with allowing his female servant to sell wine on Sunday while people were on their way to church, even when the last bell had been rung. De Loges protested that he had expressly forbidden her to do so, and the unnamed servant confessed to selling some wine to a woman who was adamant that she do so even after the last bell for the sermons. Calvin and the other assistants simply told the two not to do it again.[114] While the cobblers' "sin" might be construed as working on Sunday in general, de Loges and his servant had sold wine during a service, and the strong impression is that if they had sold wine before or after the service, they would not have been brought before the Consistory. The bottom line is that the prohibition against work was not a high priority for the Consistory, which was not particularly strict in its application.

The Consistory registers also indicate that people were not strictly forbidden to seek mundane diversions on Sundays. Calvin thought that taking part in moderate amusements on Sundays was permissible, and he himself was known to bowl occasionally on Sunday afternoons.[115] As we will see in the following chapter, young men got in trouble for taking part in martial games on Sundays because they were supposed to attend catechism at that time. The fact that the games were held on Sunday afternoon, however, did not itself provoke the ire of the Consistory. From the Consistory's perspective, the key was to refrain from working and playing during church services.

Religious Compliance

When reading the Consistory's minutes, one often has the impression that these disciplinary institutions were trying to impose certain forms of behavior that were widely unpopular among the population at large. One must always remember, however, that these registers, like all court records, are skewed toward the negative. People who enthusiastically embraced and quickly conformed to Reformed piety were not likely to be summoned. Church attendance was mandatory, and throughout Calvin's ministry the Consistory convoked people who were truant. These people, however, represented a very small fraction of the residents of the city and the dependent countryside. Moreover, the effectiveness of the Consistory depended to a very large extent on the collaboration of the rank and file. The pastors, elders, and *dizeniers* were not nearly numerous enough to watch over the behavior of all Genevans. Apart from self-denunciations, authorities depended to a very large degree on the willingness of residents of Geneva to denounce others who were straying from the straight and narrow path. Unfortunately from the historian's perspective, consistory records, like those of the

Inquisition, almost never give the names of the accusers.[116] But the frequency of such denunciations demonstrates that most people in Geneva supported the goals of the Consistory.

Testimony of witnesses often reveals that many laypeople shared the convictions of the pastors and elders that certain forms of behavior should be suppressed. As we have seen, many residents felt that it was their moral responsibility to rebuke blasphemers, even publicly. Moreover, in one case, seven witnesses, three men and four women, affirmed that they bluntly told a group of women riding in a cart outside the city to stop singing unseemly songs.[117] The registers of the Consistory provide more examples of women and men who conformed, often even enthusiastically, to Reformed mores than those who actively resisted them. In August 1548, the Consistory interrogated Aimé Dunant, obviously a man of modest means, as to why he no longer diligently attended church and even the *congrégations*, the weekly Friday morning meetings of pastors that were open to the general public to discuss Scripture and theology. When Calvin and his colleagues opined that it seemed that he no longer had "any affection for the word of God," Dunant protested:

> He is not ceasing to have affection for the word of God, knowing that it is the lamp of the faithful that shines the light for them. [It is also] the path by which the Christian must direct his steps. But one time, he heard a sermon one Friday at [the church] of Saint-Gervais and afterward went to the congregation where he stayed a rather long time. When he returned [from the congregation], here came a man named Jacques Duval, a Parisian of the same profession [as Dunant], who reproached him, saying that it is the business of a rich man to go to the congregations and stay there until ten o'clock, and that it would be better if he worked to provide for his small children since he was poor. Aimé replied to him that he certainly wanted to work to provide for his small children, but [to do] that he would never give up following the word of God so long as God gave him the blessing [to do so].[118]

People called before the Consistory regularly stressed their attachment to the Reformed faith—it would have been most impolitic to do otherwise—but this exclamation went far beyond what the pastors and elders expected of the rank and file. Though it was unusual for a layman to express such an avid interest in Scripture and matters of faith, there were Genevans who were deeply tied to the Reformed faith, evident in the fact that laypeople typically comprised over 60 percent of the attendees at the weekly *congrégations*.[119]

Women and the Reformed Faith

One can also find many examples of women who were much more devout than their husbands. Convoked for domestic discord in October 1550, Jeanne Bryden complained of her husband's debauchery and reputedly cited Scripture and writings by Calvin to convince him to forswear his sinful ways.[120] In June 1559, the shoemaker Guillaume Rens and his wife, Philippa, were convoked for their domestic quarrels and insults. Guillaume was clearly more culpable than Philippa, whom he constantly berated and insulted. Testimony further revealed that while Guillaume was chronically absent from the sermons, Philippa faithfully attended them, a habit that angered her husband. Apparently Philippa sometimes tried to recount to her husband the sermons she had heard, which provoked him to tell her derisively that she should go take the place of "Mister Colladon," a supposed reference to Pastor Nicolas Colladon. When questioned by Calvin and his colleagues, however, Guillaume admitted saying those words but insisted, not very convincingly, that he was referring to the attorney Germain Colladon, a cousin of the minister, because his wife was acting as if she were arguing a case with him. Witnesses also indicated that Philippa recited Scripture to her husband when trying to persuade him to treat her better.[121]

Quite interesting was the probe into the actions of Jacquème Egipte in May 1557. When an unnamed woman questioned her about her faith and asked if she knew why God had created her, Egipte admitted that she crudely replied, "Eat shit" (*Mache merde*). Egipte regretted saying these words and now asked for mercy from God and the *seigneurie*. The Consistory referred her to the Council, which sentenced the repentant Egipte to one day in jail.[122] Significantly, the entry in the registers concerning Egipte comes right after inquiries about two other women who had shown disrespect toward pastors when they conducted visitations just before Easter. Appearing where it does in the minutes, Egipte's case might mean that the unidentified woman was herself actively participating in the visitation alongside the pastor or, perhaps more likely, that she took it upon herself to tutor Egipte (whether she wanted this assistance or not) in preparation for the upcoming pastoral visit. What is beyond dispute is that she wholeheartedly embraced the Reformed faith.

There was actually a precedent for a woman openly proselytizing to other women in Geneva with the approval of reformers. A former nun from Flanders, Marie Dentière was a convert to Protestantism and resided in Geneva with her second husband, the pastor Antoine Froment, from 1535 until her death in 1561. In August 1535, accompanied by the reformers William Farel and Pierre

Viret, Dentière entered the convent of the Poor Clares in Geneva to exhort the nuns to leave the monastic life and to reject celibacy. We know of this incident from Jeanne de Jussie, a nun and the eventual abbess of that community, who described this encounter years later, complaining about a false "nun ... with a devilish tongue ... named Marie Dentière ..., who meddled in preaching and in perverting pious people."[123] Dentière also had the distinction of being the only woman to publish a work on theology in Reformation Geneva. In 1539, she wrote *A Very Useful Epistle*, dedicated to Marguerite of Navarre, sister of King Francis I of France, and this publication represented "the first explicit statement of reformed theology by a woman to appear in French."[124] Writing the *Epistle* after Calvin and Farel had been expelled from Geneva because of their rigid stand on discipline, the author, identified as "a Christian woman of Tournai" (Dentière's hometown), aggressively criticized both the magistrates and the pastors for their treatment of these reformers. She proclaimed to Marguerite, "though we are not permitted to preach in congregations and churches, we [women] are not forbidden to write and admonish one another in all charity. . . . I wish to write this letter ... to give courage to other women detained in captivity ..., as I was, for the word of God. And principally for the poor little women [*femmelettes*] wanting to know and understand the truth, . . . that from now on they be not internally tormented and afflicted, but rather that they be joyful, consoled, and led to follow the truth, which is the Gospel of Jesus Christ."[125] Natalie Zemon Davis has aptly described Dentière's claim to want to teach the Gospel only to other women as "modest fiction."[126] Referring to numerous key female figures in the Bible, the ex-nun defended her right to expound on Scripture:

> Some might be upset because this is said by a woman, believing that this is not appropriate since woman is made for pleasure. But I pray you to be not offended; you must not think that I do this from hatred or from rancor. I do this only to edify my neighbor, seeing him in such great, horrible darkness, more palpable than the darkness of Egypt. Nevertheless, if it please you to consult and diligently examine the texts cited here . . ., comparing them to holy scripture, with good judgment, you will find even more than what I say here.[127]

Viret and Farel clearly condoned her aggressive efforts to convince the Poor Clares to leave the convent, and Calvin no doubt appreciated her criticism of the Genevan leaders responsible for his expulsion. That said, Calvin did not envision women having an active role in the propagation of the faith and definitely disapproved of them proselytizing in public.[128]

In Geneva women were also less likely than men to delay in asking to be readmitted to the Supper. In her work on Dutch Reformed churches, Judith Pollman found that being permitted to participate in the Supper affirmed a woman's moral good standing in the community. Dutch women were accordingly much more willing than men to submit to the discipline of the consistories; doing so amounted to restoration of their honor.[129] Similar attitudes may help explain why Genevan women more willingly asked to be readmitted to communion than men did.

More broadly, it should be noted that far more Genevans, male and female, wanted to take communion than tried to avoid it. The meetings prior to the Supper were dedicated in large part to requests from excommunicants to be readmitted to the sacrament. In order to handle the intense activity just before the celebration of communion, the Consistory instituted the practice, starting in April 1542, to meet twice, on Tuesdays and Thursdays, during the week before the celebration of the Supper.[130] The number of such petitions far eclipsed the number of residents who shunned taking communion.

All told, the Consistory aggressively tried to enforce regular church attendance and to combat all forms of religious noncompliance in Calvin's Geneva. We can conclude that women in Geneva were more reluctant than men to give up certain Catholic traditions such as saying prayers to the Virgin Mary or celebrating Christmas. Some women and men resisted, either actively or passively, the efforts of the pastors and the Consistory to effect change in piety among Genevans. Calvin and other authorities would brook no insubordination, but they were not unduly harsh when confronted with people who seemed genuinely repentant about having strayed from the straight and narrow path by attending Mass in Savoy, for example. The members of the Consistory also did not appear overly concerned when faced specifically with female noncompliance; their sexist attitudes meant that they expected less from and were less threatened by female nonconformists, which could result in more lenient treatment for them. Moreover, the many requests to be readmitted to the Supper indicate that the overwhelmingly majority of both women and men wanted to comply with Reformed mores.

This evidence can also be compared with the findings of other historians regarding the success of the Reformation. In the 1970s, Gerald Strauss challenged the assumption that the Reformation was a catalyst for dramatic change, amounting to a revolution in religious practices that affected the lives of people in all social classes. On the basis of records of visitations of rural parishes, Strauss found that peasants were ignorant of and even hostile to the Lutheran faith and that their piety was thoroughly imbued with magic even several decades after the conversion to Protestantism. He concluded that the Reformation was a failure.[131] On the basis of research on Zurich's rural parishes, Bruce Gordon also found that the teachings and discipline of the clergy had little effect on the laity, at least during the time of Heinrich Bullinger.[132] By contrast, Amy Nelson Burnett is more sanguine in her assessment of the success of the pastoral ministry in Basel. On the basis of visitation records, she finds that the Reformation was indeed a success in both town and country: by the early 1600s even Basel's rural population had assimilated the basic tenets of the Reformed faith and showed a certain hostility toward Catholicism.[133]

The evidence from Geneva definitely skews more toward the success than the failure of the Reformation. First, contrary to the arguments of Strauss and of the French historian Jean Delumeau,[134] evidence does not support the contention that Genevans were not truly Christian prior to the Reformation.[135] Although, as will be seen in chapter 5, there were elements of folk religion that certainly resembled magic, one cannot equate the religion of the rank and file, even in the countryside, with magic or paganism with just a thin veneer of Christianity. Calvin and his colleagues would never be wholly satisfied with the religious knowledge and the piety of the lay men and women of Geneva, and, as we shall see in the coming chapters, the clergy and laity were not always on the same page as far as what constituted sinful behavior. That said, the unavoidable impression is that the rank and file assimilated the basic tenets of the faith and could distinguish acceptable (from the Reformed perspective) from unacceptable religious rituals and practices. As will be seen, the residents of neighboring rural communities were slower in giving up certain practices that were deemed superstitious but even they definitely seemed to have fully embraced Protestantism by the end of Calvin's lifetime.[136]

It is well known and not at all surprising that Protestantism encountered less resistance when the Reformation came from below rather than from above by an act of the state,[137] and one must remember that Geneva had converted by means of a unanimous vote of the General Council, comprising all citizens. While the fact that the vote was taken publicly surely deterred some crypto-Catholics from voting against the measure, the fact remains that Genevans collectively chose the Reformed faith. Quite quickly during Calvin's ministry, the residents of his adopted city truly became Reformed.

CHAPTER 3

Educating and Disciplining the Young

T HE RAPPORT BETWEEN PARENT and child, with the possible exception of that between spouses, is probably the most fundamental and influential of all human relationships. In the Reformation era, various thinkers, both Protestant and Catholic, showed a great deal of interest in child-rearing, believing that the proper raising of children and youths was a crucial means of building a pious Christian society. As Europe was bitterly divided over religion, Genevan leaders, like those of all confessions, saw the need to indoctrinate the young in order to lead them down the straight and narrow path and protect them from unacceptable beliefs.[1] As we saw in chapter 2, the Consistory of Geneva had a pedagogical as well as a disciplinary role, as it strove to ensure that Genevans attended the sermons regularly and were able at the very least to recite the Lord's Prayer and the Apostles' Creed. They hoped that all residents would learn the basics and internalize Reformed morality, and Calvin and other leaders realized that this goal depended to a considerable extent on inculcating discipline from an early age. Calvin had agreed to accept the ministry in Geneva on the condition that magistrates place their full support behind the catechism and the Consistory, which bore witness to the importance he gave to both pedagogy and discipline.

This chapter will examine the Consistory's interest in child-rearing and parenting. As we will see, Calvin and his colleagues did not hesitate to intervene if they felt that residents were not performing their parental duties well or if children and youth appeared to be going astray or were not respecting the commandment to honor one's mother and father. The actions the Consistory took involving the young of Geneva show the manner in which its pedagogical and disciplinary roles could be closely intertwined.

Baptism

Baptism is life's first important rite of passage for Catholics and Calvinists alike. Though Reformed Protestants kept the sacrament of baptism, there were some significant changes in the way it was conceived and administered, as evidenced by several cases brought before the Consistory.[2] Among the most tangible changes was the obligation that all baptisms be conducted publicly in a church by a pastor, as seen in the summoning in May 1542 of Amied Darnex. A resident of the village of Satigny, Darnex had waited six years to have one of his children baptized, and all magisterial reformers were quite concerned about delayed baptisms, which they associated with Anabaptism. When appearing before the Consistory, Darnex explained that his daughter, Clauda, had actually been baptized at birth by a woman, most likely a midwife. Recently, however, a friend told him that such a baptism was invalid, prompting Darnex to have the child baptized again, this time in church by a clergyman. Since they viewed baptism as a condition sine qua non for salvation, Roman Catholics had long allowed midwives to baptize infants if death appeared imminent. Darnex himself had feared that his young daughter was not going to survive and testified that his wife did indeed die as a result of the girl's birth. He also pleaded ignorance that such baptisms were forbidden. Indeed if his daughter was actually six years old in 1542, then he had not violated Genevan law; in response to appeals from Farel, the Small Council forbade baptism by midwives only in January 1537. Nonetheless, the Consistory showed no leniency toward Darnex and recommended that he receive appropriate remonstrances, publicly confess his sin, and be sent to prison. Out of fear of Anabaptism, the Consistory further asked that public announcements be made to uncover any other children who had yet to be baptized.[3] The severity of this sentence may stem more from this strong rejection of Anabaptism than from the unauthorized baptism several years earlier.

Other cases further indicate that some residents of Geneva, like many Catholics, were convinced that the souls of unbaptized babies could not be saved. In June 1542, Nicolas Baud of the village of Peissy and an unnamed grown son were convoked because of actions surrounding the recent birth and death of another son of Nicolas. They testified that following the birth of the stillborn child, the elder son took the baby's body to Seyssel, a village on the Rhône River in nearby Catholic Savoy. He went to the bridge in front of the chapel of Notre Dame, where miracles had allegedly taken place. Hoping himself for a miracle, Baud had the body of his baby brother baptized there and buried it immediately thereafter. The son showed a certain defiance toward Calvin and the Consistory when he declared that had the baby already been buried, he would have dug him up to take him to Seyssel for a postmortem baptism. He added that he had no money to have Masses said there for the soul of his deceased sibling. Eventually, though, the younger Baud begged for clemency, asserting that he had erred and now viewed his previous beliefs as mere fantasies. Following the Consistory's advice, the Small Council ordered the *châtelain* of Peney to place both Nicolas and his son under arrest.[4]

Both these cases demonstrate that some residents in Genevan territory had assimilated Catholic views on baptism.[5] The practice of baptizing the deceased existed in parts of Europe from 1387 into the twentieth century, being most common from the fifteenth through the eighteenth centuries. In France, there were 260 sanctuaries, most of which were consecrated to the Virgin, where people baptized the bodies of deceased children. Such postmortem baptisms, which usually occurred immediately after the death of the child, had been known in pre-Reformation Geneva. Stillborn children had been baptized at Nôtre-Dame de Grâce at Geneva's Augustinian monastery until the Small Council forbade these "false miracles" in May 1535. In light of Catholic theologians' belief that one could not be saved without baptism, the actions of Darnex and the Bauds made perfectly good sense. Rejecting this view, Calvin insisted that baptism was the sign of one's "purgation" but not the actual means by which one is justified. For Calvin, children who died without baptism could be saved, provided they were heirs to the Kingdom of God.[6] This attitude is patently seen in the Consistory's rebuke of Claude, the wife of Nicolas Mestral, and of Jeanne Dupuis because the former allowed her child to be baptized by a midwife (apparently Dupuis). Calvin and colleagues avowed that this error stemmed from "the great infidelity of thinking that if the children of the faithful do not have an external sign, they perish." On the contrary, the Consistory insisted, "The children of the faithful are saved, even as the faithful are certain that God is their God and the God of their children."[7] Quite striking, however, is the fact that so few in Geneva reacted in the manner of Claude Mestral. Genevans overwhelmingly conformed to the requirement of public baptisms in church; only four times during Calvin's ministry did the Consistory uncover baptisms performed by women, the last involving the Mestral child in 1548.[8]

Similarly, there was little apparent opposition to certain changes in the church ritual of baptism itself. In pre-Reformation Geneva and in Catholic France, fathers often did not attend their children's baptisms out of the belief that their presence brought bad luck.[9] In 1550 a woman, seeing a man taking his child to be baptized, declared that she would rather have the devil take her baby away than have the child carried to the baptism by the father.[10] In the same year, a certain Jacques Vallentin expressed his disapproval that Pastor Cop had taken his own child to be baptized.[11] In his ecclesiastical ordinances for rural parishes, Calvin felt compelled to write in 1546 that, barring a legitimate excuse, fathers were supposed to attend the baptisms of their children, a clause that he had not written in the city's ecclesiastical ordinances of 1541, implying that he had been unaware of the practice of fathers not participating in their children's baptisms. Be that as it may, no sign of conflict is found in any Consistory register after 1550, showing that Calvin had little difficulty changing this habit.[12]

It also must be noted that the Consistory registers do not reveal only non-compliance among Genevans. In May 1543, the carpenter Michel Cochet and his wife, Françoise, appeared before the Consistory in response to an inquiry concerning the birth and baptism of their child. Upon learning that her mother was on her deathbed, the pregnant Françoise returned to her native Savoy to tend to her. While there, Françoise gave birth to a child but, she claimed, refused to allow the baby to be baptized *à la papisterie*. If relatives did baptize the child in a Catholic rite, she insisted that it was without her knowledge and consent. Moreover, a week prior to their appearance before the Consistory, Michel and Françoise had their child baptized at the church of La Madeleine at the age of five weeks, and Françoise insisted that the godfather who carried the child to the baptism was indeed "faithful." She added that for having rejected Catholic baptism, she inherited none of the goods belonging to her mother.[13]

That the Cochets reacted to Protestant baptism differently from others, such as Darnex and the Bauds, is understandable. The Cochets were both originally from Catholic Savoy and, one can surmise, almost surely emigrated to Geneva for purposes of religion. They probably arrived in Geneva already firmly attached to Protestant convictions. The fact that they both successfully recited prayers and the credo in the vernacular showed that they had assimilated some of the most important external expressions of Reformed piety. Darnex and the Bauds, by contrast, lived in rural communities that had previously been subject to the bishop of Geneva and were now subordinate to the city itself. Throughout Europe, rural inhabitants tended to be less educated, more strongly attached to various aspects of popular religious traditions, and less attracted to Protestantism than urban dwellers. The reluctance of some rural Genevans to embrace Protestant innovations in baptism is therefore not surprising.

In Calvin's Geneva, the baptism of children did occasion many bitter quarrels between parents and clergy over the selection of names. Throughout Christian Europe, the choice of names for children had always been the prerogative of parents and godparents.[14] Calvin and other pastors demanded that Genevans give only biblical names to their children and aggressively tried to eliminate the names of certain saints. The competing aims of clergy and parents in the selection of names exploded in a number of acrimonious conflicts in the 1540s and 1550s.

Among the earliest and best documented of the bitter disputes surrounding baptism involved the son of the barber Amied Chappuis. In August 1546, Chappuis and several friends and relatives went to the church of Saint-Gervais to celebrate the baptism of this son, whom he wanted to name Claude in honor of a relative. Claude, however, was also the name of a local saint whom Genevans had long venerated. As they later explained to the Small Council, the pastors decried the existence of an "idolatrous" chapel in honor of Claude just seven leagues from Geneva. While conducting the baptism, the officiating pastor declared that the child would be named Abraham. Stunned by what they perceived as an abuse of pastoral power, many people in church were furious, including Hippolyte Rivet, a goldsmith and member of the Council of Two Hundred. Though apparently unrelated to the child, Rivet argued most vociferously with the minister over who had the right to name the boy. When the pastor attempted to impose a name on the child, Chappuis and others refused to allow the baptism to continue, taking the child out of the minister's hands before he could finish the rite. The pastor avowed that in the shouting and confusion that followed, an unidentified person rhetorically asked whether Saints Peter and Paul were any better than Claude. When he appeared before Calvin and other members in late August, Chappuis in effect denied that his son had actually been baptized by the pastor. He asserted that the pastor erroneously said, "I baptize you in the name of Abraham," and never got around to saying the decisive words, "in the name of the Father, Son, and Holy Ghost." Reproached for persisting in calling his son Claude, Chappuis defiantly proclaimed that, if denied the right to name his own son, he would wait until the boy was fifteen years old before baptizing him.[15]

Among those involved in this case, Boniface Nevet well reflected the outrage of many Genevans who viewed the pastor's actions as a violation of traditional parental privileges. Interestingly, Nevet was the wife of Claude Vouvrey, who served as the Consistory's *officier*, the person who actually went out to summon people to appear before the morals court. As a midwife, Nevet, prior to the conversion to Protestantism, may well have performed some baptisms on children who appeared on the verge of dying. After members of the baptism party stormed out of Saint-Gervais, they went to Chappuis's home, where Nevet reportedly said over the child, "I baptize you Claude, in the name of the Father and the Son." Nevet, however, denied this accusation, and the Consistory limited itself to remonstrances.[16]

In response to this disputed baptism, Calvin and the other ministers appeared before the Small Council on August 27 to complain about Chappuis and others who named their children Claude. Some magistrates, though, were wary of the zeal with which Calvin and other ministers proscribed names as idolatrous or superstitious. Nonetheless, even though Calvin's position of leadership in Geneva was not entirely secure until 1555, magistrates came down in favor of the pastors in this and other cases. After serving a few days in prison, a "repentant" Chappuis was released on September 2 and required to listen to "good remonstrances," to confess publicly his errors and beg for mercy from God before the Consistory, and to pay his expenses. At Calvin's request, the Council banned the use of the name Claude and mandated that parents could choose only among those names found in the Bible. In November 1546, the Small Council asked Calvin to draw up a list of prohibited names, which was to be made known throughout Geneva.[17]

The creation of that list did not, however, put an end to such conflicts, as was evident in May 1548, when the Burgundian cabinetmaker André de La Roche brought his son to be baptized in the church of Saint-Pierre. During the ceremony, the godfather, Jean-Baptiste Sept,[18] announced that the child was to be named Balthasar. But Michel Cop, the officiating pastor, rejected this because it was on Calvin's list of prohibited names. (Traditionally Balthasar was believed to be the name of one of the magi, though this does not appear in the Bible and was therefore considered superstitious.) Cop did baptize the boy but proclaimed that his name would be Jean. This caused an uproar in church, with the child's grandfather yelling that Cop was not worthy of baptizing the boy and that he himself could do it just as well. Several other people present, including some prominent Genevans, bitterly complained about Cop's actions. According to witnesses, the secretary of the Small Council, Philibert Berthelier, soon to become a bitter enemy of Calvin, loudly castigated Cop in church, and the *châtelain* of Jussy, Nicolas Gentil, avowed, "We have already put up with too much. We have let too many things be governed by [the French pastors]." The controversy continued to rage for days to come. De La Roche was heard insisting that his son had not really been baptized and that he would take the boy "a hundred leagues away" rather than have him named Jean. A witness further revealed that an unidentified man declared in front of de La Roche's house, in obvious reference to the pastors, "We have to kill them all in the next two weeks, put down their heads and bodies. We have had enough!"[19] In spite of this vitriolic rhetoric, in the end the critics of the pastors were forced to back down. De La Roche and his father-in-law were briefly imprisoned for their harsh words against Cop and were obliged to accept the name Jean.[20]

These disputes over the naming of children pitted the native Genevan laity against the French clergy. Calvin and other pastors viewed the names of saints, among others, as utterly inappropriate for Christians. Genevans were understandably upset, however, at being told that their own names were linked to paganism and superstition and could not be passed on to their children and godchildren. Many natives, including members of influential families, expressed their anger and frustration at what they perceived as pastoral arrogance, but Calvin eventually succeeded in eradicating names such as Claude. While Claude had been the third most common name for both girls and boys in Geneva, it disappeared during the course of the sixteenth century. More broadly, while saints' names represented 43.3 percent of the names of boys and 49 percent of the names of girls in pre-Reformation Geneva, these figures fell to 3.2 percent and 1.8 percent, respectively, of the names given in the 1560s. Diametrically opposed was the trend for biblical names: while just over half the babies born in the years immediately prior to the Reformation were given biblical names, 97 percent of those baptized in Geneva in the 1560s received names from the Bible.[21] Their actions were often heavy-handed, but pastors succeeded in effecting conformity in the baptizing and naming of children.

The Religious Education of Children

In an era of intense religious conflict, both Protestant and Catholic thinkers were quite concerned about the religious indoctrination of the young, deeming it essential to teach children right Christian doctrine and to protect them from the errors of heresy. Who, though, was largely responsible for this religious education? Was that the responsibility of parents, the clergy, or magistrates? With his break with Rome, Martin Luther became convinced that the family, not the church, was to be the most fundamental "school for character." Luther, Calvin, and other reformers strongly encouraged religious education in the home, promoting private family devotions and exhorting parents to lead the religious instruction of their children.[22]

As for the roles of men and women in domestic religious pedagogy, Luther viewed the male household heads as "bishops in their homes" and thus responsible for the religious education of family members, often including their wives as well as children.[23] With their decisive role in child-rearing, however, one might expect mothers to have been entrusted with very important responsibilities in the religious education of their offspring.

Several cases brought before the Consistory reveal much about the roles of mothers, fathers, and clergy in the religious education of children both before and after the conversion to Protestantism. When the Consistory asked people who taught them the prayers and creeds they recited, the most common response was their parents or, less often, one of their parents. For example, when the Consistory asked Jeanne Begaz to recite her prayers, she said that she knew how to pray "only in the manner in which her father and mother had taught her" and proceeded to recite the credo, the Ave Maria, and other prayers in Latin. The Consistory ordered her to attend the sermons and catechism lessons and to learn to pray in the vernacular.[24] Likewise, convoked in April 1543 for speaking favorably about festivals, saints' days, and other "papal ceremonies," Thibauda Le Guex affirmed that she knew "how to pray as her father and her mother taught her" and recited the Lord's Prayer and the Ave Maria in Latin.[25] These and other cases clearly show that a degree of religious education in the home was already well established prior to the conversion to Protestantism. At the very least, children memorized Latin prayers, such as the Pater Noster and the Ave Maria, largely under the tutelage of their parents.[26]

These and other examples suggest that religious pedagogy in the home was not necessarily the responsibility of women on the eve of the Reformation.[27] After the conversion, the registers suggest that the pastors and elders deemed the male household head principally responsible for the religious instruction of the family, an attitude that was shared by members of French consistories.[28] At times the Consistory convoked men and asked them how they instructed both their children and their wives on religion. For example, in March 1543 Claude de Miribello and his wife, Pernette, were called before the Consistory. Authorities suspected that they, especially Pernette, maintained certain Catholic rituals, though Pernette denied, among other things, that she said the prayers of the rosary. In response to a question, Miribello insisted that he taught his wife and children to pray to God alone, adding that they did not pray for the dead or to the Virgin Mary. The Consistory admonished Miribello to instruct his wife and children still further, even though Pernette successfully recited the confession and the Lord's Prayer in the vernacular.[29]

In February 1543, Matthieu Gathsiner, an innkeeper from Bavaria, appeared on suspicion of serving fish to guests during Lent, a form of fasting that Protestants rejected as pagan and unbiblical. Professing the desire to live according to the Reformation, Gathsiner claimed that he and many of his guests ate meat in the inn but that he also had to give the "papists" what they wanted (presumably fish). Asked to recite the confession and the Lord's Prayer, Gathsiner could say only the latter in Latin and German. Members of the Consistory instructed him to learn the confession before Easter and to take his wife and children to catechism lessons on Sundays. He was also told that he should instruct his guests in matters of religion and have a copy of the New Testament available for them.[30] Ideally, the travelers who stayed with Gathsiner were to participate in devotions and Bible readings similar to those that should be practiced in Genevan households. Simply put, while people learned prayers from both their mothers and fathers before the Reformation, Calvin and other members of the clergy obviously wanted to enhance the role of the patriarch in the religious education of the household.[31]

As the cases of Begaz and Gathsiner show, the Consistory often mandated attendance at catechism, which indicates that for Calvin and his colleagues, religious education in the home did not suffice. In Reformation Geneva, the catechism would indeed play a decisive role in the religious education of youth. The catechism, which outlined clearly and succinctly the principal benefits of Reformed Christianity, was intended to inculcate discipline among the believers. Throughout Reformation Europe, Protestants and Catholics published a large number of catechisms, many of which, to be sure, were intended for home use, in which a parent would read questions to a child, who was to memorize the appropriate answers.[32] But from the beginning, members of the Consistory were convinced that instruction in the home needed to be supplemented by formal catechetical instruction, the program of which was divided into fifty-five lessons over the course of a year. In Geneva children and adults were required to know the basics of the catechism before they could take communion. There was no set age in Geneva for starting the catechism, just as there was no fixed minimum age for taking communion; to participate in the Supper, children had to reach the "age of discretion," which was generally understood to be around ten. Those attending the catechism might be as young as five or six but might be ten, twelve, or even older. Catechetical lessons were held at all three churches on Sundays at noon, and these sessions were actually as much a church service as a lesson per se. It had its own liturgy, by which catechumens would learn, sometimes through singing, the Ten Commandments, prayers, the Apostles' Creed, and so on.[33] The catechism in Geneva and elsewhere still relied on the memorization of answers to specific questions, and the active involvement of pastors ensured that the young were being exposed to the desired religious beliefs and practices. One can rightly argue that Calvin's strong emphasis on catechism actually meant that the responsibility of the religious education of the young was shifting away from the household to the church.[34] This theory finds support in the fact that the Consistory's inquiries about how men instructed their families in matters of religion—so common in the Consistory's earliest sessions—had largely disappeared by 1550. As catechism lessons became more pervasive, Calvin and his colleagues demanded less often that men instruct their wives and children.

Conflicts over the Catechism

As the above cases indicate, Calvin, like other Reformed leaders, placed considerable importance on religious instruction through the catechism. In 1537 Calvin published his first catechism, which provided a brief summary of the tenets of the faith and stressed the importance of learning the Lord's Prayer, the Apostles' Creed, and the Ten Commandments. Calvin insisted on mandatory catechetical instruction as a condition for his return to Geneva in 1541, the year that also witnessed the reformer's much longer second catechism, which would remain a key source for doctrinal standards for the city during the next two centuries, and the passing of the ecclesiastical ordinances, which mandated that all children in the city and the countryside attend catechetical sermons at noon on Sundays.[35] Several shorter catechisms would follow in sixteenth-century Geneva, and these show that the city's pastors had rather modest expectations concerning children's required level of knowledge before they could be admitted to the Supper.[36]

Although since its inception the Consistory stressed the importance of catechetical lessons, often requiring adults to attend if they were unable to recite their prayers, it did not experience any major conflicts concerning catechism until the late 1550s. At that time, either there were unprecedented numbers of youths who skipped the Sunday lessons or, more likely, the Consistory only then began aggressively pursuing the youths, virtually all of whom were males, who were truant from catechism.[37]

One source of conflict was the habit of many Genevan youths of participating in martial games on Sunday afternoons. As early as May 1550, the Consistory admonished several Genevan boys for skipping catechism in order to celebrate rowdily *papeguai*, a festival that included contests in archery and firing the arquebus in order to choose the king of archers or arquebusiers.[38] In October 1560, the Consistory summoned François Des Eaux, a fencing master whose lessons coincided with the catechism, and told him that he must not accept any pupils under the age of eighteen.[39] Nonetheless, Genevan boys continued to participate in the Sunday competitions, as evidenced by the Consistory's request of June 12, 1561, that the Small Council take measures.[40] Even those adolescents who were not fencing or shooting arrows or arquebuses were not necessarily attending catechism. Others were convoked for playing skittles, billiards, and quoits when they should have been learning the catechism.

While previously those truant from catechism were simply admonished to be more diligent in their attendance, beginning in the late 1550s boys who were playing instead of learning the catechism were regularly subjected to corporal punishment. The Consistory's first such sentence was passed in December 1558 against nine boys who were playing *marc* on ice—a game that apparently resembled curling—condemning them to be sent "to the teacher at school to be beaten with rods in order to reform the youth and set an example for others."[41] In November of the following year, four boys were caught playing quoits during catechism. The Consistory asked that Theodore Beza, the regent of the school, have them whipped and that the Small Council interrogate the youths, described as coming from good families, to learn the names of the other boys playing with them; the latter then were to be taken to the hospital to be caned as a lesson for all Genevan youths.[42] In the weeks that followed, two pastors out on patrol found eight boys playing billiards and two others who were just wandering about during the time of the catechism lessons. Several of these boys were also not attending school, and Calvin and his colleagues sent them all to the Small Council, which complied with the Consistory's recommendation and ordered that the boys be taken to the school (*collège*) for a whipping as an example to all the other children and pupils.[43]

In March 1560, the Consistory expressed its concern to the Small Council about the growing problem of truancy from catechism, calling for officers to be sent all over the city and its environs to find those who were absent. Special mention was made of many who acted as if they were going to catechism but instead remained near the doors of the church, laughing, shouting, and just being rowdy. The Consistory demanded that such miscreants be taken to the school to get a whipping.[44] Though corporal punishment was usually administered at the school or hospital, the Consistory at times ordered fathers to beat their sons who skipped catechism lessons, occasionally further requiring that they send their sons to school.[45] The Consistory would also brook no disrespect for the regular worship service. In 1559 three boys, the fathers of two of them, and the grandfather of the other were all summoned because the boys had not shown due reverence, as they had laughed and babbled throughout a sermon. The Consistory ordered one of the men to take his son—evidently considered the ringleader—to the Small Council in order to be whipped with switches. Failing to do so, the father himself would be punished.[46]

So great was the concern about attendance at catechism that members of the Consistory themselves began patrolling the streets and knocking on doors during the lessons to catch people who were truant. In August 1559, for example, two lay members of the Consistory, Claude Chicand and Pierre Dance, along with Pierre Alliod, who served as the Consistory's secretary, were conducting a "visitation" and knocked on the door of the home of the widow Jeanne Abram, which also served as a tavern. She did not respond to their order to open the door, but the three representatives of the Consistory observed many people fleeing her home by running upstairs and going out on the roof while others hid in some rooms in the back of the house. The Consistory excluded her from the Supper, and the Council ordered her jailed and denied her the right to run a tavern.[47]

Truancy from catechism continued, and in September 1560 the Small Council officially mandated that visitations should be increased, ordering that two lay assistants of the Consistory, each accompanied by "a lookout and an officer," patrol the streets and neighborhoods of Geneva every Sunday during the catechism in order to catch those not attending.[48] This practice led to a dramatic increase in the number of actions against absenteeism. The assistants found many groups of boys who were playing or just wasting time but often were able to identify only one or two of them before the boys fled. In such cases, the Consistory sent those who were identified before the Small Council, where they were obliged to identify their playmates; all of them were then sent "to the *collège* or to the hospital if they are big to be whipped with rods."[49] Upon discovering a group of truant boys, the Consistory assistants were known to take the hats off the heads of as many boys as they could reach. The boys then had to go to the school to retrieve their hats, after receiving a good caning.[50] In March 1561 the Consistory forbade the city's gatekeepers to allow youths to leave the city after Sunday dinner, the time when they should be learning their catechism.[51]

The next year actually witnessed an uptick in the number of youths caught skipping catechism, no doubt a result of more aggressive actions against truancy. In April 1562, the Consistory called "a great multitude" of youths who were caught outside when they should have been in church. The Consistory admonished them all and advised Jean Aubert, a lay member of the Consistory, to tell their fathers that they must give their sons a whipping.[52] In June of that year, even the son of a minister—Jean Conrad, a young man from Basel—was guilty of taking part in such games (on the Sunday before the Supper no less).[53] In November of that year, "several" young men appeared, all accompanied by their parents, for wandering about when they should have been at catechism.

When told that they should punish their sons, one father, the baker Jacques Pinget, went up to his son and slapped him in the face. Far from approving of this action, Calvin and his colleagues interpreted the slap as showing contempt for the Consistory and referred him to the Council, which sent him to jail for twenty-four hours.[54] In March 1562, the lay assistant Jean Aubert, an elder and lay member of the Consistory, found the three children of Jean Dumas fooling around outside when they should have been at catechism. The three were there with their mother, but the father was in Provence where he had been for a year and a half. Members of the Consistory ordered that the mother should give the three a caning but then decided that Aubert should administer the blows instead, probably because they believed that the mother was unwilling or unable to mete out an adequate form of corporal punishment.[55]

The aggressive searches made by Genevan officials probably increased attendance at the weekly sessions but also resulted in more active resistance to catechism. Many who did attend were apparently disruptive. In October 1562, the Consistory requested that the lieutenant post officers at the church entrances and in the churches themselves "to impose silence" during catechism sessions but still complained about the tumult in February 1563.[56] Worse still, there were cases of open rebellion, such as the "great number of children" who threw stones at the doors of a church during catechism lessons; these youths were all to be caned, some at school and others by their fathers in the presence of one of the Consistory assistants.[57]

Authorities would never be entirely satisfied with the behavior and participation of Genevan youth in the catechism. At the meeting of May 11, 1564, just two weeks before Calvin's death, the Consistory again urged the Small Council to ensure that the city's gatekeepers enforced the ordinances concerning youths "who go do crazy things outside of town instead of going to catechism on Sundays."[58]

These various cases cause us to ponder a number of questions. Why was there so much resistance to the catechism? Why was this resistance basically found only among boys? And why did catechism truancy cases, unlike baptism irregularities which largely disappeared by the early 1550s, first become numerous only in 1559? Caution of course must be used in considering noncompliance. Young people who did not object to catechism lessons—undoubtedly the large majority of Genevan youths—did not appear before the Consistory. Still, the quantity of cases and the persistent complaints of the Consistory members surely derived from the refusal of a significant minority of Genevan youths to attend catechism.

Certainly a major factor was that Calvin and his colleagues were making an unprecedented effort to have all youths attend the lessons. For years, Calvin and the Consistory had apparently turned a blind eye toward the many Genevan males who frequently skipped catechetical sessions, often with their fathers' approval, in order to take part in martial contests. Since his position in Geneva was not entirely secure until 1555, Calvin had probably been somewhat reluctant to insist too much that Genevans forswear these martial contests—in and of themselves important training for the defense of the Republic—in favor of learning the catechism. With his detractors all vanquished and having already won a number of battles—over baptism, the selection of names, prayers to the Virgin Mary and to saints—Calvin could now turn his attention to attendance at catechism. The traditional Sunday afternoon games were also an obvious reason why only four girls were among the many youths convoked for missing catechism, since girls were not trained in the military arts.[59]

The active resistance to attend catechism probably also reflected lingering resentment of some locals toward the powerful influence that Calvin and the other French pastors wielded in Genevan society. True, the Consistory minutes give no explicit testimony that truancy from catechism sessions stemmed from antagonism to Calvin and his colleagues. But following the defeat of the Perrinistes in 1555, on the one hand, it would have been most impolitic for anyone openly to express opposition to Calvin; on the other hand, it seems implausible that all enmity toward the French pastors simply vanished with the exile of Calvin's most aggressive critics.

The Secular Education of Children

It was certainly not by chance that the upswing in catechism truancy cases coincided with some very important changes in education in Geneva. With their emphasis on the reading of Scripture and the study of the catechism, Protestants in general hoped to make a certain level of education available to everyone. They strove for universal literacy, which, however, was not realized anywhere in the sixteenth century. On May 21, 1536, at the same time that Geneva opted for the Reformation, the General Council ordered mandatory elementary education, a goal that would not be met for centuries. Prior to the conversion to Protestantism, the city, with input from the bishop, ran a *collège*, which allowed students to study Latin, beginning with the basic rules of grammar and extending to the lower levels of secondary education. This school came to an end in 1536, replaced by the Collège de Rive, first housed in an abandoned monastery. The

Council chose the director and provided him with a set sum, which he used to purchase appropriate materials and to hire two or three teachers to assist him with instructing the pupils, all boys. Magistrates set the cost of tuition at three sous per trimester but mandated that poor students be instructed free of charge. The school was not divided into classes based on the years of instruction, and headmasters repeatedly complained about the inadequate resources. Latin was still the principal subject studied, though Greek and the singing of Psalms were also part of the curriculum.[60] Starting in the 1550s students could also choose to study Hebrew, which further reflected the significant part played by sacred studies in this *collège*'s curriculum. Calvin, however, viewed this institution as far too independent of the Company of Pastors, which, he argued, ought to have the exclusive right to choose the teachers. He and other pastors complained that secular leaders were neglecting the schooling of the young and decried that classes were no longer held in one locale but rather were dispersed throughout the city. Though there was a noticeable increase in the number of pupils from the pre-Reformation era, Calvin was disappointed that the Collège de Rive served only a small percentage of Geneva's young.[61]

Many Genevans wanted to provide their children, especially their sons, with the best possible education, and until the late 1550s, the schooling available in Geneva left something to be desired. In August 1542 the shoemaker and innkeeper Jean Corajod was convoked because he had sent his son to school in a Catholic area. Originally from Savoy, Corajod had been naturalized and had become a fairly prominent figure in Geneva, having served as *dizenier* from 1534 into the 1540s.[62] His son was attending the Collège de La Roche in Savoy, which had an excellent academic reputation and trained some future leaders of the Jesuits.[63] Though he confessed that his son was guilty of "idolatry" at that school, Corajod protested that he had not sent his son to La Roche because of "papistry" but rather because the Genevan schools were unsatisfactory.[64]

In February of the following year, Jean Bennar and his wife, Loise, were convoked for the same reason. A potmaker and innkeeper, Bennar was also a rather prominent citizen, serving on the Council of Two Hundred. Bennar explained that he sent his son to La Roche simply for the educational opportunities and to get him away from the boy's mother. He was obviously unhappy with the rapport between his wife and son, but we do not know if he deemed her overly indulgent, harsh, or negligent. When the Consistory told him to bring his son home, Bennar requested that the boy be allowed to stay at La Roche until August since he had paid for tuition until then. The Consistory, however, insisted that he bring his son home by the middle of Lent. The cases of Bennar and Corajod show that for some Genevans the desire to remain true to Reformed principles, be it real or feigned, could conflict with the wish to give their sons the best possible education.[65]

The Consistory likewise took a very dim view of people sending their daughters to work in Catholic areas. In 1559 it twice convoked Pierre Danel of the village of Jussy because his daughter was working as a servant for Danel's brother and sister-in-law in Lyon. Following the orders of the Consistory, Danel twice went to Lyon to retrieve his daughter but twice returned without her, armed each time with an attestation from a notary, which averred that Danel's brother refused to relinquish his niece who, in effect, had not fulfilled the term she was contractually bound to serve. The Consistory, however, found that these notarial documents actually exacerbated Danel's guilt rather than exculpated him. Finding that he was shirking his paternal duties, the Consistory excluded Danel from the Supper and referred him to the Council to be punished.[66]

The late 1550s were decisive for the educational institutions of Geneva. Following decades of underfunding and a chaotic turnover among teachers and rectors, the old Collège de Rive was closed, replaced at the instigation of Calvin by the Genevan Academy, which first opened its doors to students in 1558 and was officially inaugurated the following year, when magistrates accepted the *Ordre du Collège de Genève*, authored principally by Calvin.[67] The Academy was divided into two parts: the *collège* (*schola privata*, also known as the *grande école*), consisting of seven grades that offered secondary and some primary education; and the Academy proper (*schola publica*), the forerunner of the University of Geneva, which offered higher learning in theology aimed especially at training pastors. The language of instruction at the *collège* was Latin. Like the *collège* that preceded it, the Academy was not open to females and served only a small minority of Genevan boys. Boys who attended *petites écoles*—vernacular schools that offered instruction in reading, writing, and arithmetic—were surely far more numerous than those attending the *collège*.[68] Even the villages were obliged to hire schoolmasters to provide vernacular instruction to children, and magistrates insisted that everyone in the villages had to pay taxes to cover the salaries of the teachers.[69]

It must be stressed that there were far fewer educational opportunities in and around Geneva for girls than for boys. There existed a few neighborhood schools where girls received some very basic instruction in reading the Bible and perhaps in writing and arithmetic. Otherwise, apart from private instruction from tutors among affluent families, most females could hope for nothing beyond possibly acquiring some rudimentary reading skills through the mandatory learning of the catechism.[70] In this regard, girls were apt to be more motivated than boys to attend Sunday afternoon catechism.

The Schools and Discipline

Starting in the late 1550s, we begin to see actions against boys or their parents for not attending school. In April 1564, Jeanne, the widow of Guillaume de Fernex, and her son Pierre appeared because the lad, with his mother's complicity, was not attending the *collège* as the Council had required. The mother apologized but since Pierre, described as a libertine (*debauché*) refused to promise to go to school, the Consistory asked the Small Council to send him (and other boys who had abandoned their studies) to the *collège* and recommended that the entrance to the school be overseen by a doorman, apparently to make sure that students did not just come and go as they wished. Theodore Beza and the Marquis Caracciolo were entrusted with making the case to the Council of the need to oblige parents and especially guardians to send their sons and protégés to the *collège* "because it would be a great pity for those who have thus profited [from an education] to lose themselves."[71]

The same period also saw the first appearance of students being summoned for being disrespectful to teachers. In January 1559, two boys appeared before the Consistory because they had told others that their regent, Master Jean Barbier, had blasphemed and cursed them. Because there were variations in the boys' testimony and since no other pupil heard the purported curses, the Consistory concluded that the boys had fabricated the story to defame Barbier. Since Barbier asked that the boys be shown clemency because of their youth, the Consistory limited itself to giving the boys a scolding, denying them the next communion, and requiring them to get on their knees to beg forgiveness from God, members of the Small Council, and Master Barbier.[72]

In a number of cases students or their parents complained that teachers were physically abusive, and frankly the evidence is overwhelming that masters could indeed be quite violent in their treatment of pupils. The most extreme case involved Pierre Moussard, brother-in-law of Sebastian Castellio and teacher at the Collège de Rive. There were numerous complaints about Moussard's abuse; most notably, in 1547 a man protested to the Council that Moussard, who also led children in the singing of Psalms at the church of Saint-Gervais,[73] had beaten his son so severely that the boy died of his injuries. The Council ordered the lieutenant to investigate, though authorities never brought charges against Moussard, who retained his teaching job for several years.[74]

Claude Dravod and Pierre Bron appeared before the Consistory after Dravod had taken his son out of school. The armorer Dravod declared that Master Pierre Duc, the current regent of the Collège de Rive, had beaten his son "three or four times every morning for a week."[75] Bron reported that another teacher, Master Jean de La Barre, had beaten a boy so severely that the lad was seriously injured.[76] Though de La Barre was not summoned, Duc appeared before the Consistory and confessed "that he had indeed beaten Claude Dravod's son but not viciously as he claimed."[77] Duc further complained that Dravod and Bron together came to the school and caused quite a disturbance, loudly criticizing Duc's treatment of the boy. To avoid a scandal in front of the pupils, Duc tried to get the men to leave but Dravod refused, saying that he had as much right to be there as Duc did. Then, according to Duc, Dravod "grabbed his son and gave him a slap, telling him that he would no longer go to school." After Dravod admitted as much, the Consistory ruled:

> Master Pierre Duc is to be remonstrated that he treat his pupils well and that he continue [to serve as teacher] in the grace that Our Savior has shown him. And as for Sieurs Dravod and Bron, they are to be sent before *Messieurs* [of the Small Council] to be punished with the recommendation that they be ordered to go to the school to confess the wrong they have committed before Master Pierre and the pupils in order to better keep the children in fear.[78]

Authorities acceded to this recommendation and added that Dravod must continue sending his son to school so that the boy would not be "ignorant" like his father.[79]

This defense of teachers' power vis-à-vis pupils was also evident in the case of Pernon, the wife of Martin de Ville. In April 1559, she was called by the Consistory because she did not want her son to be punished by the regent and had thus removed him from the *grande école* to put him in another school. The Consistory ordered that she bring her son to the *collège*'s regent to be punished; otherwise, both mother and son should appear before the Small Council the following Monday.[80] Quite simply, students were supposed to defer to teachers, who enjoyed considerable leeway in using corporal punishment to maintain discipline and, so they believed, to promote learning.[81]

It is clear that educators themselves were not always on the same page when it came to the corporal punishment of pupils. In May 1550, the Council named Louis Enoch rector (*maître d'école*) and expressed concern about the lack of discipline among pupils and even a degree of insubordination of the teachers toward the headmaster.[82] Enoch zealously undertook reform of the school. In April 1551 he had a physical altercation with one of his teachers, a certain Mr. Leger, over the rector's penchant for whipping students. Under questioning by lay authorities, pupils reported that one day recently, the cantor had arrived to lead the children in singing. When some of the children were slow to come for this lesson, Enoch sent for them and began beating them as soon as they arrived. Leger intervened, telling Enoch that he must not beat the boys since they had arrived as quickly as possible and had not had the chance to finish their lunch. The angry Enoch told Leger to leave and warned that he would whip him with switches just as he had done to the children. When Leger refused to go, Enoch reportedly grabbed him by the arm, provoking Leger to grab Enoch's beard with one hand and to reach for his dagger with the other. Leger, however, proved to be no match for Enoch, who threw him on the floor. The headmaster then ordered students and his wife to assist him in pulling down Leger's pants and proceeding to whip his buttocks (*par le cul*). Leger pressed charges against Enoch for this battery, though apparently later dropped them.[83] The fact that there was no judicial decision against Enoch implies that Genevan authorities did not disapprove of Enoch's physical abuse of the children or even of his whipping the teacher's bare buttocks in the presence of the pupils. Interestingly, three years later, the headmaster Enoch dismissed Pierre Moussard, the aforementioned teacher whose physical abuse reputedly resulted in the death of a child, for excessive violence, and replaced him with Pierre Duc, who, as we have seen, definitely did not spare the rod.[84] In April 1556 Enoch was named a pastor in the city—and consequently a member of the Consistory[85]—and Duc was appointed pastor in the village of Russin in 1561, which shows unequivocally that neither man suffered a loss of reputation for the abuse they perpetrated at school.[86]

The dismissal of Moussard does demonstrate that despite the numerous examples of abusive behavior, one finds exceptional cases in which Genevan authorities took action against teachers whose corporal punishments were deemed excessive. In August 1563 Theodore Beza and the rector of the *collège* reported to the Small Council that there were rumors that Claude Bardet, the teacher of the first grade, was so brutal in disciplining students that he had practically killed one and badly injured another. Bardet denied the charges, but *Messieurs* had him arrested and ordered an investigation.[87] While the testimony of pupils and of their parents revealed that Bardet did not beat any child to the point of death, he was definitely extremely abusive with the boys, who were described as aged seven to nine. At various times, Bardet, a native of Beauvoisin in France, had beaten pupils in the face and on the head with sticks. Though he denied some of the accusations, Bardet confessed to others, including admitting that he once shoved a stick in the mouth of a student and then ripped it out so abruptly that he knocked out a tooth; the boy also suffered some serious wounds on his buttocks from Bardet's whippings. The teacher's blows drew blood from some of the boys, including one whom he punched in the face, and one lad remained bedridden for five or six days after a beating. The boys recounted that the teacher resorted to corporal punishment because they were not learning their lessons well; one boy indicated that he had incurred the master's wrath when he erred on "two or three words" in a lesson. Authorities condemned Bardet to ask forgiveness for this abuse and fired him from his position as schoolmaster.[88] The tenor of this investigation indicates that both parents and authorities objected to the excessive nature of this corporal punishment. The magistrates allowed and to a considerable degree even encouraged teachers to discipline students by whipping them on their buttocks but did not accept striking children in the face and on the head.[89]

Cases pertaining to school attendance and behavior also show that schooling was now playing a greater role in the lives of growing numbers of Genevan boys. Although there was still a problem with attendance, members of the Consistory definitely wanted all boys to get some formal education, a goal that extended, as we have seen, to the sons of peasants in the surrounding countryside. In August 1559, the *châtelain* of Céligny was told to bring the guards, minister, and schoolmaster of that village before the Small Council to be ordered to make sure that Céligny's youth and children started attending school.[90]

While Calvin and others surely hoped that everyone would be able to read the Bible, schools offered more than just these basic skills. Teachers were to promote Reformed morality and inculcate discipline among the young, whose natural tendency, Calvin believed, was to sin. While some parents objected to the corporal punishment that was so prevalent in the schools, others saw schooling as a means of instilling discipline in their dependents. This was the case in May 1562 when Aimé, son of the late Claude Levrat, was brought before the Consistory by his own guardian, the secretary Mugnerin. Mugnerin complained of the boy's laziness and of his unwillingness to attend school—the boy had even said that he would rather kill himself than go to school. Facing Calvin and other Consistory members, Aimé confessed uttering those words and said that he was now ready for schooling. The Consistory declared that he would indeed go to school where the rector would see that he get an exemplary caning. The boy was also required to get on his knees and ask forgiveness of his guardian and his mother.[91] In response to a summons, Pierre Chappe brought his son, who was constantly getting into fights and did not want to go to school. The exasperated Chappe said that he chastised the boy as much as he could and that even others had beaten the youth, but his behavior had not improved. The Consistory gave Pastor Louis Enoch, the aggressive former regent of the school, the charge of giving the boy a good caning.[92] Obviously the pastors and elders and probably most parents had faith that if one subjected youths to enough corporal punishment, they would eventually forswear their wayward behavior. As these and many of the above catechism cases show, schools now played a most important role in disciplining the young—as we have seen, on many occasions, the Consistory sent boys to the school to receive corporal punishment for misdeeds that were committed elsewhere. Indeed, for Genevan authorities, the *collège* was an appropriate venue to punish wayward young men even if they were not students there.[93]

The fact that rebellions against catechism lessons were strongest beginning in the late 1550s is almost surely linked to the increased emphasis on schooling at this time. While the Consistory became more adamant in attacking truancy from catechism, more Genevan boys were also being pressured to attend school. The Consistory registers make clear that resistance to school and catechism was in no way motivated by religious convictions—there is no evidence that any of the youths or their parents were closet Catholics or Anabaptists or found Calvinist doctrine morally objectionable. Rather, a good number of boys simply preferred playing to praying. As more boys were spending time in classrooms during the week, they surely became more resistant to additional instruction on Sundays.

More important, the increased emphasis on catechism and school together showed the Consistory's determination to lead Geneva's youth down the straight and narrow path, both religiously and socially. Those who learned the catechism and attended school were believed much less likely to get in trouble. Genevan leaders viewed learning to read and write and assimilating the content of the catechism as important in and of themselves but also viewed them as protection against debauchery and idleness and as fundamental pillars for a disciplined Christian society.[94]

Disciplining the Young and Generational Conflicts

As many of the above cases show, the Consistory, believing that parents, especially fathers, should play a decisive role in disciplining their children, was quite willing to intervene and order fathers to punish their sons and daughters for their misdeeds. Several scholars have insisted that the Protestant Reformation enhanced patriarchy and believed that instilling the need of sons and daughters to obey their fathers—and of wives to submit to their husbands—was a vital means of reforming church and society in sixteenth-century Europe. Learning to obey one's father helped inculcate obedience to magistrates and other social superiors.[95]

Genevan authorities were also quite willing to step in to defend the interests of parents and stepparents vis-à-vis rebellious sons and daughters. In December 1557, for example, Jean Gautier appeared before the Consistory complaining that his son, Laurent, who was about sixteen, was disobedient, refused to go to church, and did nothing other than betting money *au marc et au pallet*. He added that Laurent had defiantly declared that he would rather serve a "papist" than his father, whom he contemptuously called an "executioner" in the presence of others. Jean offered a partial confession to these accusations, and the Consistory excluded him from the Supper and referred him for punishment to the Council, which ordered that he be whipped at the hospital in the presence of the pupils as an example.[96] After her mother struck her on the shoulder, Jeanne Dupuis threatened to hit her back and told her mother "to go to the devil." For these actions, secular authorities in July 1558 sentenced Jeanne to three hours in the stocks and to do *réparation* to her mother.[97]

As the Gautier case shows, some Genevans actively sought the assistance of the Consistory and the Small Council to make their rebellious sons and daughters submit to parental wishes. When Jean Chenu, merchant and citizen, complained in 1561 that his son Aimé refused to obey him at all, the Consistory asked the Small Council to "send [the boy] to the hospital to be beaten with rods."[98] In July 1563, a widow brought her son to the Consistory, complaining that he entirely ignored her commands and had insulted her, calling her "stupid." For his insubordination, the Consistory sent the boy to the Small Council, which had him jailed.[99]

As these verdicts suggest, when faced with generational conflicts Calvin and Genevan authorities more often than not sided with the parents. In July 1560 Jean Barrois and his wife appeared, bitterly complaining about Faronne, Barrois's disobedient thirteen-year-old stepdaughter (his wife's daughter from a previous marriage). They claimed that she repeatedly ran away from home, did not obey them at all, and wanted to return to Roman Catholicism. Two neighbor women testified that the teenager was indeed rebellious but also said that they did not want to see her punished, insisting that the parents treated the girl too harshly. One of these neighbors reported once seeing the girl, bleeding, locked in a room by her parents, and she reportedly had threatened to kill herself. The

Consistory ruled that these women should mind their own business and not try to correct this couple when they disciplined their daughter. While they did advise the mother and stepfather to bear their daughter's infirmities more patiently, they also referred her to the Small Council, which agreed to send the girl to the hospital to receive a caning.[100] Five months later, Barrois was again appearing before the Consistory, complaining that, notwithstanding the punishment she had received, Faronne was still running away from them and hiding in "holes" from which it was impossible to extract her. Barrois reported that at that very moment, Faronne was hiding in a niche in their attic, where she had been ensconced for three days. The Consistory asked that one of the syndics be notified immediately so that an officer could go and retrieve Faronne and put her in jail until the following day. The Council agreed to allow her stepfather and mother to hold the girl under house arrest so that she could no longer run away or cause further scandal.[101] Although authorities at first seemed to think that the parents were at least partly responsible for the girl's rebellion, by October 1560 they had clearly concluded that this was almost entirely the girl's fault.

It is important to note that the Consistory recognized that parents at times were unduly harsh and convoked some for child abuse, a type of action that, like those concerning catechism and school attendance, became more common in the late 1550s. In August 1559, for example, the Consistory recommended that a woman be imprisoned on bread and water for having brutally beaten a small stepchild, who was badly bruised on the arms, sides, and thighs.[102] The following year it convoked Claude, wife of Pierre Gardet, who, while drunk, beat her daughter in the face, causing her to bleed considerably.[103] Pierre Arlod viciously beat and kicked his son, screaming he would kill him. During one beating, Arlod kicked the youth to the ground each time he tried to get up, outraging several onlookers.[104] The Consistory strongly rebuked the cabinetmaker Brie Clavel and his wife for their cruelty, which nearly drove their daughter to suicide.[105] In June 1563 Philippa Crespe was ordered to stop abusing her children—her daughter claimed that when her father was not present, Philippa was wont to beat her all night.[106] In December of the same year, four women testified having witnessed François Vigneron and his wife, Esprite, brutally whip and beat their small, sickly child twice in the same day, first by the father, then by the mother. For this "cruelty," the Consistory excluded the couple from the Supper and ordered them to stop abusing their child.[107] In March 1562 Jeanne, the wife of the miller Pierre Abraham, was excluded from the Supper and placed in the stocks for two hours for having slapped and thrown to the ground her three-month-old baby while arguing with another miller.[108]

When a master took on apprentices, servants, or other young employees, he assumed a responsibility toward them that was akin to paternal authority. Just as parents were not to use excessive force in disciplining their children, masters were supposed to show restraint toward their servants. Called before the Consistory in May 1558, George Ogier freely admitted to whipping a servant girl six days in a row. Ogier was upset because he had found a new job for her, but her new master soon fired her for theft. Since then, Ogier found yet another position for her but required that she return to him to be whipped daily for three days. The Consistory found this punishment extreme and referred him to the Small Council, which limited itself to admonitions.[109] By contrast, the pastors and elders at times obliged masters to discipline their employees. When Marc Camut admitted in March 1563 that he had been drinking with his friends rather than attending the afternoon church service, the Consistory mandated that his master, the armorer Raymond Curtet, punish—presumably corporally—the young man in the presence of certain members of the Consistory.[110]

Child abuse could come in a variety of forms. When Claude Thomas found his young son crying, he discovered that his wife had given the boy, her stepson, a crust of bread covered with tar over which she spread butter. Appalled at this behavior, the Consistory forwarded the case to the Small Council, which sent the stepmother to jail.[111] In May 1561, Jeanne, the wife of the gunpowder maker Jean Theysier, tried to make her rebellious son go to school by throwing stones at him. Though desiring that all youths attend school, Claude Chicand, a member of the Consistory, witnessed the stone-throwing and reproached the mother. The Consistory limited itself to admonishing Jeanne for her violence and for telling Chicand he could not prevent her from correcting her son.[112]

In Geneva and elsewhere in Europe, Protestant authorities stressed the need for parents, especially fathers, to take parenthood seriously and to discipline their children. They were well aware of the need to avoid the excesses at both ends of the spectrum—fathers and mothers must not be abusive, overly indulgent, or, as we will see below, negligent.[113] Like authorities elsewhere, though, Calvin and his colleagues clearly preferred that parents err on the side of discipline.

Parental Neglect

The Consistory convoked some parents for neglecting their children. In December 1551, Julianne, the wife of the ribbon maker Jean Murgiet, had to appear before the Consistory following the tragic death of her infant. Julianne had placed the baby in a cradle, leaving her five-year-old daughter in charge and locking the two young children in their abode. When the mother returned, she discovered that the cradle had tipped over, resulting in the baby's death. Several neighbors had earlier reproached her for not paying adequate attention to the baby, and the Consistory issued strong remonstrances that she admit her fault.[114] Fortunately Calvin and his associates did not always wait for a tragedy to occur before taking action against negligent parents. In February 1564, François Richard found Gonette, the widow of Jacques Pape, drunk and asleep by the fire, which put her small child at great risk of falling into the fire. This was not the first time that she had been found drunk, and the Consistory excluded her from the Supper and sent her to the Council to be punished, though it recommended that it take into consideration that she was a poor widow and have her "drink some water."[115] In saying this, the Consistory was suggesting that Pape be subjected to water torture in lieu of a jail sentence, apparently because, as a poor widow, she would have no means of caring for her child while in jail.[116]

The Consistory showed considerable interest in a particular form of child neglect or abuse involving the sleeping arrangements of babies. In early modern Europe, it was not unusual for mothers or wet nurses to sleep in the same beds with infants. Moralists decried this practice because the woman might roll over and smother the child, either accidentally or intentionally. In January 1551, when the Council asked the Consistory what punishment should be imposed on the mothers and wet nurses who were responsible for such deaths, the Consistory opined that there was no need for an ordinance per se and recommended judging these deaths on a case-by-case basis.[117] The Consistory convoked a number of women following such infant deaths. In 1556, the wet nurse Nicole, wife of François Ligrin, appeared before the morals court because of the suspicious death of a three-month-old girl she was nursing. Nicole confessed that during a recent night when the baby started crying, she picked up the child and put her next to herself in bed. She later transferred the baby, once asleep, back to her cradle. Since it appeared the baby had been smothered, the Consistory ordered the wet nurse to confess her error in church after the sermon and sent her to the Small Council, recommending three days jail on bread and water.[118] Having already been chastised by the Small Council, Jeanne, wife of Jean Barlemon, received the Consistory's admonitions for having slept with and suffocated her baby.[119] In 1557 Genevan authorities condemned the wet nurse Étiennette Mignol to spend three hours in the stocks in front of city hall and then to be banished under pain of the whip for having rolled over and suffocated the child who was in her care.[120] Alarmed by the number of such deaths, the Small Council and the Consistory in the early 1560s contemplated whether a new, more aggressive law was needed to deal with these "rollover" deaths, but such accidents continued to be a problem in Geneva for over a century to come.[121]

Parental neglect could also include not helping children, especially sons, learn a trade. In April 1561 the Consistory scolded the pastry chef Jean Papillier and his wife for failing in this area, alleging that the son was not doing anything other than carrying around a *charret*, a board game. The father expressed the desire to have his son learn a trade but said that it would cost too much, a reference to the payments that were needed to set up a young man in an apprenticeship. The Consistory declared that the Papilliers must ensure that their son get instruction in a trade regardless of the cost and referred them to the Council, which sought to know what trade the son wished to pursue.[122]

Calvin and the other assistants were particularly upset by the treatment that the youth Mathelin Rosier received at the hands of his mother, Amande, and stepfather, the knife sharpener Michel Dufour. On September 4, 1561, Rosier appeared before the Consistory to receive admonitions for having allegedly struck his mother, for which he had already spent time in jail. Buoyed by a strong letter of support from Geneva's armorers, which he submitted to the Small Council the same day, Rosier claimed that he had suffered a gross injustice at the hands of his mother and stepfather. Denying that he ever hit his mother, he charged that his parents simply wanted to get rid of him. He added that they gave him a coin (*un teston*) and a pair of shoes and sent him to the "papist" French town of Nantua where he eked out a living for a while. Rosier avowed that they were motivated by Dufour's own need for work and that he himself had already surpassed his stepfather in the craft of knife sharpening. At this point, the Consistory decided that all three should abstain from the Supper and should be questioned the following week.[123] When they all appeared on September 11, the Consistory asked Amande Dufour if she had indeed renounced her own son—who had been born out of wedlock—by claiming that he was her nephew and was named Jean rather than Mathelin. She tacitly admitted as much but maintained that this was not done out of malice. As for the physical mistreatment, she asserted that her son had indeed grabbed her by the ears but conceded that she was not sure that he had done this on purpose. The Consistory concluded that Amande had maliciously and falsely accused her son of a crime in order to "send him to the gallows" and that her husband had also acted "in bad conscience." The couple was excluded from the Supper and sent to the Council, which condemned them to six days in jail.[124] Calvin and his associates found the false accusations and the mother's renunciation of her own son to be egregious forms of parental neglect and cruelty.

Jacques Simond was summoned for a unique form of parental neglect: failing to provide ample supervision for his son, Laurent, who was mentally deficient. In January 1552, the Consistory issued remonstrances to Jacques because he had allowed his son to present himself for the Supper even though he was "very simple in spirit." The father was told to work in tandem with a pastor to ensure that the son receive appropriate instruction in matters of faith.[125] Eight years later, the Consistory reprimanded Simond because he had not kept his feeble-minded son shut in their home as both the Consistory and the Council had required, since "our Lord wanted to give [this son] to him." Simond had been allowing Laurent "to wander about here and there; even on the day of the Supper, he came into the temple of Saint-Pierre, taking half of the Supper, that is, the bread and not the wine." When Simond protested that he did not know what to do with the son, whom the scribe designated as "out of his mind," the Consistory curtly replied that he must do what was necessary or the Council would take charge of this situation.[126] Although the concerns of Calvin and company were heightened by what they perceived as a lack of respect for the Supper, they clearly desired that those with intellectual disabilities for the most part be kept out of sight. Failing to do so was, in their eyes, a form of parental failure.

The Moral Supervision of Children and Youths

Parental neglect could also take the form of inadequate moral supervision. Bernardine Plantemps, the widow of Georges Plantemps, had to account for the behavior of her two nubile daughters: they frequented young men unchaperoned, and one of them was believed pregnant.[127] In August 1559 the Consistory became quite concerned when four women testified about seeing a brother and sister, aged seven and five respectively, playing together nude in a lascivious manner. The Consistory strongly rebuked the mother for putting up with this behavior and ordered that she take the children the next day after the sermon to the hospital where they were to be whipped with rods. Failing to do so, she was to be sent to the Small Council to be punished herself as a rebel.[128]

Fearing sexual improprieties, Calvin and the Consistory were also very concerned about the sleeping arrangements of older children. Philiberte, the widow of François Epaula, was scolded for sleeping in the same bed with her two sons, who were described as "big" boys.[129] Following the death of her husband, Claude Dannel and her son, Georges, slept in the same bed for fifteen months, for which the *châtelain* of Jussy briefly imprisoned them. The mother apologized, saying that her illness had been the cause of this sleeping arrangement. Mother and son were warned that if they resumed sharing the same bed, they would be punished for incest.[130] The family of Jean Du Montley also had to account for their sleeping arrangements before the Consistory. At first, the Du Montleys' son and daughter were sleeping in the same bed. When told that was forbidden, Du Montley started sleeping in the same bed with his son and his wife with their daughter. The Consistory, however, said that such an arrangement was worse still. The Du Montleys explained that due to their poverty, they simply did not have enough beds for their children to sleep alone. Ordered to stop these practices, the Du Montleys promised to comply.[131] In March 1563, a man and his adult daughter admitted to sharing the same bed along with her small child— she insisted that the child slept between her and her father—for two months because of the cold. The Consistory warned the father to stop this "scandal," insisting that "honesty must take precedence over necessity."[132]

Predictably, the concern over the sharing of beds extended to servants. Pierre Garmejean and his servant, Pernette Gervais, had to appear before the Consistory because the two of them regularly shared the same bed along with Garmejean's wife. Both admitted as much but insisted that no sexual activity took place. Since the servant girl was medically examined and found to be "intact," the Consistory limited itself to admonitions, forbidding the girl to stay in their house any longer.[133]

Ever since its founding, the Consistory aggressively attacked what it considered dissolute behavior and was particularly determined in pursuing adults who encouraged or at least facilitated the debauchery of Genevan youth and children. An obvious case in point was the widow Madeleine Petet, who was suspected of encouraging her daughter to become a prostitute.[134] Pernette Bresson, the wife of Antoine Damereau, was rather imprudent in sharing her ideas about conception with the daughters of two Genevan ministers. In 1562, Bresson worked as a private tutor, teaching reading and writing to two girls who boarded with her: Aimée, the daughter of Raymond Chauvet, as we have seen perhaps the most volatile of Geneva's pastors; and Rachel, the daughter of the late pastor Jean de Saint-André and now the stepdaughter of Antoine Calvin, the reformer's brother.[135] A laughing Bresson once told her protégées that to have beautiful children, they must think of a handsome person at the time of conception. She added that if she were going to conceive a child, she would make sure to think of Theodore Beza! We of course cannot know if Bresson was being sincere or ironic—given her laughter, we may suspect the latter—but when questioned by judicial authorities, she insisted that she meant no harm and that in referring to a handsome man, she meant to stress the "wisdom and doctrine" a man might possess, adding, "quite happy would be the mother who could have a child like Mr. Beza." Though the analogy is far from clear, Bresson explained that this issue came up when she was describing for her pupils the story of Jacob who asked for all the black sheep and spotted goats as his wages (Genesis 30:32). The girls reported that their teacher also said that a painter from her native France had said that when trying to conceive a child, one should always look at a beautiful picture.[136] These statements show that Bresson was quite familiar with sixteenth-century learned opinions that a mother's thoughts and imagination at the time of conception or early pregnancy directly affected the physical appearance of her children.[137]

Bresson was also the source of scandal because she was openly frequenting Jean Chartier, whom she wanted to marry, in the presence of her pupils. She was not yet divorced from Damereau, who had abandoned her ten years earlier and had sent no news of his whereabouts. She insisted under oath that she and Chartier had never had sexual relations, though she admitted that she had continued to see him even though Antoine Calvin had ordered her not to. For her scandalous words and actions—particularly unacceptable because of the proximity of the girls from good families—Bresson was sentenced to a whipping and then banished from the city in May 1562. In September 1563 she and Chartier wrote to request permission to return and marry in Geneva, but the Consistory told them that Bresson was persona non grata and they would have to marry elsewhere.[138]

Conclusion

The registers of the Consistory show significant changes over the course of the first two decades of its existence in cases dealing with childhood and youth. In the early years, Calvin and his colleagues were most concerned about eliminating "papist" vestiges, as seen in their attention to baptism and the naming of children. By the late 1550s, however, those with strong Catholic sympathies had long since succumbed or departed.[139] With the defeat of the Perrinistes in 1555, the reformer could become bolder and the Consistory more invasive, demanding compliance in attending catechism and school and freely intervening to establish the proper rapport between parents and children in Geneva. The Consistory actually wielded greater authority in dealing with youths than with adults. Although it technically had no power to mandate any secular penalties, the Consistory, as we have seen, quite often imposed corporal punishment on Geneva's young without referring them to the Small Council. Like parents and teachers, the Consistory could subject Genevan youths to whippings without the permission of the Small Council. Moreover, the Consistory even took action against youths for behavior over which it technically had no jurisdiction. For example, in June 1563, it subpoenaed Claude Bouchier and his friend, Thibaud Boson, because the former had stolen some money from his father, Jean-Nicolas Bouchier, to buy three purses, one of which he gave to Boson, and a small knife. The Consistory told the regent and pastor Enoch that he should see that the two boys be given a whipping at the *collège*.[140] Similarly, in May 1561 when Jean, the son of the late Nicolas Gillard, threatened to stab another boy, the Consistory sent him to the Council to be whipped at the *collège* in the presence of all the other pupils and of his mother.[141] Although theft and threats of violence were generally not under the purview of the morals court, Genevan magistrates apparently agreed with the pastors that the Consistory could assume exceptional paternalistic powers in trying to correct the misbehavior of children and youths.

In this regard, the Consistory's actions involving children stand out from virtually all other types of cases brought before it. A recurring theme in this study is that in dealing with a wide range of moral misdemeanors, the Consistory resembled a form of mandatory counseling service more than a tribunal. The Consistory felt duty bound to nurture healthy rapports among family members, at times laying the blame on one party but seeking above all repentance and reconciliation. In dealing with rebellious youths, the Consistory still aimed at reconciling the wayward with the Reformed community but did so in a more heavy-handed or paternalistic way and was essentially functioning like a tribunal.

More broadly, members of the Consistory, like Protestant and Catholic leaders throughout Reformation Europe, viewed patriarchy and paternalism as the most effective means of promoting Christian doctrine and stability in the household and society. Convinced that humans, tainted by original sin, were more inclined to do evil than good, Protestant theologians and magistrates saw the need for paternalistic discipline and leadership in matters of religion within the household.[142] Calvin and his colleagues on the Consistory viewed their role as that of "fathers" to the rest of society, providing guidance and coercion to their "children" in order to establish and maintain their strong faith and a well-ordered society. The principal means of religious education in Geneva were the sermon and catechism, and the Consistory bore the responsibility of ensuring that its residents were attending church and learning the catechism. While indoctrination through catechism and schools nurtured discipline, the Consistory, through its admonitions, censures, and excommunications, employed extensive coercive powers to implement effectively social discipline in Geneva.[143] Calvin and his colleagues demonstrated a faith in corporal punishment as a means of promoting good behavior that is shocking to many twenty-first-century observers. Though they were known to attack abusive parents, they more often stepped in when they believed that parents and guardians were being too lax in regard to discipline. Their strictness undeniably shows that the Calvinists of Geneva were extremely interested in children and child-rearing: the authorities themselves could not possibly be accused of being indifferent or neglecting the children of the Protestant Rome.

Moreover, the efforts of the Consistory, combined with the mandatory catechetical instruction, were successful in producing a laity that was informed on the basics of the faith. Tom Lambert has persuasively argued that in less than a decade, the large majority of residents had successfully assimilated the minimum knowledge needed to be admitted to communion and had accepted the Reformed teachings on these matters.[144] More broadly, with its defense of mandatory schooling, the Consistory was also contributing to a more literate and better educated population, especially among males.

Controlling Lust and Regulating Marriage

THIS CHAPTER FOCUSES ON another side of family life: the control of sexuality and marriage. Since lust was one of the seven deadly sins and adultery was prohibited by one of the Ten Commandments, Protestants and Catholics agreed that sexual relations were supposed to take place only within the confines of marriage. The Consistory, working in conjunction with the Council, had jurisdiction over matrimony and illicit sexuality, and actions pertaining to these matters represented a very significant portion of its activity.

In Geneva and elsewhere, Protestants modified marriage in a few ways. To form a binding marriage, they insisted on witnesses, parental permission (at least until a certain age), the publication of the banns (usually announced by a pastor from the pulpit on three consecutive Sundays), and a church ceremony. They reduced the impediments to marry based on consanguinity and affinity (being related by blood and marriage, respectively) and eliminated the prohibition of matches involving people related through godparentage. Denying that marriage was a sacrament, Protestants also introduced the possibility of divorce and remarriage on very limited grounds. Rejecting the moral superiority of celibacy, Protestant leaders also afforded pastors the right to marry.

This last change affected Calvin in a personal way. In 1540, with encouragement from Martin Bucer, Calvin married Idelette de Bure, the widow of a former Anabaptist, in Strasbourg. Though it was certainly not a love match, Calvin appeared to become genuinely attached to her and mourned her death in 1549. He does not seem ever to have seriously considered remarrying, and he spent the rest of his life residing with his brother Antoine and his family in the house provided for the reformer.[1] In Reformation Europe, disciplinary institutions, be they consistories or bishops' courts, prosecuted sexual relations outside of marriage with varying degrees of efficiency, ruled on the validity of claims of betrothals, and adjudicated disputes between spouses. As we shall see, in enforcing sexual morality and promoting stability in marriages, the Consistory of Geneva put much more emphasis on its disciplinary than its pedagogical roles.

Illicit Sexuality

Most scholars see the Reformation as a watershed in the control of sexuality and marriage. Denouncing the Catholic Church as corrupt, Protestant reformers rejected the ideal of celibacy—in the *Institutes* Calvin bemoaned the centuries-old "superstitious admiration of celibacy"[2]—and excoriated the toleration of concubinage and prostitution. They created new institutions, such as consistories, to adjudicate matrimonial disputes and to prosecute sexual activity outside of marriage. In response to the Protestant challenge, the Counter-Reformation also introduced greater moral rigor and regulated sexuality much more closely than before.[3] Even scholars who stress continuity from the late Middle Ages agree that the Reformation witnessed greater intensity in prosecuting cases of fornication and adultery.[4]

In considering the control of sexuality, we must remember that all disciplinary bodies, including Reformed consistories and the Catholic Inquisition, were entirely masculine institutions.[5] The consistories' personnel—the officer who summoned people to appear, the assistants themselves, and the scribe who recorded the proceedings—were all men who aimed to enforce ecclesiastical ordinances and municipal edicts that were drawn up and passed by men only. In Geneva, the Consistory referred anyone it deemed deserving of a secular penalty to the Council, another all-male organization. Women are found in the consistorial minutes as defendants, witnesses, and plaintiffs, but given its composition, appearing before the Consistory can hardly be said to be a gender-neutral process. This raises the question of whether it treated men and women differently for the same sins or misdeeds.

In many places, among the most common of consistorial actions were those taken against illicit sexuality,[6] and this trend held true in Reformation Geneva. In handling cases of fornication and adultery, the Consistory of Geneva, like most Protestant disciplinary institutions, generally did not appear to maintain a double standard.[7] Authorities pursued male and female fornicators with the same aggressiveness—males actually comprised almost 60 percent of those convoked for fornication or adultery in Geneva for the years 1568–1582[8]—and usually assigned the same penalties to them. From its inception, the Consistory aggressively attacked fornication, and as with all sins, its ultimate goal was to convince those guilty of fornication to repent, forswear their sinful ways, and beg God for forgiveness. When the Consistory reproved a couple for their fornication in 1548, it explicitly exhorted them to "repent, recognize their faults, and henceforth walk in newness of life, demonstrating signs of repentance, with the heart touched by the Holy Spirit so as to weep and receive the grace of God."[9] First-time unmarried offenders were excluded from the Supper, and the Council typically sentenced them to three days in jail on bread and water.[10]

For years, though, the Consistory tried to increase the severity of the penalties against adultery, fornication, and blasphemy, and Calvin exhorted leaders throughout Reformed Europe to attack these and other sins with greater rigor.[11] As noted in chapter 2, after the defeat of the Perrinistes and with encouragement from Calvin, the Small Council and the Council of Two Hundred issued new edicts concerning illicit sexuality and blasphemy, but the General Council rejected them as too harsh.[12] The text of the proposed edict against *paillardise*, a generic term for illicit sex—does not exist,[13] but the Consistory's investigation of Jacques Nepveu suggests that it called for capital punishment for adultery. Nepveu was among those protesting in the General Council, and members of the Consistory summoned him on November 26, 1556, because they were not at all happy with his public reactions to the edict they supported.[14] A week later, witnesses alleged that, alluding to Leviticus (20:10), Nepveu insisted that in Geneva one must not embrace the severe rules of the Old Testament that condemned adulterers to death.[15] Calvin, the Consistory, and the Small Council would brook no criticism of their goal of cracking down on illicit sexual relations.

It is clear that in practice authorities began imposing more severe sentences for *paillardise* starting in 1556, even though the city's ordinances did not officially change. For example, in March of that year the servant Pernette Rey confessed that she had fornicated and was pregnant by a certain Alexandre Moine. Calvin and his colleagues excluded her from the Supper and sent her to the Council, which condemned her to six days in jail, double the traditional penalty for those convicted of fornication for the first time.[16] In April 1557, the Consistory summoned Humberte Farin, a domestic servant from Savoy who had been in Geneva for less than a year, on suspicion of fornication. Though she denied the charge, the Consistory was convinced of her guilt and referred her to the Council, which sentenced her to six days in jail and then banishment.[17] This palpably shows increased severity toward fornication, and banishment was far more likely to be imposed on a foreigner, especially one who was a recent arrival, than on a native of Geneva.

Some Genevans decried the punishments for fornication as too severe. In April 1557 the miller Pierre Pape got into trouble for complaining about ministers' severity toward *paillardise*. He told others that he did not want to be his daughter's executioner and pointed out that God forgave King Solomon for his fornication. The ministers, he claimed, reproached others for their faults but remained silent about their own. Subjected to a criminal investigation, Pape confessed to judicial authorities that he had erred in speaking thus.[18]

In Geneva as in other Reformed areas,[19] getting married did not exculpate a couple who had engaged in premarital sex. The Consistory and Council had always punished couples who had sexual relations before marriage, but in the late 1550s they started imposing harsher sentences for doing so. In 1557, Henri Fournier and his wife, Nicolarde Guex, were excluded from the Supper and sentenced to six days in jail for having had sex before marriage, the child being born six months after the wedding. So while fornicators had previously been sentenced to three days in jail, by the later 1550s the Council had doubled this penalty for first-time offenders, even married couples whose transgression was evident only by the birth of a child within a few months of the wedding.[20] In September 1559 the Consistory subpoenaed the needle-maker Pierre Choerlac and his wife, Claude, because their baby was baptized six months and two weeks after their wedding. The couple both tried to argue that the child was born premature, and if not, Pierre averred, then the baby must have been fathered by another man. A week later, the couple returned to the Consistory and admitted that they had sexual relations before the wedding. Calvin and his colleagues sent them to the Council to be punished both for fornication and for having initially lied to the morals court.[21] In Geneva, religious and lay authorities paid close attention to the dates of weddings and baptisms.[22]

In another case, the fiancée was visibly pregnant even before the couple married. When the hatmaker Nicolas Du Vernet and Catherine de La Chambre appeared in 1562, they affirmed that they had made promises to marry and that Catherine was now pregnant, and the Consistory accordingly excluded them from communion and sent them to the Council for punishment. Quite significantly, though, the Consistory affirmed that being denied access to the Supper did not preclude them from getting married at that time.[23] Though people excluded from communion could not serve as a godfather or godmother and thereby present a child at baptism, in some cases it was possible for people to marry in Geneva before being readmitted to the Supper.[24] This reflected the Protestant denial that marriage was a sacrament. In the same year, though, Genevan magistrates mandated that couples who had engaged in premarital sex had to ask for forgiveness in church at the time of the wedding.[25]

An interesting and rather complicated case of fornication and deception involved Gabriel Fornier and his wife, Jeanne, both of the village of Jussy, who first appeared before the Consistory in November 1561 because their child was born just six months and ten days after the wedding. For his part, Gabriel asserted categorically that he had not had sexual relations with Jeanne before the wedding. Jeanne claimed they had sex three days before the wedding, an assertion that he flatly denied; even if true, this could not possibly account for the healthy full-term baby she gave birth to. When they appeared for the third time—the Consistory referred her to the Council after her second appearance—Jeanne confessed that the father of the child was not Fornier but rather her former master, Bernard de Chambet, dit Fenna, of the village of Corsinge. She added that it was Fenna who had been instrumental in arranging her marriage to Gabriel. Notwithstanding this deception, Fornier declared that he was willing to remain married to Jeanne, provided that she not be subjected to corporal punishment or lose her honor, that the child be given to Fenna to be raised, and that she cease all contact with her former master. Although she may well have been devastated at the prospect of giving up her baby, the registers reported that she was happy with this arrangement and begged for mercy from Fornier, God, and the Council. Calvin and his colleagues excluded her from communion and required her to give the baby to Fenna, and they left open the possibility that Fornier might press charges against Fenna in pursuit of his own "interests."[26]

There are a number of things worth noting about this outcome. On the one hand, the Consistory was itself mandating that Fenna, who was probably married, raise the child he had fathered out of wedlock in his own household. This was something over which the Consistory, in theory, had no jurisdiction and provides further evidence of its extending its institutional reach after the late 1550s. In this case of fornication and deception, the Consistory was also relatively gentle in its treatment of Jeanne. The sentence said nothing about disciplining her for having lied under oath during her first two appearances. Although, as usual, the assistants did not explain how they arrived at their sentence, we can assume that a major reason for being less severe with her was Fornier's willingness to remain married. We cannot know how Jeanne felt about Gabriel's demand that she give up the child to Fenna, but it would be most surprising if this caused her no emotional distress. The Consistory's specific statement that it recognized Gabriel's right to press additional charges against Fenna might mean that the Forniers could keep the child and sue Fenna for child support. Civil authorities' decision on this matter lends itself to this conclusion, as Fornier was allowed to submit a bill to be reimbursed by Fenna for all expenses they had incurred by the birth of the baby.[27]

This case shows one way that Reformed Protestantism, which in many respects enhanced patriarchy, could bring certain benefits to women. Calvin and other Reformed leaders strongly affirmed that men were, by divine decree, the heads of households and responsible for the welfare of all members of their families, including children they fathered outside of marriage. Consistories, in conjunction with secular authorities, made much more aggressive efforts than their Catholic counterparts to oblige men to support all the children they produced. At times this meant that they raised their illegitimate offspring in their own households, at others that they provided financial support to the mothers of their children born out of wedlock. Reformed leaders wanted to avoid illegitimate children becoming a financial burden on the state, but the Consistory of Geneva also took actions against men who, in order to shield themselves and their families from dishonor, had sent their illegitimate children to be raised outside Geneva. In so doing, Calvin and his colleagues showed not only that they wanted these children to be brought up Protestant rather than Catholic but also that they expected men to recognize their faults and fulfill their responsibilities as fathers.[28]

Actions against *paillardise* provide further proof that to a considerable degree, the Consistory depended on the cooperation of the laity to investigate possible sins committed in the Republic. Unless the elders or pastors personally witnessed sins being perpetrated, they were dependent on the rank and file to bring them to their attention. This held true for consistories in other Reformed areas,[29] and rarely do the registers in Geneva and elsewhere identify the people who notified the consistories about infractions. A study of consistories in Languedoc suggests that women, through gossip, were helping establish what was acceptable behavior and were actively engaged in policing morality, especially in regard to the sexual behavior of other women. While trying to strengthen patriarchy, consistories, according to this argument, were unintentionally providing important avenues for female agency by policing behavior through gossip.[30]

In Geneva, women surely played a significant role in the policing of mores. We know that ample numbers of women were called as witnesses to purported sins, be they sexual or otherwise. The sheer volume of actions against sexual indiscretions was possible only with the cooperation of Geneva's laity, both male and female, and Sara Beam argues that women often served as "moral arbiters," asserting that women rather than men most often reported inappropriate relationships in Geneva.[31]

Evidence suggests that authorities were less successful in nurturing self-control among Genevans in their sexual relations than in certain other areas of behavior. Along with quarrels, *paillardise* would remain among the most common causes for being summoned by the Consistory. True, the illegitimacy rate remained low, but this could in part be explained by the fact that women who became pregnant outside marriage at times left to give birth in order to avoid detection and punishment.[32]

Adultery

Adultery, involving at least one party who was married, was understandably considered a more serious sin and crime than the fornication of two single people. Although ministers and magistrates might have supported in theory the death penalty for adultery, such sentences were quite rare in Calvin's Geneva. Nevertheless, as with simple fornication, authorities demonstrated increased severity toward adultery starting in the later 1550s. In 1562, for example, magistrates mandated that Jacques Lombard, a married rural laborer guilty of adultery, be whipped through the streets until he bled, despite being described as rather advanced in age.[33] In May 1564, shortly before Calvin's death, the Consistory questioned Gaspard Rocca and his maidservant, Guillaume Trottier, on suspicion of illicit sexual relations while his wife was away. Rocca, a native of Italy, denied actually having sexual relations with Trottier though he did admit that on one occasion he tried to seduce her, expressing repentance for having thus forgotten God and "abandoned himself to the devil." Notifying the Council of their misbehavior, the Consistory admonished them both and excluded them from the Supper.[34] Convinced that they were indeed guilty of adultery, *Messieurs* condemned Trottier to fifteen days in jail and ordered Rocca to ask for forgiveness from God and justice and to spend two hours in the stocks in front of city hall. When he refused to recognize his error before the elders of the Italian congregation in Geneva to be readmitted to communion, he was further sentenced to be whipped publicly.[35] The sentences indicate that authorities viewed Rocca as guiltier than Trottier; be that as it may, in light of her vulnerability vis-à-vis her master, Trottier's fifteen-day jail sentence seems unduly harsh to the modern observer, and it stands in stark contrast to the sentence, described above, of Jeanne Fornier, whose master arranged the marriage to another man after he got her pregnant. In the case at hand, it is important to note that, though guilty of adultery, Rocca was not banished and indeed was whipped only because he continued to deny the charges after being convicted.

In December 1557, the Consistory investigated the miller Pierre Girod of the village of Petit-Saconnex on suspicion of committing adultery with one and perhaps two married women, as witnesses reported seeing him with those women in very suspicious circumstances.[36] Although none of the parties confessed to adultery, the Small Council deemed the evidence sufficient to order that Girod be banished for life from Geneva under pain of the whip, a rather harsh sentence for a crime which frankly had not been proven beyond a reasonable doubt.[37] Girod's experiences also demonstrated that Genevan authorities often shortened sentences of banishment. When he approached magistrates in March 1559 and expressed remorse for his previous actions, Girod was readmitted to the Republic.[38] Cases of people who were allowed to return to Geneva regardless of a sentence of banishment for life were quite common. In early February 1564, Cathérine Brinon, the wife of Nicolas Mollet, was also whipped and banished for having committed adultery with François Lehan. Her banishment was very short, however, as she was back in the city and petitioned (unsuccessfully) to be readmitted to the Supper by the end of March 1564.[39] Her husband's apparent forgiveness probably explains in part the willingness of Genevan authorities to allow her to return.

Not surprisingly, authorities, as noted, were far less likely to banish a person who enjoyed citizenship in Geneva than someone who had immigrated to the city. In 1560 the butcher Pierre de La Planche, a citizen, confessed to committing adultery with a married woman. De La Planche expressed remorse for his actions, and the Council of Two Hundred decided to commute his sentence of being whipped and banished to nine days in jail and a fine of twenty-six florins.[40] Though the tenor of this decision seemed to imply that the normal punishment for adultery was a whipping and banishment, magistrates actually meted out a range of penalties for adultery but rarely banished a citizen for this crime.

There were exceptional cases in Reformation Geneva in which adulterers were actually put to death. In August 1560, Anne Lemoine, the wife of Pierre Bernard, and their servant Antoine Cossonex from Rouergue in southern France were convicted of having an adulterous affair. In addition to illicit sexual relations, they were guilty of other misdeeds. She had physically assaulted her husband and stolen things from him to give to her lover, while Cossonex had also attempted to rape the Bernards' daughter. Authorities sentenced her to be drowned and him to be decapitated.[41] In January 1561 Nicolas Lenepveux was sentenced to be decapitated for having committed adultery with several women.[42] In July of the same year, civil authorities passed sentence against Bernardine Neyrod, who was the daughter of Pierre Neyrod, a notary and citizen of Geneva, and the wife of Claude Antoine Dumolard, a naturalized citizen. As a recidivist adulteress, Bernardine was condemned to be drowned in the Rhône River, whereas her paramour, Pierre Dugerdil, a first-time offender, was to be whipped until he bled and then banished under pain of death.[43] Adulterers in Geneva could thus be obliged to pay the ultimate penalty for their sins, and laws were passed in several other Reformed territories that prescribed death for adultery, though in all locations capital punishment for adultery was rare in practice.[44]

A few features of these death sentences are worth noting. In most such cases, the people who were sentenced to death were recidivists; authorities concluded that these individuals, far from mending their ways, were incorrigible. Serial adulterers could be sentenced to death whether they were male or female, though adulteresses were more apt to be drowned, male adulterers to be decapitated. Sonia Vernhes Rappaz has written a very interesting article on death by drowning, a new method of capital punishment that was introduced in Geneva in 1558 and imposed for the last time in 1619. Assigned for crimes "against nature," this new penalty was considered a less painful method than burning and was especially, though not exclusively, imposed on female offenders.[45] The case of Lemoine and Cossonex stood out in that there is no evidence that either of them had previously committed adultery. Why were the magistrates so severe in handling this particular case? Apart from the additional misdeeds they committed, authorities were probably especially upset that Cossonex worked as a *serviteur* for Lemoine and her husband, Pierre Bernard. It could be that they viewed this as a particularly heinous sin because it violated the trust that Benard had bestowed by having Cossonex work and (one assumes) live under their roof. If so, then Genevan authorities were guilty of a double standard, as there were numerous cases of married masters impregnating their female servants, none of which resulted in a capital sentence. It is quite possible that class bias played a role and that authorities viewed adultery as a greater sin if it involved a man rather than a woman of lower status than the couple.

In 1566, two years after Calvin's death, Genevan magistrates passed stricter laws against illicit sex, and those ordinances definitely revealed a double standard in the treatment of adultery. Although these ordinances prescribed capital punishment for both parties in cases of double adultery—i.e., involving two married people—women received harsher sentences for other forms of *paillardise*, and adulterous affairs between masters and mistresses with their servants were specifically subject to harsher treatment; tellingly, adulterous relations between female servants and their masters resulted in more severe penalties for the former than the latter.[46] Liliane Mottu-Weber has persuasively shown that the double standard for women actually worsened in Geneva from the sixteenth to the eighteenth centuries, and female servants became even more vulnerable vis-à-vis their masters. While magistrates in the Reformation era expected masters to offer a type of paternal protection to their domestic service, in the late 1700s they were known to banish a female servant (and her child born out of wedlock) while exonerating entirely her master, whom she accused of rape. Like Calvin and his colleagues two centuries earlier, the Consistory in the eighteenth century wanted men and women to receive roughly the same treatment for the same sexual misconduct. The Council, however, looked much more askance at adultery perpetrated by married women than by married men.[47] Both during and after Calvin's time, capital punishment for adultery was only randomly imposed.

When lacking iron-clad evidence of illicit sexuality, the Consistory of Geneva, like other Protestant morals courts, convoked people for scandalous *fréquentation*. These were police actions against a man and a woman, usually one of whom was married, who were suspected of having an unwholesome relationship because they spent too much time together. Typical of this genre was the summoning in August 1553 of Matthieu Monetier because he was seeing too much of Jeanne Rachey, the wife of Otto Chautemps, in direct violation of Chautemps's express wishes. The Consistory reprimanded Monetier and warned him to stop seeing Rachey or risk being condemned as a *paillard*.[48] The Consistory wanted to be proactive by preventing all potential illicit laisons. Such actions also provide further evidence of the support the Consistory received from the laity in Geneva. Though some decried the penalties against *paillardise* as too severe, barring an out-of-wedlock pregnancy or getting caught in the act the Consistory could attack cases of illicit sexuality only if they were brought to its attention. This was most obviously the case when dealing with accusations of *fréquentation* since by definition they lacked proof of actual sinful activity. The Consistory depended on the accusations of ordinary folk to attack illicit sexuality and almost all other sins under its purview.[49]

Rape

Some cases heard by the Consistory or by the Council clearly show that Genevan authorities recognized rape as a crime that was distinct from the sin of fornication. In August 1557, magistrates sentenced Alexandre Vincent from Paris to be whipped until he bled and then banished for life for having attempted to rape the daughter of his employer,[50] and two years later Nicolas Retout of Normandy received an identical sentence for attempted rape.[51] In June 1562 a man was ordered to be drowned for having raped a twelve-year-old girl.[52] Though the Consistory ordinarily did not have jurisdiction over acts of violence, which were under the purview of the Small Council, one can nonetheless find cases of alleged rape or attempted rape in the registers of the Consistory. Such a case involved Pernette, the servant of the apothecary Louis Loue, who in December 1550 accused the miller Jean Theysier of making aggressive sexual advances toward her several times, most recently on the previous Saturday when he threw her on the ground and reputedly beat her when she resisted. As in modern criminal cases, some men accused of rape tried to discredit their accusers by attacking their moral probity. While various individuals affirmed seeing Pernette crying and showing signs of having been beaten, many witnesses had close ties to Theysier, including his own wife, and tried to discredit Pernette as being prone to dancing and other "dissolute" activities. For its part, the Consistory gave enough credence to Pernette's accusations to call for a thorough investigation, and the Council accused Theysier of being strongly suspected of fornication and violence.[53]

If Pernette at least could think that Calvin and his associates were taking her accusations seriously, that most definitely was not so for Jeanne Laurence "Susanne" Billot; the manner in which the Consistory handled her case strongly offends modern sensibilities. Summoned in June 1559, Billot affirmed that three years earlier the governors of poor relief had placed her in the service of Guillaume Prevost, who dabbled as a merchant and lacemaker. Shortly after she entered his service, the two of them left the city and wandered about to Neuchâtel and elsewhere, often sleeping by the side of the road. Billot claimed that three months earlier, Prevost had raped her, drawing his sword on her and swearing that he would kill her if she did not do as he pleased. The two made their way back to Geneva, though Prevost had by now left the city again. At the time of her appearance, Susanne was only thirteen years old and, questioned by the Consistory, affirmed that Prevost had sexual relations with her during a period of three months. Susanne begged for mercy, but the Consistory excluded her from the Supper and sent her to the Small Council to be punished for having fornicated with her master.[54] Apparently city council members initially hesitated to punish the girl, as twice in the following three weeks the Consistory repeated its recommendation that she be punished for fornication. In the end, the Council complied and sentenced Susanne to jail, accepting the notion that a girl of (at most) thirteen was culpable of taking part in consensual sex with her master.[55]

The attitude here of religious and lay leaders is quite troubling. In Reformation Geneva there was no prescribed minimum age for sexual activity in the same way that, as we shall see, there was no set minimum age for marriage if parents consented. How Calvin and his colleagues could have viewed this child as culpable is mind-boggling, and the contrast with the sentence against Alexandre Vincent, whipped and banished for the attempted rape of his employer's daughter, is striking. One cannot help speculating that members of the Consistory were less concerned with the welfare of poor, orphaned girls who had been wards of the state than with those from middle-class families.[56]

Same-Sex Relations

Sexual acts between members of the same sex were considered serious crimes—specifically crimes "against nature"—which ordinarily were not under the jurisdiction of the Consistory but rather went directly to the Small Council. We find, though, occasional brief references to such acts in the registers of the Consistory. On December 20, 1554, the Consistory minutes dedicate just two sentences to a case of sodomy (*bogrerie*) in which five boys were implicated. Declaring that they wanted "to keep this case secret," the assistants ordered the schoolmaster to keep close watch over the "children" until they could notify the Small Council to restore order.[57] The parents of the youngest boys involved asked permission to punish their sons themselves, and the Council agreed that the youngest two, Paul Tarex and Gabriel Pattu, would be beaten by their parents in the presence of the Council before being released to their families. The three others, Daniel Requin, Jean Goula, and Jean Levet, were to be taken to the jail where they were to witness the burning of themselves in effigy and be beaten by the schoolmaster. Then they were to be chained to the wall and jailed in separate cells for three months and then whipped again before being released.[58] Genevan authorities considered homosexual acts to be an abominable sin and a crime against nature and believed that these boys deserved both severe corporal punishment and a substantial jail sentence. Had they been adults, they most likely would have been sentenced to death, the fate of several (though not all) men convicted of sodomy in Reformation Geneva.[59]

In October 1561, the Consistory summoned two youths, Pierre Tornier and Pierre Malliet, from the villages of Bourdigny and Satigny respectively, for apparently simulating a sexual act together for laughs. Questioned, they admitted that Malliet mounted Tornier and that the latter said, "If I were a pretty lass, you would wreck my pussy." Tornier admitted that he had taken communion since that act, whereas Malliet had not. The Consistory ordered that Tornier be excluded from the Supper and told Malliet that he dared not take communion without first receiving its permission. It also sent them both to the Council, which sentenced them to a whipping at the hospital.[60] The language and sentence both indicate that these young men were feigning rather than actually taking part in a sexual act; otherwise, they would have received a much more serious punishment than a beating. Studies have shown that authorities in certain other regions of Europe, as in Geneva, were increasingly severe in prosecuting cases of sexual relations between males in the early modern period.[61]

There were rare instances in which the Consistory investigated lewd behavior between women. In sixteenth-century Europe, it was rather common for people to share a bed, a practice that, as we saw in the previous chapter, Genevan authorities tried to prohibit for all people other than married couples. Occasionally their fears of sexual activity appeared well founded. In November 1557, the Consistory convoked the apothecary Jacques Prudhomme's chambermaid Jeanne Serain and his daughter Charlotte to testify against Jeanne-Marie Mallet, the widow of Jean Libernet, who had also worked as a servant for Prudhomme. Jeanne and Charlotte both recounted that when the three of them were lying together in one bed, Jeanne-Marie would often speak of the sexual prowess of her fiancé, bragging that his member was as big as an arm. She told Serain that if she knew what she were missing, "she would not wait to sleep with men, and it was a shame that she was waiting so long." Serain also affirmed that Jeanne-Marie "showed her her shameful parts and had her touch them with her hand, and in the same way [Jeanne-Marie] put her finger in [Jeanne's] shameful parts." Charlotte confirmed these accusations against Serain, and the Consistory asked the Council to arrest and incarcerate Mallet immediately.[62] Following an investigation, the Council decreed that Jeanne-Marie Mallet was to leave the city within twenty-four hours and was banished for life from Genevan territory under pain of the whip.[63] Undoubtedly the reason that only Jeanne-Marie was punished was that at forty, she was much older than Jeanne and Charlotte, whose ages were not given but were clearly youthful; all concluded that she seduced Jeanne (and perhaps Charlotte too) and not vice versa.[64]

In August 1563, the Consistory investigated another case that involved one woman's attempt to seduce another. Pierre Deverneto described an incident that took place about two weeks after Easter in 1563, in the village of Avully at the home of Genise Pugin. Louise de La Rue, who was married, was serving as a wet nurse for the Pugins. De La Rue recounted that when she saw Blanche, the wife of Antoine Firmin, looking at herself in a mirror, she told her that she was quite beautiful, whereupon Blanche grabbed Louise, flung her on a bed, threw herself upon her, and roughly rubbed her body against hers. De La Rue called out for help from Antoine Deverneto, Pierre's mother, who came to the rescue and pulled Firmin off the wet nurse, who was quite upset by the attack. For her part, Firmin emphatically denied these accusations and claimed that it was de La Rue who forced herself upon her.[65] The following week other witnesses confirmed the accusations against Blanche. Interestingly, the Consistory decided to exclude from the Supper not only Blanche Firmin but also Pierre Deverneto and Louise de La Rue. Without saying so explicitly, the Consistory clearly found Firmin guilty of a lascivious attack on another woman (and also of singing bawdy songs), but it specifically rebuked Deverneto and, by implication, de La Rue, for "having revealed this out of envy and malice, as is clearly evident, and also for the lapse of time" since the actions took place.[66] As we will see in chapter 7, accusations were not to be made out of malice, and the Consistory viewed the lengthy delay as problematic.

There was clearly a real difference between how authorities adjudged same-sex relations between men and between women. True, the Consistory and the Council abhorred lesbian activity and definitely viewed it as a sin against nature. Mallet was indeed banished for life, and in 1559, in a case that bypassed the Consistory entirely, a servant girl, Jacquema Gonet, was condemned to be drowned after having seduced Esther, the fifteen-year-old daughter of her master. In that case, the jurist Germain Colladon, a close associate of Calvin, declared that Gonet had committed "abominable acts of sodomy and a sin against nature." The decisive factor behind that capital sentence, however, was almost certainly that both Jacquema and Esther sexually abused Nicolas, Esther's half-brother, who was only about eight years old. On this occasion, Genevan authorities condemned crimes involving children as the most "unnatural" of sex crimes.[67] It is worth stressing that notwithstanding her aggressive sexual assault, Blanche Firmin was only excluded from communion and not even referred to the Council. All told, it is hard to escape the conclusion that authorities looked upon sexual relations between men with much greater abhorrence.[68]

Why the difference? In Scripture, the condemnation of sexual relations between males appears much more overt than between females. The most explicit passages that condemned homosexual relations are both found in Leviticus: "No man is to have sexual relations with another man; God hates that" (18:22); and "If a man has sexual relations with another man, they have done a disgusting thing, and both shall be put to death" (20:13). While these passages condemn male homosexual relations as an abomination, they make no mention of lesbian activity. Though the Apostle Paul bemoans the "shameful passions of women," he is less explicit than in his reference to male homosexual acts. Decrying people who know God but have gone far astray, Paul writes, "Because they do this, God has given them to shameful passions. Even the women pervert the natural use of their sex by unnatural acts. In the same way the men give up natural sexual relations with women and burn with passion for each other. Men do shameful things with each other, and as a result they bring upon themselves the punishment they deserve for their wrongdoing" (Romans 1:26–27). Although Scripture may not provide an unambiguous condemnation of lesbianism, that almost certainly was not the principal reason for the perceptible disparity in the treatment of men and women guilty of intimate relations with members of the same sex. Just as Calvin and other theologians understood the prohibition in Matthew (5:32) against divorcing one's wife except for adultery to extend to unfaithful husbands, so they could interpret biblical injunctions to include lesbian as well as male homosexual activity.

The discrepancy more likely stemmed primarily from the belief that a sexual rapport between two males was a greater abomination because of deep-seated understandings of gender differences. Considered the weaker vessel, a woman who had sex with another woman may have been guilty of taking part in an "unnatural" act, but this did not violate her gender, as religious leaders understood it, to the degree that a homosexual act contravened the gender norms for a man. By his nature, a man was not to be passive and be penetrated by a sexual partner; that was the role of women. Both the "active" and "passive" male partners were guilty of taking part in actions that were construed as pulling men down to the level of women. More was expected of men, and they were accordingly liable to suffer greater consequences for giving in to "unnatural passions." Since less was expected of females, they did not have as far to fall and the penalties for same-sex activity were therefore less severe than for males.

Dancing

Though dancing had long been tolerated by Catholic authorities, Reformed leaders viewed it as a form of lewd behavior that could lead to fornication. Accordingly, from its creation, the Consistory convoked people who were caught dancing. Clearly some people had trouble giving up dancing—and popular songs for that matter—and this was particularly true in the Genevan countryside. Dancing seemed to be considerably more common in the countryside than in the city, either because it was more deeply rooted in the rural population, because it was more difficult to surveil daily life in rural as opposed to urban settings or, most likely, because of a combination of both.[69] In July 1551, Marin Du Molard and others of the village of Cologny got in trouble because many people (around fifty) reputedly danced the *virollet*, a circle dance, at his wedding festivities.[70]

Dancing, however, was not exclusively for peasants. Many Genevans, even some from influential families, enjoyed dancing, especially at weddings. In 1557 the Consistory, specifically stating that it made no exceptions for social rank, admonished François Beguin, a syndic, for allowing dancing at his wedding celebration.[71] We have reason to believe that some city dwellers held wedding parties in the countryside to be able to dance without being detected by authorities. In the summer of 1551, the notary Jacques Blondel, who had already served as *auditeur* and was later elected a member of the Small Council in 1556, syndic in 1560, and lieutenant in 1566,[72] was accused, along with many others, of dancing at his wedding. Blondel denied that anyone danced at the celebration, but the fact that it took place in Faucigny in Savoy could mean that he wanted to be away from the surveillance of Genevan authorities.[73] In any event, that Blondel's appointments to high office occurred after the purge of the "libertines" in 1555 suggests that even some very dedicated Reformed Protestants did not believe that dancing, especially at weddings, constituted a real sin.[74]

As early as February 1547, Genevan authorities passed ordinances expressly for the Genevan countryside, which included an article mandating that anyone caught singing profane songs and dancing the *virollet* was to be sentenced to three days in jail.[75] It likely reflected the fear that rural inhabitants were more prone to dancing than urban dwellers, but authorities were usually much less severe in dealing with dancing, regardless of where it took place, than this ordinance mandated. The Consistory more often than not limited itself to admonishing those who danced and occasionally excluded them from the Supper.

Starting in the later 1550s, lay authorities did impose secular penalties on some people who were guilty of dancing. In March 1558, the Consistory heard a case of several people who sang and danced in the countryside near the border with Savoy, and the Council ordered four of the women involved to ask for forgiveness and to pay a fine of ten écus each.[76] At almost the same time, lay authorities showed even more rigor by sentencing two men to three days in jail and a fine of five florins for dancing the *virollet* with some women at another gathering.[77] In the fall of 1560, the Consistory registers referred to a large number of people who were caught dancing, which led lay authorities to undertake a criminal investigation; this incident involved more than fifty people, most of whom were sentenced to one or two days in jail and a fine.[78] In May 1564, the Consistory initially suspended from the Supper six women and girls and one man because they had danced at a fair but immediately backed away from that decision and, convinced of their repentance, granted the request of five of those women to be readmitted to communion.[79] These variations show that, as with its handling of fornication, the Consistory took a firmer stand against dancing after the defeat of the Perrinistes in 1555, at least temporarily. Toward the end of Calvin's life, however, its members were relenting a bit; though still viewing dancing as a sin, they obviously did not view it as a major threat to Geneva's collective morality and again limited themselves to admonitions to the truly repentant.

Although men comprised the large majority of those summoned before the Consistory for all reasons, women were easily in the majority among those accused of dancing.[80] This does not appear to be simply a product of the gendered prejudices of this all-male institution. As we have seen, religious and lay authorities did not hesitate to take action against men who danced, and they were more apt to reserve the harshest penalties for male rather than female dancers, most likely because they expected more of men. The overrepresentation of women and girls among those accused of dancing almost certainly reflected a greater interest in dancing among them. This was also one activity for which the pastors and the laity were not on the same page, as many residents obviously did not view dancing as incompatible with a life of piety, an attitude shared by some Reformed Protestants in France, Switzerland, and Scotland.[81]

The Formation of Marriage

An important innovation in Protestant Europe in regard to family life was the rejection of the so-called clandestine marriage. Since the twelfth century, canon law had held that consent alone sufficed to form a marriage, which Catholics considered a sacrament. A valid marriage did not require a public ceremony. Though it was a sin to marry without the publication of the banns or the benediction of a priest, by orally consenting to marry a couple formed a valid and binding marriage.[82] Moreover, the age at which one could legally contract a marriage was fourteen for boys and twelve for girls.[83] Having attained these ages, adolescent boys and girls theoretically could contract binding marriages without the authorization of their parents and without the presence of witnesses.

Protestant reformers rejected clandestine marriages because they undercut the authority of parents and because they could be the source of legal complications, since there might be no witnesses to prove an alleged promise to marry. Wherever Protestantism took hold in continental Europe, authorities required for a marriage to be binding not only the freely given consent of both parties but also the publication of the banns, the presence of witnesses, parental consent until a certain age, and a wedding ceremony in church. In 1545 Calvin drafted marriage laws, which served as the basis for the ecclesiastical ordinances on marriage that were eventually adopted in Geneva in 1561.[84] In addition to the presence of witnesses to marriage promises, Calvin required parental permission—in reality, almost always paternal permission—to marry until the age of

24 for men and 20 for women, which were changed to 20 and 18, respectively, in the ordinances. Calvin's marriage laws were actually in effect long before 1561, as magistrates evidently wanted to test the new laws for a few years before actually committing to them.[85]

The records of many, though not all, consistories and other matrimonial courts show that disputed marriage contracts were the most common form of matrimonial litigation in the sixteenth and seventeenth centuries.[86] These involved cases in which one party came before the Consistory to attempt to prove—or occasionally to disprove—that he or she had a binding contract to marry another person. Contrary to what one might expect, women did not always comprise the majority of plaintiffs to enforce alleged marriage contracts. Women did file three-fourths of these suits in Basel, but men comprised the majority of such plaintiffs in Neuchâtel.[87] In Geneva and most other areas, prior to the Reformation, such issues pertaining to marital validity would have been under the purview of the bishop's court.[88]

Even before the adoption of the ordinances, Geneva's Consistory, like those elsewhere, consistently declared alleged promises of marriage null if there were no witnesses. In September 1550, the Consistory summoned the cobbler and citizen Thomas de Cusinens concerning alleged marriage promises and fornication with the widow Jenon Basset, who was pregnant. Only on his third appearance did he admit having sexual relations with Jenon, but he steadfastly denied promising to marry her. Though he conceded giving her two rings, a gesture associated with marriage engagements, he swore that they were not given in the name of marriage. Since there were no witnesses to the reputed promises, the Consistory ruled them invalid but excluded Cusinens from the Supper and sent him to the Council, which sentenced him to jail for *paillardise* and, more important, required him to assume financial responsibility for the baby.[89] Genevan authorities were obviously showing some sympathy for Basset's plight, but since no one witnessed the alleged spousals, this did not constitute a binding marriage.

The Consistory and Council consistently stressed the importance of parental permission to marry. In March 1558 Geneva's secular authorities condemned the minor Michel Binot to six days in jail for having entered promises of marriage in Savoy without his mother's permission (his father was deceased). When the Council referred this case to the Consistory, it predictably declared the contract null.[90] When a person's father was deceased, one had to receive permission from a designated guardian, who served in loco parentis. This was the case in 1560 when the saddler Jacques Paquier protested that a neighbor, Jeanne Huet, had arranged a marriage between her son, René, and his niece, Marie, without his permission. Marie, who claimed to be eighteen or nineteen years old, admitted that, with much encouragement from Jeanne and her two daughters, she had accepted René's marriage proposal. Since she was underage (according to Calvin's guidelines) and her uncle had not been consulted and was opposed, the Consistory declared the marriage null and instructed Paquier, acting as if he were her father, to give his niece a good whipping—an unusual sentence for a contested marriage contract!—for entering into this agreement so lightly. The assistants excluded René, Jeanne, and her two daughters from the Supper and sent them to *Messieurs* to be punished, and they forbade Marie and René to socialize with each other.[91]

The Consistory was sometimes known to oblige people to get their fathers' permission to marry even if they were well over twenty-five. In 1563, when the minimum age to marry without parental permission was twenty for males, Vincent Parent from Arras in northern France asked the Consistory for permission to marry a woman he had proposed to two weeks earlier. He explained that he had been prevented from celebrating the marriage because he did not have explicit permission from his father. Parent explained that he was thirty years old and that he was quite certain that his father would consent, adding that his father was now old, poor, and blind. A week later, five men appeared as witnesses on his behalf. Some were character witnesses, noting that Parent was an "honest man" who wrote sermons, which suggests that he may have been one of the men who were tasked with writing down in shorthand the sermons of Calvin while he preached (and later transcribing the full text).[92] Two of them had met Parent's father in Arras and affirmed that he was elderly and poor, and one of them even corroborated Vincent's claim that he had sent money to his aged father, which would certainly show that the son was not financially dependent on him. The Consistory ruled that he could marry on the condition that he provide within three months an attestation of his father's consent.[93] The bottom line is that pastors and secular authorities preferred that people consult their parents, especially fathers, before marrying regardless of their age and their parents' health and financial status.

Though it defended parental authority in the formation of marriages, the Consistory also demanded that fathers not abuse this authority in their sons' and daughters' selections of mates, clearly seen in its handling of a disputed marriage contract in November 1561. The *châtelain* of Saint-Victor sent to the Consistory Pernette, the daughter of Antoine Guignet from Feigères in Savoy and Claude Mestral of the village of Landecy. Both freely admitted having sexual relations, which resulted in Guignet's being pregnant, though Mestral initially denied her claim that he had promised to marry her. The Consistory suspended them from the Supper and advised the *châtelain* to punish the couple for *paillardise*. Since there was no proof of the engagement, the Consistory ordered them to appear before the Council where Mestral was to swear that no promises were made, exhorting him, however, to think hard and examine his conscience before taking that oath.[94] Admonished about his own conscience, Mestral declined to take the oath before the Council. Later, though he still told Calvin and his colleagues that he had not proposed to Guignet, Mestral now expressed the willingness to marry her if his father and mother consented.[95]

A week later, the couple appeared again along with Mestral's father and other relatives. When asked if he consented to the match, the father said that under no circumstances would he give Claude permission to marry since he had an older son. When asked how old Claude was, the father indicated that he was about eighteen while Claude himself said he did not know. Calvin and his colleagues ordered Claude, Pernette, and other family members to leave the chamber while they questioned the young man's father. The assistants strongly urged him to allow the marriage to take place since it was now clear to them that Claude had indeed made marriage promises with Pernette. The elder Mestral refused, however, saying that this marriage would be the ruin of the family. The Consistory decided to refer the matter again to the Council and advised that since the father was opposed, the marriage contract was null. Since the father had behaved "as a barbarous man here in the Consistory, saying that he simply did not want his children to marry," the Consistory also asked the Small Council to declare that henceforth, if any of the Mestral siblings should fall into another sin, including *paillardise*, the blame should be placed on the father. Moreover, since the father did not want to consent to this marriage, Claude should be given the freedom to marry whomever he wished "as if he had no father." In effect, the Consistory found the father's opposition to the match totally unfounded and was proclaiming that, if the Council agreed, Claude and Pernette should be allowed to marry; the father had so misused his paternal authority that the son should be freed of it.[96] It is rather surprising that the Consistory took this stand on the misuse of paternal authority, since the son was only eighteen, well under the minimum age at which he could marry without parental consent. It differs drastically from the case of Vincent Parent, the thirty-year-old from France who was obliged to show that his father approved of his marriage. Also surprising was the Consistory's opinion that the father should be deemed responsible for any future illicit sexual behavior of his children. One can accuse the members of the Consistory of being inconsistent or praise them for being flexible, but they certainly did not believe in a one-size-fits-all solution when considering parental permission in disputed marriage contracts.

When marriage promises had been properly made without conditions and in the presence of witnesses and, if applicable, with parental permission, couples could not simply decide not to go through with the wedding if one or even both parties had a change of heart. In Geneva, as in other Reformed areas such as Neuchâtel, authorities insisted that promises that had been properly made had to be respected.[97] This is seen in an unusual case from August 1559 involving Pernette Giron of the village of Onnex and Jean Des Moilles, originally from Savoy and now residing in Onnex. The *châtelain* sent them to the Consistory because they had fornicated, resulting in Pernette being pregnant, and allegedly had made marriage promises. Des Moilles confessed to these accusations, whereas Giron confessed to fornicating but insisted that she had not consented to marry Jean. When Calvin and the other assistants asked her if she wished to marry Des Moilles, Giron replied that she would if this were "agreeable to God and her relatives." The Consistory accordingly ruled that they should return a week later along with Pernette's brothers to hear their opinion on the marriage.[98] The following week the two appeared with Pernette's three brothers: Martin, Richard, and Mermet Giron. When first asked if they agreed to the marriage, the brothers avowed that they did not because Des Moilles was a foreigner without assets and believed that he might take her away to live in a "papist" area. Des Moilles, though, insisted that he intended to remain in Genevan lands, if so willed by God and *Messieurs*. Pernette persisted in saying that she did not want to marry him if her relatives were opposed. The Consistory told the parties to discuss the matter among themselves and to come back in an hour. When they returned, the brothers Giron said that they now agreed to the match provided that Des Moilles assumed financial responsibility for the marriage and that Pernette wanted to marry him. When Pernette declared that she did not want him as her husband, the Consistory told her that since she had said the previous week that she would marry Des Moilles if her relatives concurred, she was bound to marry him because her brothers now supported the union. The couple was to be sent to *Messieurs* to be punished for fornication, and the first publication of the banns was to be made the following Sunday.[99] Pernette in effect had conditionally accepted Jean's marriage proposal, and since the condition had been met through the consent of her brothers, she and Des Moilles were to be wife and husband.

To the modern observer, it seems cruel and imprudent to force people to marry someone they no longer desired as a spouse, but this amounted to a continuation of the tenet from canon law that marriage contracts were binding from the moment of consent, not just from the consecration in church.[100] Moreover, once a couple had made marriage promises, they were required to proceed with the wedding in an expeditious manner. In November 1561, the Consistory convoked Claude Pirasset and Julienne, the widow of Claude Guichard, because the couple had been engaged for three or four months. They explained that an aunt's illness had impeded them from celebrating the wedding but promised that they would marry as soon as the aunt's health was restored. The Consistory told them to get married shortly, or the Small Council was to be notified.[101] Calvin and his colleagues did not like long engagements.

The Annulment of Marriage Promises

Although couples were generally required to respect marriage engagements that had been made properly, it was possible to be released from them under certain circumstances. In August 1556, Toussaint Alliet and his daughter appeared before the Consistory along with her fiancé, Claude Fornier. Alliet affirmed that the couple had made proper marriage promises, but Alliet alleged that after agreeing to marry his daughter, Fornier left Geneva for an extended period, during which he contracted a venereal disease. Alliet asserted that Fornier had been badly disabled by this malady and he feared that his daughter would contract the same illness should they go through with the marriage. Accordingly, he asked that she be released from the promises. Observing that Fornier was quite poor and in bad health, the Consistory referred the matter to the Small Council and recommended that, if Fornier did indeed have a venereal disease, this bond should be dissolved since this was "only an engagement."[102] Since his illness was blatant, the Council released her from the promises and even banished Fornier as undocumented.[103] Although certainly not easy to nullify marriage promises, it was definitely less difficult than receiving a divorce for a marriage that had already been celebrated. Had one of the parties contracted a venereal disease after the couple had actually married, it would have been much more difficult to terminate this union, even though the illness was itself proof of adultery, which was recognized as a ground for divorce by virtually all Protestant reformers. In this case, appearing just once before the Consistory and the Small Council sufficed to terminate this engagement. As with divorce litigation, this termination was based on matrimonial guilt, whereby one party was clearly guilty and the other innocent.

Genevan authorities at times took it upon themselves to intervene in marriage contracts because of the age of one of the parties. While they defended the rights of fathers over their sons' and daughters' choices of mates, they demonstrated concern over fathers who pushed their children to marry before they were adults. In August 1558 Amied Badel, François Venier, and André Du Monthey, all from the village of Chancy, had to appear because of an alleged promise to marry between Badel's (unnamed) son and Venier's daughter, Nicolarde, who seemed quite young. The men claimed that she was baptized about fourteen years ago, and Nicolarde herself testified that her mother, who had died just two weeks earlier, told her she was fourteen, though she acknowledged that she had never participated in the Supper.[104] Asked to return the following week with documentation, the parties presented the marriage contract which, Calvin pointed out, revealed that Nicolarde was only twelve years old. The Consistory ruled that the girl was absolutely incapable of marrying since she had neither the requisite "spirit, sense, nor discretion" to do so and had not taken communion for the first time. The assistants referred this matter to the Small Council with the request that Nicolarde be obliged to wait to marry until she was mature enough, both in body and spirit, and had participated in the Supper. The Consistory delegated to Calvin the responsibility of going to the Council to express concern about girls who were entering into marriage agreements as early as the age of twelve, which was far too young. The Consistory asked *Messieurs* to enforce the edict on the minimum age to marry and, if no such law existed, to create one.[105] Calvin made his case two days later, and the Council decried that among "certain peasants" some girls were getting married quite young and mandated that only those girls who had received communion would be allowed to marry; this would serve as a sign that that they were capable of making reasoned decisions. Considering that children as young as eight were sometimes allowed to take communion, this declaration was essentially meaningless in establishing a minimum age for marriage.[106]

If child brides were a cause of concern, authorities were also troubled by marriages involving fiancés of widely disparate ages, at least when this involved an older woman and a younger man. To give an extreme example, on New Year's Eve 1556 Bartholomée d'Orsières and Louis de Crouz were summoned because of their marriage engagement. Already twice widowed, d'Orsières was about seventy years old, whereas her would-be fiancé, who was employed as her *serviteur*, was only twenty-five or twenty-six! Members of the Consistory were appalled at this match, but the couple expressed the desire to live and die as husband and wife. The Consistory sent them to the Council and asked Calvin and two lay members to petition *Messieurs* to prohibit such scandals, "which even pagans do not tolerate, by which the order of nature would be shattered, as women should not marry men who are not near their own age, and those who are beyond the age of bearing children should not be married to young men."[107] The Council was equally shocked and, following the Consistory's request, declared the marriage null because it was against nature, adding that de Crouz wanted to marry his employer not for the principal goals of marriage, such as having children and "other consolations," but out of desire for riches.[108] Three years later authorities likewise annulled the "scandalous" marriage of the Frenchman Jean Baudet and Pernon Soutier from the village of Jussy because she was forty while he was only twenty.[109]

By contrast, the Consistory allowed marriages that involved men who were much older than their brides. True, Calvin was outraged in 1558 when his erstwhile friend and mentor, William Farel, at sixty-nine married a girl of about sixteen in Neuchâtel. But while this caused a scandal and essentially ended the rapport between the two reformers, Calvin opined that there was nothing to prevent the marriage once the banns had been publicized.[110] When in 1576 Genevan authorities adopted ecclesiastical ordinances that officially proscribed marriages between spouses of widely disparate ages, they continued to be primarily concerned about women who were older than their husbands.[111]

Since Reformation Geneva attracted many refugees and other immigrants, especially from France, authorities sought to verify that cohabiting couples who had recently arrived were truly married. In August 1550 the Consistory issued a statement asking the Council to consider passing an ordinance concerning such new arrivals, and the following Monday the Council duly issued an edict proclaiming that to avoid the sin of *paillardise*, all couples who were recent immigrants had to provide proof that they were legitimately married.[112] The Consistory showed itself to be somewhat flexible when dealing with what were essentially common-law marriages involving ex-priests. Just two months after the publication of this edict, the Frenchman Pierre de Marillac was admitted as an *habitant* in Geneva and within days appeared with his wife, Marie, before the Consistory to ask that their marriage be recognized as valid. Marillac came from an affluent, illustrious family in Auvergne—one brother was a member of the Parlement of Paris, another the superintendent of finances, and a third the archbishop of Vienne and formerly the king's ambassador to Geneva—and he himself had served as abbot of the prestigious Potigny Abbey.[113] Thanks to his prestigious name, Marillac's conversion itself amounted to a coup for the Reformed cause in Geneva. Marillac affirmed that he and Marie had been together for four years but had not been formally married. Questioned separately, Marie told the assistants that she was from the French town of Chinon and did indeed want to be married to Marillac, with whom she had three children, only one of whom was still alive. The Consistory asked the Small Council to approve the recognition of their marriage.[114] Another very impressive public relations coup was the conversion of Jacques Spifame, formerly Bishop of Nevers and before that *recteur* of the University of Paris and a member of the Parlement of Paris. Several years after embracing Calvinist doctrine, Spifame came to Geneva and, on the same day he was granted residency in the city, asked that his marriage be recognized as valid. The Consistory did so in just one session.[115] In these cases, there was no question of punishment for fornication, almost certainly because marriages of Catholic clergymen were forbidden everywhere, a ban that Protestants emphatically rejected.

Police Actions against Married Couples

Calvin and other religious leaders, both Protestant and Catholic, viewed marriage and the family as the most fundamental building blocks for a pious well-ordered society. Accordingly, Calvin and the Consistory showed a special interest in assuring that relations among family members were healthy and stable. The Consistory's most common cases involving married couples were not petitions for divorce—as we shall see, divorce was rare in Reformation Geneva—but rather police actions in which the Consistory convoked one or both spouses to question them about alleged inappropriate behavior. Some of these involved couples who just could not get along, and whose quarrels had become public knowledge.

In dealing with marital strife, the Consistory's goal, as with its handling of all disputes and quarrels, was pacification and reconciliation. Clearly the Consistory's registers represent only a small part of the efforts of pastors and elders to establish and maintain order in Genevan society. Calvin and his associates undoubtedly made many more efforts to calm troubled waters outside the Consistory than through it. Occasionally the registers can actually provide a glimpse of such extra-consistorial efforts to promote order within households. In November 1561 the weaver Claude Besson and his wife, Philippa, were supposed to appear before the Consistory because of their quarrels; they had already been summoned a number of times for their domestic turmoil, which Claude blamed on Philippa's penchant for drink and violence toward his daughter from a previous marriage.[116] When the Bessons did not appear, Calvin explained that the couple had come to see him at his abode a couple days earlier and he reconciled them and bade them to return home. The Consistory concluded that the reconciliation that Calvin effected superseded the need to appear before the morals court.[117] Reconciling quarreling parties was the goal, and if it could be realized without the intervention of the Consistory, so much the better. Clearly the Bessons also viewed Calvin as an effective moderator who could facilitate the settling of their differences.[118]

Quite common were police actions against domestic violence, one of the few types of consistorial actions that were clearly made primarily for the benefit of women. That said, as we shall see, the protection from abusive husbands that the Consistory offered women was limited. Calvin and other leaders firmly believed that men wielded authority over their spouses and tolerated a degree of corporal punishment in the correction of wives. In August 1548, for example, the eminent Genevan chronicler François Bonivard was called before the Consistory for purportedly beating his wife, Jeanne Darmeis, and frequently having loud arguments with her. Bonivard freely admitted that he had beaten Darmeis but only because she had disregarded his order to stop seeing a certain man. The Consistory decided that under these circumstances, the corporal punishment was justified and advised the wife that "she must conform to the will of her husband and, since he had forbidden her to associate with the other [man], she should not have ignored his order. For this reason, she has been admonished to live in a Christian manner with her husband."[119]

Husbands such as Bonivard who were entirely vindicated for beating their wives were a very small minority, however. The Consistory often convoked wife-beaters, which shows that Calvin and his associates deplored domestic violence and the social unrest that it caused. More common was the treatment shown toward Marquet Du Jusse and his wife, who were summoned in July 1556. The wife, whose name was not given, appeared in court with her face badly bruised from a beating. Du Jusse admitted to the abuse but complained that she had the habit of criticizing him for not having any money. The Consistory forbade the couple to take communion and warned that if the discord continued, they would be sent before the Small Council to be punished.[120] In December 1559, two members of the Consistory and the secretary went to the abode of Amied and Georgea Vulliet to investigate allegations of domestic violence, questioning the couple and their maidservant. Amied admitted that he had beaten his wife so severely that she had been bedridden for the past nine weeks, during which time he had not deigned to go into her room even once to see how she was doing, a dereliction of duty that the Consistory deemed contrary to nature, God, and justice.[121] He defended himself, though, by saying that once he had been sick in bed for six weeks, and Georgea had never come to see him. The Consistory entrusted Pastors Beza and Chauvet and the elder Jacques Blondel with the responsibility of going to the Vulliet household to rebuke them for their faults and induce them to reconcile. Failing to do so, the couple was to be excluded from the Supper.[122] In this case not only did Vulliet not spend a day in jail, he was not even sent before the Small Council for his extreme domestic violence. The Consistory sought only a reconciliation for this couple who clearly were living separately in the same abode. In March 1560, Claude De Luc, owner of the tavern La Croix Verte, had to appear along with his wife, Jeanne de Sales, and their employee, Louis Bonivard. Testimony revealed that De Luc was often drunk and violent and had recently beaten his wife and even thrown her into the fire. When Bonivard intervened on her behalf, De Luc beat him up, causing some cuts that required stitches. The Consistory admonished them all to live well and told De Luc to return in a month to see if he had mended his ways enough to take Easter communion.[123] Members of the Consistory clearly believed that De Luc was largely culpable for this discord and that his violence was habitual and excessive, but they did not send him to the Council.

Most of the cases of domestic violence ended thus: admonitions to the husband to stop beating his spouse and to the wife to obey her husband. This was generally true even in cases of severe violence. In two of the most extreme cases, the Consistory censured two men—one in 1542 and another in 1561—for having beaten their wives so severely that they put out one of their eyes. On both occasions, however, the Consistory also ordered the women to obey their husbands and to live peacefully with them; neither man spent a day in jail for this brutality.[124] In all the above cases, Calvin and his associates scolded both parties, not just the physically abusive husband, and more often than not, the violent husband was not even referred to the Small Council, let alone jailed.[125]

The few exceptions to this rule generally involved cases in which the violence appeared life-threatening. The mason Humbert Revilliod and his wife, Huguine, first appeared for their marital discord in 1552,[126] and four years later Revilliod was arrested and accused of trying to strangle Huguine. The later incident did not even appear before the Consistory, but Revilliod was briefly jailed and authorities undertook a criminal investigation of his violent actions. A male witness reported that one evening, some women came running asking him to come to the rescue of a woman. He burst into Revilliod's abode and freed Huguine from her husband, who was strangling her with her scarf. Under questioning, Revilliod acknowledged that he had beaten Huguine but only because she had contradicted him; he denied that he tried to strangle her. Six days later, the Revilliods appeared before the Council, which issued strong admonitions to both of them.[127] In this case, an enraged husband did spend a few days in jail for almost strangling his wife—she allegedly at one point tried to jump out a window to escape his violence—but the admonishments show that judicial authorities clearly viewed Huguine as partly responsible for the marital discord. Late in Calvin's ministry, one can find a few cases of men being briefly jailed for domestic violence that was apparently less extreme than that perpetrated by Revilliod. The pinmaker Grégoire Poncenet, whom the Consistory had previously censured and excluded from the Supper for physically abusing his wife,[128] was sentenced in February 1560 to six days in jail and warned that he would be banished should he again resort to such violent attacks.[129] Calvin and his colleagues could get quite upset if they learned that an abusive husband had threatened his wife with further violence if he were called before the Consistory. In July 1562, the Consistory sent François Sarrasin to the Council after he confessed to threatening to break his wife's arms and legs if he had to go before the morals court for his mistreatment of her. The Council sentenced him to three days in jail.[130] In this case, the anger of authorities probably stemmed more from Sarrasin's attempt to undercut the Consistory's work than from the physical abuse itself.

In December 1561 several witnesses testified against Jean Pradaire for his brutal treatment of his wife, Jeanne. For fifteen years he had been subjecting her to brutal beatings and jealously vilifying her, calling her a slut and a whore. Witnesses reported finding her, whom they described as "virtuous and honest," lying in bed covered with bruises and with head injuries. They had seen him choking her and jumping on her and kneeing her in the abdomen. Previous admonitions had been in vain, so the Consistory, deeming Jean entirely responsible for the disorder in the Pradaire household, excluded him from the Supper and sent him to the Council.[131] Pradaire spent three days in jail for his mistreatment of Jeanne, but the couple was back at the Consistory four weeks later in January 1562. This time Jean presented himself as the aggrieved party and complained that Jeanne held it over him that he had been jailed and refused to do anything for him, a charge that she did not deny. The Consistory heeded his request and, notwithstanding the years of abuse, issued sharp admonitions to Jeanne to obey her husband.[132] The pastors and elders expected women like Jeanne to put years of abuse behind them and to obey and live peacefully with their husbands. All told, while the Consistory strongly embraced patriarchy and the belief that women must obey their husbands, it did make serious efforts to stop domestic violence. More often than not, however, these interventions failed, and a woman was expected to stand by her man and not rouse his anger.

There were also some examples of women being summoned for domestic violence. Most often, this involved cases in which the Consistory censured both the husband and the wife for their violence. Sara Beam has found that most of the reported female violence in Geneva took place in the household and was investigated by the Consistory rather than by civil authorities. For the years 1553–1554, almost a third of the Consistory's investigations of domestic violence included women as perpetrators.[133] Moreover, evidence may imply that Calvin and his colleagues could get even more upset with wives who beat their husbands than vice versa. Such was the case with Marquet Petex and his wife, Jacquèmine, who appeared several times for their marital strife. At times both of them were guilty of violence, and in January 1562 the Consistory demanded that they reconcile and do their duties toward the other spouse or be sent to the Council.[134] The couple appeared again in June of that year, with Marquet complaining that Jacquèmine had beaten him when he was suffering from a recent illness. For those actions, Calvin and his colleagues excluded her from the Supper, and lay authorities sentenced her to six days in jail, a harsh verdict compared to the treatment of most violent husbands.[135]

Divorce

In the long run, the most significant change in marriage law that Protestants made was the introduction of divorce and subsequent remarriage. As early as the patristic period, Roman Catholic theologians argued that marriage was indissoluble, a view inspired at least in part by the belief that it was a sacrament: to many theologians, divorce appeared tantamount to undoing the grace bestowed by God through the sacrament of marriage. Catholics did recognize the possibility of annulment, a declaration that a real marriage had never existed because of pre-existing impediments, such as being related by blood or marriage, premarital impotence, deception concerning one's status, and sexual relations after betrothal between a fiancé and a third party. Catholic law also allowed the possibility of a legal separation, which did not permit either party to remarry.[136]

All Protestants denied that marriage was a sacrament, a vehicle of grace, and virtually all agreed that there was no scriptural basis for the idea that marriage was indissoluble. Calvin and other Reformed theologians believed in the possibility of divorce on limited grounds, most notably for adultery, the only ground found in all divorce doctrines and legislation among continental Protestants. Most Protestant reformers and matrimonial courts also recognized desertion or the prolonged absence of a spouse as a valid ground for divorce, based on the assumption that, after an extended period of time, the absent spouse was likely dead. Divorce in these cases in many resembled a "substitute death certificate" for the absent spouse, and canon law had also allowed the possibility of terminating a marriage, on the presumption of death, after an absence of several years—Pope Celestine III (1191–1198) set the waiting period at seven years, which was the most commonly prescribed period.[137]

Like consistories elsewhere, the Consistory of Geneva had jurisdiction over cases of divorce, which remained quite rare in the sixteenth century, a trend found throughout Europe.[138] As mentioned above, divorce at this time was based on matrimonial guilt—one party had to be guilty, the other innocent, with no collusion. Although marriages occasionally were terminated for other reasons, such as impotence, which, as noted, could have justified an annulment for Catholics, almost all divorces in Geneva and throughout Reformation Europe were awarded on the grounds of adultery or desertion.[139] Genevan authorities generally did not make it easy to obtain a divorce even if a spouse was blatantly guilty of adultery. A good example involved Jeanne Dupuy de Montbrun and her husband, Gaspard de Theys, the *seigneur* of Clelles, a village in the Alpine region to the south of Geneva. The first mention of this couple was in November 1557 when "Noble" Gaspard de Theys appeared before the Council and asked that *Messieurs* oblige Dupuy to return to live with him in France and to bring their two young daughters with her. She protested, however that she had fled "papism" and chose to serve God by coming to Geneva, where she had converted to the Reformed faith and feared that she would be in danger of being burned if she returned to France. The Council decided to ask certain members of the Consistory to investigate and specifically asked the opinion of Calvin. Facing the reformer and his colleagues, Jeanne declared that she should not be obliged to return to Gaspard since he had committed adultery and fathered a child with another woman; she averred that he had kept a mistress ever since their marriage, an accusation that he denied. The Consistory initially responded by declaring that Dupuy had not acted properly by abandoning her husband, but it took her accusations of adultery seriously and gave her six weeks to prove them. If she failed to do so, she was to return to him with their two children.[140]

Thus began a long process that ended in divorce about a year and a half later. In February 1558, de Theys made another petition to the Council, which referred him again to the Consistory, though he claimed that the members of the Consistory could not be his judges, no doubt because he was Catholic and French and therefore should not be subject to Reformed pastors and elders.[141] In December of the same year, Jeanne came before the Consistory and demanded a divorce on the ground of adultery, seeing that he kept a "young wench" under the same roof with him. Several witnesses affirmed that he led a life of debauchery, and some avowed that he had fathered two children with two different maids and that he had even "bought" a young woman in Valence in the Dauphiné for four hundred florins to do with as he pleased.[142] In January and February of the next year, she provided documents proving his adultery, and the Consistory decided she deserved a divorce and sent her to the Council.[143] Before she could actually obtain the divorce, however, the Consistory obliged her to announce this decision to her husband in France and to the Parlement of Grenoble.[144] Jeanne Dupuy received the response from the Parlement three weeks later. After studying this document and asking the opinion of Calvin, the Consistory finally decided to award Jeanne the divorce on March 23, 1559. It also ruled, however, that she should wait a year before remarrying in order to avoid all scandal, based in part on the fear of making Geneva look like a place where one could go to get a divorce.[145] Herself of noble lineage, Jeanne really did not want to wait that long; she and the Italian Count Julio de Thiènes, a refugee from Vicenza, made several requests to shorten that waiting period so that they could marry. Eventually, based on the Consistory's recommendation, authorities agreed to shorten the period to six months and allow the couple to marry. For having continued to see Count Julio though she had been forbidden to do so, Jeanne was sentenced to three days in jail, though out of deference to her new fiancé, authorities allowed her to spend her sentence in the city hall rather than the jail.[146]

The case of Dupuy versus de Theys reflected in a number of ways Reformed standards in dealing with marital breakdown. The Consistory's initial reaction showed that a woman was supposed to stay with her husband and to follow him in almost all circumstances. Even her claim that she had come to Geneva to flee "popery" was an insufficient ground to remain separated from her husband. (As evidence that her family was strongly attached to the Reformed faith, her brother, Charles Dupuy de Montbrun, was a highly successful Huguenot military leader and a key player in the "Maligny affair," a Protestant conspiracy to seize the city of Lyon in 1560.[147]) Calvin himself once wrote a letter to a Protestant woman in which he bluntly told her that she must not leave her physically abusive Catholic husband unless her life were truly in danger.[148] Dupuy's suit also shows that if the evidence of adultery was overwhelming and the innocent spouse had in no way consented to the adulterous rapport, then she or he could have the divorce. Apart from the more comfortable jail sentence that Jeanne received, the noble status of all parties probably did not have much of an impact on the rulings of the Consistory and the Council. Women were expected to remain with their husbands regardless of their social status, and proven adultery was a viable ground for divorce provided there was no collusion between the spouses.

If a person had sexual relations with their spouse while knowing that he or she had committed adultery, the coition was interpreted as a sign of forgiveness and the innocent spouse no longer had grounds for divorce. This policy was common throughout Protestant Europe and is evident in the handling of the case of the hatter François Raviot and his wife, Jeanne Vertier. Having committed *paillardise* and produced an illegitimate child with a servant,[149] Raviot fled Geneva and now lived in Pont d'Arve, a small community just outside Genevan borders. In June 1562, Raviot sent a request asking the Consistory to grant him a divorce or to oblige Vertier to come join his household. A week later Vertier told the assistants that she absolutely did not want to go live with him,[150] and the next time the couple appeared in the registers was in November when Raviot again asked that Vertier be required to join him or at least to let him know if she wanted to divorce him. Under questioning, Jeanne conceded that on one occasion she had sexual relations with François after knowing that he had committed adultery. The Consistory then asked her if she could affirm if he had sexual relations with his paramour after she had had intimate relations with him on that one occasion. Since she could not provide proof that her husband had committed adultery after that one incident, the Consistory sent her to the Council and declared that she should be required to follow her husband.[151]

Without clear proof of adultery, it was almost impossible for someone to terminate a marriage on that ground and to receive permission to form another one. An important exception to this rule, however, was the suit filed by Antoine Calvin, the brother of the reformer, against his wife, Anne Le Fert. The brothers Calvin had already accused Le Fert of adultery in 1548 but since the evidence was deemed insufficient, the couple had to reconcile.[152] On January 7, 1557, Antoine Calvin appeared before the Consistory, accompanied by his brother who was in effect providing him with legal counsel, even though, as noted in the introduction, Calvin had previously asserted that everyone should appear before the Consistory without legal assistance. Antoine was again filing for a divorce, accusing his wife, who was already incarcerated, of having committed adultery with Pierre Daguet, formerly employed as the reformer's *serviteur*. The Consistory immediately referred the case to the Small Council and asked *Messieurs* to provide "good and speedy justice." Wielding considerably more power than he had nine years earlier, John Calvin was successful this time, even though the evidence of adultery was frankly quite weak. Several witnesses affirmed seeing Le Fert and Daguet together when her husband was absent, but no one could provide any proof of sexual relations between the two. Daguet had already left Geneva for Lausanne and protested his innocence in two letters, and Anne herself never confessed to adultery, even though she was twice subjected to torture. Nevertheless, thanks to this "speedy justice," on February 15 Antoine Calvin received a divorce and permission to remarry, and Anne Le Fert was banished from the city under pain of the whip.[153] Given the paucity of evidence, a lesser personage almost certainly would not have been successful in this suit.

In Geneva and elsewhere, when a marriage was terminated because of adultery, the innocent spouse, be it the husband or wife, received custody of the children. This custom was reflected in the case of Firmin Givaudan from 1560. Givaudan was married to Marie Choyrade, who had been whipped and banished for having an adulterous affair with Pierre Mottu. Far from wanting a divorce, Givaudan forgave her and petitioned the Council and Consistory to allow her to return to Geneva, adding that he needed help raising his children, of whom he now had sole custody. Specifically saying that they were taking into consideration the children and the husband's willingness to forgive her, the Consistory referred the case to the Council and recommended that she be allowed to return, though warned that if she strayed again, Givaudan would be banished along with her. Without stating so, Calvin and the other assistants probably justified such an arrangement because Givaudan was responsible for bringing a convicted adulteress back to the city.[154]

As noted, it was possible to receive a divorce for desertion, but this required waiting many years, chastely, with no news from the absent spouse. In April 1558 Clauda Dupuis asked permission to remarry because her husband, Antoine Guillermin, had abandoned the household twelve years earlier. She presented witnesses, including some of Guillermin's own relatives, who agreed with Clauda that he had dissipated all their assets and had deserted her a dozen years ago. They all agreed that Dupuis was an "honest woman" who had not given Antoine any reason to leave. Because of this strong testimony, the Consistory and the Council ruled in her favor, granting her the divorce in June 1558, though the Council condemned her to three days in jail for "having hastened" to become engaged to another man without permission.[155] Having already waited twelve years, Clauda was probably not too happy about this sentence, but the marriage was allowed to proceed. The testimony of her good conduct was crucial; had she already had sexual relations with her new fiancé—and there is no evidence that she had—then authorities most likely would have rejected her request.[156] In light of the Protestant reformers' diatribes against the celibate life—they asserted that the majority of humans were incapable of following such rigorous abstinence—it seems rather cruel and inconsistent of them to force someone to live chastely for years and wait patiently to see if the absent spouse returned. Barring evidence of the absent spouse's death or adultery, however, authorities in Geneva and elsewhere in the sixteenth century only rarely awarded divorces for absences of less than seven years or so.[157]

Although most cases of willful desertion involved absent spouses whose fate was unknown, a few cases involved so-called religious desertion, whereby a Catholic wife refused to follow her Reformed husband who moved to a Protestant land. By far the most famous such case was that of the Marquis Galeazzo Caracciolo (1517–1586), a member of a great Neapolitan noble family. His conversion (around 1541) amounted to a real coup for Reformed Protestantism, as he was the nephew of Gian-Pietro Carafa, who served as inquisitor-general at the founding of the Roman Inquisition and later as Pope Paul IV (1555–1559), a fierce opponent of Protestantism. Received as an *habitant* in Geneva in 1551, Caracciolo was instrumental in the creation of the Italian church in the city and, after receiving citizenship in 1555, twice served on a city council and became a member of the Consistory in 1560.[158] When he came to Geneva, Caracciolo left behind his wife, Vittoria Carafa, the daughter of the Duke of Nocera, and their six children. Caracciolo eventually sought a divorce on the basis of desertion when she persisted in refusing to leave Italy and join him. The justification for such a claim was based on a very liberal interpretation of a passage from 1 Corinthians (7:12–15) in which the apostle Paul sanctioned divorce between Christians and pagans (but not between different types of Christians). Calvin was uneasy with this request—there was never a hint that Vittoria might have been guilty of adultery—and initially advised Caracciolo to remain celibate. Having lost great wealth in the form of the family lands he left behind, Caracciolo was unwilling to make this additional sacrifice and filed for divorce on April 6, 1559. Maintaining that she "abandoned" him solely because of religion—though she undoubtedly would also have been reluctant to give up the comforts of aristocratic life in Italy—Caracciolo stressed the Pauline privilege based on 1 Corinthians. After he produced nine witnesses who affirmed that he had made every effort to persuade Vittoria to join him, Calvin expressed his support and advised that the marquis should send a formal summons giving her one last chance to comply. With the support of the Council and the Consistory, Calvin drafted the document, and Vittoria's written response arrived in Geneva in August 1559. The Consistory recommended that he be granted a divorce, the Council concurred, and Caracciolo officially received the divorce in November and remarried the following January.[159] For giving up great material wealth for the sake of his faith,

Caracciolo was a hero to Calvinists but a disgrace to family members in Italy, who suffered terribly as a result of his departure and apostasy.[160] This divorce was certainly facilitated by the great prestige enjoyed by the plaintiff.[161]

Evidence from Reformed areas, including Geneva, consistently shows that adultery was cited as a ground for divorce much more often by male than by female plaintiffs, whereas women comprised the majority of those who filed for divorce for desertion.[162] Why the contrast? The most common proof of adultery was the birth of an illegitimate child; quite often these involved married women whose husbands were away for extended periods and returned to find their wives with babies they could not possibly have fathered. By contrast, if an unfaithful husband did not actually get caught in the act, he ran the risk of being discovered only if his partner revealed his name. Consistory records also show that the number of men convicted of adultery was much larger than the number of women who divorced their husbands for their infidelity. This could have meant that women were indifferent about their husbands' infidelities, that they were hurt but willing to forgive their husbands' foibles, or that they feared the economic consequences if they suddenly found themselves without a male head of the household. In support of this last hypothesis, it is important to note that rarely do the registers indicate how the divorced woman was to be supported henceforth. The silence in most cases on the question of financial settlements accompanying divorces provides a clue that there may have been strong economic incentives to remain married. Most likely, the majority of women could not afford to separate from their husbands. A case before the Consistory provides palpable evidence of how even severely battered women feared being abandoned by their husbands. In a case previously alluded to, the Consistory in August 1542 convoked Claude Soutier and his wife, Martina, because of their domestic turmoil. Four months prior to this appearance, Claude had beaten Martina so severely that he blinded her in one eye. Martina, however, had not wanted to appeal to the authorities out of fear that Claude would get angry and abandon the household, leaving her and their children destitute.[163]

A theory stressing the importance of economic concerns fits comfortably with the fact that abandonment was the most common ground for divorce cited by women. Often these women complained that their husbands had left them with no financial support. If their husbands had left behind few assets, clearly there were no economic deterrents to divorce. The sole financial hope for many was to remarry. Moreover, religious and secular authorities in Geneva definitely wanted to avoid having children become wards of the state. On one occasion, the

Consistory complained because a woman had *not* filed for divorce against her husband. In March 1560 Calvin and his associates questioned Marie, the wife of Leger Foret from Auvergne, as to why she had not divorced her husband, who had been whipped and banished for attempted rape. The Consistory's main concern was that the couple's two children not become a burden on the state. Marie indicated that she followed him as far as the Genevan village of Saconnex but then returned to the city. Calvin and his colleagues would have preferred that she divorce Foret or stay with him in exile. The Consistory specifically asked the Council to find a means of obliging the banished Foret to provide financial support for his children, because Geneva "must not receive in all cases the children of all those who leave them, especially those who lead bad lives."[164]

Significantly, cruelty was not a ground for divorce; indeed nowhere in Europe in the sixteenth and seventeenth centuries was cruelty or domestic violence considered a justification for divorce. Members of consistories disapproved of excessive domestic violence and, as we have seen, took steps to deter it, but cruelty, unlike adultery, did not undercut the very essence of marriage as they understood it. This attitude is evident in the Consistory's handling of the turmoil between Amied Gaillard and his wife, Clauda, of the village of Avusy. For years the couple did not get along at all, and Gaillard's violence—witnesses even accused him of ordering male servants to beat his wife—pushed Clauda to abandon the abode so often that the couple in effect had been living separately for much of the past seventeen years. Because of her living apart, Gaillard asked for a divorce and complained that his father had forced him to marry Clauda, who was twenty-two years his senior. The Consistory paid no heed to this request, suspended them from the Supper in December 1563, and ordered them to live together in peace.[165] When they requested readmission to communion on May 25, 1564, two days before Calvin's death, the couple first said that they were getting along well. But then Clauda added that since their last appearance, Gaillard had beaten her every week up until the current one and that for the past two years she had been sleeping with the hens rather than with him. Fed up with this same old story, the Consistory sent husband and wife to the Small Council again with the request to establish order in the Gaillard household and to get the couple to stop causing problems for both the Council and the Consistory.[166]

Protestants had rejected the judicial separation, which Catholics had allowed, because they viewed it as unfair to the innocent spouse. Barring grounds for divorce, most obviously adultery, couples were expected to live together until death did them part. Only once during the ministry of Calvin did Genevan

authorities grant a separation, and that case involved a man, Bertin Beney, who
had repeatedly been reproached for domestic violence that was so extreme that
his wife's life was in danger. Even Beney's own father testified that his son had
put her in chains and drawn his sword against her. In 1553 Louise Liffort, his
long-suffering wife, was permitted to go live with her mother indefinitely, and
she finally received a divorce in December 1555, but only because Beney was convicted of adultery.[167]

In the sixteenth century, women who were the victims of domestic abuse
would have been much more likely to receive separations in Catholic rather than
in Protestant areas.[168] Catholic judicial authorities had long approved of granting
separations on certain grounds, including abuse. Protestant reformers believed
that it was immoral to subject innocent parties to indefinite separations which
forbade remarriage, but in the absence of the very limited grounds for divorce—
essentially adultery and abandonment—they expected married couples to live
together as long as they both lived.

Conclusion

In its goal of promoting a godly and stable society, the Consistory definitely put
much emphasis on overseeing marriage and sexuality and was generally quite ef-
ficient in intervening in these areas. Church and secular officials were aggressive
in pursuing illicit sexuality, aptly seen in the punishments meted out to couples
whose premarital sex was proven only by the birth of a child within nine months
of marriage. For the most part, Genevans did not maintain a double standard in
dealing with male and female miscreants and probably made greater efforts to
oblige men to provide support for children they fathered out of wedlock than
did their counterparts in Catholic areas. Notwithstanding the requirement of
parental permission and the presence of witnesses, there was more continuity
than change in the control of matrimony. Couples still had to respect marriage
promises that had been properly made, and though divorce was now possible,
it was rare. The protection that the Consistory and the Council afforded married women was quite restricted. Indeed, women who were in abusive marriages
would almost certainly have found more relief in Catholic areas, in the form
of separations, than in Calvinist Geneva. Calvin and his associates decried domestic violence and rebuked abusive husbands, but in the end required women
to obey and reside with their spouses. Although evidence of a double standard
comes more from the registers of the Council than from those of the Consistory,

on the basis of the actions concerning marriage and sexuality it is difficult to contend—as has been argued for Bern—that there was a strong alliance between women and the Consistory in Calvin's Geneva.[169] When we consider their plight vis-à-vis seducers or abusers, not too many women would have viewed the Consistory as their protector in Reformation Geneva.[170]

CHAPTER 5

Superstitions, Magic, and Witchcraft

THE SIXTEENTH AND SEVENTEENTH centuries witnessed the most intense witch-hunting in European history, and in Geneva cases of purported maleficent witchcraft were ordinarily under the purview of the Small Council, not the Consistory.[1] The Consistory did, however, investigate accusations of magic and superstitions, which in turn could lead to suspicions of witchcraft. Evidence from the Consistory records can shed light on whether Genevan authorities believed that those who engaged in magic were merely ignorant people in need of reform or servants of Satan who posed a real threat to social stability, morality, or even Christianity itself. A comparison of the Consistory's actions against magic and superstition with those of its Catholic counterpart, the Inquisition, will shed further light on whether there was a specifically Calvinist mindset in handling cases of magic and superstition. In this regard, we can ponder whether evidence from the Consistory provides any support to the claims of some scholars, most notably Max Weber, that Calvinism contributed to a certain disenchantment of the world, resulting in a world essentially devoid of occult powers.[2]

Divination and Therapeutic Magic

When we think of early modern magic, the image that immediately comes to mind is the witch who casts evil spells. Although allegations of witchcraft could go directly to the Small Council, as we shall see, the Consistory did hear a few cases of alleged *maleficia*. Far more common, however, were activities involving other forms of reputed magic or superstitions. The Consistory, for example, admonished those who sought the services of diviners to foretell their future, an action condemned by both Protestant and Catholic theologians since anyone engaged in divining was guilty of hubris by trying to attain knowledge that was accessible to God alone. In June 1548, the Consistory admonished Odette, the wife of Jacques Conte, and Henriette Mercier, the wife of Aimé Pilliod, because they had gone to see some "Saracens" to have their fortune told, which is an "abomination."[3] Three weeks later, the valet Pierre Chambet appeared for the same offense. The record reveals that when the Saracens informed him that he had only three months to live, Chambet was so terrified that he actually became quite ill. The Consistory gave him "salutary and Christian remonstrances."[4] In combatting divination, the Consistory typically limited itself to admonitions.

Among the most common cases of magic heard by the Consistory, as with the Inquisition in Italy and Spain, were those involving therapeutic magic.[5] In these cases, people allegedly consulted a healer (*guérisseur*) who used remedies deemed superstitious to cure illnesses. A typical case of therapeutic magic involved Ayma Du Chabloz, the wife of Pierre Du Foin, who appeared before the Consistory in April 1543 to answer for certain forms of healing that she allegedly performed on children and adults. Defending herself, Du Chabloz claimed that she cured people of *gormoz*, a skin disease. She insisted that she learned to cure various ills from a physician in Piedmont and denied that one of her remedies included a novena that consisted of the recitation of prayers and other devotions for nine days in honor of Saint Felix. Du Chabloz acknowledged that she had cured a man named Buclin of *gormoz* but contended that it was an herb, not Saint Felix, that made him well and denied advising Buclin to pay thirteen déniers to have a Mass said on his behalf. Du Chabloz also claimed to have cured a girl in Savoy of an unnamed illness and admitted that she had abstained from communion at Easter because she was curing a woman and two girls of unspecified ailments at that time. The Consistory exhorted Du Chabloz to attend sermons regularly and referred her to the Small Council.[6]

Du Chabloz's appearance before the Consistory is interesting for a variety of reasons. Calvin and the other members were obviously trying to eliminate forms of healing they deemed superstitious. Particularly pernicious, in their view, were efforts to restore people's health through appeals to saints and the saying of Masses. Du Chabloz herself maintained that her methods were scientifically based, as witnessed by her claim that she learned her methods from a physician and that a patient was healed by an herb rather than by a saint. Her own testimony, however, undercut her tacit denial that her healing abilities stemmed from the manipulation of the supernatural. The fact that she abstained from taking communion because she was administering cures implied that there was something morally suspect about them. Had she been doing nothing but prescribing herbs or trying to restore a patient's humoral balance, she surely would have had no qualms about taking communion. Notwithstanding her claims to the contrary, Du Chabloz's attempts to heal people apparently included some form of appeal to the supernatural. Though they of course fully endorsed praying to God the Father on behalf of people's health, members of the Consistory were firmly opposed to any healing practice that smacked of pagan or "papist" superstition, which explains the Consistory's decision to send Du Chabloz before the Small Council.[7]

In July 1563, Jean Perret, who was from Savoy but now lived in the Genevan countryside, identified himself as a physician and professed to cure sick people by using all sorts of herbs. He maintained, for example, that he had cured a girl of epilepsy and claimed to have learned that remedy from some Jews in Germany. He also volunteered that to cure someone of colic, he would prescribe the afflicted to carry some mistletoe and herbs in his or her handbag. If one's eyes were hurting, Perret recommended washing the eyes with an infusion of sage. Convinced that his "cures" were superstitious, the Consistory sent Perret to the Council and recommended that it prosecute him, forbid him to conduct such practices in Genevan territory, and banish him if he continued to do so.[8] A few months later, the Consistory received a report that Perret continued coming into Genevan lands and prescribing his cures. He reputedly tried to care for two sick pigs but his "cures" ended up killing them, and he insisted on being called "the diviner."[9]

This and other actions against therapeutic magic shed light on, among other things, attitudes toward femininity and masculinity. On the one hand, Perret's case shows that the Consistory and Council did not hesitate to take actions against men who were prescribing cures that were considered superstitious or magical. On the other hand, women were in the majority (twelve out of nineteen) of those called before Calvin's Consistory for allegedly engaging in such cures.[10] Although this may in part reveal the prejudices of the male authorities who passed judgment, it also reflected the fact that women bore the primary responsibility of tending to the sick.[11] An excellent example of such a case involved the widow Jeanne Fassoret, who had already been cited in the Consistory for being a healer (*guérisseuse*) in 1547, 1550, and 1551.[12] In 1553, Fassoret was summoned as a witness in the case of Guillauma Gros, who was accused of adultery and of having contracted a venereal disease. When asked if she had provided cures to Guillauma, Fassoret replied that she had not because Ami Gros, Guillauma's husband, was a dishonest man and that the couple habitually did not pay for services they received. She did say, however, that she "taught them how they had to deal with this illness," adding that the malady afflicting Guillauma was definitely syphilis. She also unabashedly confessed that she had treated about twenty other sick people.[13] When she first appeared for this case,

Fassoret certainly gave the impression of being an expert witness. She spoke as if she were a physician, and it certainly seemed that the Consistory itself took her testimony quite seriously, accepting it as evidence that Guillauma Gros had indeed committed adultery. By contrast, five weeks later, in July 1553, the Consistory convoked Fassoret to reproach her for her "hypocrisies and superstitions in examining and trying to heal the ill."[14] To a certain extent, the registers suggest that members of the Consistory themselves had difficulty in distinguishing acceptable medical treatment from superstitious remedies.[15]

Those who patronized healers included some prominent figures in Reformation Geneva. In November 1547 the Consistory convoked Don Guillaume Velluti and his wife for similar reasons. This proved to be a particularly delicate case since Velluti was a very prominent member of the Genevan community, having served as a member of the Council of Two Hundred. More important, as a former elder in the church Velluti had actually been a member of the Consistory for the years 1544–1546. In spite of his recent tenure, Velluti was anything but deferential when he appeared before it. The Consistory accused the Vellutis of resorting to witchcraft to cure their son, an accusation they emphatically denied. Velluti testified that when their son fell ill, they sent for a Frenchwoman who had been residing in Geneva for a month. Velluti insisted that this woman cured the boy and that he would have died without her intervention. Using rather coarse language, he defiantly added that if he knew of a physician at the far end of the earth (*aux cul du monde*) who could cure his son, he would send for that person. He further asserted that he did not see the woman make the sign of the cross over his son—a gesture that Calvin and his colleagues would have rejected as a Catholic superstition—and proclaimed that at the risk of the damnation of his soul, he did not believe that she was an *herege*, a term derived from heretic that meant witch but could also refer to healers.[16] Members of the Consistory strongly rebuked Velluti for the extremely arrogant manner in which he was addressing them, adding that they were especially disappointed since he had previously been a member of that body. The Consistory's actions against Velluti demonstrate that it considered the clients of healers just as guilty as the healers themselves.[17]

A similar case involved Colette Grasset and her servant, Clauda Natey, who were summoned along with witnesses in 1550 for having attempted a cure deemed superstitious. Both admitted that they, along with another woman, killed a chicken in an effort to cure Grasset's ailing son. The servant admitted that they bled the chicken over the child and made several signs of the cross with this blood on the boy's head, adding that her mistress said that in past times they

would have had Masses said for his health. The mother of the child admitted
that they put the dead chicken on the boy's stomach and then gave thirteen déniers to honor God but said nothing about the signs of the cross or the desire to
have Masses said. Limiting itself to admonitions, the Consistory simply scolded
the parties and told them that this amounted to "sorcery, enchantment, and
charms." Like the Velluti case, this involved a well-established Genevan family,
as the father of the child was Pierre Savoie, the son of a former syndic.[18] The
vague reference to the coins (thirteen déniers) was apparently part of a popular
cure known to a number of Genevans. At almost the exact time of this case, the
widow Françoise Blaisetta and Mia, the wife of Pierre Du Perri, admitted that
they put thirteen déniers around the neck of Blaisetta's sister, who was afflicted
by what they referred to as the illness of *Sainct Alloys*. Here, too, the Consistory
did nothing beyond reproaching these women, with Blaisetta receiving an additional admonition for having initially denied the charges to the Consistory.[19]

Calvin and his colleagues were not particularly severe even with those who
ignored their initial calls to stop engaging in therapeutic magic. In August 1563,
the mason Blaise Coplet was accused of using a charm as a remedy for his chronic
colic. He freely admitted that, on the advice of another man, he was cured of his
ills by placing some herbs and roots in a leather pouch, which he kept on his
person. Under questioning, Coplet admitted that two pastors, Michel Cop and
Nicolas Colladon, had already warned him to stop indulging in such cures because they amounted to "pure sorcery." In spite of his blatant disregard for their
directives, the Consistory limited itself to admonishing Coplet.[20]

In February 1563, the Consistory asked the widow Jeanne Favre why she was
"crazy." When she replied simply that her spirit was "mixed up," Calvin and
the other assistants insisted that "God sends afflictions to people to make them
aware of their sins." André Simon, the brother of Favre's late husband, denied
that he had sent her to "witches and diviners" or had resorted to any other "superstitions" to cure her. At this point, though, Favre herself asked permission to
go where she could be cured, a thinly veiled request to consult with practitioners
of therapeutic magic. The Consistory categorically refused this request. Since
the members believed that her troubled mental state had resulted from some
quarrel, they limited themselves to admonitions and suggested that the Council take into account the poverty of Favre, the mother of four children.[21] One
sees in this case the Consistory's rejection of magical cures, its belief that God
inflicts sufferings on people, and its relative lenience in dealing with reputed
cases of magic.

The Healing Fountain

A specific form of superstitious curing that became prominent among consistorial actions involved water from a fountain in Saint-Cergue, a village in the Pays de Vaud near the border with Burgundy.[22] The water from this fountain was believed to effect miraculous cures for a variety of illnesses, and during Calvin's ministry at least thirty-two people were convoked for allegedly fetching, giving or selling to others, or drinking water from that fountain. Interestingly, thirty of these people were convoked during a twelve-month period, the year lasting from October 1556 to September 1557 (the other two appeared in May 1559). The absence of such cases prior to this period almost certainly does not mean that Genevans had not been seeking miracles from the fountain of Saint-Cergue then; rather, Calvin and his colleagues were either unaware of the existence of this fountain or, more likely, simply chose their fights one at a time and did not try to crack down on this practice until they had succeeded in curbing practices that they deemed more pervasive and threatening, such as saying prayers to the Virgin Mary or fasting during Lent. We can surmise with confidence that it was no coincidence that these actions first appeared not long after the defeat of the Enfants de Genève. With the position of Calvin and the Consistory more secure, they could assert themselves more aggressively.

Typical was the Consistory's treatment on October 1, 1556, of the foundry worker François Duclo, the first person questioned concerning this fountain. Although he appeared repentant before the Consistory, the minutes indicate that when he had first been reproached (probably by a pastor), he had defiantly retorted that he had been cured by the water of Saint-Cergue, be it by God or the devil. The Consistory rebuked him, forbade him to take communion, and sent him to the Small Council with the recommendation that he be banished from the Republic.[23] Though condemning this "idolatry," the Council deemed banishment excessive and sentenced Duclo to three days in jail, obliging him to return to the Consistory upon his release to receive more remonstrances.[24] The Consistory's hard line against those who tried to use the healing powers of this fountain is also evident in the case against Aimé Plonjon, who appeared the same day as Duclo. A member of a prominent Genevan family, Plonjon confessed that he had sent his servant to get some water from the fountain because he hoped to cure the fevers that were afflicting his son. He reported that after his son drank the water, the fevers went away for a week but, sadly, the boy died on Sunday, four days before Aimé's appearance. The grieving father was forbidden to take communion and was also sent to the Small Council, which on October 5, just eight days after the death of his son, sentenced him to three days in jail.[25]

Almost everyone who used the water from the fountain of Saint-Cergue for healing purposes in any way received a similar sentence. Typically the Consistory admonished the guilty parties, excluded them from communion, and sent them to the Small Council with the expectation that they would spend three days in jail. Although one might suspect that humble peasants living in the country surrounding Geneva were most apt to attempt such healings,[26] many residents of the city also sought cures, including, as we saw in the case of Plonjon, members of some prominent families. In April 1557, Jeanne Bellot, the wife of Jean Chautemps who had served as syndic, admitted that she had given water from the fountain to a sick woman, and the Small Council did not hesitate to send her to jail for three days like all the others.[27]

Genevan lay authorities undertook a criminal investigation of the citizen Jean Levet and his wife, Jeanne, for having gone to the fountain to fetch some water in hopes of procuring miraculous cures. The Levets both spent a day in jail and under questioning, Jean affirmed that because he was ill, the couple had gone to the fountain with another man the previous fall. He added that there were many people present, though no priest, and that they said prayers and participated in a number of "ceremonies." People also planted about sixty crosses around the fountain, apparently a type of votive offering. Levet acknowledged that he drank his fill of the water while there, and he and his wife admitted that they brought a bottle of this water back to Geneva, giving about a half glass each to four women and two men. Authorities were convinced that the couple was engaged in a Catholic "superstition"—notwithstanding their insistence that no priest was present and Jeanne's claim that they recited only the Lord's Prayer and the credo—but released the couple with the understanding that they must reappear if called.[28] This testimony indicates that at certain times large groups of people gathered at the fountain hoping to get water for cures.

Cases involving healing fountains stand out from other actions against therapeutic magic in two ways. First, the Consistory and Small Council showed greater severity in dealing with these cases than with others—although other forms of superstitious cures usually merited admonitions and exclusion from the Supper, those who drank the water or gave it to others, as we have seen, typically also had to spend three days in jail; on one occasion, the Consistory even recommended banishment. The most likely explanation for this greater severity is that Calvin and his colleagues associated the reputed powers of healing fountains, more than other superstitious cures, with Catholic practices and beliefs. At times the Consistory registers specifically refer to using the water from the fountain as a form of "idolatry," a term also applied to simply attending Mass. Common in many parts of Europe, fountains or wells with curative powers were almost always associated with saints and had their roots in paganism.[29] Reformed leaders throughout Europe aggressively sought to eradicate anything that smacked of paganism or the veneration of saints. By the later sixteenth century, the Roman Inquisition would likely have taken similar actions against the above cures that involved killing a chicken or hanging coins around the sick person's neck, but it would have allowed the drinking of water from a fountain associated with an officially approved saint.[30]

Another way fountain cases contrasted with other types of therapeutic magic is that while women were in the majority of those accused of taking part in other forms of magical cures, men outnumbered women twenty-two to ten among those whom the Consistory summoned for using or distributing water from the fountain. Why the difference? The most obvious reason is that getting to the fountain required traveling about thirty-five kilometers (twenty-two miles) north of Geneva, and men tended to travel much more than women. This also simply involved procuring water from the fountain rather than preparing remedies that might be elaborate, which more closely resembled the preparation of food and other forms of care that women were likely to perform. It is even possible that the prevalence of men may have incited Calvin and his colleagues to be more stringent in handling the fountain cases: no doubt expecting women to be more prone to believe in such superstitious activities, authorities may have been particularly alarmed by the number of men involved. The registers do not, however, give any explicit sign that this was a motive behind the greater severity toward this kind of cure—the registers of both the Consistory and the Council rarely express a motive for a particular punishment—and sentences for men and women were identical.[31] The disappearance of such cases from the Consistory records probably meant that the intense actions of 1556 and 1557 were largely successful in deterring Genevans from seeking miraculous cures for their ills from any fountain.[32]

Therapeutic Magic and *Maleficia*

Other cases show that therapeutic magic could readily lead to suspicions of *maleficia*. In March 1552, Jean Billiard and his wife, Jacquème, were accused of consulting a *guérisseuse*, the so-called good witch (*la bonne herege*) of the village of Challex in the neighboring Pays de Gex. The healers whose services Genevans sought were more often than not women and were usually from villages outside Genevan territory, no doubt because such healing could be exercised with less fear of being discovered by authorities. Appearing before Calvin, Billiard explained that their son had been quite ill and in fact recently died. Like others, he sought aid from this woman in Challex, and he was careful to refer to her as a physician (*une medicine*) who offered remedies in the form of "herbs and medicines." Billiard freely admitted that he aggressively forced Jeanne Pya, the wife of François Chapuis, to leave her own home. He believed that Pya was responsible through witchcraft for his son's sickness and death, and testimony revealed that Pya had indeed visited the sick boy, perhaps to offer cures similar to those provided by the woman from Challex. Appearing in court, Pya conceded that she had gone to see the boy but emphatically denied that she was a witch, an accusation that was first made by none other than the good witch of Challex. Notwithstanding Billiard's use of the term "physician," he obviously believed that the child's ills were supernatural in origin, and the "good witch" clearly believed that she could identify the author of *maleficia*. The Consistory referred the couple, another man, and Pya to the Small Council and expressed concern that the Billiards had sought the services of the "witch" of Challex and, quite interestingly, that they had impugned the "honor" of Jeanne Pya. Calvin and his colleagues were clearly skeptical that the boy had died of a maleficent spell and viewed Pya more as the victim of defamation than as a witch.[33]

A similar case took place in August 1555, when René Bastard, a former guard, was quite ill. His brother's wife sent for a man identified as Jean de Verne, known as the good witch of Challex (evidently the residents of that Savoyard village had a penchant for healing!). De Verne reputedly came to the village of Bourdigny, where Bastard lived, and provided some herbal beverages, which the sick man drank for four or five days. De Verne also informed him and other family members that a neighbor, Michel Dufour, was responsible for this illness through a maleficent spell. This was the source of a bitter quarrel, as Bastard and other relatives called Dufour a witch and the latter in turn cursed his accusers with blasphemous words. Although the two men appeared to be ready to reconcile at their first appearance before the Consistory, two weeks later they were still quarreling. In that appearance, Bastard said he still thought that Dufour had made him ill through witchcraft—a belief shared by his two sisters-in-law—while Dufour was furious at being called a witch. The Consistory required Dufour to cry for mercy from God and kiss the earth for his blasphemy and excluded both men and Bastard's sisters-in-law from communion.[34]

In cases such as these, people accused of practicing white magic and the parties who patronized them tried to portray the *guérisseurs* as physicians. Bastard was quick to point out that de Verne prescribed an herbal concoction, and his sister-in-law who went to fetch de Verne claimed in court that she did not believe he was a witch, a view that was contradicted in the same session when Bastard himself referred to de Verne as a "good witch."[35] In August 1563, the pot-maker Nicod Hanse explicitly referred to Jean Perret, the man who claimed to have learned cures from German Jews, as a physician.[36] Although most of those accused of being *guérisseurs* lived outside Genevan territory and thus could not be brought before the Consistory, in February 1556 Rolette de Saxe, a widow from Gex living in the village of Bons in nearby Savoy, was suspected of being such a healer. She defended herself before Calvin by saying that she was the daughter of a physician and had been around sick people all her life, implying that her methods were anything but superstitious. Although she protested that she did not prescribe medicines, a woman who had used her services insisted that de Saxe was known as "the good physician" and claimed to have personally witnessed her cure, through medical means, patients for whom more traditional doctors had given up all hope. The Consistory told de Saxe to stop dabbling in medicine or be sent before the Small Council and admonished the other woman.[37]

Likewise in April 1560, the Consistory summoned Jean Morand of Choully for using "diabolical words" to kill the midges that were devouring the wheat. He confessed that he had a recipe for a concoction made up of certain herbs and roots that he cooked in water, which he then tossed on the insects when they landed on the walls, uttering some words as he did so. He added that he had learned this formula from a Jew in France. François de Roche, a lay assistant of the Consistory, asserted that Morand had told him that he could also treat problems with vision and hearing, cure sick horses, and find lost objects.[38] When he returned the following week, Morand said that he did not actually believe in the efficacy of the words he spoke when trying to kill midges. Pressed further, Morand added that if the person or persons cooking the potion believed in Jesus Christ, it could be used to their advantage. Moreover, he now said that he had learned this from a *baptized* Jew. In his cure for bad vision, Morand claimed that he would put sage on a person's eyes and then pronounce the following words: "May Jesus Christ restore your vision just as he did for Saint Peter and Saint Paul." By inserting these Christian elements, Morand was no doubt hoping that the Reformed authorities would find his remedies more palatable. Far from accepting them, the Consistory admonished Morand for his superstitions and sorcery and excluded him from the Supper.[39] The Consistory's usual lenience in handling such cases was evident in the fact that Morand was not referred to the Small Council and was readmitted to communion in August, since Calvin

and associates were convinced that Morand had repented of his previous superstitions.[40] Saying that a cure worked only if one believed in and prayed to Jesus
Christ did not suffice to persuade Genevan pastors and elders that various cures
were acceptable. In rejecting them, the Consistory certainly could be construed
as contributing to a desacralization of mentality. To be sure, Calvin and his colleagues most definitely did not put an end to belief in the occult—the Consistory was still convoking people for matters related to magic and superstition in
the early seventeenth century[41]—but they nonetheless can be viewed as paving
the way for a more secular mentality.

The Professionalization of Medicine

In dealing with cases of healings, members of the Consistory showed their
firm resolve to root out various forms of magic and superstition. They clearly
viewed as anathema any attempt to meddle with the supernatural even if the
desired goal, restoring a person's health, was perfectly acceptable. These various
cases mirrored changing attitudes toward the use of healers and the practice
of medicine. European medical professions lacked clear standards for training
and licensing during most of the medieval period, when both men and women
worked as medical practitioners. Until the foundation of the medical guild in
1569, the Small Council had the exclusive authority in Geneva to settle medical
disputes and to issue licenses to surgeons, apothecaries, and physicians. As Philip
Rieder has noted, the standards for awarding licenses were rather flexible even
after the passing of the *Ordonnances médicales* of 1569.[42] Be that as it may, the
Consistory clearly was promoting the professionalization of medicine in Geneva
even before the passage of those ordinances. Calvin and his colleagues believed
that when a person was sick, one should send for a physician or a surgeon, a person who had received advanced training in the medical fields. The overall trend
in sixteenth-century Europe was likewise toward professionalization whereby
only people who had received medical degrees from a university had the right
to be called physicians. The Consistory consistently took action against any un-
qualified male who tried to cure people, and since women were excluded from
all institutions of higher learning at this time, they by definition could not be
physicians. Similarly, though they did not receive a university education, by the
mid-sixteenth century apothecaries generally underwent standardized formal
training through apprenticeships that excluded women from their ranks.[43] In
Geneva women did not have access to secondary education, much less advanced
training in medicine.

In the sixteenth and seventeenth centuries, when Europe experienced the most intense witch-hunting ever, women were far more likely than men to be accused of witchcraft. Members of the Consistory almost certainly shared the contemporary prejudice that women were more prone than men to make pacts with the devil. Nonetheless, in spite of the references to *hereges* and vague accusations of witchcraft, Consistory authorities gave no indication that they believed demons were in play in any of these cases. Although they disapproved of the *guérisseuses*, members of the Consistory clearly did not view them as devil-worshippers.[44] In dealing with illnesses, Reformed Protestantism eliminated a host of methods that had long been embraced in popular European culture and thus forbade not only forms of white magic but also appeals to the supernatural that Catholics accepted, such as prayers to the saints and votive offerings. Interestingly, the defendants in these cases at least acted as if they had assimilated these views on healing. Du Chabloz defended herself by claiming to be practicing medicine rather than praying to saints; the Vellutis asserted that their son was healed through the woman's knowledge of herbs, not by appeals to supernatural intervention; Billiard emphatically referred to *la bonne herege* as a physician; and Rolette de Saxe pointedly mentioned that her father was himself a physician. They knew that, in the view of the Consistory, illness was in the domain of medicine, and they all at least paid lip service to that same belief.

Witchcraft and Other Forms of Magic

Calvin and his colleagues definitely believed it was possible to cast maleficent spells with the help of the devil, and they accordingly were not always dismissive when people expressed suspicions of witchcraft.[45] In June 1552 Pernette Morel appeared with a man and a woman, complaining that the latter two had accused her of being a witch. Though denying that charge, the others asserted that Morel was quite rude and haughty, and Blaise Phillibert added that about a year ago her eight-year-old daughter suddenly fell quite ill just an hour after Morel had gotten quite angry with the girl, and later died of this malady. Though the Consistory sent Morel to the Small Council, it was as much for having not taken communion for some time as for this suspicion. Significantly, the Council did not charge her with witchcraft.[46] In August 1562 the Consistory took the initiative and asked the lieutenant to investigate Jacquème Galley, who was suspected of having caused, through witchcraft, a boy's leg to wither.[47] When Galley appeared before Calvin and the other assistants, she denied the accusation. Since there was no proof, the Consistory ruled that this matter must be left to the judgment of

God and that Galley should abstain from the Supper if she was guilty; otherwise she should come "in all humility" to take the sacrament. Galley declared that she would take it with a clear conscience.[48]

A very interesting case involved a man who actually made accusations against Calvin himself. Benoît Perrotel, a purse-maker originally from Calvin's native Picardy, was subject to a criminal investigation for having claimed that the reformer was able to read his mind through the black arts. In this investigation, Calvin confronted Perrotel in October 1550 because he allegedly had told others on several occasions that Calvin was a diviner who communicated with demons (*ayant participation avecq les dyables*). Perrotel, who had been granted residency in Geneva four months earlier,[49] replied that he did not specifically say that Calvin was communicating with "the Enemy." He did affirm, however, that while listening to Calvin preach, he felt as if Calvin was reading his mind. Perrotel opined that since all prophecies ended with the Passion of Christ, Calvin's knowledge of his thoughts must have come through demonic revelation. Perrotel even recalled the precise moment when he started hating the reformer. He frankly admitted that he strongly desired two different women, and while delivering a sermon on a Monday, Calvin, he claimed, looked first at him and then at one of those women, leading him to conclude that Calvin had perceived and thwarted his libidinous yearnings. Convinced that he had been out of his senses, Perrotel asserted that he now believed that Calvin was a good man. Seeing his contrition, the Council condemned him to three days in jail and to appear before the Consistory to be censured.[50]

It is understandable that authorities did not take seriously Perrotel's claims that Calvin must have been benefiting from demonic powers, but in other settings his allegations could have resulted in counter-accusations of harmful magic against him. In this case, however, Genevan authorities treated this as a simple case of defamation of character, which could deter people from accusing others of witchcraft, especially if the accused was a very prominent person.

In considering accusations of *maleficia*, Calvin and his fellow Consistory members exhibited a greater degree of skepticism than certain other Genevan authorities, particularly those associated with the surrounding countryside. In February 1554 a couple from the village of Peney appeared before the Consistory because the *châtelain* had prevented them from marrying on account of rumors that she was a witch who was responsible for the deaths of a neighbor's chickens. The Consistory curtly told the *châtelain* and the village pastor, Jacques Bernard, to do their duty and allow the marriage to be celebrated.[51] In November 1561 Calvin and his associates summoned Martin Canard, a resident of the city, for possessing a book of charms. Canard affirmed that he had found the book in the common privies, and the Consistory simply ordered that the book be burned immediately. It did not admonish Canard, exclude him from the Supper, or refer him to the Small Council.[52]

Quite significant is the fact that in this age of intense witch-hunts, the Consistory on a number of occasions actually defended suspected witches and even censured their accusers for defamation of character. In October 1560, Pierre Dupuis alleged that he was having no problem drawing wine from a vat but that it suddenly stopped flowing upon the appearance of Gonin Besson, which caused Dupuis to suspect that Besson was a witch. Dupuis admitted that he asked Besson to show him his "mark," a reference to the mark the devil purportedly left on the body of a witch upon entering a diabolical pact. The Consistory admonished Dupuis for taking this so lightly and being so suspicious.[53] As for Besson, the Consistory was satisfied with his claim that he had no idea why Dupuis's wine stopped flowing and had absolutely nothing to do with it. Basically ignoring the accusations of witchcraft, Calvin and his associates denied Besson access to the Supper but only because he had blasphemed.[54] In May 1562, the Consistory called three women for spreading rumors that Jean Perollet and his wife, Pernette, were *sorciers*, alleging that Jean had even been beaten up on those suspicions. The Consistory issued stern admonitions to the three for levying false charges, and they promised to cease all such talk of witchcraft concerning the Perollets.[55] Later that month, a boy named Robert Picquet appeared before Calvin and his colleagues for having warned other children to stay away from Antoina Pelerin, the wife of a glassmaker, because she was a witch who was responsible for the death of a child. The Consistory confronted him with the woman who, he claimed, had told him about Pelerin's maleficent actions. When she denied telling the boy that Pelerin had caused anyone's death, Picquet then said that yet another woman had been his source of information. Since there were inconsistencies in his testimony, the members of the Consistory ordered that Picquet be given a caning for having lied to them.[56] In short, the Consistory appeared more concerned with witchcraft accusations as a form of slander than as real diabolical threat.

The Consistory and the Inquisition on the Handling of Magic

As noted, consistories have been of special interest to scholars who support the confessionalization paradigm. Proponents of this theory argue that starting in the later sixteenth century, the Lutheran, Catholic, and Reformed faiths

employed similar methods to inculcate appropriate Christian beliefs and practices. As the state reputedly assumed the central role in bringing about confessional uniformity within its borders, consistories in France, Switzerland,
and the Netherlands and the Inquisition in Spain and Italy all endeavored to
root out religious beliefs and practices deemed inappropriate, and scholars have
rightly pointed to similarities in this regard between the Reformed Consistory
and the Catholic Inquisition.[57] A comparison between the Roman Inquisition
and the Consistory of Geneva is quite germane. In 1542 Pope Paul III founded
the Roman Inquisition or Holy Office as a means of combatting Protestantism. A Congregation of cardinals served as the Holy Office's supreme court,
which closely oversaw a large number of regional inquisitions throughout Italy.
Although the Consistory's jurisdiction did not extend beyond the boundaries
of the Republic, Reformed Protestants elsewhere looked to Calvin's Consistory
as a model for their morals courts.

How did the cases of purported magic of Calvin's Consistory compare with
those of the Inquisition? On the one hand, both the Consistory and the Inquisition heard more cases of alleged therapeutic magic than of *maleficia* and
were unusually mild in dealing with accused witches. On the other hand, cases
of reputed love magic were quite common in Italy but almost totally absent in
Geneva. Actions against spells *ad amorem* were the Inquisition's most common
action against superstitions in parts of Italy in the late sixteenth and early seventeenth century.[58] In Calvin's Geneva, however, the Consistory records reveal
only two fleeting allusions to love magic, both of which were tied to opposition
to marriage engagements. In November 1552 a man alleged that his son's fiancée,
who he claimed was beneath their station, had "enchanted" his son by giving
him a concoction to drink. The Consistory exhorted the father to give his consent to the marriage and admonished him for being "superstitious."[59]

Another case vaguely related to love magic was that involving François and
Mie Sangmaistre, who were summoned in June 1559 because two different chambermaids working for them had committed fornication. The second servant was
a certain Françoise, who, desperate at having been jilted by her fiancé, Claude
Fichet, himself a former servant of the Sangmaistres, had tried to jump into a
well, provoking the Small Council to sentence her to a whipping. The Sangmaistres claimed that they were in no way responsible for their servants' misbehavior
and that Fichet had tried to seduce one of their previous chambermaids, which
led them to fire him. They claimed, though, that he was able to enter into their
home by magical means as he had spent time in Germany where he served "an
enchanter or a magician [*tragiteur*] from whom he learned how to pass freely"

in and out of houses. Paying no attention to these allegations, the Consistory simply enjoined the couple to watch over their servants more diligently than they had in the past.[60]

Also quite common in early modern Italy but very rare in Geneva were cases against superstitious attempts to discover lost objects or buried treasure.[61] An exceptional case of this nature involved Jean Goy of the village of Russin in August 1563. The local minister informed the Consistory that three years earlier Goy reputedly had found through divination a harrow that a peasant had lost, and the peasant paid Goy two florins for his services. Goy admitted finding that tool but said that the two florins were payment for a barrel he had sold.[62] The following week, however, witnesses from Russin affirmed that Goy had been paid for finding the harrow. Gabrielle Bocquet claimed to have heard Goy boast that he was a diviner and could find lost objects and that he had demon familiars to which he gave only coal to eat. The Consistory excluded Goy from the Supper, and though it did ask the Council to have the *châtelain* of either Peney or Saint-Victor investigate, Calvin and his colleagues did not seem overly concerned about this man, despite the reference to the coal-fed demons that assisted him.[63] This case, the likes of which were common in Italy, was almost unique in Calvin's Geneva.[64]

Why the dramatic difference between the types of magic found in Geneva and Italy? It is quite possible that spells to win another's love or to find lost treasure were not part of popular magic in Geneva and its environs even before the Reformation took hold. Another factor, however, almost surely played an important role. People whom the Roman Inquisition convoked for magic were quite often guilty of the abuse of the sacraments or, more often, of sacramentals, referring to ceremonies, benedictions, exorcisms, or objects that resembled or were related to the sacraments. In the celebration of the Eucharist, Roman Catholic doctrine holds that, once consecrated, the host is transformed into the body of Jesus and is therefore sacred. In early modern popular culture, the consecrated host was commonly believed to be endowed with supernatural powers, and experts on demonology affirmed that both consecrated and unconsecrated hosts could be used for magical purposes, especially in regard to love magic.[65] In early modern Catholic Europe, popular opinion also held that the physical sacramentals—items such as bread, water, oil, or salt, which had been blessed or exorcised by priests—wielded supernatural power. Various objects associated with the Eucharist, such as the altar cloth or the corporal on which the priest placed the consecrated host, were believed to possess healing power, as did objects that were placed illicitly beneath the altar during Mass.[66] If they fell into the wrong hands, these same objects could be misused, as holy candles, oil, or wine could purportedly be employed in love magic or other spells.

Protestantism, especially Calvinism, has often been portrayed as being quite hostile to rituals as it promoted the interiorization of religion. Scholars such as the historian Peter Burke and the anthropologist Mary Douglas have argued that Protestantism ultimately even contributed to Western culture's rejection of rituals. As Douglas argues, with the Protestant Reformation, ritual "became a bad word signifying empty conformity," which she linked to "the Reformation and its complaint against meaningless rituals, mechanical religion, Latin as the language of cult, mindless recitation of litanies."[67] A number of scholars have taken issue with this stand, however. Susan Karant-Nunn has argued that important changes in rituals took place in Lutheran Germany, but this did not equate to the interiorization of all piety. For example, although Luther believed that one is saved by faith alone and that the believer can do nothing to influence God in matters of salvation, Karant-Nunn affirms that Lutherans—especially through their belief that communicants ate Christ's flesh and drank His blood—nonetheless nurtured the notions that God was approachable and that humans could even "act in ways to obtain His benefit."[68] Robert Scribner, a pioneer in the history of popular religion, has described the Protestant Reformation in Germany as a ritual process, as evangelicals rebelled against Catholicism through rituals of parody, disruption, and iconoclasm.[69] In her exemplary study of the religious culture in Reformation Scotland, based on kirk session minutes, Margo Todd rejects as untenable previous historians' depiction "of reformers vigorously discarding all external forms, rituals, garb and symbols in favor of an interior focus on conversion and correct doctrine." She insists that "far from being discarded, external forms and ceremonies remained crucial to the protestant conquest of hearts and minds." Indeed, to a certain extent she attributes the success of the Scottish Reformation to the kirk's achieving "a balance between preservation and innovation in ritual and outward forms."[70] Likewise, in his brilliant examination of the celebration of the Supper, Christian Grosse shows that Calvin's Reformation did not eliminate rituals; rather it altered rituals and the liturgy, most notably in their relationship to the Word as it was preached.[71]

While these various scholars have rightly noted the important ritualistic elements that survived in the Reformed faith, it is nonetheless undeniable that Calvin's Reformation greatly reduced the number of acceptable rituals, and this definitely had an impact on people's understanding of access to God and the supernatural. Protestantism eliminated five of the seven sacraments and all but eliminated sacramentals. The sermon had replaced the Eucharist as the center of worship in Geneva, and communion was celebrated just four times a year. Reformed worshippers did not believe that Christ was present in the bread and wine. Calvin and his fellow pastors certainly did not believe that access to God and the supernatural could be facilitated through the misuse of communion bread or any other object, and the rank and file in Geneva apparently quickly assimilated this belief. Not one person was convoked during Calvin's ministry specifically for procuring communion bread or wine with the explicit hope of using it for magical purposes. There were rare cases, such as that involving Jean Gatens, which might have involved such a motive. At the celebration of the Supper at Pentecost in 1560, Gatens, rather than eating the bread immediately, reputedly held onto it and was going to receive the cup when Calvin actually snatched the bread from his hand. Gatens was admonished that he must be better instructed before the celebration of the Supper in September, and Calvin himself took it upon himself to tutor Gatens.[72] It is likely that the assistants suspected that Gatens was going to misuse the communion bread, but they made no mention of magic and obviously were not unduly concerned by his actions. Just after Christmas in the same year, members of the Consistory also expressed their dismay that right after the celebration of the Supper, people were practically pouncing on the platter to take the unused bread. The pastors and elders ruled that henceforth no one was to touch the bread so long as the platter was on the communion table. Once it was removed from the table, however, those in attendance were welcome to help themselves to the bread, presumably just for consumption.[73] In expressing fears of excesses, the Consistory showed that it was concerned about decorum in church, not about magic. Had they truly feared that someone might try to use the bread in a spell, Calvin and other members certainly would not have allowed anyone to take it, a practice that was itself worlds away from the Catholic custom of carefully preserving consecrated hosts in a tabernacle. Simply put, misusing the communion elements for magic was not a problem in Geneva.[74]

In a similar fashion, Genevans appeared to have quickly accepted Calvinists' rejection of exorcism, itself an important sacramental. Calvin and other Reformed leaders certainly continued to believe that demons could possess a person's body,[75] and they prescribed prayer and fasting, but not exorcism, as appropriate weapons against demon possession. The Consistory records reveal only one case of a person who likely sought the services of an exorcist. In late May 1554, a widow in the village of Laconnex admitted that she had taken her twenty-year-old daughter to Annecy in Savoy, where they attended Mass and sought a cure for the girl's demonic possession; demons supposedly possessed her heart, having entered her body through an apple she had eaten. Although the word "exorcism" does not appear in the registers, the fact that the mother admitted to "conjuring" the devil leaves no doubt that she was seeking relief through exorcism. The Consistory excluded her from the Supper and referred her to the Small Council with the recommendation that she not go to jail but be obliged to ask for mercy from God in church as an example to others for this offense.[76] The relatively mild reaction of the Consistory probably reflected the belief that Genevans were little inclined to resort to exorcists.

Historians have considered the possible impact that access to exorcism had on witch-hunting. In his monumental book on religion and magic in England, Keith Thomas saw an inverse relationship between the availability of various remedies, including exorcism, and the hunting of witches. In England, as in Geneva, the conversion to Protestantism greatly restricted the number of possible spiritual remedies for alleged evil spells and possession, which he claims opened up the possibility of more trials of witches.[77] By contrast, the records of the Holy Office suggest that exorcism could actually serve as the spark that could ignite a local witch-hunt in Italy, as some exorcists in effect acted as witch-hunters. The Holy Office, especially the Congregation of Cardinals in Rome, served as a brake on such aggressive actions[78] In her work on seventeenth-century France, Sarah Ferber found that Catholics were ambivalent toward exorcism, but her findings definitely lend themselves to the conclusion that exorcisms, particularly those performed in public, could contribute to witch-hunting fervor.[79] In the case of Geneva, the evidence from Calvin's Consistory does not suggest that eliminating exorcism resulted in a rash of accusations of witchcraft.

Witchcraft and Reconciliation

As we will see in chapter 7, the Consistory of Geneva went to great lengths to reconcile feuding parties. Calvin and his colleagues sought reconciliation even when the conflict was based on suspicions of witchcraft. Two widows from the village of Peney appeared in June 1552 for a quarrel that stemmed from one accusing the other of having cast a spell so that an apple tree no longer bore fruit. Paying no attention to this accusation, the Consistory simply gave their pastor the task of reconciling the two parties.[80] An even better example of this desire for reconciliation is found in a case from May 1548 when the Consistory subpoenaed Humbert Aubert, a law enforcement official (*officier*) in the village of Genthod. Aubert explained that the reason he had not been taking communion was that he harbored very strong feelings against his neighbor Claude Venarre, who he believed was a witch. Previously Aubert had rented a field from Venarre for the price of six florins. When Venarre leased the field to someone else, Aubert successfully filed suit to get his money refunded. According to Aubert, Venarre then menacingly predicted that he would regret that action. Shortly thereafter, when encountering Aubert's young son who was walking down a path with his little sister, Venarre supposedly grabbed the boy and stopped the children so he could pass them. The boy then told his sister, "Cursed be that man; he has really cooked me."[81] According to his father, the child took ill almost immediately and died within twenty-four hours. A mark on his body, similar to a black hand, was found on his body, supposedly where Venarre had touched the boy. When the *officier* wanted to press charges, Venarre initially fled the village but later returned. In the presence of Calvin and his associates, Aubert proclaimed that he wanted to provide evidence to prove that Venarre was guilty of witchcraft. Listening to all the reasons that Aubert found to suggest that Venarre was a servant of the devil—including the fact that the man was very ugly—the Consistory referred the matter to the Small Council and opined that if Venarre truly was a witch, he should not be allowed to stay in Genevan territory. At the same time, though, members of the Consistory rebuked Aubert who, far from loving his enemies, had such a "hard heart" (*le coeur sy gros*) that he could not forgive his neighbor. Urging him to forgive Venarre with all his heart, they told him that "he must recognize the good will of the Lord and His providence and not act like the dog that bites the stone which has been thrown at it, because all things happen to us by the will and providence of the Lord."[82] Taken to its logical conclusion, this strong providential attitude would seemingly eliminate all actions against witchcraft; if all unfortunate events were willed by God, how could one possibly convict anyone for manipulating supernatural powers for evil ends?[83]

Conclusion: Providence, the Supernatural, and Science

All told, the Consistory was remarkably mild in dealing with cases of magic. True, the period under study may have slightly predated the most intense witch-hunting in Europe in the late sixteenth and early seventeenth centuries. And Geneva did execute a number of people for witchcraft—a person was put to death in Geneva for witchcraft as late as 1652, and the city's last witchcraft trial took place in 1681. As William Monter has found, however, Geneva's execution rate was exceptionally low, and the most intense hunts were associated with the alleged spreading of the plague.[84] A major factor behind the Consistory's and Geneva's relative lenience vis-à-vis suspicions of magic and even witchcraft was surely the Calvinistic emphasis on God's omnipotence, aptly seen in its exhortation to Humbert Aubert that God wills all events.[85] Calvinists elsewhere declared that the greatest sin of witches was the belief that their spells were the actual cause of harm, insisting that an angry God was ultimately responsible for all misadventures. In a similar way, consulting a *guérisseur* was reprehensible because it implied that one could undercut God's power.[86] Also important, however, was the manner in which Calvin and his associates perceived the very function of the Consistory. As repeatedly noted, in dealing with a wide range of moral misdemeanors, the Consistory usually was less interested in punishing troublemakers than in bringing them back, contrite, into the Reformed community.[87]

The Consistory's handling of cases of magic and superstition can be juxtaposed with certain provocative theses that scholars have been put forward. Some of the writings of John Calvin himself seem to lend support to Weber's thesis about the disenchantment of the world. Concerning the notion of sacred space, for example, he asserted in the first edition of the *Institutes* that places of worship

> do not by any secret sanctity of their own make prayers more holy, or cause them to be heard by God. . . . [T]hose who suppose that God's ear has been brought closer to them in a temple, or consider their prayer more consecrated by the holiness of the place, are acting in this way according to the stupidity of the Jews and the Gentiles. In physically worshipping God, they go against what has been commanded, that, without any consideration of place, we worship God in spirit and in truth.[88]

In a commentary on Genesis, the reformer insisted that the faithful could worship anywhere they wished, since the "inward invocation of God neither requires an altar, nor has any special choice of place."[89]

Certain historians have gone even further than Weber's "disenchantment" thesis and have argued that Calvinism helped promote the growth of modern science. Quite important in this regard was the thesis of Robert K. Merton, who argued in 1938 that Puritanism nurtured scientific inquiry by expressing the need to uncover the orderliness of God's creation, thus providing a religious motivation for pursuing scientific research.[90] In his *Religion and the Decline of Magic*, Keith Thomas argued that the Reformation in England marked a decisive turning point that witnessed the separation of religion and magic, which eventually allowed for the triumph of science and technology.[91] A key critic of this view was Robert Scribner, who avowed that Protestantism did not play a pivotal role in the processes of desacralization and secularization and that it promoted a vision of the world that was still permeated by the supernatural.[92] The trend among most historians has been to lean more toward Scribner and to see continued belief in access to the supernatural among Protestants, as witnessed by their strong belief in diabolical power and by the tendency of some of them to treat Bibles and other objects as amulets and to view churches and cemeteries as sanctified space.[93] Some scholars have expressed doubts specifically about the purported connections between Calvinism and science, rightly pointing out that there was a wide range of opinions among Calvinists pertaining to science and that ideas that could promote a more scientific mentality were not unique to people of the Reformed tradition.[94]

Contrastingly, examining the works of a wide range of theological authors over a period of centuries, church historian Euan Cameron finds that Protestantism introduced a fundamental change in the understanding of the relationship between the performance of rituals on the one hand and the salvation of the individual soul on the other. With his strong emphasis on God's providence, Calvin believed that the will of God was behind every action of the devil, who in effect served as God's executioner. Calvin and other Protestants came to believe that the age of miracles was over, and if misfortunes, including demonic afflictions, were willed by God, it was inappropriate to try to resist them through supernatural or ritualistic means.[95]

Calvin and his supporters strongly rejected the idea that God was utterly transcendent. This is evident in the Consistory's reaction to an extraordinary incident when a bolt of lightning struck and destroyed a cross placed high on the tower of the church of Saint-Pierre. Echoing remarks made by the city council,[96] the Genevan chronicler Michel Roset provided a vivid description of this event:

> On the point of the church tower of Saint-Pierre, there remained a large cross, on top of a big copper ball, which God struck down by lightning on August 10, [1556,] around nine o'clock in the morning. The lightning made two round holes in the ball, about two fingers wide, and then entered the cross through its shaft . . ., which was all covered by tin and burned down to the clock. There were present a dozen journeymen who fought the fire with great courage and temerity. The embers were falling all blazing and aflame on their heads, and the height and challenging nature of the site could have caused them to fall in all ways if God, through His grace, had not miraculously saved them and the whole city . . . without any damage, other than the summit where the cross was, which caused several to say that God had taken this action to purge the church of such vestiges. Shortly

thereafter, they had a cross removed which was on the tower of [the church] of Saint-Germain, since it was a disgrace that such a cross, as a mark or sign of papal devilry [*diablerie papale*] had been left.[97]

As this passage indicates, a number of people in Geneva interpreted this lightning strike as a sign of divine disapproval of the cross that Reformed Protestants considered idolatrous and a vestige of popery. But when Jean Beljaquet heard the bookseller, Philibert Hamelin, expressing this opinion, he mocked the latter (in Greek!), saying that he "was just a fool and a heretic" and that Beljaquet "would show him through dialectic that, on the contrary, God does not get involved in such affairs." Calvin and the other members of the Consistory were not at all happy about the opinion expressed by this erudite gentleman. For them it was entirely unacceptable to deny that the lightning bolt which struck the "idolatrous" cross was an act of a judgmental God. They excluded him from the Supper and referred him to the Council, before which Belajaquet apologized and confessed to having spoken inappropriately.[98]

Regardless of the occasional incident of this nature, the evidence from the Consistory nonetheless lends credence to the contention that Calvinism contributed to a certain disenchantment of the world. Moreover, these records are precisely the type of documents favored by Scribner, who believed that Reformation historians had paid far too much attention to the musings of theologians and not enough to the mundane experiences of ordinary folk. The registers of the Consistory and its treatment of magic, superstition, and religious rituals show in effect a reduction in access to the supernatural. Calvin and other Reformed Protestants embraced a form of piety in which God was far more transcendent than Catholics had envisioned. Calvinists did not witness apparitions of the Virgin Mary, nor did God work miracles through Protestant saints. Christ was not physically present in the Supper, nor did Protestants genuflect and make the sign of the cross when they passed in front of the (now removed) altar.[99] Post-Tridentine Catholic leaders tried to eliminate some of the excesses associated with the veneration of saints, but they still insisted that one could pray to saints and especially to the Virgin Mary as a mediator to God. While Protestants believed that God was not swayed by pilgrimages, Catholics continued to go to fountains and sanctuaries dedicated to saints in hopes of miraculous cures.[100] As we have seen, when faced with cases of therapeutic magic, Calvin and his associates maintained that when people were sick, they should call a physician. Pastors did of course minister to the sick in Geneva, but they had nothing to offer them other than prayers and consolation. Moreover, although Calvin and his colleagues certainly believed in the reality of witchcraft and the possibility of selling one's soul to Satan, they showed remarkable skepticism when confronting accusations of *maleficia*. It does not seem like too much of a stretch to suggest that this change in mentality eventually could help stimulate the search for scientific, as opposed to supernatural, explanations for mundane phenomena such as illnesses.[101]

As a result, although definitely not intending to do so, Calvin and the other members of the Consistory were contributing to a certain desacralization of mentality with the manner in which they reacted to cases of alleged magic and witchcraft. They were unwittingly paving the way for the highly secular mentality of the eighteenth century that was evident in Genevan judicial actions against magic, which by then were extremely rare. In the 1700s Genevan authorities prosecuted people not for manipulating occult powers but for swindling gullible people through the sale of reputedly magical means of getting rich or finding stolen items. Interestingly, the victims in these cases were all foreigners from Catholic lands. In 1773, for example, magistrates tried Moise Morié, a recidivist who sold to a humble Savoyard a book with instructions on forcing rebellious spirits, such as Lucifer, to assist in finding treasures, winning the affection of women, and so on. In summing up his arguments, the prosecutor expressed his dismay that there were still some people who were so superstitious as to believe in magic. Even more, he was indignant that there were other people who nurtured such superstitions in order to take advantage of the naïveté of simple folk and deprive them of their goods, actions that differed little from theft.[102] The attitudes that Calvin and his colleagues revealed in handling allegations of magic in the mid-sixteenth century represented a decisive step toward this skeptical mentality.

CHAPTER 6

Promoting the Industrious and Sober Lifestyle

THE CONSISTORY WAS A quasi-tribunal, but many forms of misbehavior were not under its purview. Most actions that we today would recognize as crimes—theft, assault and battery, homicide—ordinarily would not have been subject to the Consistory's scrutiny and would have gone directly to the city council. In a similar way, most financial offenses and disputes would not have come before Calvin and the other assistants. The lieutenant oversaw much civil litigation and lesser offenses, and the Council generally had the final say on misdeeds of an economic nature.[1] That said, the Consistory did prosecute a number of "sins" that were related directly or indirectly to economic activity in Calvin's Geneva, attacking certain practices and promoting others.

Indolence (*acedia*) was one of the seven deadly sins that medieval Catholic theologians had long preached against. Although, unlike the Ten Commandments, the seven deadly sins are nowhere specifically listed in the Bible, there are scriptural passages that inveigh against these various iniquities, including sloth. Although they almost never made specific references to the Bible, Calvin and his colleagues could have cited various scriptural passages against indolence, such as "Work hard and do not be lazy. Serve the Lord with a heart full of devotion" (Romans 12:11). Calvinism has long been associated with a strong work ethic, and this connection was already quite evident in Reformation Geneva. The Consistory, in tandem with the Council, strongly encouraged industriousness and vigorously attacked laziness and the squandering of assets among all residents. Members of the Consistory could also have pointed to Scripture as a justification for taking actions against avarice, another of the seven deadly sins. In Hebrews 13:5 one reads, "Keep your lives free from the love of money, and be satisfied with what you have. For God has said, 'I will never leave you; I will never abandon you.'" And the Apostle Paul warned about the dangers of too much love for money: "But those who want to get rich fall into temptation and are caught in the trap of many foolish and harmful desires, which pull them down to ruin and destruction. For the love of money is a source of all kinds of evil. Some have been so eager to have it that they have wandered away from the faith and have broken their hearts with many sorrows" (1 Timothy 6:9–10). Late in his ministry, Calvin and his colleagues, still working in conjunction with the Council, started summoning people specifically for economic infractions such as usury and price gouging, which they associated with greed. These actions allow us to ponder the possible connections between Calvinism and economic development. In Reformation Europe, Calvinism tended to appeal to people of the middle class, especially merchants, and this raises the question, which has been debated at length, as to whether Calvinism contributed to the growth of capitalism.

John Calvin himself was, to a certain degree, of two minds about the accumulation of wealth. On the one hand, he noted, "By its nature wealth does not prevent us from following God, but human nature is so depraved, it is almost certain that those who are well-off will choke on their riches."[2] He asserted that God "has commended frugality and temperance to us and prohibited luxuriating wantonly in abundance." Calvin was adamant that "the rich, whether through inheritance or their own industry, should bear in mind that what is left over is meant not for intemperance or luxury but for relieving the needs of brethren."[3] On the other hand, he insisted, "Riches in themselves and by their nature are not at all to be condemned; and it is even a great blasphemy against God to disapprove of riches, implying that a man who possesses them is thereby wholly corrupted. For where do riches come from, if not from God?" He also accepted the uneven distribution of wealth, asserting that "the varying mixture of rich and poor" was determined by divine providence.[4] According to William Bouwsma, the reformer was "particularly opposed to 'plundering the rich' in order to 'deal humanely with the poor.'"[5] Calvin viewed private property as fundamentally important to society, spoke favorably of merchants, and approved of loans at interest, provided the rate did not "contravene equity and brotherly union."[6] The son of a notary, the reformer believed that being of middling status and wealth was preferable to being rich or poor. "How much more useful and desirable for us," he proclaimed, "is a moderate fortune, which is at least more peaceful and neither exposed to storms of envy nor liable to dark suspicions."[7]

If he was somewhat ambivalent in regard to riches, Calvin left no doubt about where he stood in regard to work. In a sermon, he proclaimed to his congregation, "We are born to work. God does not intend us to be lazy when we are living in this world, for he has given people hands and feet, he has given them industry.... [I]t is certain that we must apply ourselves to some [form of] labor."[8] In a commentary on the Gospel according to John, Calvin railed against idleness: "When we see what a short interval of life is allotted to us, we ought to be ashamed of languishing in idleness."[9] In another commentary, Calvin opined that there was "nothing more disgraceful than a lazy good-for-nothing who is of no use either to himself or to others but seems to have been born only to eat and drink."[10] In light of the reformer's exhortations to industry and thrift and his warnings against luxury, an examination of the Consistory's actions regarding financial activities can be most interesting and fruitful.

The Weber Thesis

A little over a century ago, Max Weber presented his famous thesis that Protestantism, especially Calvinism, nurtured the spirit of capitalism. Calvinists embraced double predestination, which meant that one could do nothing to attain salvation. But, according to Weber, they believed that being able to perform good works consistently was a good indication that one was saved; thus one did not perform good works to be saved, but good works could be interpreted as a sign that one was among the elect. Weber could have found support for his thesis in Theodore Beza's *Shorter Catechism* (1573), in which he wrote, "good works are for us the certain evidences of our faith" and provide "certainty of our eternal election."[11] Among the various good works that one could perform was applying oneself to one's calling. Calvinists stressed that everyone, not just monks or other clerics, had a calling and that all people were to apply themselves with religious dedication to their vocations. Weber argued that for Calvinists "tireless labor in a calling was . . . the best possible means of attaining . . . self-assurance" that one was among the elect.[12] In pursuing their callings, Calvinists accumulated wealth but eschewed luxury, choosing rather to reinvest their profits in their businesses. This ascetic lifestyle, Weber maintained, strongly nurtured the capitalistic spirit.[13]

This thesis engendered a great deal of debate among historians and even more among sociologists, but Weber, his supporters, and his critics concentrated very heavily on Reformed Protestants of the later sixteenth and especially the seventeenth centuries, most notably the Puritans of England, a group on whom Weber based much of his thesis.[14] As Erik Midelfort has aptly argued, "Weber thought that English Puritans came to emphasize God's implacable decree well beyond what Calvin had taught, with the result that believers, trapped in the 'grandiose consistency of the doctrine of predestinations,' fell into what Weber characterized as 'a feeling of unimaginable inner loneliness of the solitary individual. The question of eternal salvation constituted people's primary life concern during the Reformation epoch, yet they were directed to pursue their life's journey in solitude.'"[15]

Among the many scholars who weighed the possible connections between Calvinism and capitalism, the church historian Karl Holl argued that Calvinism was actually opposed to capitalism through the mid-seventeenth century, after which time Puritans in England and New England became more receptive to capitalistic endeavors.[16] By contrast, writing in 1912, the German Protestant theologian Ernst Troeltsch found that the economic ethic of Calvinism merged much more easily with capitalism than did Catholicism or Lutheranism. Calvin not only placed great value on work and denigrated luxury but also extolled trade and industry, an attitude which Troeltsch attributed directly to the situation in Geneva. A small city surrounded by hostile neighbors, Geneva, according to Troeltsch, was home to small-scale capitalistic ventures that could be tempered by thrift, loyalty, and charity, thus avoiding the excesses of large-scale capitalism which Calvin would have had trouble supporting. While Calvinist groups believed that labor and profit were not intended for purely personal gain, Troeltsch asserted that "in these Christian circles, and in them alone, was it possible to combine modern economic activity with Christian thought."[17] More recently, some studies of Scotland and Puritan New England support the view that Calvinism contributed significantly to capitalistic developments in those regions.[18] Other studies, however, offer only limited support to Weber. In his work on New England, James Henretta concludes that while Calvinism appealed to both merchants and religious intellectuals in the seventeenth century, this attraction was something of an aberration and that by the eighteenth century, Calvinism was in decline while capitalism was on the rise.[19] Looking at Calvinists in North America, Mark Valeri finds that the first generation of colonists were rather conservative and found much to criticize in the emerging market economy. He asserts, however, that Puritans embraced a moral pragmatism in regard to economics and by the late seventeenth century accepted the new economy, even using some of the same scriptural passages to defend the market economy that their forefathers had used to attack it.[20] Insisting upon the need to make direct comparisons between the economic experiences of Calvinists and Catholics, Philip Benedict offers a useful analysis of marriage contracts in seventeenth-century Montpellier and finds that in the early 1600s, Huguenots were wealthier than Catholics and that a higher percentage of Protestants were learned professionals or merchants. Examining the work profile across the seventeenth century, Benedict found that a much higher percentage of Huguenots were merchants and a much lower percentage were officeholders or professionals in the 1660s compared to the first decade of the seventeenth century. At first glance, these findings might lend support to Weber, but Benedict argues that Huguenots gravitated to commerce simply because they had lost political clout and faced growing hurdles to holding office or working in other professions. Moreover, the marriage contracts show that while Calvinists from the start tended to be more affluent than Catholics, members of both confessions benefited equally from the growth in prosperity in the seventeenth century, a finding that does not fit readily with the Weber Thesis.[21]

While the Puritans have been the focus of much research on possible links between Protestantism and capitalism, it is nonetheless important to go back to the roots of Calvinism in Geneva to examine such potential connections, and the Consistory records can be most useful in this inquiry. Did the Consistory take actions that might encourage industriousness and the accumulation of wealth and inhibit idleness and profligacy?

Calvinist Attacks on Idleness and Prodigality

Even before the creation of the Consistory, Calvin and Genevan leaders demonstrated that they abhorred idleness and prodigality and insisted on the need to follow an industrious, frugal lifestyle. In June 1537, a year after embracing the Reformed faith, the city council proclaimed that throughout the entire year, residents of Geneva were to work every day except Sundays. The announcements of this policy, made in every district of the city, warned that those not complying would be fined, with higher fines on men than women and on the rich than the poor.[22] Later, as has been mentioned, whenever December 25 fell on a Thursday, Calvin and other members made it a point to convene the Consistory as usual. In Calvin's Geneva, as in many other Protestant states, begging was forbidden by statute, and guards were regularly stationed as deterrents at church doors, where beggars were likely to go in search of alms.[23] With the strong support of Calvin, magistrates passed an edict in 1549 that ordered "that nobody give themselves over to fornication, drunkenness, vagabondage, or foolishly wasting time . . ., but that all work according to their capacity."[24]

As noted, the Consistory was known to convoke people who were lazy or wasted material goods. Like similar institutions elsewhere, the Consistory of Geneva summoned far more men than women for laziness and dissipation of goods. This disparity reflected the reality that women and men had vastly different professional opportunities. Men were expected to be the principal breadwinners, and they had far greater opportunities than women did to make a decent living. While females most definitely worked long hours and made indispensable contributions to the early modern economy, they generally did not go through formal apprenticeships. Moreover, in urban areas where Reformed Protestants so often lived, the work of women tended to be performed at home—in their own homes or in the homes of others, most often in domestic service—where indolence was less likely to come to the attention of authorities.

Typical was the action taken against Pierre Dolen, who was convoked in October 1542 for "wandering about and wasting time." The scribe noted cryptically that Dolen, "Answers that he works when he has employment, and very willingly when he has it. And that he goes to the sermons when he can, and that he has to watch the house when his wife goes to the sermon."[25] These terse remarks in many ways capture the essence of some of the Consistory's principal concerns: worship and work. Calvin and his colleagues believed that time was a gift from God that must not be wasted and that work was edifying, attitudes that epitomized for Weber the connection between asceticism and capitalist spirit.[26] They were also confident, perhaps naïvely so, that regular attendance at sermons was not only the principal means of instilling right doctrine in the minds and hearts of Genevans but also a crucial means of inculcating sober industry in the daily lives of common folk. The following January a weaver named Bocard appeared before the Consistory, accused of not working, wasting his family's assets, and not attending the sermons. Bocard was admonished to work assiduously, govern his household well, and attend church regularly.[27]

These cases show that the Consistory attacked laziness from its inception, but such actions became much more common in the late 1550s, after Calvin's position in Geneva was fully secured (though they were never as numerous as cases of illicit sexuality and blasphemy). In November 1558, for example, the Consistory rebuked Michel Bonivard of the village of Vandœuvres and ordered him to "work for a living without spending his goods in laziness and in filing suits, as *Messieurs* have ordered him and [as they] always advise all their citizens, Bourgeois, and [legal] residents."[28] The words that the Consistory carefully chose in rebuking Bonivard indicate that the civil and religious authorities regularly exhorted everyone in Geneva to be industrious and to eschew prodigality as well as indolence. In censuring Benardin Buffet in December 1559, Calvin and the other assistants declared that it was "most scandalous" that he was not providing for his children and spent a lot of time running around with a male friend.[29] In January 1559, the Consistory rebuked Pierre Masson, who had served as a mercenary without permission, for lounging about playing *marc* and other games. Labeling him a "vagabond" who went off to war, Calvin and his colleagues referred Masson to the Small Council, which sent him to jail.[30] Louis Janin of the village of Cologny appeared for wandering about aimlessly and "wasting his time" in the city, playing sword games and squandering money and wine on bets on *marc* and other games. As admonitions alone did not succeed in changing his behavior, the Consistory sent him in June 1559 to the Small Council, which limited itself to admonishments.[31] In May 1560, Dominique, the son of Pierre Ferrier, appeared as a recidivist before the Consistory, having already been censured for making bets and leading a dissolute life. This time he admitted that his father had trusted him with six hundred écus when he sent him on a business trip to Genoa, but the younger Ferrier had spent all that money in brothels and such. The Consistory sent him to the Council as incorrigible.[32]

Games and Profane Songs

These cases clearly show that Genevan leaders were concerned about unwholesome pastimes, most obviously gambling and games of chance, which they deplored because of the waste of time and assets they involved.[33] In September 1542, the Consistory convened the carter Jean Collomb and the blacksmith Henri Giron for gambling, even on Sundays, in the stable where they worked. Proclaiming that gambling is a form of blasphemy, Calvin and his fellow members obliged the two men to promise that they would no longer gamble nor allow gambling among their "poor young journeymen," who had families to support.[34] In December of the same year, it came to the Consistory's attention that Jean Goula, himself a former syndic and prosecutor, had been secretly gambling with others. Civil authorities showed the importance they gave to this crime by coming down hard on Goula, condemning him in January 1543 to spend six months in jail with a chain attached to his leg and to be indefinitely denied all honors, such as holding any office.[35] The next month the Council sentenced four other men who had been gambling with Goula to one month in jail.[36] These unusually severe jail sentences clearly demonstrate that the judicial authorities believed that gambling could be a major source of social disorder. The harsh sentence against Goula can probably be attributed to the authorities' higher expectations of a former syndic, local political rivalries, or a combination of both.

Zealous in fulfilling his duties, Lt. Pernet Des Fosse in April 1551 asked the Council what actions should be taken about the youths of the city who were leading dissolute lives, "gallivanting in the taverns, [playing] games, [singing] dishonest songs." The Council proposed sending the four syndics to every neighborhood in order to look for such delinquents, though it does not appear that the magistrates followed up on this recommendation.[37] The Consistory, by contrast, aggressively attacked such cases of immoral behavior in that year, as it summoned many people for playing games of chance or singing profane songs. In August 1551, for example, Calvin and the other assistants reprimanded Jean Favre, the host of the Griffon tavern, for his scandalous life, which included games and other forms of "dissolution." Favre apologized and confessed that on several occasions, people had indeed played games at his establishment but that it was only for drink.[38] In saying this, Favre was apparently claiming that in his bistro, people were making bets with wine rather than with money, though the pastors and elders would have found this, too, totally unacceptable. When the pastry cook Georges Lionnet was subpoenaed in February 1551 primarily on suspicion of fornication, the Consistory also questioned him as to whether people played cards or sang "dishonest songs" at his place. Lionnet, who, like Favre apparently ran a tavern, denied the singing but admitted that sometimes haberdashers (*merciers*) did play cards for drinks.[39] Even worse for Calvin and his colleagues were the actions of Otto Chautemps and his wife, Jeanne Rachey, who were accused of allowing inappropriate songs and blasphemies at their inn.[40] In Geneva, those who oversaw public establishments were required to make sure that their customers respected Reformed mores, which included a ban on games and mundane songs.

Many Genevans plainly liked playing games and did not want to give them up, as Calvin and his colleagues continued to show a special concern for games of chance three years later, when the Consistory convoked the barber Pierre Biolley and the pastry cook Michel Chevalier for their debauchery, especially their penchant for games. Both were specifically accused of having lost money by making bets on dart games. Confessing their faults, the two were referred to *Messieurs* of the Small Council, to whom the Consistory expressed its concerns about the growing problem of games throughout the city. More than once that year Calvin went to the Council to protest the problem of games, and the Council responded by forbidding playing games for money, especially during the sermons or catechism lessons, under pain of a fine of sixty sous and three days in jail.[41] Regardless of these efforts, in Reformation Geneva there would always be some people who continued to take part in such games.

Although it was particularly concerned with gambling, the Consistory viewed playing cards and other games of chance with opprobrium even when no bets were involved. In March 1562 the Consistory complained to the Council that the lieutenant was not punishing card-players unless they were playing for money.[42] In the next four weeks following that complaint, fifty-six men—including the *châtelain* of Jussy—appeared before the Consistory to receive admonitions for

taking part in card-playing, having already been punished by the lieutenant.[43]
Quite amusing was the appearance in February 1560 of fifteen people from a
village outside Geneva—fourteen men and the hostess of the inn where they
played—who were admonished for playing cards while waiting for a pastor to
come preach to them.[44]

It is important to note that while leaders in Geneva were strongly opposed
to games of chance, especially since they were so often tied to gambling, they
certainly did not forbid all forms of play. François Albois owned and operated
a tennis court (*jeu de peaume*). The Consistory had no problem with Genevans
playing tennis at Albois's court, but in 1559 it objected that he kept it open right
up until the last ringing of the bells for sermons, both on workdays and on Sundays.[45] Calvin and his colleagues did not even object to Genevans playing tennis
on Sunday, provided that their games did not in any way interfere with attending
church services. In this regard, Calvin was far less strict than some contemporary
and future Reformed Protestants in interpreting the commandment to remember the Sabbath and keep it holy.[46]

Drunkenness

In promoting the pious, industrious life, Calvinists took aggressive actions
against drunkenness, which they, like Catholics, considered a sin. The Consistory accordingly made serious efforts to combat excessive drinking, as seen
in its censuring Pierre Bernardet for his habit of drinking to the point of not
knowing what he was doing; most notable was a very violent incident when he
tried to kill his wife and child. Bernardet confessed that he was given to drink
and begged God for mercy for his sins, but the Consistory's assistants were most
dismayed that he seemed tipsy even while appearing before them.[47] Bernardet in
fact proved to be an incorrigible drunk, as he appeared several more times before
the Consistory for his excessive drinking. In November 1559, Calvin and his
colleagues, exasperated with his latest excesses, which included exposing himself
to some girls while inebriated, referred Bernardet to the Council, which ordered
him banished to "purge the city of such villainy."[48]

Less dangerous but quite disruptive were the actions of Claude Furjod, Geneva's gravedigger. In September 1559 the Consistory reported that Furjod did
not show up to accompany a body to the cemetery even though he had chosen
the time to meet with the family and others who wished to accompany the body
to the graveyard. Several officials looked all over for him, and after an hour one
found him, totally drunk and gnawing on a piece of cheese. He confessed and

promised to mend his ways, but the Consistory excluded him from the Supper, while the Council threatened to fire him and send him to jail for a day.[49]

As with all offenses, drunkenness was of greatest concern when it caused a public scandal. In July 1563 the Consistory became quite upset by the drunken actions of a male servant identified only as Claude. On the previous Sunday, Claude confessed that while relieving himself from a bridge, he urinated (perhaps unintentionally) upon a man who was drawing water from the river below. On the Sunday before that, Claude, while apparently inebriated, vomited in church from the balcony onto the people below. The Consistory excluded the servant from the Supper and sent him to the Council, which sentenced him to three days in jail, after which he was to cry for mercy in the church of Saint-Gervais, where he had gotten sick.[50] Getting drunk usually did not merit being required to do reparation, but vomiting in church was a desecration of the service and a scandal for all present. In November 1562, the Consistory expressed its alarm at the pervasive problem of excessive consumption of alcohol. The Consistory asked the Small Council to renew its efforts to combat drunkenness and even suggested that the problem was so great that a separate Consistory should be established to deal exclusively with alcohol abuse.[51] No serious attempt was ever made to create such an institution, but the assistants' concern was no doubt based on a real problem. It is very important to stress that Genevan authorities were concerned with the *excessive* consumption of alcohol. Unlike the temperance movements in nineteenth-century England or North America, they never advocated complete abstinence from alcohol, a fact that is obvious in the Consistory's summoning Aimé Plonjon for selling foul-tasting wine for use in the Supper.[52]

Dissipation of Goods

On numerous occasions, the Consistory asked the Small Council to take aggressive action to ensure that people, usually men, not squander their assets. François Rosset, originally from Lucerne but living in the village of Choulex, filed a complaint against his son-in-law, Rolet Mege of the village of Pressy. According to Rosset, Mege beat his wife (Rosset's daughter), did not attend church regularly, and had not fulfilled his promise to come live in Geneva, preferring rather to wander about and dissipate his goods. Mege admitted to being truant from church and to beating his wife, though, he protested, not until she bled. He also confessed in part to the other accusations, and Calvin and his colleagues excluded him from the Supper and sent him to the Council, which should order him to stop selling his assets and to appoint a guardian to ensure that he not do so. They also told him to stop beating his wife and to come live in the city "where he could effectively take care of his possessions."[53] Four months later, in March 1560, Rolet Mege was before the Consistory again for having sold a piece of land for one hundred écus, another example of dissipating his estate, and for still refusing to come to Geneva where his father-in-law had arranged for him to learn a trade to earn a living. Excluding him from the Supper again, the Consistory referred him to the Council, which rebuked him and jailed him for three days.[54] Two months later, the Consistory again ordered Mege to get to work,[55] but he apparently really was intractable, as he continued to have run-ins with the Consistory in the years to come for being irresponsible, profligate, and violent toward his wife.[56] Mege obviously never became an industrious member of Genevan society, but the Consistory's persistent efforts to get him to shape up were quite impressive.

In considering the case of Pierre Rosset in May 1562, the Consistory provided some very specific details that showed that he was dissipating his goods by entering into some "crazy" deals (*folles paches*). Rosset, a blacksmith, had recently purchased on credit a large quantity of wheat at five florins, six sous per *coupe* (2.25 bushels or 79.35 liters),[57] which he immediately resold for cash at four florins, four sous per *coupe*. The entry adds that Rosset had recently "devoured" three or four hundred florins of his own assets. Accordingly, the Consistory asked the Small Council to appoint a guardian without whose consent Rosset would not be allowed to form any contract.[58] In April 1561, Gaspard Vuillet, an elder and lay assistant of the Consistory, declared that Gabriel Levet was a terrible domestic manager who regularly did not have anything to eat unless he sold off some pieces of furniture or other assets. When he did so, he was wont to go to Pont d'Arve, a village just outside Genevan jurisdiction, where he squandered all his money on food and drink (making "*grand chere*"). According to Vuillet, when his children protested that they were dying of hunger, Levet told them, "That's exactly what I want, that you die." Appalled by this behavior, the Consistory recommended that the Small Council seize his assets and appoint a guardian to administer them.[59]

Calvin and his colleagues became increasingly convinced that Geneva was plagued by an ever-growing number of lazy, irresponsible men. On March 21, 1560, the Consistory bemoaned the fact that "in this city, there are many lazy people and vagabonds who do nothing other than carry their swords about in the streets."[60] Among those mentioned was Pierre Du Boulle, whose name appears in the registers several times for laziness. In January 1562, the Consistory accused Du Boulle of not wanting to do anything other than "hitting the streets" in the city. Since he was in good health, the assistants told him that he was to work "as God commands" and as mandated by Genevan edicts.[61]

Evidence from the registers indicates that at least some residents of Geneva embraced the notion that laziness was a serious sin. When the Consistory summoned Dominique Monathon in October 1559, testimony revealed that three French booksellers living in Geneva had rebuked him for being lazy. Referring to the sermons they had heard, they told him that the apostle Paul had declared that anyone who does not work should not eat (2 Thessalonians 3:10). Monathon threatened one of those men and proclaimed that Calvin and the other preachers could not know what Paul's intentions were. The Consistory denied him access to communion and sent him to the Council. It is revealing that lay residents of Geneva felt free or even compelled to criticize others for not working.[62]

Although almost all actions against laziness or squandering were aimed at men, the Consistory occasionally summoned women for idleness or profligacy. It admonished and excluded from the Supper Claude Rebitella, a young woman who rebelled against her mother by refusing to help in the house and to go out and work as a domestic servant.[63] In May 1560, Henri Morel complained about his wife's drunkenness and profligacy. Pastor Pierre Viret affirmed that Morel's wife had been a poor chambermaid when he married her, and she immediately began depleting his resources. The Consistory admonished her and excluded her from the Supper but also told Morel that he must "make her live soberly and oversee her vocation." Interestingly, it also instructed him that whenever he was obliged to travel out of town, he must not leave any money with her but rather should give it to one of his neighbors to purchase necessities.[64] In September 1561, the cobbler Vidal Gibellin accused his wife, Louise, of doing nothing in the household and of selling all sorts of personal possessions—furniture, bed covers, a long coat, copies of the Psalms and New Testament—all so she could indulge in gluttony. The Consistory issued harsh remonstrances to her and excluded her from communion.[65] In December 1559 Marguerite Bordière and Barbe Grégoire were sent to the Consistory by the directors of the hospital, which oversaw poor relief, because these two women did not go to church and complained that the alms they received were insufficient. After hearing from them and from Pastors Chauvet and François de Collonges, the Consistory recommended that they be allowed to stay in Geneva provided that they not be a charge to the hospital or the Bourse française, the charitable fund especially for natives of France; rather, they must work for a living and make sure that their children work, too.[66] This was one of strongest statements in the registers of the Consistory that the poor were expected to work.

Likewise, in April 1560 the members of the Consistory were not at all pleased when the widow Huguette Charrey was quoted as saying that the governors of poor relief were "very quick to take [money] but very slow to give [alms]" and that the alms she received amounted to "shit."[67] Charrey asked for mercy and admitted to speaking crudely and derisively about the quantity of the alms she received but claimed that it was her daughter who uttered the first sentence critical of the Bourse. The Consistory decided to notify the governors of the Bourse that they should "not give [Charrey] anything for a long time and let her fast for a while" since she had "vilified" the alms that were given to her.[68] When Charrey's daughter admitted that she had complained about the Bourse, the Consistory referred her to the Council to be sent to the hospital to be whipped in the presence of her mother.[69] For Calvin and his colleagues, poor relief was a privilege, not a right. Moreover, by instructing the governors of poor relief for the first time not to give alms to certain people, the Consistory was assuming greater authority than ever before.

The Consistory again took it upon itself to deny alms to a person deemed unworthy in October of the same year. After having spent some time in jail for beating his wife, the traveling merchant Bernard Jomard abandoned her and their children without providing them any sustenance while he roamed about aimlessly. The Consistory exhorted him to get his life back on track and to recognize all his faults but also told the governor of the Bourse des pauvres not to provide Jomard with any financial assistance so that he would be forced to find work.[70] The Consistory's displeasure with Jomard is entirely understandable, but one might fear the unintended effects on his children and wife, the innocent victims of his misbehavior. The fact that Jomard did not appear again before the Consistory might mean that its "tough love" had the desired effect.

Members of the Consistory and the Small Council were on the same page when it came to poor relief. In July 1559, lay authorities concluded that two couples from the Dauphiné came to Geneva for the sole purpose of asking for alms in the city and even took the liberty of going to private homes begging for help. The four were banished from the city under pain of the whip if they ever returned.[71] In 1562 Geneva's magistrates concluded that out of laziness, Louis Imbert, originally from Nice, had for years used lies and deception to obtain support in Geneva and elsewhere that should have gone to those who truly needed this charity. Authorities ordered that Imbert be whipped through the streets of Geneva and then banished from the Republic under pain of death.[72] For both the Consistory and the Council, poor relief was to be given only to those who were truly deserving and did not have the means of working to make a living.

Geneva was a prime example of how the Reformation, both Catholic but especially Protestant, was a catalyst for significant changes in poor relief, which became more centralized and (to a degree) secularized, characterized by bans on begging, strong partiality for the "deserving" poor, and efforts to promote work and training.[73]

It is worth pausing to note that the Consistory convoked more men for certain sins—clearly seen for those examined in this chapter—and more women for others. As has been noted, these variations often do not appear to be simply a product of the gendered prejudices of this all-male institution. In Geneva men comprised the large majority of people who were accused of drunkenness, blasphemy, and violence.[74] Men probably were more prone than women to overindulge in alcohol, gamble, blaspheme, and commit violent acts, and they were certainly more apt to commit such indiscretions in public. Almost all those accused of wasting time and money in taverns and of gambling were men.[75] Taverns were essentially a male domain, whereas women who imbibed too much were likely to do so at home and might thereby escape the notice of the Consistory. Most broadly, consistories everywhere tended to exclude from the Supper far more men than women, no surprise since men dominated public life and consistories generally resorted to excommunication when misbehavior resulted in public scandal.[76] The evidence from consistories shows that in Reformed as in Catholic areas, conflicts between men often ended in physical violence, whereas quarrels between women were much more likely limited to verbal disputes or, at worst, less violent forms of physical altercations.[77]

Promoting the Sober, Industrious Life among Youth

In dealing with cases of laziness, prodigality, drunkenness, and the like, the Consistory was most concerned not with women or mature males but rather with young men. Calvin and his colleagues believed that it was essential to direct youths down the straight and narrow path and that it was much easier to effect change in the behavior of the young than the old. Religious and secular authorities especially wanted to steer young people away from bad habits before they became ingrained, to the detriment of themselves and of Genevan society. In December 1559, the Consistory considered the case of Jean de Gex. The young de Gex, a citizen of Geneva, was quite poor, and had been given room and board at the hospital, received some schooling, and was set up as an apprentice to the sheath-maker (*gainier*) Antoine Du Mont. De Gex, however, had abandoned his apprenticeship before he had fulfilled his obligations to his master and left to live in Catholic Annecy (though he claimed he never went to Mass). Upset that he had shown no appreciation for all the help he had received, the Consistory excluded him from the Supper until he reformed and ordered him to be sent to the hospital to receive a caning.[78]

In October 1560, the Consistory expressed its alarm and sent to the Small Council a list of forty-four young men who led lives of debauchery and hedonism. They were described as loafers (*fainéants*) who did not want to do anything other than wander about aimlessly and consume the small amount of goods left to them by their parents.[79] Among the forty-four was Amied Lambert, the son of a former city council member, who had appeared earlier in 1560 for having left Geneva to be a mercenary; in that occupation Lambert was guilty of attending Mass and of "going to wars here and there," where he was exposed to scandalous behavior and much blasphemy. Excluding him from the Supper, the Consistory sent him to the Council to be obliged to stay in Geneva and to learn a trade.[80] Though Calvinists have never been known as pacifists, they looked down upon mercenaries and viewed fighting just for money as a most unwholesome occupation. In December 1558, Jean Pascard of the village of Céligny appeared because he had gone to fight as a mercenary for the king of France in Picardy, and the Consistory presumed that, like other soldiers, he spent his time fornicating, getting drunk, and stealing. Since his return, he had been doing nothing but going to taverns and spending the money he brought back from the war. Excluding him from the Supper, the Consistory sent him to the Council, which, predictably, rebuked him and sentenced him to three days in jail.[81]

In the case of Amied Lambert, the Consistory may have especially wanted to dissuade him from performing mercenary work because he came from a good Genevan family. About a month after he was listed as one of the Geneva's notorious young loafers, Lambert asked for permission to leave the city to go to Genoa to learn a trade and serve as an apprentice in making taffetas, claiming that he was mired in poverty because of creditors' claims on his late father's estate. Asked for its opinion by the Council, the Consistory told Lambert that he was already "depraved enough without going to Genoa, where impiety abounds." To avoid becoming worse off morally, he should stay at home and learn a trade. Protesting that he had nothing to do in Geneva, Lambert was sent again to the Council with the recommendation that he be constrained to remain and learn a trade. If he persisted in his desire to leave, he should be persuaded to go somewhere other than Genoa, to a city where he could serve God (i.e., to a city that was not Catholic).[82]

In 1561 the Consistory subpoenaed Jacques Pertemps for doing nothing but hunting and leading a life of leisure. He had expressed the desire to go to Lyon, but the Consistory averred that this was only because he could not always find friends in Geneva to join him in pursuing a life of debauchery. Accepting the admonitions, Pertemps promised to obey his mother and his guardian and to get a job to make a living.[83] The Consistory called Jean Quey on suspected fornication with a maidservant and for being lazy and profligate. Forbidding him to associate with the woman, Calvin and the other assistants sent him to the Small Council with the recommendation that he not be allowed to touch any of his assets without the consent of his guardian, Claude de La Maisonneuve, who was to serve as a father to Quey. De La Maisonneuve was to take possession of all the money Quey had and all the IOUs he had incurred; living far beyond his means, Quey had borrowed heavily. Quey was to learn a trade and put an end to his drifting, and was forbidden to enter into any contracts without the knowledge and consent of his guardian.[84] In short, with the full support of secular authorities, the Consistory took aggressive actions, starting especially in the late 1550s, to get young men to learn a profession and to work.

Genevan religious and political leaders also wanted to make sure that young women were actively engaged in work. By far the most common form of work for women outside their own homes was domestic service. In December 1561 lay authorities undertook an investigation of Françoise Lossier, apparently an orphan as she had been raised by the hospital. Magistrates were dismayed that though the hospital had placed Lossier with several masters, every one of them fired her after a couple of days and sent her back because she did not want to work. Authorities asked her why this was so since she was grown up and no longer a small child. The unhappy Lossier had even expressed the desire to do away with herself, but far from showing any sympathy, the magistrates mandated that she be given a whipping and then sent to perform hard labor on the city's fortifications. They also ordered the hospital not to give her anything to eat unless she performed the work expected of her.[85] Similarly, in March 1564 the Consistory summoned three young women, Loise Conte, Pernette Jaillod, and Jeanne Dupra, for being lazy, irresponsible, and rebellious. All of them were staying at the hospital and were disobedient and disrespectful to the master of the hospital. They had been placed as servants with different masters but had all been fired for poor performance, and Dupra had actually been jailed briefly for theft. The Consistory excluded all three from the Supper and warned that if their behavior did not improve, *Messieurs* of the Council would be notified.[86]

The Consistory also aggressively pursued adults who encouraged or at least facilitated the debauchery of Genevan youth and children. The widow Madeleine Petet, dite Carmentrande, appeared before the Consistory several times in the spring of 1553 because she had set up a tavern where young people—the minutes actually referred to them as "young children"—gathered to drink excessively, waste their parents' money, and sing scandalous songs. This behavior even took place during the sermons and late at night. The Council severely admonished her and warned that she would lose her license to keep a tavern and would be banished from the city if she did not stop corrupting the youth.[87] In 1560, the Consistory admonished the tavern-keeper Georges Courtillet for contributing to the "debauchery" of some young men, most notably a young boarder who had abandoned his apprenticeship to become a tailor and was leading a very shiftless life.[88] Calvin and his colleagues believed that youths should complete their apprenticeships, which they viewed as an important means of instilling a good work ethic in these young artisans and setting them on the path to being productive adults.

When admonitions and exclusion from the Supper did not suffice, by the early 1560s the Consistory consistently recommended aggressive actions against youths who were profligate or lazy. A good example involved Jean Bergier, the son of the late Pierre Bergier, himself a martyr for the Reformed faith in France. Calvin and his colleagues depicted Jean as a lazy young man who lacked focus in his life and was quickly depleting his modest assets as he drifted back and forth between Geneva and other cities. Three uncles reported that they had set him up in apprenticeships in Strasbourg and elsewhere to learn to be a potter or a saddler, but he kept leaving and returning to Geneva without completing his training. Bergier admitted as much, and the Consistory excluded him from communion and advised the Small Council to oblige him to learn a trade and to require his relatives to make sure that he stayed with that occupation. If he persisted in doing nothing, the Consistory advised the council "to whip him to put him on the right road if that is possible, because he is no longer a child. But if he still does not want to do anything, let him return to school like a silly person to be whipped with switches by six schoolboys . . . in order to try to set him [straight] and to make him follow in the footsteps of his father who died as a holy martyr."[89] This was the only occasion during Calvin's ministry that the Consistory proposed having fellow schoolboys administer a whipping to a youth.

In pursuit of their fervent desire to put idle young men to work, the Consistory believed that a period of hard labor might be the tough love needed to turn loafers into industrious workers. In June 1560 Bernard de Chenelat appeared before the Consistory along with his wife, Claude, and their son for their scandalous domestic life. Among other issues, the Consistory was concerned because the son had abandoned the apprenticeship his father had arranged for him. The assistants decided that the son and Claude's son by a previous marriage were so disobedient that they asked the Council to sentence them both to a period of hard labor.[90] In 1562 Mermet Pascard got in trouble for having thrown up in church while inebriated and for being a loafer. When reproached for being a "vagabond," Pascard responded, "Give me work!" Not pleased with this intemperate answer, the Consistory sent him to the Council, which agreed to make him and others work on the ramparts and to have him taken to the hospital to get a whipping.[91] Convoked in July 1563 for being lazy, Jean Roy admitted that he had sold off goods to pay debts but said that he was working as a night watchman. Not satisfied with this answer, Calvin and his associates referred him to the Council, advising that Roy be obliged to work "in the ditches like a galley slave" and then be shown "charity" by making him learn a profession.[92]

Attitudes toward Luxury

As we have seen, while Calvin and other Reformed leaders did not believe there was anything inherently evil in riches and luxuries, they feared that excessive desire for material wealth could be detrimental to spiritual health. Too much attention to riches could hinder spiritual growth and keep people from showing charity. As noted above, Weber maintained that in addition to promoting industrious behavior, Calvinists were apt to reinvest the capital they accumulated through their labors rather than spend it on themselves. Although at no time during Calvin's tenure did the Consistory specifically exhort Genevans to invest their assets, we have seen that the Consistory had long convoked people who dissipated their fortunes.

Late in Calvin's ministry, the Consistory started taking aim more often at people who wasted their money on luxuries. It would be erroneous to assume that Calvin and the Consistory introduced the campaign against luxuries in Geneva. The first sumptuary law in Geneva dated all the way back to 1430, and though he consistently warned of the dangers that riches posed to the soul—especially through the sins of vanity and pride—Calvin himself recognized that what constituted luxury was relative and initially expressed a certain skepticism about laws spelling out exactly what things were and were not acceptable. Nonetheless, he came out in support of rules prohibiting excesses in certain areas, most obviously in the areas of clothing, hairdressing, and the conspicuous consumption of food, and authorities passed several sumptuary laws in Geneva in the sixteenth century, the first in 1558. Although the surveilling of luxuries was supposed to be under the purview of the lieutenant, one can find a number of actions taken by the Consistory against various luxuries during Calvin's time.[93]

Calvin and other ministers showed a special interest in suppressing knee breeches (*chausses découpées*), which were rather popular among some Genevan men, especially young men who were active in military companies. Breeches had in fact been a source of contention for many years. In April 1543, the Council passed an edict which prohibited making or wearing breeches and imposed a fine of sixty sous on anyone in violation of this injunction.[94] This prohibition notwithstanding, in 1547 authorities took note that the *capitaine général* Perrin, among others, regularly sported such breeches,[95] and in May of that year Geneva's arquebusiers asked for and received permission from *Messieurs* to wear the breeches during the martial arts celebration of *papeguai*.[96] The next day Calvin, accompanied by his fellow ministers, went to the Council of Two Hundred and delivered a harangue about this concession. Expressing his concern about the increasingly "great disorder" in the city, especially among young people, the reformer offered a retort to those who protested that the Bible says nothing about knee breeches: both Scripture and the law mandate that "all accoutrements" that are made except out of necessity are a source of "pride" and therefore "are against God and [are] of the devil" and therefore must not be tolerated. In response, Perrin and another official again asked that arquebusiers be allowed to wear the ceremonial breeches on the one day a year the *papeguai* was celebrated. The Council of Two Hundred, however, sided with Calvin and declared that the ordinances must be respected. Though the Council added that although it would forgive those who had previously violated the edict, henceforth wearing breeches would result in a fine of ten florins.[97]

While there were laws on the books against such luxuries, it was only relatively late in Calvin's ministry that the Consistory started taking actions against people for indulging in them. In 1563 it called the itinerant merchant Estienne Havet for domestic discord and for pursuing a life of leisure and luxury, which exacerbated tensions with his wife. The Consistory accused him of wasting time playing tennis and recklessly spending money on himself. Binot admitted having bought some breeches made at a cost of eight écus, a considerable sum. He explained that he had needed this fine attire in order to lease a farm in France. Calvin and his associates admonished Havet to avoid the scandal of luxury and other vices.[98] Although they seemed most concerned with men's expensive attire, in November 1562 Genevan magistrates sentenced a woman, Nicolarde Croy

Sellet, to pay a fine of twenty sous and to ask forgiveness of God and justice for wearing a headdress woven of gold and silk that violated the sumptuary laws.[99]

In May 1564, the Consistory expressed its grave concern that so many Genevans, even those of modest means, were given to luxurious clothing, most notably the expensive breeches. It accordingly delegated Theodore Beza and the elder Marquis Caracciolo to communicate to the Small Council the urgent need to suppress these excesses.[100] The following month the Council did reissue the sumptuary ordinances that prohibited various forms of luxurious clothing, including the controversial trousers.[101]

As mentioned above, the sumptuary laws also targeted the excessive consumption of food, especially when associated with weddings or other banquets. In April 1559, the year after the sumptuary law went into effect, several important Genevan authorities themselves got into trouble because of a banquet deemed excessive. Most prominent among those implicated was none other than the lieutenant, "Noble" Jean Pernet, who ordinarily had jurisdiction over those who violated the sumptuary laws. Pernet, five police investigators (*auditeurs*)—Jeanton Genod, André Embler, Guillaume Macard, François Chasteauneuf, Pierre Guerid—and the Council's bailiff, Lupi Tissot, were all guilty of having a banquet at the expense of the state with more courses than were allowed by the edicts. Judicial authorities declared that it would be a disgrace to allow this to go unpunished, to turn a blind eye to the laws being broken by those responsible for enforcing them. They accordingly strongly admonished the seven men and condemned them all to a fine. Four days later, authorities rejected the request of the lieutenant and the others for a reduction in the fine. The seven were obliged to pay thirty florins, which went to the funds of the hospital.[102] Dealing with someone of very modest means, the Consistory convoked in April 1564 Jeanne, the widow of Guillaume Hayot, because she spent excessively on her daughter's wedding even though she was receiving alms from the Bourse des pauvres.[103]

The baker Pierre Choupin was subject to a criminal prosecution in July 1563 for baking white bread, which was forbidden in Geneva as a form of luxury. Choupin was a recidivist and was also guilty of failing to put his identifying mark on the bread and for selling the bread at too high a price. Declaring him incorrigible, judicial authorities deprived him of the use of his oven, which they ordered demolished, and denied Choupin the right to sit on the Council of Two Hundred.[104] Similarly, on December 31, 1562, the Consistory called Michel Binot for having sent away his female servant while keeping his lackey. Plenty of Genevans had female servants, but male servants were considerably more expensive, a luxury that the Consistory believed Binot and his wife could not afford. He protested that the fifteen-year-old boy had served him since the time Binot was recovering from a gunshot wound in Lyon. The Consistory told him, however, that he was to dismiss the boy and to find a master who was willing to give the young man an apprenticeship.[105] As the previously mentioned case of Louise Gibellin showed, the Consistory occasionally even attacked gluttony. It summoned three men in 1559 for having eaten (together with another man) three dozen pastries. The Consistory condemned all three to be excluded from the Supper and sent them all to the Council to be punished. It expressed special contempt for one of them, Humbert Chappotet, who, rather than providing for his own children, "prostituted himself with such gluttony, losing all humanity."[106]

Quite simply, Genevans were expected to follow a sober lifestyle, which included not only working hard but also dressing modestly, eating moderately, and living within their means. The fines imposed on the lieutenant for the excessive meal shows that judicial authorities shared Calvin's abhorrence of excessive consumption. Evidence indicates, however, that after Calvin's death magistrates were decidedly less enthusiastic than the pastors in trying to curb Genevans' luxurious tastes and were less aggressive in enforcing the sumptuary laws.[107]

Usury and Price Gouging

Throughout the Middle Ages, theologians, lawyers, and popes condemned as a sin the practice of usury, which was originally defined as lending money at any interest. True, the condemnations of Aquinas or Pope Clement V did not prevent people from lending money at interest in the Middle Ages, and certain Catholic thinkers, such as the thirteenth-century canonist Hostiensis, asserted that charging interest was not a sin under certain circumstances.[108] While Luther rejected interest on a loan as a violation of natural law, Calvin declared in a treatise *On Usury* (1545) that there is no scriptural basis for a total prohibition of interest. He made a pragmatic defense of charging interest on loans, provided they were not contrary to "equity and charity." Morally speaking, Calvin found that charging interest for money lent was as justifiable as receiving rent for land leased. Ultimately he defended loans at interest provided that they benefited both parties and were in harmony with the Golden Rule.[109]

In Calvin's Geneva, there were no institutions for lending money, so people in need of a loan had to seek it from other private individuals. Such loans were quite common and perfectly legal, provided the interest charged was not excessive. The legal limit in Geneva was 5 percent, raised, with Calvin's support, to 6.67 percent in June 1557.[110] Clearly, however, loans at higher rates were quite common.

The Consistory convoked people who lent money at excessive interest and occasionally even those who received such loans. One finds actions against usury from the beginning of the Consistory's existence, but they became much more common in 1557, when over twenty people were questioned about making usurious loans.[111] One of the more detailed investigations of usury involved Laurent Peccouz, a native of Savoy. Although he initially denied the accusations, Claude Roch affirmed that Peccouz had lent him sixty florins for a year and charged him fourteen florins in interest, which amounted to an annual rate of 23.3 percent. Peccouz admitted lending or selling on credit quantities of grain to various people. He confessed, for example, to lending Jean Du Villard a *coupe* of wheat at six florins, even though, he conceded, the current market value of wheat was four florins per *coupe*. He defended this rate by saying that he had not expected to be repaid for quite some time. Members of the Consistory excommunicated Peccouz and sent him to the Small Council, asking that it "unleash . . . the ire of God in imposing justice on [Peccouz] and others like him who bring great scandal to the church."[112] In May 1562, the Consistory rebuked Jean-François Armand both for his usury and for offensive words concerning the effects of his moneylending. Armand confessed that when someone reproached him for his usurious loans, he blithely replied that he did not worry about the lives he was destroying, "provided that he got his own pleasures in this world." The Consistory sent Armand to the Council to be judged for this usury. For his "scandalous words," the Consistory excluded him from communion and obliged him to do public reparation.[113]

In the same month, members of the Consistory convoked Antoine Roch, the son of Claude mentioned above, for extortion or fraud, though they did not use those terms. Roch had intended to purchase a cow from an unidentified widow and had even borrowed money from a neighbor to that end. He was quite unhappy to learn that the widow had already sold the cow to another man. Since he felt that the two of them had already come to an agreement on the sale of the cow, Roch demanded and received thirty sous from the widow to cover the money he had borrowed, even though he had actually borrowed only twenty-one sous. Under questioning, Roch admitted that he even managed to get the widow to pay for a meal for himself, his father, and several others. The Consistory declared that Antoine was to return the thirty sous to the widow and ordered him, his father, and their tablemates to reimburse her for the costs of the large meal.[114] The Consistory was understandably showing concern for the widow whom the Roches were taking advantage of, but in this case it was also asserting jurisdiction over cases it did not traditionally have. At no point did the Consistory mention that Roch was to be sent to the Small Council; Calvin and his associates simply took it upon themselves to order the restitution of this money, another example that the Consistory was flexing its muscles in unprecedented ways in the early 1560s.[115]

The Consistory convoked far more men than women for usury, but there were some females in Geneva who apparently sought to make handsome profits through moneylending. In March 1564, the Consistory called the widow Clauda Darbignier of the village of Dardagny. Among her accusers was a man who maintained that Darbignier had lent sixteen florins to him and his fiancée on the condition that they pay her back twenty florins, a rate of 25 percent. Another man indicated that he had borrowed money from her at usurious rates but that Darbignier had insisted that they complete the transaction in neighboring Gex in Savoy through a third party, a shrewd though ultimately unsuccessful attempt to avoid detection by Genevan authorities. On another occasion, the same man had borrowed money from Darbignier using as collateral some pieces of land, which she sold to others after he could not repay his debts. The same man borrowed from her forty florins against another piece of land he owned, a transaction she later transformed into a payment of two *coupes* of wheat, which he was still paying back at the time of his appearance in court. At this time, the Consistory decided that it would defer judgment on this matter until the civil case against Darbignier was concluded before the *châtelain* of the village of Peney. Apparently not yet convinced of her guilt, the Consistory advised Darbignier that she should reflect seriously as to whether she should take communion at Easter, which was rapidly approaching.[116] This last warning reflected, once again, Calvin's conviction that it was a sin and a desecration to take communion without having first confessed and repented of one's serious sins, an idea embraced by Catholic writers for centuries.[117]

Françoise Chevillion, who lived in the nearby village of Neydens in Savoy, was summoned in October 1556. Facing Calvin and his colleagues, Chevillion conceded that she had lent money or grain to various individuals but insisted, in a rather unconvincing manner, that this did not involve interest "as far as she knew." The Consistory sent Chevillion to the Small Council for the alleged usury,[118] and the Council's handling of her case shows that the sexism of authorities could occasionally result in more lenient treatment toward women. Religious and judicial authorities assumed that women were the weaker vessel and that some of their actions might be undertaken in ignorance. Accordingly, authorities might be more prone to pardon certain crimes and misdemeanors if they were committed by women rather than men. In the case at hand, the Council ruled that "seeing that [Chevillion] is a woman and that she has been warned, on this occasion she will receive serious admonitions."[119] The tone of this sentence implies that the Council was cutting Françoise some slack because of her sex. A man convicted of usury would likely have received a jail sentence.

A case from June 1560 showed that usury and profligacy could go hand in hand. The Consistory summoned Michel Bonivard for lending fifteen florins to Roz Doctet and obliging him to repay him seventeen and a half florins just two months later, which would amount to a whopping annual interest rate of 100 percent. The testimony of both men revealed that once Doctet paid Bonivard the interest, the two residents of the village of Vandœuvres together came to Geneva where they squandered the money eating and drinking at an inn before finally purchasing a quantity of rye. The Consistory admonished Doctet but referred Bonivard to the Council to be sent to jail for his usury and especially for his squandering of goods, adding that he should receive from Doctet only the principal of the loan, fifteen florins.[120]

The Consistory also took actions against price gouging. In November 1563, it summoned three men from the village of Dardagny for selling wheat at inflated prices. The three admitted that they had purchased eight *coupes* of wheat around Easter time at a price of nine florins, six sous per *coupe*, and then sold that wheat to fourteen people at eleven florins per *coupe*, a markup of 15.8 percent in a matter of weeks. Moreover, some of the peasants were so desperate for grain that they purchased the wheat not with cash but with land. The three price gougers, though, made sure that the transfer of land involved fields that were outside Genevan territory, under the suzerainty of the canton of Bern, hoping that this would not "come to the attention of *Messieurs*" of the Small Council. Blasting the three men for wanting "to cut the throats of poor people," the Consistory denied them access to communion and referred them to the Council, which sentenced each to three days in jail and a fine of twenty-five florins to go toward the hospital.[121] These actions reflected a continued attachment to the moral economy, which forbade setting prices deemed excessive, especially in regard to essential commodities such as wheat.

Similarly, when the Consistory handled an alleged case of rebellion against rural officials, it showed remarkable sympathy toward the plight of peasants and the financial burdens they faced. A man named Gonin from the village of Sionnet was sent to the Consistory by his pastor and the *châtelain* of Jussy, Claude Testuti, for the "malicious and scandalous words" he uttered when the *châtelain* came to collect wine for the tithe. When the *châtelain* ordered him to open every barrel and draw a measure from each, Gonin admitted that he got angry and told the officer, "I think that you belong neither to God nor the devil." Gonin indicated that of the twenty-four *septiers* he possessed, he had to give two *septiers* less six quarts. The Consistory rebuked Gonin for the intemperate words to the *châtelain* and his two assistants but added that since Testuti and his accomplices "are imposing intolerable exactions [on the villagers] and we presume that they are even making a habit of this, it is advised to notify *Messieurs*, who are requested to restore order and that it pleases them no longer to permit their officers to exercise such tax-farming as the peasants and subjects do not dare contradict them, but are still tyrannized by them."[122] It comes as no surprise that contributions to the church in Geneva continued to be mandatory just as they had been under Roman Catholicism. Collection of the tithe, however, was now in the hands of lay officials, but the pastors, whose salaries came from these contributions, and elders of the Consistory expressed alarm at the burdens that were being imposed on the humblest members of Genevan society, the peasants of the dependent countryside. Part of this concern was almost certainly based on fears of corruption, the suspicion that the *châtelain* and his collaborators were taking from the peasants for their own benefit. Still, it is important to note that the quantity of wine taken, by Gonin's own count, was less than 10 percent of what he possessed. It is also impossible to know for how long this wine had been in his possession; if some of it was several years old, it likely had been subject to earlier collections, and the *châtelain* was thus guilty of double taxing. The fact that the Consistory was basically accusing a state official of extortion and of tyrannizing peasants shows a frankly unexpected concern for the plight of the Geneva's subject peasantry. Calvin and his colleagues reacted angrily against the possibility that these taxes could contribute to the impoverishment of the most vulnerable elements of Genevan society.

One can also find evidence that the Consistory favored increasing the share paid in taxes by wealthier people. In May 1562, the Consistory received a report from the minister of the village of Chancy about a tax imposed on the locals to pay for a schoolmaster to teach the children of the village. The tax, established by the city council, was a levy of eight sous on "the poor" but "only" ten sous on the more affluent. The Consistory asked the Small Council to put Chancy's financial house in order.[123] The strong implication is that the Consistory felt that the more affluent members of this village should not be paying only 25 percent more than the poor. In an era when regressive taxation was the norm in Europe, the Consistory was in favor of having more progressive tax rates so that the better off members of society would pay a greater share in taxes.

The Consistory also showed a certain sympathy for the plight of a poor widow and her children. When questioned in early March 1561, Martine, the widow of

Jean Mermier, was unable to recite the credo or show any knowledge of the tenets of the faith. The Consistory excluded Mermier from communion at Easter and told her to learn the basic tenets before Pentecost. Since she received alms from the hospital, the Consistory at first indicated that it would ask the Council to threaten withholding the alms if she did not make progress. The Consistory then took a step backward and was unusually explicit in describing changing its decision: "then since we heard that she has many children and that it is to them, not her, that the alms are given, it has been revised that nothing be said about taking [alms] from her; rather she will just be sent to *Messieurs* on Monday, who shall be notified that she has not received the Supper in eighteen months."[124] In this case, the Consistory clearly felt that the ignorance of the mother was no reason to subject her children to further deprivation.

Conclusion

So, on balance, where did the Consistory stand in regard to promoting industriousness? Could the actions of Geneva's religious and secular authorities be seen as nurturing the spirit of capitalism? On the one hand, the Consistory's actions on usury and price gouging definitely show that Calvin and his associates were uneasy with many aspects of capitalism. They certainly did not trust the "invisible hand" of the market, whereby the conjunction of self-interest, competition, and supply and demand would supposedly result in an effective allocation of resources and enhance the overall wealth of a society. Implicit in their actions was strong support for the "just price," a belief widespread in the sixteenth century and inherited from medieval thinkers. Abhorring prices and interest rates that they deemed excessive, they did not approve of people exclusively pursuing their own economic self-interest. Though Calvin and his associates in many ways did support capitalistic values, they also insisted that the pursuit of profits be tempered by charity, trust, and social welfare.[125] It would have been almost unthinkable for a theologian to have argued otherwise at this time. Calvin and his colleagues would have been far ahead of their times if they had advocated a free market economy based on the absolute freedom of individuals to pursue their economic goals. It must be noted, however, that after Calvin's death, when the pastor Nicolas Colladon denounced Genevan magistrates from the pulpit for raising the interest rate for government exchange to 10 percent, he was expelled from the Company of Pastors, now led by Beza, and from the city. The ministers' approval of the hike in the interest rate clearly showed that they were moving away from the notion of the "just price."[126]

On the other hand, the evidence is overwhelming that Calvin and his associates demanded a strong work ethic among Genevans. They aggressively attacked laziness and the squandering of assets, actions that dovetail nicely with Weber's *Spirit of Capitalism*. To be sure, Catholics had long considered sloth a deadly sin.[127] But being lazy in and itself was never grounds to be sent before the Inquisition in Italy, Spain, or Portugal. Confessors could demand acts of penitence before granting absolution to lazy confessants, but the degree of social control offered by the confessional was a far cry from that of Geneva's very intrusive Consistory. Likewise, sumptuary laws and the actions against luxuries definitely promoted a form of intra-mundane asceticism described by Weber. The fact that the Consistory's investigations often stemmed from denunciations by neighbors suggests, moreover, that many rank and file Genevans approved of the strict discipline promoted by their religious and political leaders.

Weber's explanations for this austere discipline do not apply in their entirety to Calvin's Geneva. His emphasis on vocation implies that Reformed Protestants promoted very strong work identity. While members of the Consistory often instructed people, particularly young men, that they should learn a trade, they also insisted that everyone should be willing to change lines of work if employment could not be found in their profession. This is seen in its actions against Pierre Rosset, the man mentioned earlier who had bought wheat on credit and resold it for less to get cash. In September 1563, Rosset was called again because he was acting like a "bum" and not working. He protested that presently there simply was no work for blacksmiths like himself. Far from buying that excuse, the Consistory referred him to the Small Council with the recommendation that he be obliged to go work on the ramparts to support his wife and family.[128] Digging ditches and similar unskilled labor was preferable to not working. Likewise, the Consistory rebuked the youth Philippe Gervais for being a "sluggard" who dropped out of his apprenticeship to be a goldsmith. Gervais insisted that he had received his master's permission to end his apprenticeship and that he really wanted to be a clothier (*drappier*) rather than a goldsmith. Excluding him from the Supper, the Consistory sent Gervais to the Small Council, asking that he be made to work "in one way or another."[129] Genevan leaders' encouragement of job changes when people were faced with shifting market conditions is not easily reconcilable with a strong belief in calling.[130]

The evidence from Calvin's Geneva suggests that Weber also exaggerated the belief in predestination. For Weber, the fear of being among the reprobate was supposedly a major incentive for people to perform good works, including dedicating themselves wholeheartedly to their callings as a sign of election. Although predestination has often been depicted as the very essence of Calvinism, Calvin rarely mentioned this theory in his sermons and clearly did not expect the laity to know much about it. Calvin authored the Geneva Catechism of 1542, which was written in question/answer format and was reissued in several subsequent editions. Widely used in Geneva and other Reformed areas, the Geneva Catechism barely mentioned the doctrine of predestination. Of the 373 questions asked of catechumens, there was basically just one that pertained, in a rather allusive manner, to predestination. When asked, "What is the Church," the catechumen was supposed to reply that the Church consisted of those believers whom God had elected or predestined to eternal life. Quite significantly, this catechism did not say a word about reprobation, the predestination of the damned.[131] Similarly, the Heidelberg Catechism of 1563, probably the most popular catechism in the history of Reformed Christianity, referred obliquely to predestination only once in the exact same manner, equating the Church with the elect and making no mention of reprobation.[132] Reformed Christians in Geneva and elsewhere obviously were not learning about the theory of double predestination from studying the catechism. As Weber pointed out, predestination was less prominent in Calvin than in later Reformed thinkers, aptly seen in the work of Beza or in the canons of the synod of Dordt, and argued that the need for reassurance became quite strong only in the seventeenth century.[133]

The evidence from the registers of the Consistory, even those dating well after the time of Calvin, suggest that most Genevans gave little thought to predestination. Although, as noted in chapter 2, the dispute over predestination and free will between Calvin and Bolsec generated considerable interest, Genevans were much more likely to be convoked for taking part in forbidden rituals, such as making the sign of the cross, than for espousing an unacceptable theological belief. Moreover, as will be seen in chapter 7, the Consistory occasionally notified sinners that they risked damnation if they took the Supper without being in the proper state of mind, an attitude that is not easily reconciled with the Calvinist doctrine of predestination. Simply put, it seems most unlikely that the doctrine of predestination played a significant role in nurturing the spirit of capitalism in Reformation Geneva.

All things considered, though, there does seem to be have been in Reformation Geneva a certain "elective affinity" between Calvinist piety on the one hand and the spirit of capitalism on the other. Religious and secular leaders emphasized a very strong work ethic—the only "holidays" in Calvin's Geneva were the fifty-two Sundays in a calendar year, resulting in a dramatic reduction in the number of days off—and a sober lifestyle, which eschewed luxuries and the squandering of assets. Even if much of Weber's thesis now seems discredited, it is hard to believe that the very impressive economic growth Geneva experienced over the next two centuries—interestingly, based to a large degree on the production of luxury goods for export to Catholic countries—was not in any way facilitated by the discipline championed by Calvin and his Consistory in the sixteenth century.[134]

CHAPTER 7

Conflicts, Reconciliation, and the Confession of Sins

MOST OF THE MATTERS over which Calvin's Consistory had jurisdiction would not be subject to judicial authorities in the Western world today. Indeed, most of the behaviors that concerned the Consistory would not be considered crimes or even misdemeanors in the twenty-first century. They usually involved infractions we would consider private matters that might merit moral opprobrium—or rarely, civil litigation—but certainly not criminal sentences. Among those issues were quarrels. The ecclesiastical ordinances of 1541 that mandated the creation of the Consistory said nothing about its role in settling disputes.[1] The registers nonetheless show that quarrels made up a considerable percentage of cases heard from its earliest days: if disputes between spouses are included, they comprised about 15 percent of all cases during its first year, rising to about 30 percent starting in 1546 and remaining at roughly that percentage for the remainder of Calvin's ministry. Among the approximately 4,000 actions that the Consistory of Geneva took against conflicts during Calvin's time, about 59 percent involved conflicts within families and 39 percent disputes with people outside the family.[2] Indeed, wherever they were established, consistories tended to be an important medium for the resolution of conflicts, which were often among the most common cases heard.[3] Religious leaders in Geneva and elsewhere were quite concerned about hatred, which they viewed as impeding piety. Specifically, members of the Consistory were convinced that it hindered prayer and the sacrament of communion.

Quarrels

In Geneva, as in any society, an insult or defamation could set off a quarrel. In handling disputes, Calvin and his associates did not tolerate insults and, if convinced that one party was clearly at fault, did not hesitate to oblige that person to confess his or her guilt and to ask for forgiveness from the aggrieved party.[4] In 1550 Jean and Clauda Du Villard accused Jean de La Rue of having gravely insulted them by calling Clauda a whore and her husband a cuckold. Although he first defended himself by saying that Jean Du Villard himself had claimed that Clauda had been unfaithful, de La Rue, reacting to the Consistory's strong admonitions, finally admitted that he was at fault. He was required to get on his knees in the Consistory chamber and confess his error, acknowledging that the Du Villards were good people whom he had greatly offended. At the request of Jean Du Villard, the Consistory also ordered de La Rue to repeat this act of *réparation* in the neighboring Savoyard parish of Neydens, which was under the suzerainty of Bern. De La Rue promised to make such a confession in the presence of the pastor of Neydens.[5] The Consistory obviously viewed de La Rue as wholly responsible for this dispute.

This example notwithstanding, when it addressed personal conflicts and sought to reconcile those in dispute, the Consistory, as noted repeatedly, resembled a counseling service. Its members were much more interested in settling differences than in assigning blame to one of the feuding parties. In these and in almost all cases heard by the Consistory, we see Calvin as pastor rather than theologian. The testimony found in the registers provides occasional glimpses of Calvin and other pastors trying to reconcile feuding parties outside the Consistory, and summoning people before it only after their previous efforts had failed.

A good example occurred in October 1561 after a pastor had tried to reconcile the saddler Aubin Goujon with others immediately after a sermon in the church of La Madeleine. This matter appeared before the Consistory only because Goujon became quite angry and refused to accept the pastor's admonitions in church. Goujon had been feuding bitterly with his wife, her parents, and his employer, at least partly because his wife's dowry had not been paid in full.[6] A similar case involved Jean Mouton from Provence, who accused the book peddler Jean Parent of defamation of character in 1559. According to Mouton, himself a pastor, Parent had denounced him in the city of Nîmes as a fornicator, adulterer, and hedonist and was now making the same claims in Geneva, solely because Mouton did not want to pay Parent eighteen sous for a New Testament. Rather than summoning Parent to appear before them, members of the Consistory ordered that Mouton and Parent appear together the next day, a Wednesday, at the end of the sermon at the church of La Madeleine. There they were to encounter Pastor Jean Macard, who would be preaching, as well as Amblard Boulard and Antoine Duverney, both of them elders and lay assistants of the Consistory. Together they would all try to work out a resolution to this conflict.[7]

When disputes reached the Consistory, the pastors and elders consistently strove to settle personal disputes, including those involving married couples—as we saw in chapter 4—and others who were closely related. In 1548, for example, two adult sisters, Pernette Ramel, the widow of Michel Sept, and Pernette, wife of Nicolas Drouet, had to appear before the Consistory because of their hard feelings toward each other. The scribe recorded that, after hearing the admonitions, the sisters showed signs of good will toward each other.[8] In a similar manner, in 1556, Pierre Ferrière and his wife had a major conflict over money with their daughter, Claire, and her husband, Renaud Four. Without in any way investigating the monetary issues that were the source of this dispute, the Consistory simply pressed all four parties to reconcile, which they promised to do.[9] In June 1552 Guillaume Cartier was involved in a bitter quarrel with a bookseller named Odin and Odin's wife. Cartier complained that the couple had defamed him, but Odin protested that it was Cartier who had besmirched their honor. Cartier declared that he had the witnesses to prove his accusations, but before calling any witnesses, Consistory members declared they should first try to reconcile the parties. At the end of this appearance, the scribe observed that they had indeed patched things up.[10] Similarly a certain enmity had existed for a long time between Jean Bennard and François Bossey and their wives. When the Bennards were summoned in April 1554, Jean asserted that he would gladly accept the apologies of the Bosseys but categorically refused to apologize to them. Convinced that no one was blameless, the Consistory summoned both couples two weeks later. Exhorting them to "live in peace," the Bennards and Bosseys finally agreed to put aside their differences.[11] As these cases demonstrate, when confronting quarreling parties, the Consistory was usually less interested in determining the guilty party than in settling the dispute. The records for the most part are silent on how feuding parties were persuaded to reconcile, but Calvin and the other assistants obviously deemed it their duty to encourage, cajole, and warn them of the need to forgive and forget, and considered the Consistory a most appropriate forum to promote reconciliations. Christian Grosse has rightly argued that the laity in Geneva viewed the Consistory as a useful medium through which feuding parties could negotiate peaceful settlements. He sees connections between Calvin and his colleagues' efforts at mediation and those of the Council that predated the Consistory, but highlights the latter's conviction that bitter conflicts prevented the faithful from "perceiving the spiritual gift of salvation . . . which communion attested to."[12]

There was an important exception to the Consistory's usual assumption that all parties likely contributed to disputes and accordingly should apologize and forgive one another: whenever Calvin himself was involved in a disagreement, the fault was entirely the other party's. In more than twenty years of Consistory registers, there is not a trace of Calvin ever issuing an apology,[13] but there were several instances in which the reformer demanded reprisals against anyone who besmirched his reputation or challenged his authority. To give just one example, in 1546 Pierre Ameaux, a maker of playing cards, was reported as saying at a private dinner party that Calvin preached "false doctrine" and that he was an "evil foreigner" (*meschant Picard*) and that the French were going to take over the city. On March 2, the Council of Two Hundred decided that Ameaux must ask forgiveness of Calvin in front of that body. For Calvin, the council members were being far too lenient toward Ameaux, and, with the support of the Consistory, he angrily went to the Small Council and declared that under no circumstances would he agree to a reconciliation with Ameaux before the Council of Two Hundred. He also refused to preach until Ameaux had been punished publicly. After several more appearances of Calvin and his colleagues, the Council finally rescinded the previous sentence and condemned Ameaux on April 8 to perform a very humiliating procession through the streets of the city, bareheaded, carrying a torch and wearing the shirt of the penitent, and to get on his knees publicly and beg for mercy from God and justice.[14] This harsh sentence nurtured animosity toward Calvin among some residents of Geneva and helped lead to the formation of the Enfants de Genève. Apart from disputes that involved Calvin directly, which represented a minuscule percentage of the conflicts that were heard, the Consistory generally preferred promoting harmony rather than blaming one party over another.[15]

In Geneva the pastors and elders did not show a special concern for quarrels involving women, a finding that contrasts with the actions of some consistories elsewhere. In Nîmes in southern France, for example, the consistory convoked almost three times as many women as men for insults.[16] Moreover, in certain other areas, consistories called more women than men for cursing, which has been described as "a verbal form of harmful magic." A study of rural areas in early modern Bern shows that morals courts subpoenaed more men than women for "heavy cursing," but four times as many women received harsh punishments for these curses. These figures show unequivocally that judicial authorities were much more likely to associate cursing with possible harmful magic if the malediction was uttered by a female. They not surprisingly accepted the stereotype that witchcraft was predominantly a crime of women.[17] In Geneva, too, authorities viewed witchcraft as a sin more likely to be perpetrated by women, but the same cannot be said for cursing. As chapter 2 demonstrated, the Consistory subpoenaed far more men than women for a specific form of cursing: blasphemy.

Settling Differences and the Celebration of the Supper

As we have seen, the Consistory was quite interested in the administration of the Supper and regularly held a second day of sessions (on Tuesdays) in the weeks preceding the celebration of the Supper to consider the numerous requests for readmission to communion. In addition to these petitions, the Consistory also summoned those who were not taking communion because of bitter feelings toward others. On the Tuesday before Easter in 1548, Pierre Verna, the son of a former member of the Consistory, was subpoenaed because of his rancor toward a certain boatman with whom he had had some differences. Verna confessed that he hated the man and that "unless God changed his heart, he could not bring himself to forgive him." Members of the Consistory strongly encouraged him to pray to God to change his own heart so he could forgive the man and asked him to return in a week to declare if he was ready to forgive his enemy so that he could be admitted to the Lord's Supper.[18]

Having the right spiritual state of mind when taking communion was for the Consistory an essential reason to strive for the reconciliation of feuding parties and penitence for sins.[19] Calvin and the other pastors believed that one had to attain an interior peace and not feel animosity toward others in order to participate in the Supper, and Reformed communities throughout Europe desired that "all hatred and animosity . . . be exchanged for love" before taking communion, a goal that required repentance among all parties in conflict.[20] The gardener Jacques Morellet and his wife were summoned in September 1557 because of their conjugal violence. Morellet admitted having punched his wife because she had left the door open one night, which in turn let a breeze in that disturbed his sleep. Because of his quarrelsome character and the disorder in his household, members of the Consistory forbade Morellet to take communion and warned him that they would "keep an eye on him so that, if he did not mend his ways, he would be prosecuted more fully." As for his wife, she was told that, between now and Sunday, she should notify one of the ministers if she was capable of receiving communion.[21] Their concern, quite clearly, was whether hard feelings toward her violent husband would prevent her from having the proper state of mind to take part in the sacrament. Without explicitly saying so in this case, the Consistory was certainly implying that even parties who were entirely innocent could not attain peace of mind unless they forgave those who had done them wrong.

Although the visitations of all parishioners that, starting in 1550, preceded the celebration of the Supper could be the source of conflicts, they also afforded the chance to attempt reconciliations. In this regard, they were a good example of the pastors and elders' extra-consistorial efforts to maintain peace in Genevan society. To be sure, the only examples that we know of were those that failed. In March 1563 Jacques Bourdet and Jean Lefebvre, both vinegar-makers, appeared because of a bitter dispute—the former had already been punished for slander after calling Lefebvre a brigand. Pastor d'Agnon had attempted to effect a reconciliation during the recent visitation, but this was a complete failure as Bourdet again called Lefebvre a brigand and even told the *dizenier*, Antoine Duverney, that he, too, was a source of trouble.[22] In March 1562, the Consistory called two half brothers, Jacques and François Quiblet, because they had been quarrelling bitterly, and the recent attempt by a pastor and elder to reconcile the two during the visitation had failed miserably. Appearing before the Consistory, the brothers after a lengthy discussion shook hands as a sign of reconciliation, and Jacques confessed and apologized for his "rebellion" at the time of the *visite*.[23] Quite often reconciliations were marked by feuding parties "touching" each other, a common ritual in many venues, including before consistories in Geneva and elsewhere. It involved either a simple handshake or perhaps an embrace, and it was understood as a sign that both parties were pledging to put an end to all rancor and to forget the original cause of the dispute.[24]

The most common ceremonies of reconciliation for which we have records were those that took place before the Consistory. These were essentially private affairs, at which only the parties themselves and the personnel of the Consistory were present. When quarrels had been public or if the feelings were quite bitter, feuding parties were sometimes pushed to reconcile formally just before or, more often, after a church service. Such ceremonies were overseen by a pastor and one or two elders and took place in front of the congregation. The most common day for these reconciliations was Saturday, and they almost never occurred on Sunday. They rarely were scheduled for the main church of Saint-Pierre, probably out of the desire to limit the number of people in attendance, lest the feuding parties refuse to take part.[25]

The Consistory invariably denied access to communion to those who refused to reconcile with people they were quarreling with. In 1555 a servant by the name of Ayma was most irate because another female servant had accused her of having a child out of wedlock, a charge that Ayma emphatically denied. She also took offense at some unkind words uttered by the master of the other servant. When the Consistory pressed them all to reconcile, Ayma proved "obstinate" and refused. Since she did not want to mend fences with the others, she was forbidden to participate in the Supper.[26]

When the Consistory tried to effect a reconciliation between feuding parties, it sometimes had a hard time keeping the parties' emotions in check. In September 1561, Jean-Gaspard Magistri, who was then serving as Geneva's chief prosecutor, and Étienne Furjod presented themselves before Calvin and the other assistants in order to settle their differences, which had prevented them from taking communion the previous Sunday. After the Consistory exhorted them both to bury the hatchet, Magistri spoke first, declaring that "even though Furjod had greatly insulted him and caused an outrage, he was nonetheless willing to give in and show him friendship." Furjod understandably took offense at those words and declared that it was "quite easy for Magistri to settle the difference now after having insulted not only Furjod himself but also his wife and father," adding that if Magistri really wanted to end the quarrel he should not have used such combative language. Members of the Consistory tried to calm the storm and continued to urge the two to reconcile, and they finally did, shaking hands as a sign of reconciliation.[27] This case shows that even members of Geneva's elite were expected to reconcile. When the Consistory oversaw reconciliations, we cannot know whether parties genuinely forgave each other or merely went through the motions under pressure from the pastors and elders. Excluding married couples, however, we do know that it was rather rare for people, once reconciled, to return before the Consistory for the same disputes. In practice this may have meant that the parties tried to avoid each other, but it certainly suggests a degree of success in ending feuds.[28]

Although when handling disputes, the Consistory generally assumed that there was blame to go around, that rule, again, did not apply to the occasional case involving Calvin himself. In the 1540s the reformer had a long simmering feud with the bookseller/printer Guillaume Dubois, which was roughly contemporaneous to the reformer's dispute with Pierre Ameaux, described above. Having been summoned in December 1546 for a conflict with his mother-in-law,[29] Dubois, rather than accepting the admonitions, tried to defend himself, for which Calvin rebuked him harshly and called him a hypocrite. To this, Dubois angrily replied, "It is not only now that you rage against me, and I have also told you that you are a hypocrite for having hated me for a long time and nonetheless received the Supper of Our Lord."[30] To this Calvin replied that he had never hated Dubois but only his vices, which he acknowledged he had hated for a long time. The reformer accused Dubois of being a traitor to the Reformed cause by selling books at excessive prices to the faithful in France and spreading false rumors about Calvin. For insulting Calvin, the Council had Dubois arrested and undertook a criminal investigation. Two witnesses reported that Dubois had referred to Calvin as "a devil" and said that he could no sooner reconcile with him than with a demon. Dubois continued to defend himself and to criticize Calvin when he appeared again before the Consistory on December 30, 1546. Calvin was furious and proclaimed to the Council that he would neither preach nor participate in the Consistory until he was cleared of Dubois's accusations. The reformer made a formal complaint, but Dubois continued to deny any wrongdoing until, after languishing in jail for many days, he confessed to having acted wrongly. On February 1, 1547, the sentence against the bookseller was carried out: Dubois was led out of jail carrying a torch, bareheaded and dressed only in a shirt, to the city hall, where he had to beg for mercy from God and from justice, after which he was banished for a year and a day and required to pay all expenses incurred.[31] Given the harsh sentence eventually passed against Dubois, one might question to what degree Calvin's hatred was directed solely against his sins. Moreover, this case not only shows again that the Consistory's usual goal of reconciliation did not apply to Calvin but also suggests that Dubois himself fully embraced the idea that one must not partake of the sacrament if one felt hatred toward another.

In other cases, Calvin and his colleagues recognized that there were valid reasons that people might be involved in litigation, but they wanted to make sure that the parties did not harbor ill will toward each other that would prevent them from taking communion. In April 1560, in the days preceding Easter, a couple appeared because they had a conflict over finances with her mother and stepfather. The two couples were admonished to live in peace, especially since the celebration of the Supper was approaching. The four indicated that they wanted to settle their differences "by law." The Consistory opined that they were free to proceed with their civil case but should not take communion if they felt rancor toward one another. The Consistory asked Calvin and the lieutenant to try to effect a reconciliation between the generations without in any way prejudicing the couples' judicial rights if they could not come to an agreement over the financial dispute.[32] People could have outstanding differences that involved litigation and still take communion, provided they avoided bitter feelings. The Consistory made no attempt to prevent the settlement of mundane differences over money, goods, or property through proper judicial channels. It just wanted to avoid animosity.

The registers of the Consistory indicate that at least some Genevans had assimilated the idea that it was necessary to settle differences and to bear no acrimony toward others. In March 1563, the Consistory convoked Pernette Dunant, Claude Jernoz, their husbands, and six witnesses. These two women had been feuding for four years, and Robert Dunant recounted that last Sunday, "at his urging, Pernette, his wife, assembled [six women] as witnesses to the agreement [to end] the differences there had been between her and Claude" Jernoz. According to Robert, his wife "for her part asked for forgiveness on her knees from Claude," but Claude "refused to do the same" for Pernette. Following the Consistory's strong remonstrances to put an end to this dispute, because of which the two women had not taken communion for four years, the two were finally reconciled.[33]

Dunant and Jernoz almost certainly did not become good friends, but the fact that the Dunants had brought together the Jernozes and six women to observe a solemn reconciliation at which Pernette begged forgiveness from Claude revealed a very strong desire to put an end to the disagreement and to eliminate all acrimony between them. In dealing with most disputes, Calvin and his colleagues no doubt expected, perhaps even hoped that the quarreling parties would henceforth avoid each other's company; the goal of reconciliation was not to make friends out of former enemies but to eliminate bitterness. Parties in conflicts who were close family members, most obviously spouses, could not realistically avoid each other.

This desire to live in peace and above all to avoid bitterness extended to affairs in which one might sympathize with an aggrieved party's reluctance to reconcile. In February 1558, Jean de Meulle and his wife, Claude, appeared before the Consistory with their landlord, Jean Losserand. The de Meulles accused Losserand of having tried to seduce Claude on three different occasions, including once in the presence of her husband, who was very sick in bed. Losserand eventually confessed to having kissed Claude and then thrown her on the bed, though she successfully resisted these aggressive sexual advances. The Consistory excluded Losserand from the Supper, referred him to the Small Council, and advised the de Meulles "to leave the home of Losserand and not to frequent him any more so as to avoid scandals that could arise." In addition, the Consistory strongly urged the couple to reconcile and to "live in peace the two of them with Losserand, which all three promised to do."[34] Even though in this case the Consistory specifically mandated that the parties henceforth should avoid each other, asking a woman and her husband to reconcile with her would-be rapist required a very high degree of forgiveness. This decision highlights the Consistory's belief in the need for everyone, including the victim of an attempted rape, not to harbor malevolent feelings toward others.[35] When he appeared before the Council on suspicion of "*paillardise* [not rape!]," Losserand did not want to confess any wrongdoing. The Council ordered him not to associate with Claude and to confess his fault to the Consistory before taking communion again. In effect, he received no penalty beyond admonitions and exclusion from the Supper for attempted rape.[36]

Efforts to settle differences and restore peace are common in most societies, and one can find evidence of procedures for the mediation of disputes in and around Geneva dating all the way back to the twelfth century. Such efforts, though, took on heightened importance as Geneva struggled to attain independence in the early sixteenth century. In 1527, nine years before the conversion, the city council established the "peace council" (*Conseil de paix*) for the express purpose of settling disputes (and of doing so independently of the Bishop and the Duke of Savoy). It functioned for only two years and, unlike the Consistory, had jurisdiction over small monetary disputes and the power to revoke the citizenship of those who did not comply with its decisions. This precedent may explain why Genevans did not resist the Consistory's efforts to end quarrels, unlike its claims to power over the Supper.[37]

The taboo against taking communion when troubled by conflicts or sins was certainly not unique to Reformed Protestants. Many Lutherans embraced and even internalized this prohibition, as did many Catholics, both before and after the Reformation. On the basis of Lutheran visitation records from the 1580s, David Warren Sabean finds that German villagers frequently abstained from taking communion if quarrels with others caused them to have an "agitated heart."[38] In his seminal work, *Christianity in the West*, John Bossy asserts that prior to the Reformation, the greatest concern in confession for Catholics was "hatred and its consequences," and the sacrament was both collective and individual; contrition might suffice to reconcile sinners to God, but confession was needed to reconcile them to the church.[39] Stressing the importance of strengthening bonds in a community, Virginia Reinburg avows that for the Catholic laity, the Mass was more "a communal rite of greeting, sharing, giving, receiving, and making peace" than sacrifice and sacrament.[40] Although there were examples of other confessions making concerted efforts to pacify conflicts among parishioners, the efforts of Geneva's Consistory were almost surely more systematic and successful.[41]

Moderation in Rebuking Sinners

Although Genevan authorities appeared insensitive in handling Claude de Meulle's harrowing brush with attempted rape, they were known to show some sympathy to women who, they believed, had been treated too harshly by pastors or law-enforcement officers. In 1557, Françoise Gervais of the village of Petit-Saconnex was accused of blasphemy. She denied the accusations though freely admitted that she had quarreled with the guard who had insulted her by calling her a she-wolf (*louve*).[42] Witnesses affirmed that Gervais was wont to take the name of God in vain, and the guard had tried to oblige her to get on her knees to kiss the earth. The Consistory admonished Gervais henceforth to accept calmly the rebukes of officers, but it also censured the guard, declaring that he should fulfill his duties without anger and should never use his office to settle scores with those with whom he had disagreements.[43]

The Consistory demonstrated a similar attitude in a case the following year. Antoine, the wife of Gabriel Conte, complained to the Consistory that Thivent Sage, dit Matellin, had called her a "whore and slut." Matellin, who was a lay assistant of the Consistory from 1552 to 1559, acknowledged that he had told her "that she was acting like a slut" when he saw her with "a male companion who was playing and frolicking with her." Although they disapproved of her behavior, the other members of the Consistory rebuked their colleague Matellin, and advised "that the next time he should admonish [wrongdoers] more modestly and not speak so offensively."[44] Similarly, in July 1559, the Consistory rebuked Jean Maistre, who had quarreled with Nicolarde, the wife of the notary André Vulliod. Maistre, who had himself been accused more than once of drunkenness and blasphemy, admitted that he had, in the presence of others, called Vulliod an "evil woman" who was sowing discord between husbands and wives and had gotten another woman drunk. The Consistory admonished Vulliod that he must not aggressively insult people, even if his accusations were true, or make a criminal case over foibles as he was wont to do.[45] Calvin and his colleagues would not tolerate insults even if someone merited reprimands, undoubtedly because they were convinced that insults did not promote contrition or changes in behavior.

A similar case involved Claude Testuti, who served as both a lay member of the Consistory and *châtelain* for the village of Jussy. In June 1559, Testuti accused Nicolarde Du Crest of defamation and brought with him two witnesses who affirmed that Du Crest had told each of them in private that Testuti was a real hypocrite. The Consistory ordered Du Crest to apologize and beg for mercy from Testuti, but also admonished the *châtelain* for having impetuously brought this matter, with witnesses, before the Consistory. Calvin and his colleagues thought that calling someone a hypocrite in private was not a terrible sin and that Testuti should have tried to settle this difference with Nicolarde privately. As we have seen, when handling cases of insults, the Consistory usually sought a reconciliation whereby both parties forgave each other. By obliging Du Crest to ask for mercy from Testuti, Calvin and the others showed that they considered Du Crest rather than their colleague to be principally at fault. Nevertheless, by reprimanding Testuti, the elders and pastors showed a certain sympathy for women who came into conflict with heavy-handed authorities.[46] The Consistory was to be the forum to settle only those disputes that could not be worked out privately.

Authorities showed similar sympathy toward Françoise Chevillion, who lived in the nearby village of Neydens in Savoy and was summoned in October 1556. Jean Perreri, who had served as Neydens's pastor since 1545,[47] came forward and announced that when he had reproached her on suspicions of fornication and usury, Chevillion responded angrily and did not admit any wrongdoing. When she appeared, Chevillion acknowledged that she had told Perreri that she was just as good a person as he was, but this was right after he had called her an "evil woman" who deserved to be hanged (*pendarde*, a common insult in Reformation Geneva). The Consistory admonished not only Chevillion but also Pastor Perreri, obviously believing that the minister had been intemperate in the way he rebuked Françoise.[48]

While the Consistory of Geneva cannot be said to have championed the rights of women, one does find evidence that the Consistory did not tolerate men who denigrated learned women, as seen in a case from November 1559. According to witnesses, one day in the church of Saint-Pierre, Pierre Simon and Pierre Vincent were making fun of women who could read and write. The baker Germain Poil reproached those two men for their insulting words, whereupon the other two, especially Simon, physically threatened Poil. Facing Calvin and the Consistory, the two men now claimed that they were merely repeating the proverb that a woman who speaks Latin would not find a fiancé. Witnesses, however, confirmed that Simon said in church that "All women who read, all women who write and speak Latin will surely lie to you."[49] The Consistory strongly rebuked Simon and Vincent, in part because of the physical threats that they made (in church no less). By strongly admonishing the two men for making false charges against "honest women," however, Calvin and the other assistants also showed that they did not tolerate derogatory comments about learned women. The fact that the baker Poil vehemently reproved them in the presence of others also shows that some men embraced the notion that such denigration of women was totally unacceptable.[50]

Although Genevans were encouraged to report the misbehavior of their neighbors to authorities, Calvin and his colleagues insisted that denunciations not be made out of malice. When Jacquème Quiod accused an engaged couple of fornicating in April 1564, the Consistory concluded that the accusation was groundless and excluded Quiod from communion for this defamation.[51] In September 1563 Jean Losserand, the man who had attempted to rape his renter, had to be appear again for having blasphemed during a bitter argument with Étienne Benoist and Claude Patri. The Consistory issued remonstrances to Losserand for this sin but also admonished the other two men because they had revealed his blasphemy "out of hatred rather than out of good zeal."[52] Undoubtedly some denunciations were motivated by a combination of malevolence and piety, but the Consistory consistently sought to root out ill feelings among all Genevans.

Reconciling Apostates with the Church

In his writings, Calvin had nothing good to say about Nicodemites, that is, people who outwardly conformed to Roman Catholicism but inwardly embraced Reformed piety. He himself had dissembled while living in France in 1534 after the outbreak of persecution, but he made a distinction between keeping one's true views secret and openly attending Mass or participating in other Catholic rituals. Writing from the relative safety offered by Geneva, Calvin declared to his compatriots in France that they must be willing to die for their faith.[53] In spite of the reformer's hard-line stance, the Consistory could be remarkably indulgent in dealing with cases of people who, after first embracing the Reformed faith, later renounced it in France under threat of death. The treatment of Antoine Avos was typical. A former Augustinian friar from Rouen, Avos had married Marie Le Danois, herself an ex-nun. On May 23, 1555, Avos came to the Consistory confessing that while "in Paris, [he] was interrogated about his faith under oath [and] was greatly tempted and weak in his faith out of fear of being degraded and burned ... [;] [he] disavowed and abjured and denied [his faith]. Recognizing his sin, he requests to be forgiven and to be admitted to the Supper. He also disavowed his wife there." His wife also admitted to renouncing the Reformed faith in France and reported that she was "whipped through the streets of Paris and does not know why, except that they said that she had pronounced words against the faith and that she was the concubine of her husband."[54] After hearing witnesses, the assistants decided that the couple should abstain from the next celebration of communion but could receive it three months later.[55]

Appearing before the Council in September 1558, Calvin spoke of the need to have a law prescribing an appropriate punishment for Reformed Protestants who, out of fear for their lives, renounced *l'Évangile* in France and then returned to Geneva. The Council ruled that such *renunciateurs* were to do reparation, solemnly holding a torch, upon leaving church.[56] Such sentences, which had much in common with Catholic rites of abjuration of heresy,[57] tended to be concentrated in the weeks immediately preceding the celebration of the Supper and amounted to a type of spiritual purification in preparation for communion.[58] In March 1560 two men, Gérard Bernard and Barthélemy Masset, confessed that they abjured the Reformed faith in Lyon where they were condemned to be whipped and to carry a torch in a procession. They now greatly regretted their actions, and, in compliance with a recent edict, the Consistory ordered that they do reparation, which they performed in church "after the sermon and before the prayers." The next day, on Monday, they repeated their expressions of remorse before the Council.[59] In December 1560 Marin De Vergier from Chailly near Paris admitted in December 1560 that, jailed in Grenoble for his faith, he renounced Protestantism and even burned the Bible. The Consistory ruled that De Vergier was to be excluded from the Supper and to do reparation in the church of Saint-Pierre the following Sunday.[60]

In May 1560, Claude d'Anduze, sieur de Veyrac, confessed that while he was in France he, too, had abjured the Reformed faith. The Consistory used some unusually harsh language in rebuking the noble Anduze—"one reproaches him that he has behaved in a cowardly manner and has created a great scandal and that it would have been better if he had died"—but did not go beyond ordering him to abstain from communion.[61] A closer examination can explain why the Consistory used such harsh words toward Anduze. The Consistory expressed concern about Anduze and other current residents of Geneva; during the recent "tumult" (*emotion*) in France, some had managed to escape, others had been released from prison only by insisting that they were faithful subjects of the king who wanted "to live according to the Catholic faith and Church."[62] The turmoil stemmed from the Conspiracy of Amboise in March 1560, in which a number of Protestants, including several from Geneva, tried to kidnap King Francis II to remove him from the influence of the staunchly Catholic and aggressively anti-Protestant Guise family. A prelude to the French Wars of Religion, this Conspiracy was a complete fiasco and resulted in the executions of around eighty Huguenots.[63] In addition to Anduze, the Consistory questioned eight other men about their experiences in France related to Amboise. Some asserted that they had not actually been jailed, and others claimed that they were not questioned about religion but only about "the enterprise," a reference to the conspiracy. None other than Anduze admitted to renouncing Protestantism, and the Consistory strongly admonished them all to act more wisely in the future and never again to take part in an "insane enterprise" like this.[64]

One can readily conjecture that the Consistory's ire toward Anduze was more because he had incited others to take part in this conspiracy, which they viewed, at least in hindsight, as ill-advised, than because he had renounced his faith under pressure.[65]

Worth noting is the fact that on the exact same day (May 28, 1560) that Calvin and his colleagues told Anduze he should have died in prison, they showed their typical restraint toward apostasy in considering the case of Romanet Mahet. There was no hint that he was in any way involved in the Amboise Conspiracy. Having lived in Geneva and converted to the Reformed faith, Mahet recently returned to his native Dauphiné where he was "detained as prisoner for the word of God." He admitted that he renounced *l'Évangile*, embraced the "false papist doctrine," and received "their idol" (the communion host) at the instigation of a monk. He greatly repented of these actions and begged for mercy from God and *Messieurs*, affirming that he had not participated in the Supper anywhere since leaving jail. Apart from indicating that he should still abstain from the Supper (of Pentecost), members of the Consistory limited themselves to admonitions, urging Mahet not to "disguise the truth again." They said that they would watch over his behavior from then until September, implying that he stood a good chance of being admitted to the celebration of the Supper at that time.[66]

After the wars actually started, one can find cases such as that of Jeanne Raoul, who had gotten married in Geneva eight years earlier but then went to Lyon where her child was born. She confessed that the baby was baptized in a Catholic ceremony and protested that this was unavoidable since both her father and husband were absent at the time, one being a prisoner, the other a fugitive. Evidently the Consistory bought this argument and limited itself to having Raoul, now a widow, recognize her fault in the Consistory and beg God for forgiveness on her knees.[67]

Calvin and his colleagues could become rather irate when people did not fully recognize their abjuration. A case in point was Jacques Lambert, a taffeta maker from France, who was charged in December 1560 of having recently renounced *l'Évangile* in Lyon by saying, "Inasmuch as I have offended the King, I ask for his grace and accept his pardon." Lambert conceded that he said as much but that this did not involve renouncing the Reformed faith. To this Calvin vigorously retorted that the "pardon of the King" necessarily involved abandoning Protestantism and living according to "the Roman church." Calvin accused Lambert of hiding the truth and of being a liar and a hypocrite. Noting that Lambert had not even been jailed when he abjured, the Consistory excluded him from the Supper.[68] A week later, the chastened Lambert reappeared at the insistence of the

Council to recognize fully his error; he did so and begged God for forgiveness. Calvin was out of the chamber at this moment, and the other assistants were unsure how to deal with Lambert. Accordingly, they dispatched one of the other pastors to fetch Calvin. Upon his return, the Consistory decided that on the following Sunday, Lambert was to do reparation at the main service at Saint-Pierre in front of the whole congregation.[69] Apart from showing the incredible degree of deference that the other assistants offered Calvin, this case demonstrates that in spite of Calvin's initial ire, once Lambert made a full confession the Consistory basically treated him like others who had renounced their faith. For Calvin and his colleagues, one could not equivocate; one had to acknowledge fully and unequivocally one's sins or errors.

In this era, when cases of apostasy before the Inquisition in Spain or Italy could result in capital punishment, those who renounced the Reformed faith to save their lives were routinely readmitted to the community of Geneva after being excluded just one time, provided that they were truly penitent. Most, though not all, of these were also obliged to do *réparation*, acknowledging their error publicly, often before the whole church but sometimes just in front of the Small Council or the Consistory.[70] In short, notwithstanding Calvin's scathing criticism of Nicodemites, the Consistory was not too harsh toward those who had renounced the Calvinist faith when facing execution in Catholic countries. Evidently, Calvin, the Consistory, and the magistrates of Geneva did not demand martyrdom of all those facing persecution.[71]

More common than cases of individuals who truly risked persecution and martyrdom were those involving people who had converted to Protestantism when they came to Geneva and then returned to their native France or Savoy where, probably without too much pressure, they attended Mass and participated in Catholic rituals. As we saw in chapter 2, in those circumstances the Consistory demonstrated a rather surprising degree of indulgence. A good example was the case of Jacques Corson, who in December 1561 confessed:

> after having lived in this city, where he came to know the pure doctrine of the *Evangile* [and] having participated in the holy sacrament of the Supper, he returned to his country of Palluan in Berry, where he prostituted himself in idolatry, going to Mass and to the funeral of his father. Of this he is greatly repentant, requesting that he be forgiven for this offense, especially his abjuration to live as a Catholic according to the edicts of the King.[72]

The Consistory gave him strong admonitions and declared that he will be "received in repentance, on the condition that he make reparation before the celebration of the Supper in the temple of Saint-Pierre."[73] Following this reparation, Corson would not have had to abstain from communion even once though he freely admitted to having abjured the Reformed faith in France.

The Need for Confession and Contrition

Calvin and his associates also insisted on the need to confess serious sins to the Consistory (or at least to a pastor in private) and to demonstrate sincere contrition for those sins in order to have access to the Supper. This was obvious in the case of Françoise, the wife of Gaspard Gautier, who was punished in June 1560 for petty theft for taking from a peasant woman one more egg than the number she had paid for. Upon leaving prison, she was required by the Small Council to go to the Consistory to receive admonitions for this petty larceny. Facing the assistants, Gautier protested her innocence, but trustworthy witnesses provided evidence to the contrary, and the Consistory therefore denied her access to the Supper.[74] She returned in August and again in July of the next year to ask to be readmitted to the Supper, but still protested her innocence. On both occasions the Consistory rejected her request and told her the second time that she must come back "six weeks from now or at least before the Supper [of September] to make a good confession of her fault and to request to be admitted to the Supper, which had been forbidden to her because of this [sin]."[75] A month later, Claude Voutier, excluded from the Supper for having prayed to the Virgin Mary, asked to be readmitted to communion which, she claimed, "had been denied to her for having been wrongly imprisoned for having simply talked about the Virgin Mary." Since she still felt that she was innocent, the Consistory rebuked her by telling her that "instead of coming here to confess her fault, she comes to justify [herself]." The assistants accordingly denied her request and advised that "she look to better recognize her fault between now and Christmas; otherwise she will be proclaimed in the temple" as an excommunicant. While leaving the chamber, Voutier defiantly vowed that "she would go take [the Supper] elsewhere"; for this "rebellion," the Consistory referred her to the Small Council to be punished and extended her exclusion from the Supper.[76]

An even more striking example involved Claude Mauris, the widow of Raymond Favre of the village of Jussy, who appeared several times for suspected fornication and for a bitter quarrel with another woman. Since she refused to admit any guilt, the Consistory not only denied her request to be readmitted to the Supper in May 1560 but also ruled that she was to be "proclaimed aloud excommunicated in front of and in full view of the entire congregation by the minister who will be preaching in Jussy next Sunday since she does not want to come to repentance and remains hardened and obstinate."[77] When she returned in late August and asked for admission to the Supper of September, she still claimed that she did not understand why she was being prevented from participating in the sacrament. The Consistory angrily told Mauris that she should not return to the Consistory until she was ready to confess and that if she failed to do so, *Messieurs* of the Council should banish her since she was so rebellious and stubborn.[78] The Council indeed did banish Mauris from Genevan territory, but on Christmas Day 1561 she returned momentarily from her exile in nearby Savoy to ask the Consistory for readmission to the Supper. On this occasion she readily admitted that she had done wrong and had quarreled bitterly with another woman, with whom she almost came to blows. The Consistory ruled that after the sermon next Sunday in Jussy, she was to make a full confession of her faults before all parishioners. Once she did that, she would be admitted to the Supper. The Consistory also sent her to the Council with the recommendation that she be permitted to return to Genevan territory.[79] In short, when the Consistory was convinced that people were guilty, they needed to confess rather than protest their innocence; failure to do so could even result in banishment.

The guilty also needed to confess all, not just some of their major faults. After a fistfight in August 1563, Étienne De Lecra confessed to having struck the other man once but denied that he often got drunk. Witnesses, however, affirmed that he frequently drank excessively and that he punched his victim three times, not just once. Excluding him from the Supper,[80] the Consistory convoked him again in February of the following year for beating his wife when she urged him to go request to take communion again. On that occasion, he confessed his misdeeds only "in part," and the Consistory accordingly referred him to the Small Council. When he did petition for readmission to communion in April, the Consistory rejected the request because he still was not fully acknowledging his errors.[81]

At times the Consistory doubted the sincerity of certain confessions of sins. In March 1562, Pierre Chappuis of the village of Peissy asked permission to take communion and confessed to having sold rosaries in Flanders. The assistants told him that he would have to come back to the Consistory to give a better confession of sins, advising him that the next time he should not laugh while confessing, as he did just now.[82]

Magistrates shared the Consistory's desire to encourage all to recognize, confess, and repent of their sins. In December 1557, the Small Council introduced a most interesting practice, *le grabeau*, in which all members were required to participate in order to confess their sins:

The order to reprove or censure among the *Seigneurs* of the Small Council. It has been put forward that it would be good and expedient that we establish a certain day for each month or quarter to assemble here in an extraordinary Council, which no one must miss, . . . in order to rebuke or censure each other's errors and shortcomings in good order, zeal, . . . and fraternal charity, rejecting and ceasing all enmity and rancor . . . so that the grace of God prevail among us. . . . [A]nd all of this will be kept secret without reproaching or in any way boasting . . . or revealing anything under pain of being reputed first as in violation of the sacrament. And such an assembly and congregation must be held the first Wednesday of each month here in an extraordinary [meeting of the] Council. And we must start this next Wednesday at 6 o'clock in the morning, and once this is started, we will determine if we will proceed monthly or quarterly. . . . And may all be to the honor and glory of God.[83]

The historian Doumergue said the following about *le grabeau*: "I don't know if there was ever anything [in Geneva] more characteristic and stranger than the meeting at which members of the government admitted their faults and criticized themselves and each other. Calvin took quite seriously his ideal of the Christian state."[84] In March 1558 the scribe described Council members' efforts to encourage each other lest they stray from the straight and narrow path: "In good love and charity, all censured each other, going from the first through the last, exhorting each one about his imperfections and vices. May the Lord grant us the grace to profit well from this."[85]

One finds instances in which there was clearly some negotiation between the Consistory, on the one hand, and the petitioner, on the other, on the issue of the sincerity of the latter's repentance for sins. In December 1563, for example, André Janin of the village of Cologny asked to be readmitted to the Supper. He had been excluded because he had struck a woman who had tried to hinder him from beating one of his own children. Initially the Consistory rejected this request because it found that he was not truly repentant for his sin. He responded that "with a good heart, he asked forgiveness from God" for his misdeed. The Consistory then reversed itself and declared that he was readmitted to the sacrament.[86] The entry for this case, as for many others, is very cryptic, and we cannot know what else was said beyond Janin's confession. Suffice it to say, though, that it was quite possible for people who were petitioning for admission to the Supper to change the minds of Calvin and the others about being genuinely contrite about their actions.[87]

If convinced of the sincerity of a confession, the Consistory was quite willing to grant access to the Supper even to those who had committed the most serious sins and crimes. In December 1563, Louise Berthod of the village of Céligny petitioned to be readmitted to the Supper, having been excluded the previous August for having kicked a pregnant woman, which resulted in the death of the woman and the loss of her unborn child. Believing that Berthod was fully contrite, the Consistory ruled that she be readmitted to the Supper, provided that she recognized her fault before them just as she had already done publicly.[88] Four months after, in effect, committing manslaughter, she was thus brought back into the community of the Reformed faithful. When convinced of the sinner's repentance, the Consistory could be lenient even though it initially called for severity toward the same person.

Calvin considered it a sin and a desecration to take communion without having first confessed serious sins. In April 1551, the Consistory summoned Pernon Briset because she was pregnant and single, though she claimed that her lover had promised to marry her. She was reproached "for her fault, including having continued to receive the Supper," even though she had begun having sexual relations about Saint Michael's day (September 29).[89] In December 1560, Bernard Nerod appeared as a witness, but the Consistory was disappointed with his deposition; convinced that he had not told the truth, Calvin and the other assistants warned him that if he took communion, he would receive it as if he were a dog (*en qualité d'ung chien*).[90] Evidently, the Consistory considered taking communion without having confessed one's sins—in this case of lying to the Consistory—as itself a very serious sin, an idea embraced by Catholic writers for centuries.

For the Consistory, the sins of Pierre Berthet were an even worse form of desecration of the sacrament. He was convoked for having committed serious misdeeds on the day of the Supper, and he took communion even though he had been forbidden to do so because of his previous sins. On the meeting of January 12, 1559, the secretary wrote:

Pierre Berthet, charged with often beating his wife, even on the day of the most recent Supper. Responds and confesses that [he is guilty as charged]. Also that he took the Supper at Christmas from the hands of Mr. Dupont, minister, which had been denied to him by the *sieurs* who undertook the most recent visitation going from house to house. Therefore since he profaned the holy sacrament of the Supper by taking it, though not instructed [about religion] and in violation of the injunctions made against him, [and since these actions] showed rebellion against rather than ignorance of [the

Consistory's rulings and] add [to this the fact] that in great scandal he beat his wife the day of the Supper, it seems good to send him before *Messieurs* [of the Small Council] with the entreaty that he be punished, the Supper being again forbidden to him.[91]

This passage demonstrates the close tie between the pastoral visitation and the celebration of communion and puts in high relief the idea that to commit serious sins on the day of the celebration of the Supper or to take the sacrament without having confessed reprehensible acts amounted to a profanation of the Reformed Eucharist.[92] To emphasize the idea that committing a sin on the day of communion showed contempt for the sacrament, the Consistory was known to force people who had merely quarreled on the day of the Supper to confess their sin and express their remorse in front of the whole congregation.[93]

Despite the actions of Berthet, many Genevans evidently had assimilated the maxim that they must not take communion with a troubled conscience or if they felt rancor toward others.[94] In May 1551, Paul Humblet and Jacques Duval were involved in a suit filed before the lieutenant, a case that stemmed from Humblet's allegedly hitting Duval for having blasphemed. The celebration of the Supper of Pentecost was approaching and the Consistory accordingly asked the two adversaries if they were able to receive the Supper. Both responded that they did not wish each other ill, but Duval affirmed that "his conscience was not yet disposed to taking the Supper."[95] Likewise, the miller Jacques Pape was convened in 1548 for misbehavior, accused of beating his wife, dissipating his goods, frequenting the taverns, and singing dissolute songs. When asked if he had attended church the previous Sunday when communion was celebrated, Pape frankly admitted that he had not and had gone instead outside the city with several other men to play *charret*, a board game known in English as Nine Men's Morris. As for why he had not taken communion, Pape said he was unable to do so because he was still in a conflict with a certain man named Talabard.[96] At first glance, his reference to his quarrel with Talabard could be viewed as putting the most positive spin on why he had not taken communion—if they had known that he was bitterly angry with someone, members of the Consistory themselves would have denied him access to the Lord's Supper. But in frankly admitting to playing a game instead of going to church on Sunday, Pape most definitely was not telling members of the Consistory what they most hoped to hear. Given his anger toward the other man and his misbehavior toward his wife, Pape may indeed have felt that he was not in the right frame of mind to take communion.

In 1546, a widow explained that she had not taken communion in six or seven years because she continued to harbor much anger against the man who had killed her brother. She even admitted that she altered the words of the Lord's Prayer; rather than saying, "Forgive us our offenses, as we forgive those who have offended us," she asked God to forgive her more than she could forgive her brother's killer.[97] This and similar examples strongly undercut the claim that the Reformation's emphasis on learning prayers and the creed by rote necessarily meant that most people mechanically recited them without reflecting on the words that they uttered.[98] This case clearly involved a person whose anger, which was frankly understandable, was hindering her from both praying and taking communion.

Convoked in April 1557 because he had not taken communion in the past year, the pastry-maker Claude Comparet explained that he had abstained from the Supper because he harbored bad feelings toward Pastor François Bourgoin, dit d'Agnon, because of "certain words" that d'Agnon had uttered against Comparet's brothers, who were involved in the Perriniste riot and had both been executed in June 1555. Comparet avowed that he was "in good deliberation to leave aside all hatred." The Consistory concluded that he should wait until Pentecost to evaluate his behavior and good will and asked him to go see Pastor d'Agnon to put an end to this conflict. Did Comparet tell the truth in explaining why he had not been taking communion? It would have been most impolitic for him to tell the Consistory that he did not really care whether he participated in the Supper or not. But if he had really wanted to tell Calvin and associates what they wanted to hear, he should have said that he was ready "to join the ranks of the faithful in the reception of the Supper."[99] In this case, Comparet had every reason to be upset with d'Agnon for speaking ill of his late brothers. Both had taken part in the tumult, and one of them, François the boatman, was responsible for the only injury sustained in the fracas by striking another man with a stone. These two brothers were brutally tortured, denied the right to make a defense, and then summarily executed in a most inhumane way, due to the ineptitude of the executioner. Claude Comparet was justifiably bitter about the injustices his brothers had suffered. His anger at the aspersions the pastor cast upon them was perfectly understandable, and his refraining from taking communion—from the hands of a pastor, no less—also makes sense.

All these examples lend support to the idea that the discipline implemented by the Consistory was in effect replacing private confession that was central to the Catholic sacrament of penance.[100] Like other Reformed leaders, Calvin eliminated the sacrament of penance, and he especially rejected the sacramental absolution associated with it. At the main service on Sunday, the officiating pastor recited a collective confession of sins during which the entire congregation knelt, a ritual that stressed equality as all believers were united by their sinful nature and utter dependence on divine grace.[101] In addition to this collective generic confession of sins, Calvin also saw strong spiritual benefits in confessing sins to a minister and in receiving consolation and absolution from him. We know about the confessions of sins made before the Consistory because of its rich extant sources. But it is also clear that confessions were made to ministers in other contexts, at the time of visitations and in private meetings.

In Geneva's liturgy, the collective confession of sins was not followed by a common absolution. In outlining the celebration of the Supper, Calvin did not include in the liturgy that he introduced in 1542 a declaration of consolation and absolution right after the confession of sins, even though the formula that had heretofore been used, written by Farel, did include such an expression. It is not clear why Calvin eliminated absolution, and as Christian Grosse observes, he apparently regretted this omission, as in 1561 he recommended including absolution in the celebration of the Supper in other churches (but not in Geneva).[102] There is also ample evidence that Calvin believed in the power of private absolution, and for him and other Protestant thinkers, regardless of the context, the role of the pastor in absolution was simply to proclaim the promise of grace, as all forgiveness comes from Christ; the word of absolution is God's, not the minister's.[103] Similarly, in his work on Reformation Germany, Ronald Rittgers finds that Luther saw the utility of confessing to a pastor. The clergyman, however, now had a reduced role compared to the Catholic confessor. No longer a judge, he was more a servant to the confessants, his most important function being to pronounce absolution, words of forgiveness which were the external sign of the grace bestowed on the basis of faith.[104] Calvin and his fellow pastors also exhorted parishioners to examine their consciences, especially before the Supper, and to confess their sins to God and perhaps also to a minister. If they doubted the sincerity of the confessants' contrition, they definitely did not hesitate to tell parishioners, either in private or through the Consistory, to abstain from communion.[105]

Confessing sins, suppressing hatred, and feeling contrition are all related to self-control. Measuring the success of Calvinists' efforts to inculcate self-control is extremely difficult if not impossible to measure. One very useful indicator of a society's success in controlling anger in the population would be homicide rates, but they must be based on extremely well-preserved death records and court records. Geneva's extant archival sources are among the richest and certainly the best catalogued in all of Europe, but even they cannot provide sufficient data for reliable homicide rates for the sixteenth century. Aware of these pitfalls, Philip Benedict, though acknowledging differences of opinions among scholars, asserts that "the domain of interpersonal violence and impulse control does appear to have been one in which the pressure of the church tribunals made a difference" in areas such as Scotland, Amsterdam, and Emden.[106] A study found that the homicide rate in Geneva went down slightly from the early seventeenth century to the last two decades of the eighteenth century (death records and other sources are not sufficient to provide reliable estimates for the sixteenth century).[107] The modest though perceptible decrease in the homicide rate took place at a time when the power of the Consistory had continued its decline, which had begun in the late sixteenth century, after Calvin's death. Even if we cannot make a direct connection between the Consistory and declining violence, it is nonetheless not unreasonable to posit that Calvin's disciplinary regime nurtured self-control, which was assimilated by generations of Genevans and continued even after the decline in the Consistory's power.

Desecrating the Supper with Sin

The Consistory regularly made a point of mentioning whether a sin had been committed shortly before or after the celebration of the Supper, a clear sign that the pastors considered this a form of profanation of the sacrament. When Marie Brossard appeared in September 1555, she confessed that she had fornicated with her fiancé. The scribe made it a point to write twice that she had sexual relations with her fiancé (and had even propositioned his younger brother) on Pentecost Sunday after taking communion earlier that day.[108] In September 1557 Pierre Barbarin, who had a reputation for aggressively insulting others, was summoned for having scurrilously insulted a widow just a half hour after taking communion. Noting that Pastor d'Agnon had often admonished him to mend his ways, the Consistory excluded him from the Supper for having caused a scandal on the day of communion and referred him to the Small Council, which ordered that this "quarrelsome and shameful" man leave the city within three days and not return under pain of the whip.[109] Calvin and his associates really wanted parishioners to consult their consciences to recognize the sins they had committed and to assimilate the idea that the gravity of those sins was exacerbated if committed around the time of the celebration of the Supper, an attitude previously expressed by Catholic theologians.[110]

There were some actions that were prohibited on days on which the Supper was celebrated even though they were allowed on other days, even on Sundays, provided that they did not coincide with the sermons. Following the celebration of the sacrament at Christmastime 1563, sixteen men appeared, having already spent a few days in jail, for having participated, in violation of Geneva's ordinances, in fencing exercises on the Sunday on which communion was administered. The Consistory issued admonitions to them all and excluded one from the next Supper because it viewed him as the ringleader.[111] Such martial games were tolerated and even encouraged in Geneva because they served as training for the defense of the city-state. Sundays were the day on which such games regularly took place, but they were not to be conducted on a day on which communion was celebrated. Doing so amounted to a profanation of the sacrament, according to Geneva's pastors and elders.

The registers of the Consistory indicate that at least some of the laity in Geneva shared this idea that a sin perpetrated near the celebration of the Supper constituted a defilement of the sacrament. In January 1562, the lieutenant sent to the Consistory three men whom he had already punished for getting into a fistfight, a scandal that was witnessed by a large number of people. The three confessed their error, including Michel Dufour, who admitted that a certain passerby tried to stop the fight and reproached him for having taken the Supper earlier that day "to his own condemnation." The fact that Dufour professed that he "repented" of his actions suggests that, at least to a degree, he too had assimilated the idea that committing a sin after taking communion brought about bad consequences for one's soul.[112] Though one may question the sincerity of Dufour's expression of contrition, there is no reason to doubt the convictions of the unnamed passerby.

Occasionally the Consistory notified sinners that they risked damnation if they took the Supper without being in the proper state of mind. Ami Favre of the village of Jussy had appeared several times for blasphemy and fornication and asked to be readmitted to the Supper at Christmas in 1555. Calvin and his associates were not completely convinced that Favre's apologies were sincere but permitted him to take communion, warning him, however, of the danger of taking it if he did not truly feel remorse for his sins: "we leave him to his own conscience that he must not take [communion] to his own damnation, seeing all his faults and that we know that he is guilty; he must think about it."[113] Warning someone that he risks damnation if he takes communion though unrepentant of sins or feeling rancor toward another denotes an attitude that appears incompatible with the Calvinist doctrine of predestination. True, the Apostle Paul warned in 1 Corinthians that whoever eats the bread or drinks the cup in an unworthy manner eats and drinks judgment upon himself (11:27–29). But theologians who believe in predestination and reject salvation by works, denying that people can have any direct impact on their own destiny, cannot also believe that people can actually be damned for taking communion without being repentant of their sins.[114] Why did Calvin issue these warnings? In this case, as with his work on the Consistory in general, we are seeing Calvin as pastor rather than as theologian. Christian Grosse convincingly suggests that for Calvin and his colleagues, "unworthy communion does not itself produce divine condemnation, but it incites a feeling of guilt in that person's conscience."[115] Calvin apparently thought that the goal of nurturing reconciliation and the interiorization of Reformed morality justified this warning of damnation, which he could not have entirely believed. In such cases, practical concerns took precedence over theological precision.[116] Calvin and the other pastors certainly wanted to impress on all Genevans the need to show due reverence toward God each time they partook of the Supper, and it appears that they enjoyed a considerable degree of success. Many Genevans interiorized the idea that one must never take communion unworthily, believing that their salvation was at stake if they did so.[117]

Unwarranted Abstention from the Supper

Just as one could get into trouble with the Consistory for taking communion while in a poor spiritual state, one could also be reproached for not taking the sacrament. Excluded from the Supper since May 1554 for domestic violence,[118] the mason Martin Leschiere was called more than three years later "to confess his faults for which the Supper has been denied to him for a long time." When asked why he had been excommunicated, Leschiere replied that he did not know. Since he "is a rebel and does not want to recognize [his error]," the Consistory declared that Leschiere would remain excluded from communion.[119] Five months later, Leschiere had to return to the Consistory, accompanied by Jean-Jacques Bonivard, to account for their whereabouts at the time of the most recent celebration of the Supper. The two men responded that they had been at Pont d'Arve with another man. Since at least one of them was carrying an arquebus, one can deduce that they probably intended to practice shooting. When the assistants asked him when he had last taken the Supper, Bonivard said, "about three or four years ago" and that he had not taken it since then "because he felt hatred and rancor toward his mother." The Consistory issued the following decision:

as for Bonivard, since he has waited so long to receive the Supper, he is to be sent before *Messieurs* [of the Small Council] with the declaration that he should be punished for showing himself incorrigible. And as for Leschiere, he should similarly be sent [to *Messieurs*] since he shows and renders himself a rebel by not taking into account the Supper that has been forbidden to him; instead of doing so, he goes to pass time in Pont d'Arve, because of which he also deserves punishment. The Supper is again forbidden to both of them.[120]

Though it may appear useless to deny communion to someone who seemed in no hurry to take it, this ruling nonetheless appears to have worked in the case of Leschiere. In April 1558, he asked permission to receive the Supper and declared himself "repentant of his fault." The Consistory absolved him and gave him "good remonstrances."[121] In August of the following year, the widow Pernette de La Planche of the village of Jussy appeared, having been summoned many times over the years (first in 1551) for truancy from church and from the Supper. Her husband had died excommunicated, and Pernette reputedly let her undisciplined children run wild. Pernette was noncommittal when asked if she had come to request readmission to the Supper. Concluding that she was "incorrigible," the Consistory referred her to the Council with the recommendation that she and her children, who were rascals (*garnimentz*), be banished, adding in unusually blunt language that it would be doing the villagers a favor to remove this "scum" (*ordure*) from their midst.[122] To avoid similar cases, the ecclesiastical ordinances of 1561, reiterating an edict of 1557, ordered banishment of one year for all excommunicants who did not approach the Consistory to be reconciled to participate in the Supper.[123] This went in tandem with an edict from the previous year calling for the announcement in church of the names of those who had been admonished but had refused to mend their ways. It added that people were to refrain from having contacts with such "rebels" who had to do public *réparation* before being reintegrated into the church and community.[124]

Notwithstanding a few examples to the contrary, most Genevans clearly wanted to take the Holy Supper. As previously noted, the Consistory's meetings that took place just before the celebration of communion stood out from all others. In a typical meeting, the Consistory convoked miscreants for their alleged sins. By contrast, the meetings prior to the Supper were dedicated in large part to requests from excommunicants to be readmitted to the Eucharist. In considering these petitions for readmission, the Consistory wanted to know if the individuals were truly penitent and properly disposed to take communion again.

A good example occurred in 1559 when the *châtelain* of Saint-Victor sent two brothers and their wives to the Consistory because of a bitter intrafamilial feud that had been simmering for some time. Brothers Louis and Étienne Bourgeois and their wives, all from the village of Athenaz, appeared immediately before the September celebration of the Supper. The brothers affirmed that the two of them were getting along just fine, but their wives had been fighting—Clauda, Louis's wife, had called Étienne's (unnamed) wife a "witch," and the latter had called Clauda a "slut." The women both confessed these actions but also said that they desired to take communion the following Sunday. As a sign of forgiveness, they joined hands and asked for mercy from God and from the authorities. Since the Consistory determined that they were poorly instructed in matters of the faith, it ordered them to meet with their pastor who would provide instruction and determine if they were ready to take communion.[125] All parties involved clearly wanted to reconcile before the celebration of the Supper. The large number of petitions to be admitted to the Supper undercuts the notion that Genevans were indifferent toward participation in the sacrament. This, combined with the fact that the plurality of suspensions were for only one celebration of the Supper provides strong evidence that excluding people from communion was an effective means of discipline.[126]

A Comparison with Protestant Practices Elsewhere

It is worthwhile to compare the findings in Geneva on the efforts to effect reconciliations and the confession of sins with practices in other Protestant areas. Procedures in certain Lutheran areas both resembled and differed from those in Geneva. While Reformed theologians such as Zwingli rejected clerical absolution because they believed it undercut the belief that Christ was the sole source of forgiveness, Luther, though eventually rejecting the sacramental nature of penance, approved of confession with absolution as a source of consolation and as a means of preparing for the worthy reception of the sacrament. In northern Germany, Lutherans continued to practice private confession through the eighteenth century. Before the celebration of communion, Lutherans were supposed to meet with their pastors to be questioned about their conduct and their knowledge of the faith, a practice not unlike the visitations in Geneva that preceded communion. Unlike its Catholic counterpart, Lutheran confession, sometimes called "private exploration,"[127] did not require confessing *all* one's sins to the confessor, and confessants were not to reveal the sordid details of their misdeeds. Lutheran confession appeared to put greater emphasis on the forgiveness of sins and consolation than the Catholic sacrament.[128] The church services in some Protestant areas, both Lutheran and Reformed, started including in the sixteenth century a collective confession of sins followed (though, as noted, not in Geneva) by an assurance of pardon.[129] The pastors' visitations and the Consistory's efforts to effect reconciliation and the confession of sins together had much in common with Lutherans' meetings with pastors and private confession before communion. Though Calvin no doubt would have objected, the Genevan laity may well have perceived the Consistory's readmitting people to the Supper as a form of absolution.

If in theory Lutheran confession was intended above all as a source of consolation, pastors could also use it as a means of imposing discipline by threatening to withhold participation in the sacrament. As noted in the introduction, in developing the confessionalization paradigm, Heinz Schilling has suggested that sin became criminalized in the later sixteenth century. He also found that Lutheran churches imposed humiliating acts of penitence in front of the entire congregation, akin to acts of reparation in Calvin's Geneva.[130] In theory, excommunication and discipline in Geneva and Lutheran Germany did not involve making satisfaction for one's sins, which Protestants considered a form of works-righteousness, but these humiliating acts, as a condition for being readmitted to communion, had much in common with Catholic expiatory rites. In the second half of the sixteenth century, Lutherans in many areas of Germany also established consistories, which, along with visitations, became important tools in the effort to inculcate discipline. Preliminary research suggests that issues pertaining to marriage were the most common cases brought before these spiritual courts, though conflicts with pastors, drunkenness, illicit sexuality, blasphemy, and other moral transgressions might also be heard. I have seen no evidence, however, that Lutheran consistories might summon people simply for quarreling.[131] By contrast, wherever they were established, consistories served as peacemakers in Reformed communities, consistently aiming to promote harmony and the reconciliation of people in disputes. It is almost certainly safe to say that few Lutheran areas—indeed very few Calvinist polities—had the institutional structures that could promote social discipline as effectively as the Genevan Consistory.[132]

Conclusion

W E RIGHTLY THINK OF John Calvin as a powerful intellectual and the greatest theologian of Reformed Protestantism. One must remember, however, that for the duration of his ministry this towering intellect dedicated the better part of at least one day a week to listening to the mundane and at times even petty stories about Genevans' quarrels, insults, blasphemies, illicit affairs, marital disputes, and superstitions. Far from viewing participation in the Consistory as a burden, Calvin viewed it as a pillar of his ministry. As we have seen in this study, the defeat of the Enfants de Genève in 1555 resulted in a palpable intensification of discipline in Geneva. The Consistory pursued certain "sins," such as blasphemy and forbidden Catholic practices, with greater rigor than before and broadened the roster of sins under its purview. After 1555, there was little room for deviation from Calvinist norms. Having already succeeded in changing Genevans' behavior in certain areas, after this victory the Consistory pursued more ambitiously and more intrusively the imposition of discipline in Calvin's adopted city.

As mentioned earlier, consistories have often been depicted, notably by defenders of the confessionalization paradigm, as the Reformed version of the Inquisition. There definitely were some important parallels between the Consistory of Geneva and the Inquisition. Both institutions aggressively attacked religious beliefs and practices considered unacceptable, and both shared the primary goal of reintegrating rather than punishing sinners. Ultimately both enjoyed considerable success in bringing about religious uniformity. Anyone in Italy or Spain who denied that humans have free will ran the risk of being called before the Inquisition, while people in Geneva who said prayers for the dead or refrained from eating meat during Lent were likely to be hauled before the Consistory. The Inquisition effectively quashed Protestantism in Italy and Spain in the sixteenth century, and by Calvin's death in 1564 Geneva was the most thoroughly Reformed community anywhere.

There were, however, some very important differences between the Roman and Spanish Inquisition and Geneva's Consistory. Investigations of the Inquisition occasionally resulted in executions, whereas the Consistory, not authorized to impose secular penalties, could only admonish and, at most, excommunicate miscreants. In regard to theology and religious practices, the Inquisition demanded compliance in word, deed, and thought, whereas the Consistory was generally content with conformity in word and deed. Much more than the Consistory, the Inquisition tried to examine the minds and souls of people, regulating belief as well as behavior, a fact that helps explain the Inquisition's willingness to use torture in certain cases to uncover heresy. But, as we have seen, the Consistory constantly exhorted Genevans to examine their own consciences in order to repent of their sins and to suppress (or at least channel) feelings of anger and hatred.[1] Calvin and the other assistants definitely sought the interiorization of Reformed piety among the laity. Consistories in many ways were less aggressive than inquisitions in dealing with religious nonconformity. This should come as no surprise, since Reformed morals courts were trying to root out certain religious practices that had long been accepted or even promoted by Roman Catholicism. Moreover, while Inquisitions in Spain and Italy generally functioned farther from the front lines of Protestantism, most consistories, including Geneva's, operated in cities that were in close proximity to Catholic areas, and excessive zeal in pursuing moral shortcomings could provoke some people simply to abandon the Reformed faith and move to a neighboring Catholic community. The Roman Inquisition was founded specifically to deal with heresy, whereas Geneva's Consistory did not have jurisdiction over the most serious cases of heresy—as noted, the anti-trinitarian Michael Servetus never appeared before the Consistory. The Inquisition had jurisdiction over cases of witchcraft on the grounds that it, as a form of devil worship, was the most heinous form of heresy or apostasy, whereas alleged cases of maleficent witchcraft were ordinarily not under the jurisdiction of the Consistory (though, as seen in chapter 5, it regularly convoked people for therapeutic magic).

Witchcraft and heresy notwithstanding, the Genevan Consistory was actually a much more intrusive institution than the Inquisition and had the ability to effect greater change on the laity and contemporary society in general. During the time of Calvin, the Consistory summoned every year an estimated 5 to 7 percent of the adult population of Geneva,[2] many times the percentage of people questioned by the Inquisitions in Italy and Spain. The Inquisition generally did not have jurisdiction over misdeeds unless heresy, blasphemy, apostasy, or abuse of sacraments was alleged. Entirely independent of the Inquisition were Catholic episcopal courts, which handled a range of cases, including matrimonial disputes. In Calvin's Geneva, by contrast, the Consistory had the power to convoke those suspected of deviating from Reformed mores in any way. The many people appearing in this study who were convoked for drunkenness, dissipation of assets, laziness, or simply quarrels would not have been summoned by either the Inquisition or an episcopal court.[3] Although it could not impose secular penalties, Calvin's Consistory wielded considerable power through its authority to admit and exclude people from the Supper. It was in settings like Geneva where consistories enjoyed their greatest success through a very intrusive surveillance of society.

Considered in all its aspects, the Consistory resembled much more the Catholic confessor than the inquisitor. John Eck, Luther's famous adversary, had said in 1523 that confession was the "nerve" of the Church, whereas Calvin insisted in the *Institutes* that discipline was the "nerve" of the Church.[4] Scholars have rightly suggested that the confessor was analogous to a physician for the soul whose ultimate goal was to reintegrate the sinner into the Christian community. Thomas Tentler argued that late medieval confession offered a comprehensive system of social control, which provided both discipline and consolation for sins.[5] Some scholars find that Tentler exaggerated the social effects of confession,[6] but the Consistory of Geneva clearly did provide not only discipline but also at least a degree of consolation for sins. Having jurisdiction over a vast range of moral infractions, the Consistory more often than not was less interested in punishing miscreants than in reconciling them with the community of the faithful, with God, and with themselves. While they were most concerned with public order and eschewed minute questioning to uncover all vices, members of the Consistory, like confessors, nonetheless encouraged the rank and file to examine their consciences before taking communion. By forcing parishioners to recognize their faults and by admitting or denying them access to the Supper, the Consistory filled an important void left by Protestants' elimination of the sacrament of penance. The Consistory's weekly meetings, however, almost surely had a much greater impact on the behavior of the laity than did the annual confession of Catholics. Thanks to its tenacious efforts to root out misbehavior and personal conflicts, the Consistory was nurturing a strong sense of community.

The issue of how men and women interacted with the Consistory is a very important one. The vast majority of those who appeared before the Consistory were defendants answering a summons,[7] though in certain circumstances, people could approach the Consistory to attempt to right certain wrongs. As we have seen, some plaintiffs successfully petitioned to enforce marriage engagements, and a small number of people successfully filed for divorce on the grounds of adultery or desertion; such possibilities, however, did not appear to benefit women more than men. On the one hand, in adjudicating sins, the Consistory by and large did not maintain a double standard based on class or, with the exception of certain cases of adultery, on gender, and it did not seem to give more weight to men's testimony than women's.[8] On the other hand, it did strongly defend a form of patriarchy in which women and children were to be subordinate to their husbands and fathers. Although Calvin and his colleagues rebuked men who beat their wives, their demands that women submit to and continue living with extremely violent husbands are quite shocking to modern sensibilities. All things considered, it would be difficult to argue that there was an alliance between women and the Consistory. Accordingly, I cannot accept entirely Scott Manetsch's very positive assessment of the Consistory's relationship with the most vulnerable members of society, including women: "church discipline was employed to protect the weakest members of Geneva's society, enforcing basic norms of fairness and humanity. Consistory members served as helpers for the poor, advocates for the weak, mediators for the estranged, and defenders of the exploited and abused."[9] Although it was undeniably an important mediator, as we have seen, there were real limits to the support that the Consistory provided to the vulnerable, be they battered women, abused children, or pregnant maidservants.

It is also important to stress, however, that Calvin and the other assistants espoused concepts of femininity and masculinity that seemed to dovetail more or less with the values of the laity. One can find a few examples of women who seemed to want to break out of the constraints placed on them. Obvious cases in point were the healer/physician Jeanne Fassoret and the would-be prophets Marguerite Gannerel and Marie de La Pierre; some of the women convoked for marital discord were surely rebelling against the overbearing authority of their husbands. For the most part, though, the patriarchal hierarchy espoused by the Consistory seemed to be widely accepted by both women and men.[10]

More broadly, it is fair to say that in overseeing morality, the Consistory of Geneva functioned in both a top-down and a bottom-up manner. On the one hand, the pastors and elders definitely could be heavy-handed in trying to enforce Reformed mores, and in the early 1550s a minority of Genevans clearly resented the growing power of Calvin and his supporters. Many people obviously thought that there was nothing wrong with, say, dancing, and the aggressive efforts to forbid giving the names of saints to babies needlessly alienated a good number of locals. On the other hand, the sheer volume of cases that came before the Consistory provides prima facie evidence that Genevans in general shared the ideals promoted by Calvin and his associates. Though it was very intrusive, the Consistory itself did not have the personnel to surveil closely the daily lives of residents. It depended upon the cooperation of the rank and file to identify people who were suspected of fornicating, gambling, praying to saints, and other activities deemed sinful. We have seen examples of Genevans who took it upon themselves to rebuke blasphemers, ordering them to immediately get on their knees and beg forgiveness from God. Residents of Calvin's Geneva were in effect practicing a form of neighborhood watch. Some of those who denounced others no doubt might have been trying to settle scores with their enemies rather bringing them back to the straight and narrow path, a danger that was not lost on the Consistory. It is evident, however, that for the most part Calvin and his colleagues espoused a brand of morality that the large majority of Genevans embraced.

The Link between Calvinism and Discipline?

Ronnie Hsia, who, in his broad examination of social discipline in the Reformation, notes that while all Christian groups promoted a degree of church discipline, among the major confessional groups "moral discipline was most effectively enforced among urban Calvinist communities, due to a high degree of . . . communal participation in the supervision."[11] The fact that the Consistory depended on informants among the population at large suggests that Genevans were "participating in a community of believers who felt a measure of responsibility for each other's behavior."[12] Although the special connection between the Reformed faith and discipline is widely accepted, we should pause to consider *why* Calvinists put substantially more emphasis on discipline than did other confessional groups, especially Lutherans. Here are a few ideas to try to explain the affinity between Reformed Protestantism and discipline.[13] Luther showed very little concern for discipline, no doubt because he thought that it smacked of works-righteousness, the idea that one is saved by works. As we saw in the introduction, Calvin was definitely not the first Reformed theologian to stress discipline. When he returned to Geneva in 1541, Calvin wanted to reform not only the church but also society as a whole. He wanted to create, as much as possible, a kingdom of Christ on earth. Martin Bucer, who had himself been influenced by Oecolampadius, mentored the young Calvin during his stay in Strasbourg and later authored what was probably the Reformation's most important treatise on discipline, tellingly entitled *The Kingdom of Christ* (*De Regno Christi*).[14] Although Lutherans and Reformed agreed on so many doctrines, they had notable different emphases. In Luther's *Small Catechism*, after a review of the Ten Commandments, the Apostles' Creed, the Lord's Prayer, baptism, the sacraments, and other prayers and duties, the first question asked of catechumens is "Do you believe that you are a sinner?"[15] By contrast, in the catechism that Calvin wrote for Geneva in 1545, after first affirming that the chief end of human life is to know God, the catechumen was to proclaim that God "created us and placed us in this world to be glorified in us. And it is indeed right that our life, of which himself is the beginning, should be devoted to his glory."[16]

The sharp contrast in these reformers' catechisms in many ways epitomized the key difference in what mattered most in faith to Lutherans and the Reformed. While justification by faith alone was the very essence of Christianity for Lutherans, Reformed theologians, though certainly adhering to that doctrine, gave more prominence to the reformation of life. Such a distinction can be seen in Amy Nelson Burnett's brilliant study of early Reformation debates on the sacraments, which pitted Luther and the Wittenberg Reformation against the South German/Swiss Reformation, including figures such as Bucer, Oecolampadius, and Zwingli. She argues quite plausibly that the latter were strongly influenced by the great humanist Erasmus of Rotterdam (1466–1536), who downplayed the external aspects of the sacraments and rather stressed their ability to foster inner spirituality, which in turn should lead to good moral conduct. Burnett maintains that for Luther the ultimate goal was to die a good Christian death, by which one felt assured of salvation through justification by faith. For Erasmus, who never broke with Rome, the essence of faith was to lead a good Christian life, a message that resonated with educated urban dwellers in the sixteenth century.[17] For the Reformed, the importance of glorifying God in one's life, of putting piety into action dovetailed nicely with discipline, which, in Geneva, was not just imposed by magistrates but also supported by the community at large.

There is also good reason to believe that on the eve of the Reformation, the prevailing mores of citizens of independent city-states fit especially well with the piety and discipline promoted by the Reformed faith. In the 1960s, Bernd Moeller wrote a provocative thesis that remains relevant. Looking at the early Reformation, Moeller noted the strong appeal that Reformed Protestantism, much more than Lutheranism, had to free imperial cities. In the late Middle Ages, such cities purportedly formed "sacred societies" whereby the whole urban community stood as a unit before God with no distinction between material welfare and salvation. In the mid-fifteenth century, for example, the city council of Basel decreed that "the government of every city is established primarily to augment and support the honor of God and to prohibit all injustice and especially the grossest sins and crimes."[18] Thus even before the birth of Protestantism, independent city-states worked for the salvation of their residents through the control of morality. With this urban communal ideal already in place, cities not surprisingly opted for the Reformed faith through the direct participation of the community, quite often by means of a popular vote, as was the case in Geneva. Zwingli, Bucer, and others vigorously promoted the collaboration of church and magistrates in their cities to create the kingdom of God. In the long run, however, Moeller found that the Reformation only slowed rather than prevented the eventual decline of German free cities and concluded: "The impressive theology of the first city reformers was not passed on to a loyal or thoughtful generation on German soil, but rather to Calvin in Geneva. Expanding from Geneva it conquered new regions and different conditions and set in motion those profound changes whose historical effects are still alive."[19]

The Consistory's Success

While Bern's support was crucial in preserving Geneva's independence, the success of the Consistory undoubtedly owed much to Calvin's personality, his legal background, his organizational skills, his zealous energy, and his ability to convince magistrates to embrace his brand of Christian piety and discipline. What ultimately set Geneva apart from other sixteenth-century polities was the independent system of church discipline that Calvin devised with the Consistory at its core. Backed by the state, this system was an inspiration to Reformed Protestants everywhere.

In his first publication about the Consistory in 1972, Robert Kingdon described that institution as imposing "a kind of reign of moral terror in Geneva,"[20] but he later greatly modified that view, describing the Consistory as more akin to a mandatory counseling service than a tribunal.[21] In fulfilling its important role in trying to settle quarrels, the Consistory definitely did have much in common with a counseling service; convinced that feelings of hatred were incompatible with Christian piety, Calvin and his colleagues exhorted feuding parties to reconcile and to forgive each other, especially before participating in communion. Many Genevans assimilated this idea and refrained from taking communion if they felt rancor toward anyone else. But the Consistory most definitely was a punitive institution, and having to appear before the Consistory could be daunting.[22] Especially after 1555, Calvin and his colleagues could be very heavy-handed, and their handling of certain cases seemed unduly harsh, most obviously when they felt that their own authority or reputations were being questioned. One also cannot avoid the conclusion that Calvin at times used the power of the Consistory to settle scores with people with whom he had clashed—as has been shown, the need to reconcile and to overcome animosity did not apply to the reformer himself!

Weighing all the evidence, we cannot avoid concluding that during Calvin's ministry, the Consistory enjoyed a remarkable degree of success in reforming the mores of the Genevan laity. The Scottish reformer and founder of Presbyterianism, John Knox, had an extended stay in Geneva (1556–1559) during which he drew inspiration from Calvin. Knox, who went a step further than Calvin and explicitly recognized discipline as the third mark of the true church, described Geneva as "the most perfect school of Christ . . . since the days of the apostles. In other places I confess Christ to be truly preached; but manners and religion so sincerely reformed, I have not yet seen in any other place."[23] For a number of years after 1555, religious and political leaders clearly were in lockstep in the implementation of discipline.[24] Even if the clergy was never fully satisfied with the laity's knowledge of the faith, Genevans assimilated Reformed teachings rather quickly. Calvin and his supporters enjoyed considerable success in dissuading residents from partaking in Catholic practices and in getting them to attend church and to learn the basic tenets of the faith. Genevans accepted, for example, that babies who died without baptism were not necessarily damned, that certain periods of the year did not require fasting, and that prayers for the deceased could not influence their souls' fate. If the link between Calvinism and capitalism is still debatable, the Reformed movement definitely championed hard work and condemned sloth. One may also posit that it contributed at least modestly to modernization by embracing a strict separation of the material and spiritual realms, thereby promoting a greater "disenchantment" of the world than did other confessions.[25]

The 1570s witnessed a decline in the numbers of people appearing before the Consistory and of exclusions from the Supper. Part of this almost certainly reflected an actual decline in the power of the Consistory. Starting in the 1570s, lay officials and the clergy were no longer entirely united on how to promote morality in Geneva. In the long run, perhaps the Consistory overplayed its hand; the stricter discipline that was introduced in the mid-1550s likely led to a negative reaction among some lay leaders.[26] Compared to Calvin's era, by the late sixteenth century the morals court's authority had definitely declined vis-à-vis the Council's, and in the early seventeenth century the politically powerful were able to avoid appearing before the Consistory, which even lost its monopoly on the power to excommunicate.[27]

That said, one should avoid equating a decline in consistorial activity with a failure to achieve the goals of reformers. Philip Benedict has rightly warned of the dangers of trying to measure the impact of Calvinist discipline through quantitative analysis, even when the extant data extend over decades or centuries.[28] Is it possible to view the decline in the volume of the Consistory's overall activity as evidence of its long-term success in effecting change in the behavior of Genevans? By the late sixteenth century, the Consistory was focusing especially on quarrels between neighbors and spouses. Indeed in 1605, a minister and elder proclaimed that "the goal of the Consistory is to appease discords so that all might live in peace and harmony."[29] In the 1590s, Luca Pinelli, a Jesuit priest who passed through Geneva, expressed a very favorable impression of the moral climate in the city even though he had nothing but contempt for the Reformed faith. During the three days he spent there, he said that he "never heard any blasphemy, swearing, or indecent language."[30] After a visit to Geneva in 1610, the German pastor Valentin Andreae wrote even more glowingly of Genevans' moral probity: "There is in that city . . . as a special ornament, a moral discipline which makes weekly investigations into the conduct and even the smallest transgressions of the citizens. . . . All cursing and swearing, gambling, luxury, strife, hatred, fraud, etc. are forbidden, while greater sins are hardly ever heard of. What a glorious ornament of the Christian religion is such a purity of morals!"[31] Although this statement was clearly hyperbole—Calvin and the Consistory definitely had not laid the foundation for a sinless society—it was nonetheless true that the morals court, to which Andreae was clearly alluding, had succeeded in rooting out some of the most egregious forms of "sinful" behavior. Illicit Catholic practices had all but disappeared, and Genevans had apparently curbed their penchant for blasphemy and luxuries. Authorities were less successful in rooting out illicit sexual activity,[32] dancing, and drunkenness, and to be sure there were still quarrels in early modern Geneva. Even so, more and more residents had assimilated the notion that harboring feelings of rancor toward others was incompatible with Christian piety, not to mention counter-productive to one's own emotional equilibrium.[33]

The disciplinary regime in Geneva based on the Consistory served as a model for Reformed Protestants everywhere. It would definitely have been difficult to duplicate in other settings the degree of discipline that this small republic experienced under the leadership of Calvin and with the strong support of magistrates, especially after 1555.[34] If we think of the Consistory's impact outside Geneva, Ray Mentzer quite deftly describes the example it set for Protestant Europe:

In the end, consistories across Europe flowed from a clear Genevan model, though modifications occurred regarding membership, the presiding officials, and the institution's relationship to the state. If scholars have come to understand that the consistory was far from a monolithic institution, they have also begun to reevaluate its core enterprise, stressing a pastoral as well as punitive purpose. Altogether, the consistory did more than impose discipline and chastise miscreants. It also provided counsel and fostered virtue, seeking to redirect sinners to the path of godliness through repentance and reform.[35]

Although Reformed populations invariably fell short of the goals of reformers, there is ample evidence that consistories and similar institutions successfully effected change in a number of areas of behavior, such as greater attempts to avoid interpersonal violence. The prolonged presence of such institutions habituated people to living, to a degree that varied from place to place, under the surveillance of the pastors and elders.[36]

Even if secular leaders were not always on the same page as religious reformers, one cannot escape the conclusion that there was a strong synergy between discipline and the Reformed movement. Geneva was simply the best example of this symbiotic relationship, and the Consistory that Calvin created there—the Reformed disciplinary institution par excellence—exerted an influence that went far beyond the confines of this small republic.

Introduction

1. *Registres du Conseil de Genève à l'époque de Calvin*, vol. 1, *Du 1ᵉʳ mai au 31 décembre 1536*, ed. Paule Hochuli Dubuis (Geneva: Droz, 2003), 11.

2. Bruce Gordon, *Calvin* (New Haven, CT: Yale University Press, 2009), 64–65.

3. E. William Monter, *Studies in Genevan Government (1536–1605)* (Geneva: Droz, 1964), 5.

4. To accommodate the growing population, a fourth church, Saint-Germain, was opened in 1557; *R.Consist.* 12: xi; AEG, RC 53: 234–35 (July 12, 1557).

5. Robert M. Kingdon, "Calvin and the Government of Geneva," in *Calvinus Ecclesiae Genevensis Custos*, ed. Wilhelm H. Neuser (Frankfurt: Peter Lang, 1984), 53–54; Henri Naef, *Les origines de la Réforme à Genève*, 2 vols. (Geneva: Droz, 1968), 1: 22–25; Alfred Perrenoud, *La population de Genève du seizième au début du dix-neuvième siècle: Étude démographique* (Geneva: Société d'histoire et d'archéologie de Genève, 1979), 30, 42; Louis Binz, *Vie religieuse et réforme ecclésiastique dans le diocèse de Genève pendant le Grand Schisme* (Geneva: Jullien, 1973), 499; Thomas A. Lambert, "Preaching, Praying and Policing the Reform in Sixteenth-Century Geneva," Ph.D. diss., University of Wisconsin-Madison, 1998, 198, 201.

6. *C.O.* 9: lii; 22: 7–8; Robert M. Kingdon, "Confessionalism in Calvin's Geneva," *Archiv für Reformationsgeschichte* 96 (2005): 109–16; Lambert, "Preaching," 171–76.

7. *C.O.* 10/1: 8; Lambert, "Preaching," 215.

8. *Registres du Conseil de Genève à l'époque de Calvin*, vol. 3, *Du 1ᵉʳ janvier au 31 décembre 1538*, ed. Sandra Coram-Mekkey (Geneva: Droz, 2006), 226–36; Christian Grosse, *Les rituels de la cène: Le culte eucharistique réformé à Genève (XVIᵉ–XVIIᵉ siècles)* (Geneva: Droz, 2008), 127–28.

9. On the creation of the Consistory, see Thomas A. Lambert, Introduction, *R.Consist.* 1: xvii–xxii.

10. Although the Consistory first met on December 6, 1541, its first extant records date from February 16, 1542. Cornelia Seeger has suggested that the typical meeting lasted three or four hours. *Nullité de mariage, divorce et séparation de corps à Genève au temps de Calvin: Fondements doctrinaux, loi et jurisprudence* (Lausanne: Société d'histoire de la Suisse romande, 1989), 220.

11. See Robert M. Kingdon, "Calvin and Discipline among French and Italians"; and Mario Turchetti, "Les refuges italiens et français, avec une note sur les 'Italiens' vus par Calvin"; both in *La Réforme en France et en Italie: Contacts, comparaisons et contrastes*,

ed. Philip Benedict, Silvana Seidel Menchi, and Alain Tallon (Rome: École française de Rome, 2007), 553–62, 563–76.

12. Philip Benedict, *Christ's Churches Purely Reformed: A Social History of Calvinism* (New Haven, CT: Yale University Press, 2002), 282.

13. John Calvin, *Institutes of the Christian Religion*, 7th ed., 2 vols., trans. John Allen (Philadelphia: Presbyterian Board of Christian Education, 1936), IV.xii.5, 2: 506–7; Scott M. Manetsch, *Calvin's Company of Pastors: Pastoral Care and the Emerging Reformed Church, 1536–1609* (Oxford: Oxford University Press, 2013), 189.

14. Calvin, *Institutes*, IV.xii.8, 2: 510.

15. Calvin, *Institutes*, IV.xii.10, 2: 512.

16. For a good introduction to this subject, see Christian Grosse, "Pour une histoire comparée des disciplines ecclésiastiques réformées en Suisse," in *Sous l'œil du consistoire: Sources consistoriales et histoire du contrôle sous l'Ancien Régime*, ed. Danièle Tosato-Rigo and Nicole Staremberg Goy (Lausanne: Études de Lettres, 2004), 13–28.

17. Amy Nelson Burnett, *The Yoke of Christ: Martin Bucer and Christian Discipline* (Kirksville, MO: Sixteenth Century Journal Publishers, 1994), esp. 180–207.

18. Robert M. Kingdon, "La discipline ecclésiastique vue de Zurich et Genève au temps de la réformation: l'usage de Matthieu 18, 15–17 par les réformateurs," *Revue de théologie et de philosophie* 51 (2001): 343–55.

19. See Walther Köhler, *Zürcher Ehegericht und Genfer Konsistorium*, 2 vols. (Leipzig: M. Heinsius Nachfolger, 1932–1942).

20. See Richard Feller, *Geschichte Berns*, vol. 1, *Von der Reformation bis zum Bauernkrieg 1516 bis 1653* (Bern: Herbert Lang, 1954).

21. Thomas Brodbeck, "'Christliche Zucht' durch die Chorgerichte: Die Alltagspraxis der Sittenzucht," in *Berns mächtige Zeit: Das 16. und 17. Jahrhundert neu entdeckt*, ed. André Holenstein (Bern: Stämpfli Verlag, 2006), 243–44; Heinrich Richard Schmidt, *Dorf und Religion: Reformierte Sittenzucht in Berner Landgemeinden der frühen Neuzeit* (Stuttgart: G. Fischer, 1995); Heinrich Richard Schmidt, "Morals Courts in Rural Berne during the Early Modern Period," in *The Reformation in Eastern and Central Europe*, ed. Karin Maag (Aldershot and Burlington: Scolar Press and Ashgate, 1997), 155–81. For a good overview of the conversion to Protestantism in Bern, see Martin Sallmann, "The Reformation in Bern," in *A Companion to the Swiss Reformation*, ed. Amy Nelson Burnett and Emidio Campi (Leiden: Brill, 2016), 126–69.

22. Regula Matzinger-Pfister, "L'introduction des consistoires dans le Pays de Vaud," in *Sous l'oeil*, ed. Tosato-Rigo and Staremberg Goy, 113–23.

23. Jeffrey R. Watt, *The Making of Modern Marriage: Matrimonial Control and the Rise of Sentiment in Neuchâtel, 1550–1800* (Ithaca, NY: Cornell University Press, 1992), 52. Each parish in the principality of Neuchâtel also had a *consistoire admonitif,* which comprised the pastor, some elders, and the highest local lay official. These consistories, which kept no records, had the power only to admonish and exclude people temporarily from the Supper. Michèle Robert, *"Que dorénavant chacun fuie paillardise, oisiveté, gourmandize . . .": Réforme et contrôle des moeurs: La justice consistoriale dans le*

Pays de Neuchâtel (1547–1848) (Neuchâtel: Alphil-Presses universitaires suisses, 2016), esp. 96–105.

24. Throughout this study, any reference simply to "the Council" alludes to the Small Council of Geneva.

25. Kingdon, "Discipline ecclésiastique." For an excellent brief introduction to the Chorgericht, see Brodbeck, "'Christliche Zucht,'" in *Berns mächtige Zeit*, ed. Holenstein, 241–48.

26. For a useful brief examination of the elders who served on Geneva's Consistory, see William Naphy, "Judges and Shepherds: Consistories," in *Judging Faith, Punishing Sin: Inquisitions and Consistories in the Early Modern World*, ed. Charles H. Parker and Gretchen Starr-LeBeau (Cambridge: Cambridge University Press, 2017), 104–15. Elders were paid quarterly for participating in Consistory meetings—at a rate of two sous per session—whereas pastors received no extra compensation. Lambert opines that this could mean that the scribe was more careful about marking as present the lay members than the pastors; Lambert, "Preaching," 264n96. Mention is made of the payment for the "quartemps d'autumpne" on Christmas Eve 1559. AEG, R.Consist. 16: 245.

27. Lambert, Introduction, *R.Consist.* 1: xxii.

28. On one occasion, the minutes make a specific reference to a vote. Jeanne Deschamps admitted to attending Mass and receiving the host while visiting family in Lyon, and the Consistory admonished her and by majority vote (*la plus grand voys*) decided to send her to the Council to be punished as it saw fit. *R.Consist.* 5: 309, 327; Lambert, "Preaching," 242.

29. Christian Grosse, "Inquisition and Consistory Records: Consistories," in *Judging Faith*, ed. Parker and Starr-LeBeau, 133; Danièle Tosato-Rigo, "Registres consistoriaux et images de l'exil," *Bulletin de la Société de l'Histoire du Protestantisme français* 153 (2007): 657.

30. *R.Consist.* 3: x, 207–8. An important exception to this rule occurred in January 1557 when Calvin himself served as legal counsel for his own brother, Antoine, who filed for divorce against his wife, Anne Le Fert. See the brief discussion of this case in chapter 4; *R.Consist.* 11: 328–29; AEG, RC 53, 16v (February 15, 1557); PC 1ère Sér. 610; Robert M. Kingdon, *Adultery and Divorce in Calvin's Geneva* (Cambridge, MA: Harvard University Press, 1995), 71–97.

31. In the eighteenth century, Genevans had the right to be defended by an attorney, a clear sign that by then the Consistory was in fact a court. By that time, however, this institution was also considerably weaker than in the sixteenth century and concentrated on illicit sexuality; Grosse, "Inquisition and Consistory Records: Consistories," 137–38.

32. Calvin and his associates did show some flexibility when dealing with agricultural laborers from the dependent countryside who were summoned as witnesses (but not as defendants). In July 1559, for example, a couple was summoned from a village under strong suspicion of fornication. When the couple denied the charges, members of the Consistory called for witnesses but decided that since the harvest was in full swing, they did not want the villagers to lose time coming all the way to Geneva to testify.

Accordingly, they mandated that a *châtelain*, an official who investigated crimes in the countryside, should question witnesses there and bring the testimony back to Geneva; AEG, R.Consist. 15: 120r–v.

33. Jeffrey R. Watt, "Introduction: Genève et le Consistoire en 1551," *R.Consist.* 6: xii–xiii.

34. Robert M. Kingdon (with Thomas M. Lambert), *Reforming Geneva: Discipline, Faith, and Anger in Calvin's Geneva* (Geneva: Droz, 2012), 21. According to his biographer Nicolas Colladon, Calvin delivered all the remonstrances and admonitions. Though this was not the case, evidence suggests that he probably gave the majority of them; *C.O.* 21: 66.

35. On the two forms of excommunication—temporary suspension from the Supper and full exclusion from the church—see Raymond A. Mentzer, "Marking the Taboo: Excommunication in French Reformed Consistories," in *Sin and the Calvinists: Morals Control and the Consistory in the Reformed Tradition*, ed. Raymond A. Mentzer (Kirksville, MO: Sixteenth Century Journal Publishers, 1994), 97–128. See also Grosse, *Rituels*, 388–91. The words "excommunication" or "excommunicated" rarely appear in the Consistory records.

36. Lambert, Introduction, *R.Consist.* 1: xxiii; Christian Grosse, "La 'réparation publique' réformée: ritualization de la penitence dans les Eglises calvinistes (XVI^c–XVIII^c siècle)," in *Calvinus Pastor Ecclesiae: Papers of the Eleventh International Congress on Calvin Research*, ed. Herman J. Selderhuis and Arnold Huijgen (Göttingen: Vandenhoeck and Ruprecht, 2016), 29–50; Watt, *Making Modern Marriage*, 63, 184. Scottish consistories often imposed sentences of public humiliation by obliging sinners to sit, often wearing sackcloth, on a raised "stool of repentance" near the pulpit and facing the congregation for a certain number of Sundays; Margo Todd, *The Culture of Protestantism in Early Modern Scotland* (New Haven, CT: Yale University Press, 2002), esp. 130–43; Margo Todd, "Tribunals and Jurisdictions: Consistories," in *Judging Faith*, ed. Parker and Starr-LeBeau, 48; Geoffrey Parker, "The 'Kirk By Law Established' and Origins of 'The Taming of Scotland': Saint Andrews," in *Sin and Calvinists*, ed. Mentzer, 180–81.

37. Kingdon, "Discipline ecclésiastique," 351; J. Wayne Baker, "In Defense of Magisterial Discipline: Bullinger's *Tractatus de Excommunicatione* of 1568," in *Heinrich Bullinger, 1504–1575, Gesammelte Aufsätze zum 400. Todestag*, 2 vols. (Zurich: Theologisher Verlag, 1975), 1: 148. See also Emidio Campi, "The Reformation in Zurich," in *Companion to Swiss Reformation*, ed. Burnett and Campi, 98.

38. Michael W. Bruening, "Francophone Territories Allied to the Swiss Confederation," in *Companion to Swiss Reformation*, ed. Burnett and Campi, 377–78.

39. Raymond A. Mentzer succinctly spells out some of these differences in "Local Contexts and Regional Variations: Consistories," in *Judging Faith*, ed. Parker and Starr-LeBeau, 15–27. In the same volume, see Philippe Chareyre, "Programs of Moral and Religious Reform: Consistories," 155–66; Philippe Chareyre, "On Consistorial Diversity," in *Emancipating Calvin: Culture and Confessional Identity in Francophone Reformed Communities. Essays in Honor of Raymond A. Mentzer*, ed. Karen E. Spierling,

Erik de Boer, and R. Ward Holder (Leiden: Brill, 2018), 60–80. Mentzer and Chareyre are the premier scholars of French consistories, and various works by them are cited numerous times throughout this book. On the Netherlands, see P.H.A.M. Abels and A.Ph.F. Wouters, *Nieuw en ongezien: Kerk en samenleving in de classis Delft en Delfland 1572–1621*, vol. 2, *De nieuwe samenleving* (Delft: Eburon, 1994).

40. Todd, *Culture of Protestantism*; Todd, "Tribunals and Jurisdictions: Consistories," 40–51; Michael F. Graham, *The Uses of Reform: "Godly Discipline" and Popular Behavior in Scotland and Beyond, 1560–1610* (Leiden: Brill, 1996), esp. 83–85; Parker, "'Kirk By Law Established,'" 159–97.

41. Norbert Elias, *The History of Manners*, trans. Edmund Jephcott (New York: Pantheon Books, 1982); Gerhard Oestreich, *Neostoicism and the Early Modern State*, trans. David McLintock, ed. Brigitta Oestreich and H. G. Koenigsberger, (Cambridge: Cambridge University Press, 1982).

42. Michel Foucault, *Discipline and Punish: The Birth of the Prison*, trans. Alan Sheridan (New York: Pantheon Books, 1977).

43. Max Weber, *The Protestant Ethic and the "Spirit" of Capitalism and Other Writings*, trans. and ed. Peter Baehr and Gordon C. Wells (New York: Penguin, 2002).

44. Max Weber, *Economy and Society: An Outline of Interpretive Sociology*, trans. Ephraim Fischoff et al., ed. Guenthe Roth and Claus Wittich (Berkeley: University of California Press, 1978), 588–89, 594; Philip S. Gorski, *The Disciplinary Revolution: Calvinism and the Rise of the State in Early Modern Europe* (Chicago: University of Chicago Press, 2003), 27–28.

45. Gorski, *Disciplinary Revolution*, x.

46. Gorski, *Disciplinary Revolution*, xv, xvi.

47. Gorski, *Disciplinary Revolution*, xvi. As we shall see, in Reformation Geneva it would be difficult to argue that most actions through the Consistory were more bottom-up than top-down.

48. Contemporaries in early modern Europe often equated consistories with inquisitions, clearly seen when a Dutchman complained that the Reformed Church in the Netherlands was establishing a Genevan-styled inquisition; Charles H. Parker and Gretchen Starr-LeBeau, introduction to *Judging Faith*, ed. Parker and Starr-LeBeau, 4–5.

49. For introductions to the theory of confessionalization, see Wolfgang Reinhard, "Pressures Towards Confessionalization? Prolegomena to a Theory of the Confessional Age," in *The German Reformation*, ed. C. Scott Dixon (Oxford: Blackwell, 1999), 172–92; Heinz Schilling, "Confessional Europe," in *Handbook of European History, 1400–1600: Late Middle Ages, Renaissance and Reformation*, 2 vols., ed. Thomas A. Brady, Heiko Oberman, and James D. Tracy (Leiden: Brill, 1995), 1: 641–70. Works that weigh the applicability of this theory to different settings include: Benjamin J. Kaplan, *Calvinists and Libertines: Confessions and Community in Utrecht, 1578–1620* (Oxford: Clarendon Press, 1995); James R. Farr, "Confessionalization and Social Discipline in France, 1530–1685," *Archiv für Reformationsgeschichte* 94 (2003): 276–93; Marc R. Forster, "With and Without Confessionalization: Varieties of Early Modern

German Catholicism," *Journal of Early Modern History* 1 (1998): 315–43; Philip Benedict, "Confessionalization in France? Critical Reflections and New Evidence," in *Society and Culture in the Huguenot World, 1559–1685*, ed. Raymond A. Mentzer and Andrew Spicer (Cambridge: Cambridge University Press, 2002), 44–61; Joel F. Harrington and Helmut Walser Smith, "Confessionalization, Community, and State-building in Germany, 1555–1870," *Journal of Modern History* 69 (1997): 77–101; Allyson M. Poska, "Confessionalization and Social Discipline in the Iberian World," *Archiv für Reformationsgeschichte* 94 (2003): 308–19.

50. Gorski, *Disciplinary Revolution*, xvii. In his defense, Schilling sees Calvinism as putting special emphasis on discipline which, he claims, contributed significantly to the "making of the modern mind." *Civic Calvinism in Northwestern Germany and the Netherlands, Sixteenth to Nineteenth Centuries* (Kirksville, MO: Sixteenth Century Journal Publishers, 1991), 40.

51. On the Inquisition in its various forms, see Edward Peters, *Inquisition* (New York: Free Press, 1988); Francisco Bethencourt, *L'Inquisition à l'époque moderne: Espagne, Italie, Portugal XVe–XIXe siècle* (Paris: Fayard, 1995). On the Roman Inquisition, see especially Andrea Del Col, *L'Inquisizione in Italia: Dal XII al XXI secolo* (Milan: Mondadori, 2010); Andrea Del Col, "Alcune osservazioni sui processi inquisitoriali come fonti storiche," *Metodi e ricerche* 13 (1994): 85–105; Adriano Prosperi, *Tribunali della coscienza: Inquisitori, confessori, missionari* (Turin: Giulio Einaudi, 1996); John Tedeschi, *The Prosecution of Heresy: Collected Studies on the Inquisition in Early Modern Italy* (Binghamton, NY: Medieval and Renaissance Texts and Studies, 1991). For good introductions to the Spanish Inquisition, see Henry Kamen, *The Spanish Inquisition: A Historical Revision* (New Haven, CT: Yale University Press, 1997); *Inquisición española: Poder politico y control social*, ed. Bartolomé Bennassar (Barcelona: Editorial Crítica, 1981); Helen Rawlings, *The Spanish Inquisition* (Oxford: Blackwell, 2006). Still valuable is Henry Charles Lea's *A History of the Inquisition of Spain*, 4 vols. (London: Macmillan, 1906–1907).

52. See Andrea Del Col, "Alcune osservazioni" and "I processi dell'Inquisizione come fonte: Considerazioni diplomatiche e storiche," *Annuario dell'Istituto storico italiano per l'età moderna e contemporanea* 35–36 (1983–1984): 33–49. For a very different take, see Carlo Ginzburg, "The Inquisitor as Anthropologist," in *Clues, Myths, and the Historical Method*, trans. John and Anne C. Tedeschi (Baltimore: Johns Hopkins University Press, 1989), 156–64. For a good brief discussion of the problems and potential of Inquisition records, see Kim Siebenhüner, "Inquisition and Consistory Records: Inquisitions," in *Judging Faith*, ed. Parker and Starr-LeBeau, 140–52.

53. Judith Pollmann, "Off the Record: Problems in the Quantification of Calvinist Church Discipline," *Sixteenth Century Journal* 33 (2002): 423–38.

54. Christian Grosse, "Rationalité graphique et discipline ecclésiastique: Les registres du consistoire de Genève à l'épreuve (XVIe–XVIIIe siècles)," *Bulletin de la Société de l'Histoire du Protestantisme Français* 153 (2007): 550.

55. See, for example, *R.Consist.* 3: notes 1273, 1275, 1276; Christian Grosse, "Inquisition and Consistory Records: Consistories," in *Judging Faith*, ed. Parker and Starr-LeBeau, 129–32. There are two extant records of the meeting of Geneva's Consistory that date from October 13, 1547. Although there are variations in details, the essence of the accounts is the same, including most importantly the decisions rendered; *R.Consist.* 3: 214–20.

56. See Grosse's good defense of using these registers; "Inquisition and Consistory Records," 133.

57. For similar findings for Lausanne, see Sylvie Moret Petrini, "Ces Lausonnois qui 'pappistent': Ce que nous apprennent les registres consistoriaux lausannois (1538–1540)," *Revue historique vaudoise* 119 (2011): 148.

58. Jean-François Bergier declared that the registers of the Consistory are "la meilleure source d'une histoire des moeurs, voire d'une histoire de la société"; *Registres de la Compagnie des Pasteurs de Genève au temps de Calvin, 1546–1553*, ed. Robert M. Kingdon and Jean-François Bergier, 2 vols. (Geneva: Droz, 1962–1964), 1: 18n2; Lambert, "Preaching," 12n20.

59. William G. Naphy, *Calvinism and the Consolidation of the Genevan Reformation* (Manchester: Manchester University Press, 1994); Kingdon, *Adultery*.

60. Grosse, *Rituels*; Karen E. Spierling, *Infant Baptism in Reformation Geneva: The Shaping of Community, 1536–1564* (Aldershot and Burlington, VT: Ashgate, 2005).

61. Manetsch, *Calvin's Company*. Scholars are using these sources in some rather unexpected ways. The musicologist Melinda Latour very effectively drew on the registers of the Consistory as the basis for an article on songs in Calvin's Geneva; "Disciplining Song in Sixteenth-Century Geneva," *Journal of Musicology* 32 (2015): 1–39.

62. Robert M. Kingdon, "The Control of Morals in Calvin's Geneva," in *The Social History of the Reformation*, ed. Lawrence P. Buck and Jonathan W. Zophy (Columbus: Ohio State University Press, 1972), 3–16.

63. E. William Monter, "The Consistory of Geneva, 1559–1569," *Bibliothèque d'Humanisme et Renaissance* 38 (1976): 467–84.

64. Kingdon (with Lambert), *Reforming Geneva*. Wallace McDonald, another key collaborator on the Consistory project, performed the invaluable service of reading aloud the manuscript to Professor Kingdon and conveying the latter's reactions to Lambert.

Chapter 1

1. The only exception was Jacques Bernard, a former Genevan Franciscan who served as pastor in the city during Calvin's absence (1538–1542) and then mostly in the village of Satigny from 1542 until his death in 1559; *R.Consist.* 1: 2n6; AEG, RC 35: 447v (December 30, 1541); *Registres de la Compagnie*, 1: 59.

2. Robert Wiblé, "Antoine Froment: Le 'Livre de la Sédition,'" *Bulletin de la Société d'Histoire et d'Archéologie de Genève* 15 (1974): 272; quoting Froment's unpublished *Livre de la Sédition;* Lambert, "Preaching," 484.

3. *R.Consist.* 2: 157–59. For the text of the *Franchises,* issued by the bishop in 1387, see *Les sources du droit du canton de Genève,* ed. Émile Rivoire and Victor van Berchem, 4 vols. (Aarau: H.R. Sauerländer, 1927–1935), 1: 201–3.

4. *R.Consist.* 2: 248; AEG, RC 41: 116v, 119, 133v (June 18, 21, 22, 28, 1546); Henry Fazy, "Procès et démêlés à propos de la compétence disciplinaire du Consistoire (1546–1547)," in *Procédures et documents du XVIe siècle (1546–1547),* ed. Henry Fazy (Geneva and Basel: H. Georg, 1886), 8–10.

5. *R.Consist.* 3: 20–21; Fazy, "Procès et démêlés," 13–14.

6. See Lambert, "Preaching," 270.

7. AEG, RC 42: 68 (March 25, 1547); Fazy, "Procès et démêlés," 17.

8. AEG, RC 42: 70v (March 29, 1547); Fazy, "Procès et démêlés," 19.

9. *R.Consist.* 3: 140–41 (esp. n. 879); AEG, RC 42: 154v (June 24, 1547); Fazy, "Procès et démêlés," 21–22, 31, 45.

10. *R.Consist.* 3: 207–9; Fazy, "Procès et démêlés," 23–34, 67–69. His daughter Françoise likewise showed repentance for her previous actions.

11. *R.Consist.* 2: 191–92, 202–3.

12. "Not ne vollin pas tan avey de metre," which means, "Nous ne voulons pas avoir tant de maîtres"; Henry Fazy, "Procès de Jacques Gruet," in *Procédures,* ed. Fazy, 5–6; *R. Consist.* 2: 191n459.

13. *C.O.* 12: 546 (epistle 921); Fazy, "Procès de Jacques Gruet," 15n2.

14. *C.O.* 12: 547 (epistle 921); Fazy, "Procès de Jacques Gruet," 17.

15. The original *procès criminel* (AEG, PC 1ère Sér. 131) is in poor condition and can no longer be consulted. Henry Fazy, who wrote an analysis of this case and reproduced the pertinent documents, indicated that the fragment on which Gruet wrote these thoughts is not extant; we know about them only from documents detailing allegations against him and from a letter Calvin wrote to Viret; Fazy, "Procès de Jacques Gruet," 12.

16. Fazy, "Procès de Jacques Gruet," 17.

17. Fazy, "Procès de Jacques Gruet," 1–141; Amédée Roget, *Histoire du peuple de Genève depuis la Réforme jusqu'à l'Escalade,* 7 vols. (Geneva: Jullien, 1870–1883 [repr. Nieuwkoop: B. de Graaf, 1976]), 2: 289–312, 324–29.

18. *R.Consist.* 2: 155–56. See chapter 7 for more on the conflict between Calvin and Ameaux. Ameaux received the first fully documented divorce in Reformation Geneva; see Kingdon, *Adultery,* 31–70.

19. AEG, PC 1ère Sér. 423 (quotation); PC 2e Sér. 702; *R.Consist.* 2: 153n244; RC 41: 52v–53, 55, 72, 73v (March 16, 19; April 13, 15, 1546). De La Mare nonetheless later became a minister in territory under the suzerainty of Bern. On de La Mare's dismissal, see Naphy, *Calvin,* 59–68. On the Ameaux affair, see John-Barthélemy-Gaïfre Galiffe, *Nouvelles pages d'histoire exacte soit le procès de Pierre Ameaux conseiller d'état de Genève et ses incidents 1546* (Geneva: Vaney, 1863).

20. Grosse, *Rituels*, 365.

21. *R.Consist.* 5: 107.

22. AEG, PC 1ᵉʳᵉ Sér. 485. See also Roget, *Histoire du peuple*, 3: 283.

23. *R.Consist.* 9: 30–31; "il vouloit retorner à la papaulté pour faire bonne chiere, car icy on ne risoit point."

24. AEG, RC 41: 104 (May 31, 1546); cited in Lambert, "Preaching," 368; Manetsch, *Calvin's Company*, 175–76.

25. AEG, PC 1ᵉʳᵉ Sér. 424. *Torticol* literally meant "the neck backward" but at this time also figuratively meant "false devout, hypocrite"; *Dictionnaire de l'Académie française*, (Paris: J. B. Coignard, 1694), SV "torticolis."

26. *R.Consist.* 7: 72.

27. *R.Consist.* 7: 133–34; "mechant heretique"; "faict plus de scandalle que luy."

28. *La France protestante ou vies des protestants français*, ed. Eugène Haag and Emile Haag, 2d ed., 6 vols (Paris: Sandoz and Fischbacher, 1877–1888), 4: 260–63; Manetsch, *Calvin's Company*, 310.

29. AEG, RC 47: 174 (November 3, 1553); *C.O.* 21: 559.

30. AEG, RC 47: 179v–180 (November 13, 1553); *C.O.* 21: 561–62.

31. *R.Consist.* 8: 200–1. Though named an assistant to the Consistory in February 1552, Vulliet had himself been reproached by the Consistory many times for a variety of misdeeds including drunkenness, fornication, blasphemy, and insolence toward pastors; 7: 4n18.

32. *R.Consist.* 9: 181, 290, 315, 322, 326; 10: 8; AEG, RC Part. 9: 4v, 33 (February 18; April 8, 1555). A few months later, the Council rejected his request to return to Geneva; RC 50: 44v (November 22, 1555).

33. *R.Consist.* 9: 316.

34. Geneva was much more open to receiving refugees than other Protestant cities, a trend that has been attributed to the fact that in Geneva, "unlike in cities such as Basel, the guilds, always hostile to the threat of increased competition on the labor market, were not represented in municipal government." Philip Benedict, "Calvin and the Transformation of Geneva," in *John Calvin's Impact on Church and Society, 1509–2009*, ed. Martin Ernst Hirzel and Martin Sallmann (Grand Rapids, MI: William B. Eerdmans, 2009), 5.

35. *C.O.* 51: 537; 42: 70; 53: 270; cited in Rodolphe Peter, "Genève dans la prédication de Calvin," in *Calvinus Ecclesiae Genevensis Custos: Die Referate Des Congrès Internationalen Kongresses für Calvinforschung vom 6. Bis 9. September 1982 in Genf*, ed. Wilhelm H. Neuser (Bern: Peter Lang, 1984), 29–30; Benedict, "Calvin and Transformation of Geneva," 1.

36. AEG, RC 46: 102 (November 26, 1551). With the approval of the Company of Pastors, on March 31, 1552, the Council named Celse Martinengo of Brescia the first pastor for the Italian community; Roget, *Histoire du peuple*, 3: 221n1.

37. See Jeannine E. Olson, *Calvin and Social Welfare: Deacons and the "Bourse française"* (Selinsgrove, PA: Susquehanna University Press, 1989), 34.

38. Roget, *Histoire du peuple*, 3: 135–37.

39. See Jean-Antoine Gautier, *Histoire de Genève, des origines à l'année 1691*, 7 vols. (Geneva: Rey et Malavallon, 1896–1914), 3: 415–16.

40. On the Council of Two Hundred, see Lilian Mottu-Weber, Anne-Marie Piuz, and Bernard Lescaze, *Vivre à Genève autour de 1600*, vol. 2: *Ordre et désordres* (Geneva: Slatkine, 2006), 2: 61–77.

41. AEG, RC 47: 53v–54v (April 11, 1553); *C.O.* 21: 539; Roget, *Histoire du peuple*, 3: 288. On the office of lieutenant, see Mottu-Weber, Piuz, and Lescaze, *Vivre à Genève*, 2: 54, 126–27, 130–31, 135. Created in the fifteenth century, the *dizeniers* at first had a primarily military role—to make sure that citizens had sufficient arms in case of attack—but took on moral and religious functions as well, as the Consistory relied on them for surveillance, among other things; Grosse, *Rituels*, 250–52.

42. Lambert, "Preaching," 493–96.

43. *R.Consist.* 6: 204, 206.

44. *R.Consist.* 6: 218.

45. *R.Consist.* 8: 238.

46. AEG, RC 43: 280, 288 (January 11, 22, 1549); *R.Consist.* 5: 230n1581.

47. *R.Consist.* 5: 298; "Sieur Calvin n'est pas son prinse."

48. Calvin favored having communion monthly but went along with magistrates' wishes to follow the practice in Bern of celebrating the Supper just four times a year (celebrated each time at two different services for all three churches in the city); Grosse, *Rituels*, esp. 130, 137–40, 286–94. On the liturgy in Geneva concerning the celebration of the Supper, see Grosse, 140–51, 198–240.

49. *R.Consist.* 1: 22.

50. AEG, RC 37: 37v (March 19, 1543); Grosse, *Rituels*, 358. On resistance to the Consistory up to 1555, see Grosse, 358–69.

51. In August 1550, the Consistory asked that the Council authorize the visitation before the upcoming celebration of the Supper in September, noting that the visitations were to take place twice a year. The next day the Council decided to delay the second visitation until Christmas, since it would be easier to find people at that time. On December 15 of that year the Small Council authorized that visitation and decreed that the lay Consistory officials should take part in it; *R.Consist.* 5: 187n1296; 267; AEG, RC 45: 78v, 148v (August 29, December 15, 1550).

52. The first mention of the visitations is on April 3, 1550, when the Council declared that the pastors were to go out accompanied by a *dizenier* and by an elder to go house to house to determine who was eligible to participate in the Supper; AEG, RC 44: 352v (April 3, 1550); *R.Consist.* 5: 57n398.

53. In April 1564, the Consistory cited Cathérine, the widow of Regnauld Reguengne because "elle n'a point voullu comparoir devant Monsieur Colladon à la visite, combien qu'elle eust esté remise par le dizenier plusieurs foys"; AEG, R.Consist. 21: 43v. Though visitations in the dependent countryside began already in 1546 (AEG, RC 69: 344v, 356v [January 11, 25, 1546]), they did not appear to be conducted as systematically as in

the city. Christian Grosse has found that they became sporadic beginning in 1574, and the rural visitations were not conducted at all for the years 1582–1605; "'Il y avoit eu trop grande rigueur par cy-devan': La discipline ecclésiastique à Genève à l'époque de Théodore de Bèze," in *Théodore de Bèze (1519–1605): Actes du colloque de Genève (septembre 2005)*, ed. Irena Backus (Geneva: Droz, 2007), 60; *Rituels*, 408–12.

54. See Grosse, *Rituels*, esp. 400–7. The ecclesiastical ordinances of 1561 decreed that the visitations were to take place once a year, before the celebration of the Supper at Easter. For the years 1551–1560, the number of cases heard by Consistory peaked during the months of March, April, and May, indicating that the time surrounding Easter continued to be a period when one was to reflect upon and confess one's sins; Grosse, 421–22. On the Supper, see also Bernard Roussel, "Comment faire la cène? Rite et retour aux Ecritures dans les Eglises réformées du Royaume de France au XVIᵉ siècle," in *Les retours aux Ecritures, fondamentalismes présents et passés*, ed. Evelyne Patlagean and Alain Le Boulluec (Louvain and Paris: Peeters, 1993), 195–216; Bernard Roussel, "'Faire la Cène' dans les Eglises réformées du Royaume de France au seizième siècle (ca. 1550–ca. 1575)," *Archives de sciences sociales des religions* 85 (1994): 99–119; Lee Palmer Wandel, *The Eucharist in the Reformation: Incarnation and Liturgy* (Cambridge: Cambridge University Press, 2006). For a provocative study on the revolutionary impact of Calvinist ideas on the eucharist, see Christopher Elwood, *The Broken Body: The Calvinist Doctrine of the Eucharist and the Symbolization of Power in Sixteenth-Century France* (Oxford: Oxford University Press, 1999).

55. Grosse, *Rituels*, esp. 401, 405. Noting the connections among visitations, the confession of sins, and the Supper, Herman J. Selderhuis wrote quite aptly that for Calvin "the confessional was not thrown out, but was relocated to the living room." *John Calvin: A Pilgrim's Life*, trans. Albert Gootjes (Downers Grove, IL: IVP Academic, 2009), 88. An apprentice from Basel who lived in Geneva in the early 1560s described the visitation in this manner: "The ministers gather together the residents of six to eight households, both young and old, to interrogate and examine them, requiring them to give an account of their faith and the *Catechism* before they take the Lord's Supper." A. Gautier, "Un jeune Bâlois à Genève au XVIᵉ siècle," *Mémoires et documents publiés par la Société d'Histoire et d'Archéologie de Genève* 17 (1872): 412–16; quoted in Manetsch, *Calvin's Company*, 282.

56. *R.Consist.* 6: 99. The Consistory issued remonstrances to her and obliged her to beg for mercy from God.

57. *R.Consist.* 12: 105; RC 53: 99 (April 12, 1557).

58. *R.Consist.* 12: 116.

59. According to the historian Amédée Roget, "la plus grosse épine dans les rapports de l'Église et de l'État était toujours la question de la Cène." *L'Église et l'État à Genève du vivant de Calvin: Étude d'histoirie politico-ecclésiastique* (Geneva: Fick, 1867), 57; *R. Consist.* 3: 47n308.

60. *R.Consist.* 6: 50–51, n. 315; 56–57, 61; AEG, RC 45: 249r–v (April 13, 1551). The jail sentence was probably because he reputedly struck a man who reproached him for his blasphemy.

61. On the office of *châtelain*, see André-Luc Poncet, *Châtelains et sujets dans la campagne genevoise (1536–1792)* (Geneva: Presses Universitaires Romandes, 1973); Mottu-Weber, Piuz, and Lescaze, *Vivre à Genève*, 2: 136, 138.

62. *R.Consist.* 6: 66–67; AEG, RC 45: 249v (April 13, 1551).

63. *R.Consist.* 8: 42.

64. AEG, RC 47: 56r–v, 57 (April 14, 17, 1553).

65. AEG, RC: 47: 52v (April 10, 1553); *C.O.* 21: 539; Roget, *Histoire du peuple*, 3: 282.

66. *R.Consist.* 6: 19–20, 115–16, 123, 223; AEG, RC 46: 1, 123, 128, 129v (July 6; December 25, 31, 1551; January 1, 1552). See also Jacques Auguste Galiffe, John-Barthélemy-Gaïfre Galiffe, Eugène Ritter, and Louis Dufour-Vernes, eds., *Notices généalogiques sur les familles genevoises, depuis les premiers temps, jusqu'à nos jours*, 7 vols. (Geneva: J. Barbezat, 1829–1895), 1: 429; Christian Grosse, *L'excommunication de Philibert Berthelier: Histoire d'un conflit d'identité aux premiers temps de la Réforme genevoise (1547–1555)* (Geneva: Société d'Histoire et d'Archéologie de Genève, 1995), 105–6, 118; *R.Consist.* 2: 71n200; Naphy, *Calvin*, 170, 181–82; Roget, *Histoire du people*, 3: 149–51.

67. Perrin, Ami, in *Dictionnaire historique de la Suisse*, ed. Marco Jorio et al. (Bern: Fondation du Dictionnaire historique de la Suisse, 1998-2014), https://hls-dhs-dss.ch/fr/.

68. *R.Consist.* 6: 7, 48–49, 52–53. Berthelier and Calvin had gotten into a rather amusing conflict back in the fall of 1547. One day Calvin apparently complained from the pulpit about people coughing during a sermon. After the service, Berthelier derisively told others outside the church of Saint-Pierre that if Calvin forbade them to cough, they were nonetheless free to pass gas and belch in church ("Calvin ne veut pas que nous toussissons mais nous petrons et roterons"). Berthelier admitted that a few days before making these comments, he burped while passing Calvin in the street. Calvin became angry and declared that he had done this on purpose, although Berthelier claimed that his belch was involuntary. This disagreement with the reformer resulted in an inconclusive criminal investigation; AEG, PC 1ère Sér. 449.

69. Roget, *Histoire du peuple*, 3: 226–27; AEG, RC 46: 148v, 252v (February 7, 11, 1552).

70. Roget, *Histoire du peuple*, 3: 265–66; AEG, RC 46: 269, 270v, 273v, 280v (September 8, 9, 19; October 3, 1552).

71. Roget, *Histoire du peuple*, 3: 249; AEG, RC 46: 300v (November 8, 1552).

72. *R.Consist.* 7: 158–59; AEG, RC 46: 282v–83 (October 7, 1552); see Roget, *Histoire du people*, 3: 244–45.

73. AEG, RC 46: 283v–84v, 286 (October 8, 9, 13, 1552); *R.Consist.* 7: 186, 205–6.

74. Roget, *Histoire du peuple*, 3: 275–76. Perrin was one of very few people to serve contemporaneously as syndic and *capitaine*.

75. See, for example, AEG, RC 47: 135 (August 17, 1553).

76. AEG, Mss. Hist. 293: 75. On the office of *auditeur*, see Mottu-Weber, Piuz, and Lescaze, *Vivre à Genève*, 2: 127.

77. AEG, RC 47: 147v (September 7, 1553). See also 47: 144r–v, 145, 146, 148v, 151v, 155, 174v, 175v–176v, 177, 197v–98, 203r–v (September 1–2, 4, 8, 12, 18; November 3, 7, 9; December 21, 1553; January 2, 1554).

78. *R.Consist.* 9: 36–37; 10: 112–13. For a summary of the conflicts between Berthelier and the Consistory, see Grosse, *Excommunication*, esp. 72–97.

79. Galiffe et al., eds., *Notices généalogiques*, 2: 160; Roget, *Histoire du peuple*, 4: 197–202.

80. Roget, *Histoire du peuple*, 4: 230–31. See also Calvin's letter to Bullinger; *C.O.* 15: 678–79 (epistle 2243).

81. AEG, RC 49: 68v, 71–72v, 74, 76v–77, 77v (May 6, 9, 13, 14, 16, 1555); Roget, *Histoire du peuple*, 4: 227–33, 238, 241.

82. Roget, *Histoire du peuple*, 4: 267.

83. Roget, *Histoire du peuple*, 4: 249–55, 266–7; AEG, RC 49: 78r–v, 79–80 (May 16, 17, 19, 1555).

84. Roget, *Histoire du peuple*, 4: 249–55, 266–67, 273–76, 280–86; AEG, RC 49: 78r–v, 79–80, 85v, 86v, 96, 106v, 107v–108, 110r–v (May 16, 17, 19, 24, 25; June 3, 17, 18, 20, 1555). On the importance of the baton, see Bernard Lescaze, "Le bâton syndical de Genève: Sur un insigne du pouvoir au XVIe siècle," *Genava: revue d'histoire de l'art et d'archéologie* 20 (1972): 217–30.

85. *C.O.* 15: 686 (epistle 2245); Roget, *Histoire du peuple*, 4: 287.

86. AEG, RC 49: 117v (June 27, 1555); Roget, *Histoire du peuple*, 4: 281–82, 286–87. In and of itself, capital punishment for taking part in a drunken brawl strikes us as incredibly cruel and excessive, but the ineptitude of the executioner made it even worse. The executioner did not have sufficient strength to carry out a quick execution, and he apparently needed to hack at the Comparets' necks numerous times before succeeding, prolonging their agony.

For botching the execution, the executioner Jean Blanc was jailed for four days and then banished for a year and a day; AEG, RC 49: 122 (July 4, 1555); Roget, *Histoire du peuple*, 4: 281–82, 287–88. Far from showing any sympathy, Calvin was convinced that the protracted pain endured by the Comparets at the hands of the executioner was a form of divine judgment. He wrote to Farel on July 24, "Je suis persuadé que ce n'est pas sans une volonté spéciale de Dieu, qu'ils ont subi, en dehors du verdict des juges, un long tourment, sous la main du bourreau." *C.O.* 15: 693 (epistle 2250); trans. Roget, 4: 288.

87. *C.O.* 15: 693 (epistle 2250); trans. Roget, *Histoire du peuple*, 4: 292–93. See Sara Beam, "Rites of Torture in Reformation Geneva," *Past and Present*, suppl 7: *Ritual and Violence: Natalie Zemon Davis and Early Modern France* (2012): 197–219.

88. AEG, RC 49: 152v–153, 158v, 181 (August 6, 15; September 11, 1555); Roget, *Histoire du peuple*, 4: 298–300, 312.

89. Roget, *Histoire du peuple*, 4: 318–22. For brief discussions of the conflicts between Calvin and Bern, see Jeffrey R. Watt's introductions to the following volumes of the Consistory registers: *R.Consist.* 6: ix–xii; 7: xii–xiv; 9: xvi–xix; 10: x–xii.

90. On the course of events of 1555, see Roget, *Histoire du peuple*, 4: 245–336; Gautier, *Histoire de Genève*, 3: 563–645; François Bonivard, *Advis et devis de l'ancienne et nouvelle police de Genève* (Geneva: Revillod, 1865), 136–48; Naphy, *Calvin*, 194–99. According to Bernard Lescaze, this agitation effected a dramatic transformation in Genevan

government, resulting in more power concentrated in the hands of fewer people—the power of the Small Council increased while that of the General Council declined; Mottu-Weber, Piuz, and Lescaze, *Vivre à Genève*, 2: 61.

91. This expansion is reflected in the sheer size of the volumes immediately after the defeat of the Perrinistes. Volume 10 (1555) was 90 folios long (resulting in 300 pages, including annotations, in the published tome), whereas volume 11 (1556) numbered 108 folios (354 pages) compared to 157 folios (430 pages) for volume 12 (1557).

92. Grosse, *Rituels*, 381.

93. From 1570–1609, the average weekly number appearing went down to sixteen, indicating that Beza and his colleagues had overreached; Manetsch, *Calvin's Company*, 209–10.

94. For the years 1542–1609, Manetsch found a total of 9,256 excommunications. The suspensions started increasing after 1555, "reaching around 300 suspensions in 1559, and spiking at 681 suspensions in 1568." This was followed by a sharp decline in the early 1570s. For the years 1575–1609, suspensions averaged two per week, which is lower than that for the last decade of Calvin's ministry. He rightly notes the difficulties in quantifying excommunications; *Calvin's Company*, 199n88. Though the precise numbers cannot be known, the overall trends that Manetsch traces are no doubt accurate. On the basis of the Consistory records, Grosse found the following numbers of suspensions: 103 in 1555, 189 in 1556, 284 each in 1557 and 1558, and the peak during Calvin's ministry, 358 in 1563. These figures compare to only twelve and twenty-four for 1546 and 1547, respectively; *Rituels*, 384.

95. There were twenty-four such requests on March 31, 1556 and 33 two days later. Prior to Pentecost 1561, the Consistory heard forty-eight requests on May 20, 40 on May 25, and forty-four two days after that; Grosse, *Rituels*, 382.

96. *R.Consist.* 11: 165; *Sources du droit*, ed. Rivoire and van Berchem, 3: 32; *C.O.* 21: 644. On Calvin's insistence that lying can never be justified under any circumstances, see Raymond A. Blacketer, "No Escape by Deception: Calvin's Exegesis of Lies and Liars in the Old Testament," *Reformation and Renaissance Review* 10 (2008): 267–89.

97. In referring to the numbers of women excommunicated in the city for the years 1564–1569, Monter lumps together lying with "Scandals," resulting in a very amorphous rubric; "Consistory of Geneva," 479. For his part, Manetsch, lists lying and slander in the same category; *Calvin's Company*, 201. Slandering someone could indeed result in a summons, reprimand, exclusion from the Supper, and perhaps even a brief jail sentence. As we will see below, the same was true for those who lied under oath to the Consistory. Telling a lie under other circumstances, however, ordinarily would not result in being called before Calvin and his colleagues.

98. *R.Consist.* 5: 257–58, 275; AEG, RC 45: 145v, 147v (December 11, 12, 1550). In a sermon in 1555, Calvin inveighed against Genevans who lied to the courts even under oath, decrying that it was impossible "to tear a single word of truth from their mouths"; *C.O.* 53: 38; cited in Lambert, "Preaching," 19.

99. AEG, R.Consist. 19: 53.

100. AEG, R.Consist. 19: 60.

101. Authorities apparently deemed such a sentence excessive and condemned her to twenty-four hours in jail and to do "réparation au temple"; AEG, Jur. Pen. A3–1562: 31 (May 11, 1562).

102. *R.Consist.* 11: 119.

103. *R.Consist.* 11: 255; "Dieu don[ne] bonne vie à Messieurs."

104. AEG, PC 1ère Sér. 626.

105. *R.Consist.* 12: 277–78.

106. AEG, RC 53: 318, 338 (September 6, 21, 1557).

107. *R.Consist.* 12: 277–78; AEG, PC 1ère Sér. 672.

108. *R.Consist.* 9: 312.

109. AEG, RC 54: 95v, 97v (February 21, 24, 1558). He was reinstated as scribe a few months later because his successor was not nearly as good at taking notes; see *R.Consist.* 13–14: xi–xii.

110. AEG, RC 54: 99 (February 25, 1558).

111. AEG, P.C. 2e Sér. 1198.

112. AEG, R.Consist. 19: 175v.

113. AEG, R.Consist. 19: 180v.

114. Lay folk complained that pastors at times not only named names but also pointed their fingers at people from the pulpit; *R.Consist.* 4: 22, 125; *R.Consist.* 11: 161; Lambert, "Preaching," 364–65.

115. On Castellio, see Ferdinand Buisson, *Sébastien Castellion: Sa vie et son oeuvre (1515–1563)*, ed. Max Engammare (Geneva: Droz, 2010); Hans R. Guggisberg, *Sebastian Castellio, 1515–1563: Humanist and Defender of Religious Toleration in a Confessional Age*, trans. and ed. Bruce Gordon (Aldershot, England and Burlington, VT: Ashgate, 2002).

116. AEG, R.Consist. 18: 18ter v.

117. AEG, R.Consist. 18: 25v.

118. AEG, R.Consist. 19: 178v–79, 184. See also 187, 187 add.

119. AEG, R.Consist. 19: 209v, 210–12.

120. AEG, R.Consist. 20: 16r–v.

121. Sébastien Châteillon, *Conseil à la France désolée*, ed. Marius F. Valkhoff (Geneva: Droz, 1967); *Advice to a Desolate France: In the course of which the reason for the present war is outlined, as well the possible remedy and, in the main, advice is given as to whether consciences should be coerced, the year 1562*, trans. Wouter Valkhoff (Shepherdstown, WV: Patmos Press, 1975).

122. AEG, R.Consist. 20: 104v, 117v; Gautier, *Histoire de Genève*, 4: 372. Secular authorities admonished Michel and in an effort to suppress this book, ordered an official to go to all "boutiques des libraires." Jur. Pen. A3–1563: 53 (August 24, 1563).

123. AEG, R.Consist. 20: 127v.

124. See, for example, AEG, R.Consist. 18: 129v.

125. For example, AEG, R.Consist. 17: 62v, 68.

126. Magistrates did not give the pastors and the Consistory a carte blanche even in matters pertaining to the Supper. In 1561, the Council rejected the request of Calvin and

Viret to distribute lead tokens (*méraux*) to those who were deemed worthy of taking communion. This would have been a means of protecting the sacrality of the sacrament by preventing the ignorant and unworthy from participating. Such communion tokens were soon used in Reformed churches in France; AEG, RC 55: 185, 186v (January 30, February 1, 1561); Monter, "Consistory of Geneva," 468; Raymond A. Mentzer, "Marking the Taboo," 98; Grosse, "Rationalité graphique," 548–49.

127. It must also be noted that Calvin did have his fans. In early September 1564, just over three months after the reformer's death, Matthieu Doussin was detained for having declared that after Calvin's passing, everything had been turned upside down and that there was no longer justice in Geneva. Considering this an attack on their own integrity, *Messieurs* admonished Doussin and ordered that he ask forgiveness from God and justice; AEG, PC 1ère Sér. 1228.

Chapter 2

1. As Susan Karant-Nunn aptly noted, "No preaching, no Reformation." "Preaching the Word in Early Modern Germany," in *Preachers and People in the Reformations and Early Modern Period*, ed. Larissa Juliet Taylor (Leiden: Brill, 2001), 194–95.

2. *R. Consist.* 1: 136; Kingdon, *Reforming Geneva*, 30–38; Thomas A. Lambert, "Cette loi ne durera guère: Inertie religieuse et espoirs catholiques à Genève au temps de la Réforme," *Bulletin de la Société d'Histoire et d'Archéologie de Genève* 23/24 (1993–1994): 5–24; McKee, *Pastoral Ministry*, esp. 162–71; Grosse, *Rituels*, 268–69. See also Virginia Reinburg, "Liturgy and Laity," *Sixteenth Century Journal* 23 (1992): 526–46.

3. In his study of the diocese of Geneva in the late Middle Ages, Louis Binz did not find a single case of a priest delivering a sermon to his parish; *Vie religieuse et réforme ecclésiastique dans le diocese de Genève pendant le Grand Schisme et la crise conciliare (1378–1450)* (Geneva: Jullien, 1973), 390–92; Manetsch, *Calvin's Company*, 147.

4. Calvin averaged around eighteen to twenty sermons a month and probably delivered more than 4,000 sermons during his ministry in Geneva, over a fourth of which have been published; Manetsch, *Calvin's Company*, 150; T. H. L. Parker, *Calvin's Preaching* (Louisville, KY: Westminster John Knox Press, 1992), 62–63.

5. In rural parishes typically only two or three services a week were offered, as pastors in the countryside served two or more churches and had to travel by foot or by horse to go from one to another; Robert M. Kingdon, "The Genevan Revolution in Public Worship," *Princeton Seminary Bulletin* 20 (1999): 264–80; Manetsch, *Calvin's Company*, 148–49, 152–53.

6. On Servetus, see Roland H. Bainton, *Hunted Heretic: The Life and Death of Michael Servetus, 1511–1553*, rev. ed. (Providence, RI: Blackstone Editions, 2005); Jerome Friedman, *Michael Servetus: A Case Study in Total Heresy* (Geneva: Droz, 1978).

7. See Buisson, *Sébastien Castellion*; and Guggisberg, *Sebastian Castellio*.

8. For a good discussion of the Bolsec affair, see Roget, *Histoire du people*, 3: 157–206.

9. Jeffrey R. Watt, Introduction, *R.Consist.* 10: x–xii; *C.O.* 15: 544–45 (epistle 2175); Roget, *Histoire du people*, 4: 215–16. This was one of a number of issues that delayed the renewal of the alliance between Bern and Geneva, so vital to the latter's security. The *combourgeoisie* expired in March 1556 and was not renewed until January 1558; Eugène Choisy, *La théocratie à Genève au temps de Calvin* (Geneva: Fick, 1897), 191–93; Émile Doumergue, *Jean Calvin, les hommes et les choses de son temps*, 7 vols. (Lausanne: G. Bridel, 1899–1927), 7: 67–105; Gautier, *Histoire de Genève*, 3: 648–64; 4: 1–176; Michael W. Bruening, *Calvinism's First Battleground: Conflict and Reform in the Pays de Vaud, 1528–1559* (Dordrecht: Springer, 2005), 214–21.

10. On the basis of the Consistory registers, Robert M. Kingdon found that most rank and file Genevans viewed religion more as a set of rituals than as a creed; "Genevan Revolution in Worship."

11. *R.Consist.* 6: 220.

12. *R.Consist.* 6: 225–26, 232.

13. *R.Consist.* 6: 221; 7: 23–24, 28, 31; AEG, RC 46: 134v, 136v, 142, 207 (January 11, 14, 28; May 17, 1552); PC 2ᶜ Sér. 984. See also Roget, *Histoire du people*, 3: 221; Naphy, *Calvin*, 201, n. 39.

14. AEG, RC 46: 262v (August 29, 1552). See also Roget, *Histoire du people*, 3: 237, 239. It is unclear if Des Cassines ever was actually exiled.

15. AEG, PC 2ᶜ Sér. 1204

16. *R.Consist.* 1: 39n189; AEG, RC 35: 559, 565 (April 17, 21, 1542). On the conflicts with the Consistory of another of Castellio's sisters, Jeanne Essautier, see chapter 1.

17. AEG, R.Consist. 18: 161v–62.

18. Genevan authorities also encountered a very few people who embraced, at least temporarily, Socinianism. See, for example, the case from 1559 of Jean Bernardin, who was admonished and excluded from the Supper; AEG, R.Consist. 16: 204v.

19. Among the large number of publications on female mystics in Spain, be they "true" or "false," see Gillian T. W. Ahlgren, *Teresa of Avila and the Politics of Sanctity* (Ithaca, NY: Cornell University Press, 1996); Alastair Hamilton, *Heresy and Mysticism in Sixteenth-Century Spain: The Alumbrados* (Toronto: University of Toronto Press, 1992); Richard Kagan, *Lucrecia's Dreams: Politics and Prophecy in Sixteenth-Century Spain* (Berkeley: University of California Press, 1990); Ronald E. Surtz, *The Guitar of God: Gender, Power, and Authority in the Visionary World of Mother Juana de la Cruz (1481–1534)* (Philadelphia: University of Pennsylvania Press, 1990). For cases of pretense of sanctity heard by the Roman Inquisition, see Anne Jacobson Schutte, *Aspiring Saints: Pretense of Holiness, Inquisition, and Gender in the Republic of Venice, 1618–1750* (Baltimore: Johns Hopkins University Press, 2001); Adelisa Malena, *L'Eresia dei perfetti: Inquisizione romana ed esperienze mistiche nel seicento italiano* (Rome: Edizioni di Storia e Letteratura, 2003); and various essays in *Finzione e santità: Tra medioevo ed età moderna*, ed. Gabriella Zarri (Turin: Rosenberg and Sellier, 1991).

20. AEG, R.Consist. 17: 193v

21. AEG, R.Consist. 17: 193–94; Jur. Pen. A2: 127 (December 19, 1560)

22. AEG, Jur. Pen. A2: 127v (December 20, 1560). Authorities ordered that her assets be seized. The son was clearly a minor as authorities mandated that a *tuteur* be assigned to ensure that his assets (*son bien*) be restored to him.

23. AEG, R.Consist. 17: 204; Jur. Pen. A2: 128v–29, 129v (December 26, 27, 1560).

24. AEG, R.Consist. 17: 204v.

25. AEG, R.Consist. 17: 205.

26. AEG, R.Consist. 17: 205–6; Jur. Pen. A2: 131v, 132, (January 3, 6, 1561).

27. AEG, PC 2ᵉ Sér. 1222.

28. AEG, PC 2ᵉ Sér. 1222.

29. AEG PC 2ᵉ Sér. 1222.

30. AEG PC 2ᵉ Sér. 1222; Jur. Pen. A2: 133v (January 13, 1561).

31. AEG, R.Consist. 17: 219v; Jur. Pen. A2: 136v (February 7, 1561).

32. AEG, R.Consist. 18: 27, 32; Jur. Pen. A2: 144 (April 7, 1561).

33. AEG, R.Consist. 18: 55.

34. AEG PC 2ᵉ Sér. 1222; Jur Pen. A2: 163 (July 28, 1561). It appears likely that de La Pierre did actually return in 1563, remarried to a minister (though not John Calvin!). Marie's maiden name was Ringard, and on December 16 she appeared along with her husband, Nicolas Pinoil, "ministre de la parolle." Identified as Marie "Ringat," this woman admitted that she had previously committed some serious errors for which she had been excluded from the Supper. The Consistory acceded to her request to be readmitted to communion, giving her "bonnes admonitions" and exhorting Pinoil "de promettre qu'elle porte ung tel estat." R.Consist. 20: 174v.

35. See Allyson M. Poska, "Gender on Trial: Inquisitions," in *Judging Faith*, ed. Parker and Starr-LeBeau, 240–49.

36. Claire Guilhem found that the Spanish Inquisition consistently dismissed as crazy women who challenged male religious authorities, "L'inquisition et la dévaluation des discours féminins," in *L'Inquisition espagnole: XVe–XIXe siècle*, ed. Bartolomé Bennassar (Paris: Hachette, 1979), 197–240.

37. AEG, PC 2ᵉ Sér. 1222.

38. In France, men outnumbered women among those who converted to Protestantism. In the Netherlands, men were perhaps more likely to embrace Protestantism in the early stages of the Reformation, but once it was well established, women comprised the sizable majority of members of Reformed Dutch churches; Benedict, *Christ's Churches*, 137, 200.

39. Jeffrey R. Watt, "Women and the Consistory in Calvin's Geneva," *Sixteenth Century Journal* 24 (1993): 432–33. In its earliest days, the consistory of Lausanne also convoked far more women than men for engaging in "papist" activities such as attending Mass or possessing rosaries or images of saints; Moret Petrini, "'Ces Lausonnois qui pappistent,'" 141–42, 144. Manetsch, by contrast, found almost twice as many men as women excommunicated for "Catholic Behavior" in Geneva for the years 1542–1609; *Calvin's Company*, 201, 203–4. His definition of "Catholic Behavior" is quite broad and includes, among other things, "fighting in Catholic armies" and "manufacturing

Catholic religious objects." I find these to be decidedly different from, for example, saying the Ave Maria or celebrating a Catholic holiday.

40. *R.Consist.* 3: 9–10; Lambert, "Preaching,"

41. Kingdon, *Reforming Geneva*, 55.

42. AEG, R.Consist. 17: 139v.

43. AEG, R.Consist. 18: 116v–17.

44. AEG, R.Consist. 13: 7.

45. AEG, R.Consist. 19: 24. She had been accused of saying prayers to the Virgin Mary and for the dead in February 1551; *R.Consist.* 5: 325.

46. AEG, PC 1ère Sér. 1023; Jur. Pen. A3–1562: 16 (March 30, 1562).

47. *R.Consist.* 1: 277–78.

48. AEG, R.Consist. 16: 209.

49. AEG, R.Consist. 16: 231.

50. *R.Consist.* 12: 358. The Council gave them "grandes remonstrances." AEG, RC 53: 446 (December 6, 1557).

51. McKee, *Pastoral Ministry*, 592, 622–24. Calvin no doubt would have approved wholeheartedly of the wording about funerals in Scotland's First Book of Discipline: "For avoiding of all inconveniences we judge it best that neither singing nor reading be at buriall. For albeit things sung and read may admonish some of the living to prepare themselves for death, yet shall some superstitions think that singing and reading of the living may profite the dead. And therefore we think it most expedient that the dead be conveyed to the place of burial with some honest company of the kirk, without either singing or reading; yea without all kind of ceremony heretofore used, other than that the dead be committed to the grave, with such gravity and sobriety, as those that be present may seeme to feare the judgements of God, and to hate sinne which is the cause of death." *The First Book of Discipline*, ed. James K. Cameron (Edinburgh: St. Andrew Press, 1972), 200; Benedict, *Christ's Churches*, 507.

52. *R.Consist.* 1: 34, n. 161.

53. AEG, Jur. Pen. K1: (unnumbered page) (January 4, 1554).

54. *R.Consist.* 8: 236–37.

55. See Kingdon, *Reforming Geneva*, 111; Manetsch, *Calvin's Company*, 125; McKee, *Pastoral Ministry*, 299–310. On December 25, 1550, Calvin was rather disturbed to see the unusually large crowd assembled to hear the sermon he delivered on that day, a Thursday, and issued a stinging rebuke: "c'est une chose bonne que nous ayons ung jour en l'an auquel on nous monstre le proffict qui nous revient de ce que Jesus Christ est né au monde. . . . Mais si vous pensez que Jesus Christ soit né aujourd'huy, vous estes des bestes, voire des bestes enragés. . . . Car ung jour n'est point meilleur que l'aultre." *Supplementa Calviniana*, vol. 5, *Sermons sur le Livre de Michée; Sermones de Libro Michaeae*, ed. Jean-Daniel Benoît (Neukirchen-Vluyn: Neukirchener Verlag des Erziehungsvereins, 1964), 172; quoted in Grosse, *Rituels*, 300–301.

56. *R.Consist.* 8: 237.

57. AEG, R.Consist. 18: 190v–91, 191v, 197; Jur. Pen. A2: 188v (January 12, 1562).

58. AEG, R.Consist. 20: 168v, 169v–70.

59. He was ordered jailed for three days and warned that he would be banished if he repeated that behavior; AEG, Jur. Pen. A3–1563: 76 (December 6, 1563).

60. AEG, R.Consist. 20: 168v, 169v–70.

61. Under popular pressure, the Council finally reinstated the celebration of Christmas in Geneva in 1694 notwithstanding opposition from the Company of Pastors; Benedict, *Christ's Churches*, 495–96; Jean Pierre Gaberel, *Histoire de l'Église de Genève depuis le commencement de la réformation jusqu'à nos jours*, 3 vols. (Geneva: Cherbulier, 1855–1858), 3: 45–47.

62. *R.Consist.* 5: 283, 295.

63. *R.Consist.* 5: 149, 151,160; AEG, RC 45: 47v (July 14, 1550). Other studies have also shown that while rank and file members of Reformed churches consistently shunned crucifixes and images that were considered idolatrous, artists and artisans were not willing to sacrifice their own livelihood and continued to produce such objects for Catholic customers; Benedict, *Christ's Churches*, 486.

64. *R.Consist.* 9: 47. These men were both readmitted to communion in May of the same year, 97.

65. *R.Consist.* 12: 100.

66. AEG, R.Consist. 18: 26v.

67. AEG, R.Consist. 16: 217v.

68. AEG, Jur. Pen. A2: 60v (November 20, 1559). The Council had been more severe in July 1558 when it sentenced two women to three days in jail and *réparation* for having attended Mass in Savoy; PC 1ère Sér. 748.

69. *R.Consist.* 11: 182–83; AEG, RC 51: 254v (August 10, 1556).

70. AEG, R.Consist. 15: 158v.

71. AEG, R.Consist. 15: 158v–59, 163v–64. The Consistory excluded Gallatin from the Supper and sent him to the Council, which ordered him jailed; Jur. Pen. A2: 46v (September 4, 1559).

72. In Spain, the Inquisition also accused far more men than women of blasphemy. Allyson Poska attributes this to the Inquisition's emphasis on male self-control, but I cannot help wondering if this rather suggests that women had assimilated the notion that blasphemy was unbecoming a woman; Poska, "Gender on Trial," 246–47.

73. Such a law was passed in early modern Valangin in the principality of Neuchâtel, and the consistory there accused sixty-two men but only five women of blasphemy; Robert, *Que dorénavant*, 321.

74. *R.Consist.* 8: 135.

75. AEG, PC 1ère Sér. 435; RC 41: 242, 247 (November 15, 22, 1546); *R.Consist.* 2: 337, n. 1325.

76. *R.Consist.* 12: 224, 231–32, 233–34.

77. AEG, PC 1ère Sér. 657.

78. *R.Consist.* 6: 177, 179–80; AEG, RC Part. 4: 322 (October 12, 1551).

79. See Grosse, *Rituels*, 412–16.

80. AEG, Registres des criées et publications 1: 61–6 (March 10, 1550); *Sources du droit*, ed. Rivoire and van Berchem, 3: 530–35. Calvin aggressively called for the passing of these edicts in August, November, and December of 1551 and then again in July 1555, but every time the Council declined to take action; RC 46: 39v, 98r–v, 124 (August 18, November 23, December 25, 1551); 49: 130 (July 12, 1555); *R.Consist.* 10: 147n829.

81. AEG, RC 51: 82, 174r–v (April 6, June 8, 1556); 52: 63r–v (October 26, 1556).

82. *R.Consist.* 11: 12 (and n. 69).

83. AEG, RC 52: 94–95 (November 12–13, 1556).

84. AEG, RC: 52: 96r–v (November 15, 1556). Unfortunately, we do not know what the proposed penalties were.

85. AEG, PC 1ère Sér. 563; RC 50: 119 (February 3, 1556). As was often the case in Calvin's Geneva, a sentence of banishment for life should not be taken literally. She was clearly living in Geneva again in June 1562 when she appeared before the Consistory; R.Consist. 19: 83v.

86. *R.Consist.* 11: 321.

87. AEG, RC 52: 180 (December 28, 1556).

88. AEG, PC 2ᶜ Sér. 1114; RC 52: 183 (December 31, 1556).

89. *R.Consist.* 11: 155.

90. AEG, PC 1ère Sér. 588; RC 51: 225v, 226, 231v, 233v (July 20, 23, 24, 1556). Rime made matters much worse for himself and his family when he tried to hang himself when his neck was placed in the *collier*. Though his wife and young children begged for mercy, Rime was again ordered to spend three hours in the *collier* and then was banished for a year and a day under pain of the whip; RC 51: 238, 240v (July 28, 30, 1556).

91. AEG, R.Consist. 18: 159r–v; "il avoyt mangé le diable et ne pouvoit avaller les cornes."

92. AEG, RC 52: 127v (December 1, 1556).

93. AEG, PC 1ère Sér. 995; Jur. Pen. A2: 180 (November 21, 1561).

94. The innkeeper Otto Chautemps was actually executed for blasphemy in 1559, but one cannot help wondering if this harsh penalty was the result of the accumulation of the many offenses he had committed over the years. The son of a former syndic, Chautemps had appeared repeatedly before the Consistory and the Council for various forms of misbehavior, such as domestic violence, theft, blasphemy, and tolerating games of chance and dishonest songs in his establishment; *R.Consist.* 2: 53n94; AEG, Jur. Pen. A2: 15v (April 3, 1559); PC 1ère Sér. 741; Alfred Cartier, "Arrêts du Conseil de Genève sur le fait de l'imprimerie et de la librairie de 1541 à 1550," *Mémoires et documents de la Société d'Histoire et d'Archéologie de Genève* 23 (1888–1894): 433.

95. While Swiss consistories regularly convoked people for truancy from church, they virtually never questioned parishioners about their knowledge of prayers or the confession of faith. Sylvie Moret Petrini found that the consistory of Lausanne was strictly a disciplinary institution with no pedagogical role, a description that could also be applied to the seigneurial consistories of Neuchâtel; "'Ces Lausonnois qui pappistent,'" 139–51; Robert, *Que dorénavant;* Jeffrey R. Watt, "The Reception of the Reformation

in Valangin, Switzerland, 1547–1588," *Sixteenth Century Journal* 20 (1989): 89–104. In response to the earnest requests of Lausanne's pastors, Bernese authorities in 1558 finally allowed the consistory of Lausanne to summon people because of "ignorance" so that they could be "instruits et endoctrinés"; Bruening, *Calvinism's First Battleground*, 251; Henri Vuilleumier, *Histoire de l'église réformée du Pays de Vaud sous le régime bernois*, vol. 1, *L'Âge de la Réforme* (Lausanne: La Concorde, 1927), 665.

96. *R.Consist.* 5: 104, 243.

97. See Manetsch, *Calvin's Company*, 137–44.

98. AEG, R.Consist. 17: 46v. On the efforts of the Consistory to oblige servants to tell the truth even when this ran contrary to the wishes of their masters, see Karen Spierling, "Putting 'God's Honor First': Truth, Lies, and Servants in Reformation Geneva," *Church History and Religious Culture* 92 (2012): 85–103.

99. AEG, R.Consist. 19: 36. Chenu had not even been accompanying pastors as they conducted visitations in his district.

100. AEG, R.Consist. 19: 38, 44, 49v.

101. AEG, R.Consist. 21: 40v.

102. AEG, R.Consist. 17: 163. See also Kingdon, *Reforming Geneva*, 53–54.

103. AEG, R.Consist. 18: 52.

104. AEG, R.Consist. 18: 68v. See also Scott Manetsch "Discipline and Ignorance in Calvin's Geneva," *Unio Cum Christo: International Journal of Reformed Theology and Life* 3 (2017): 103–17.

105. AEG, R.Consist. 18: 34.

106. AEG, R.Consist. 18: 43v.

107. Kingdon and Lambert found that words meaning "prayer" occurred 488 times in the twenty-one volumes, and 305 of these were found in just the first volume (1542–1544), fifty-five in the second volume (1545–1546). They also found that the percentage of people who could successfully recite both the Lord's Prayer and the Apostles' Creed, reasonably high already in 1542, was significantly higher in 1544; *Reforming Geneva*, 54–55.

108. *R.Consist.* 1: 132.

109. AEG, R.Consist. 17: 189. Immediately after this decision, three other men appeared because they were absent from the same church service. All three men admitted that they were having a snack at the home of one of the three. Next a tavern keeper and his wife admitted that they had served dinner to some "foreigners" during the afternoon sermon. Since all of these, unlike Soutier, confessed their error, the Consistory limited itself to admonitions; 17: 189.

110. On the Wednesday day of prayer in Geneva, see McKee, *Pastoral Ministry*, 269–352.

111. Manetsch, *Calvin's Company*, 130–31; McKee, *Pastoral Ministry*, 178–87.

112. AEG, R.Consist. 16: 238v. See also Grosse, *Rituels*, 180–81.

113. AEG, R.Consist. 18: 59v; Manetsch, *Calvin's Company*, 131.

114. AEG, R.Consist. 18: 59v.

115. Benedict, *Christ's Churches*, 325.

116. True, the minutes for volume 14 are preceded by the list of the individuals summoned for each meeting in that volume as well as the names of people who called them. The latter, however, were essentially all members of the Consistory, and we cannot know who brought the alleged misconduct to their attention.

117. AEG, R.Consist. 14: 38v–39.

118. *R.Consist.* 4: 113.

119. See Erik de Boer, *The Genevan School of the Prophets: The congrégations of the Company of Pastors and Their Influence in 16th Century Europe* (Geneva: Droz, 2012).

120. *R.Consist.* 5: xix, 236–37.

121. AEG, R.Consist. 15: 115v–16v.

122. *R.Consist.* 12: 154; RC 53: 129 (May 10, 1557).

123. Jeanne de Jussie, *The Short Chronicle: A Poor Clare's Account of the Reformation of Geneva*, trans. and ed. Carrie F. Klaus (Chicago: University of Chicago Press, 2006), 151–52.

124. Mary B. McKinley, introduction to Marie Dentière, *Epistle to Marguerite de Navarre and Preface to a Sermon by John Calvin*, trans. and ed. Mary B. McKinley (Chicago: University of Chicago Press, 2004), 2.

125. Dentière, *Epistle*, 53.

126. Natalie Zemon Davis, "City Women and Religious Change," in *Society and Culture in Early Modern France* (Stanford: Stanford University Press, 1975), 82–83.

127. Dentière, *Epistle*, 76–77.

128. See Calvin's letter to Farel about an encounter with Dentière; *C.O.* 12: 377–78 (epistle 824); cited in McKinley, introduction to Dentière, *Epistle*, 19. For more on Dentière, see Irena Backus, "Marie Dentière: un cas de féminisme théologique à l'époque de la Réforme," *Bulletin de la Société de l'Histoire du Protesantisme Français* 137 (1991): 177–95; Isabelle Graesslé, "Vie et légende de Marie Dentière," *Bulletin du Centre Protestant d'Etudes* 55 (2003): 3–31; Cynthia Skenazi, "Marie Dentière et la prédication des femmes," *Renaissance and Reformation* 21 (1997): 5–18. Another woman, Anne Vaughn Lock, a Marian exile in Geneva, translated into English four of Calvin's sermons, which were published in 1560, and likened the reformer to an apothecary who could assist in healing spiritual ills; McKee, *Pastoral Ministry*, 566–67.

129. Judith Pollmann, "Honor, Gender and Discipline in Dutch Reformed Churches," in *Dire l'interdit: The Vocabulary of Censure and Exclusion in the Early Modern Reformed Tradition*, ed. Raymond A. Mentzer, Françoise Moreil, and Philippe Chareyre (Leiden: Brill 2010), 29–42.

130. Grosse, *Rituels*, 322; AEG, RC 35: 549 (April 4, 1542); *R.Consist.* 1: 26–29.

131. Gerald Strauss, "Success and Failure in the German Reformation," *Past and Present* 67 (1975): 30–63. For a variety of interpretations, see "The 'Success' of the Reformation," in *The Long Reformation*, ed. Jeffrey R. Watt (Boston: Houghton Mifflin, 2006), 201–43.

132. Bruce Gordon, *Clerical Discipline and the Rural Reformation: The Synod in Zürich, 1532–1580* (Bern: Peter Lang, 1992), 221–22.

133. Amy Nelson Burnett, *Teaching the Reformation: Ministers and Their Message in Basel, 1529–1629* (Oxford: Oxford University Press, 2006).

134. Jean Delumeau, *Catholicism between Luther and Voltaire: A New View of the Counter-Reformation* (London: Burns and Oates, 1977), esp. 175–201.

135. Kingdon, *Reforming Geneva*, 26–30; Lambert, "Preaching."

136. These findings dovetail with Manetsch's in *Calvin's Company*. On the general impact of Reformed Protestantism on piety in the early modern period, see Benedict, *Christ's Churches*, 490–532.

137. Benedict, *Christ's Churches*, 528–29.

Chapter 3

1. See Joel F. Harrington, *Reordering Marriage and Society in Reformation Germany* (Cambridge: Cambridge University Press, 1995); *Sin and Calvinists*, ed. Mentzer; Jeffrey R. Watt, "The Impact of the Reformation and the Counter-Reformation," in *The History of the European Family*, ed. Marzio Barbagli and David I. Kertzer, vol. 1: *Family Life in Early Modern Times* (New Haven, CT: Yale University Press, 2001), 123–52.

2. For a fuller discussion of the survival of Catholic baptism practices in Geneva, see Spierling, *Infant Baptism*. See also Kingdon, *Reforming Geneva*, 90–94; Manetsch, *Calvin's Company*, 257–65; McKee, *Pastoral Ministry*, 391–436; Hughes Oliphant Old, *The Shaping of the Reformed Baptismal Rite in the Sixteenth Century* (Grand Rapids, MI: William B. Eerdmans, 1992).

3. *R.Consist.* 1: 51. There is no record that these announcements were actually made. Following the break with Rome, English midwives continued to perform emergency baptisms during the reign of Henry VIII. Various reformers criticized this practice in the Elizabethan era, and baptisms by midwives became rare during the course of the seventeenth century; David Cressy, *Birth, Marriage, and Death: Ritual, Religion, and the Life-Cycle in Tudor and Stuart England* (Oxford: Oxford University Press, 1999), 64–66, 117–23.

4. *R.Consist.* 1: 75.

5. For Catholic views on baptism's fundamental role in the salvation of infants' souls, see Louis Haas, *The Renaissance Man and His Children: Childbirth and Early Childhood in Florence 1300–1600* (New York: Palgrave Macmillan, 1998), 64–69.

6. Lambert, "Cette loi," 7–8. See also Jacques Gélis, "La mort et le salut spirituel du nouveau-né: Essai d'analyse et d'interprétation du 'sanctuaire à répit' (XVe XIXe s.)," *Revue d'histoire moderne et contemporaine* 31 (1984): 361–76; Edward Muir, *Ritual in Early Modern Europe* (Cambridge: Cambridge University Press, 1997), 20–27; Barbara Pitkin, "'The Heritage of the Lord': Children in the Theology of John Calvin," in *The Child in Christian Thought*, ed. Marcia J. Bunge (Grand Rapids, MI: William B. Eerdmans, 2000), 181–86. For excellent analyses of early modern rituals pertaining to both baptism and death, see Cressy, *Birth, Marriage, and Death*; and Susan Karant-Nunn,

Reformation of Ritual: An Interpretation of Early Modern Germany (London: Routledge, 1997).

7. *R.Consist.* 4: 57; Spierling, *Infant Baptism*, 74–75.

8. *R.Consist.* 2: 271–72n952.

9. See Jacques Gélis, *L'arbre et le fruit: La naissance dans l'Occident moderne, XVIe– XIXe siècle* (Paris: Fayard, 1984), 526. The first mention of this practice in the Consistory minutes is found in November 1545, when two people from the village of Dardagny were convoked; *R.Consist.* 2: 66n174. This note from vol. 2 was the source for the discussion below of fathers not attending baptisms.

10. *R.Consist.* 5: 265.

11. *R.Consist.* 5: 14.

12. For more on the absence of fathers from baptisms, see Spierling, *Infant Baptism*, 91–93. Examining a wide variety of rituals, Susan Karant-Nunn found considerable resistance to Protestant changes in Germany; *Reformation of Ritual*, 194–201. The rural origin of some of her evidence helps explain the discrepancy between her findings and mine; the gap between popular culture and the mores of church leaders was invariably greater for peasants than for the urban laity.

13. *R.Consist.* 1: 371.

14. Cressy finds that godparents played a much more visible role in early modern English baptisms than did parents. When a child was baptized, for example, it was the godparents who told the minister the child's name, though ordinarily the parents and godparents had agreed on it in advance; *Birth, Marriage, and Death*, 149–63. My impression from the Consistory registers is that this was also common practice in Geneva. On godparentage in Calvin's Geneva, see Spierling, *Infant Baptism*, 105–57.

15. *R.Consist.* 2: 279–81, and n. 999.

16. *R.Consist.* 2: 271–72, 284–85.

17. *R.Consist.* 2: 280, n. 999; AEG, PC 1ère Sér. 431; RC 41: 184v, 185, 186, 188v, 190, 238, 242, 247 (August 27, 30, 31; September 2; November 15, 22, 1546). See also Lambert, "Cette loi," 9; and Naphy, "Baptisms," 87–97.

18. As seen in chapter 1, Jean-Baptiste Sept was a future Perriniste who fled Geneva in 1555 and was condemned to death in absentia.

19. *R.Consist.* 4: 73–75.

20. *R.Consist.* 4: 82, 88, 94; AEG, RC 43: 109, 111, 181 (June 7, 11; August 5, 1548). See also *R.Consist.* 2: 280n999.

21. E. William Monter, "De l'évêché à la Rome Protestante," in *Histoire de Genève*, ed. Paul Guichonnet (Lausanne: Payot, 1974), 146–47; E. William Monter, "Historical Demography and Religious History in Sixteenth Century Geneva," *Journal of Interdisciplinary History* 9 (1979): 412; Naphy, "Baptisms," 87–97; Naphy, *Calvin*, 144–45; Spierling, *Infant Baptisms*, 140–52. For similar disputes over the naming of children in Reformation England, see Cressy, *Birth, Marriage, and Death*, 162–63. On Catholics' preferences for saints' names, see Haas, *Renaissance Man*, 85–87.

22. See McKee, *Pastoral Ministry*, 573–92.

23. Strauss, *Luther's House*, 4.

24. *R.Consist.* 1: 145.

25. *R.Consist.* 1: 232.

26. Robert M. Kingdon, "The Geneva Consistory as Established by John Calvin," *On the Way: Occasional Papers of the Wisconsin Conference of the United Church of Christ* 7 (1990): 35; Robert M. Kingdon, "Catechesis in Calvin's Geneva," in *Educating People of Faith: Exploring the History of Jewish and Christian Communities*, ed. John Van Engen (Grand Rapids, MI: William B. Eerdmans, 2004), 296.

27. Louis Haas found, however, that children in Renaissance Florence learned their prayers primarily from their mothers; *Renaissance Man*, 138.

28. Raymond A. Mentzer, "Masculinity and the Reformed Tradition in France," in *Masculinity in the Reformation Era*, ed. Scott H. Hendrix and Susan C. Karant-Nunn (Kirksville, MO: Truman State University Press, 2008), 125.

29. *R.Consist.* 1: 190–91.

30. *R.Consist.* 1: 181–82. He reappeared twice to be queried on his progress, especially in instructing his children; 1: 190, 205.

31. Some medieval Catholic theologians also viewed the father as principally responsible for the religious education of their children. Aquinas wrote, "Now, a woman alone is not adequate to this task [of overseeing the religious instruction of young children]; rather, this demands the work of a husband, in whom reason is more developed for giving instruction and strength is more available for giving punishment." *Summa Contra Gentiles*, trans. Vernon J. Bourke (Notre Dame, IN: University of Notre Dame Press, 1975), book 3, chapter 122.

32. Hugh Cunningham, *Children and Childhood in Western Society Since 1500* (London and New York: Longman, 1995), 49–50; Steven Ozment, *When Fathers Ruled: Family Life in Reformation Europe* (Cambridge MA: Harvard University Press, 1983), 170–72; Strauss, *Luther's House*, 163; James Bast, *Honor Your Fathers: Catechisms and the Emergence of a Patriarchal Ideology in Germany, 1400–1600* (Leiden: Brill, 1997).

33. Grosse, *Rituels*, 182–83, 481–92.

34. Kingdon, "Catechesis," 294–313. See also Barbara Pitkin, "Children and the Church in Calvin's Geneva," in *Calvin and the Church: Papers Presented at the 13th Colloquium of the Calvin Studies Society*, ed. David Foxgrover (Grand Rapids, MI: Calvin Studies Society, 2002), 144–64; Barbara Pitkin, "'Heritage of the Lord,'" 186–89.

35. In the long run, the Heidelberg Catechism, attributed to Ursinus and Olevianus and first published in Germany in 1563, lent itself better to religious instruction and was much more widely used among Reformed Protestants than Calvin's; Kingdon, *Reforming Geneva*, 59–60; Lyle Bierma, "Olevianus and the Authorship of the Heidelberg Catechism: Another Look," *Sixteenth Century Journal* 13 (1982): 17–27.

36. Kingdon, "Confessionalism," 109–10; Kingdon, *Reforming Geneva*, 56–62; Manetsch, *Calvin's Company*, 265–69; Olivier Millet, "Le premier 'Catéchisme' de Genève (1537/1538) et sa place dans l'oeuvre de Calvin," in *Actes du VIIIe Colloque Jean Boisset: Catéchismes et Confessions de foi*, ed. Marie-Madeleine Fragonard and Michel

Peronnet (Montpellier: Université Paul Valéry, 1995), 209–29. In the same volume, see also Max Engammare, "Les fonctions pédagogiques des Figures de la Bible du XVIᶜ au XVIIIᶜ siècle," 313–70; and Philippe Chareyre, "Consistoire et catéchèse: L'exemple de Nîmes XVIᶜ–XVIIᶜ siècles," 403–23.

37. One hurdle in studying childhood and youth is that the Consistory records rarely mention the age of people appearing before it, and baptism records are not sufficiently well preserved for this era to determine their ages. The strong impression, though, is that most people who were truant from the catechism or from school (see the discussion below) were adolescents or pre-adolescents.

38. *R. Consist.* 5: 110, 114. See also J.-D. Blavignac, "Armorial genevois, recherches sur les armoiries, les bannières et les monnais de Genève," première partie, *Mémoires et documents de la Société d'histoire et d'archéologie de Genève* 6 (1849): 291–314. The *papeguai* was also a popular contest in Nîmes, where the consistory expressed concerns about possible excesses associated with it; Philippe Chareyre, "'The Great Difficulties One Must Bear to Follow Jesus Christ': Morality at Sixteenth-Century Nîmes," in *Sin and Calvinists*, 95.

39. AEG, R. Consist. 17: 157.

40. AEG, R.Consist. 18: 64. The Council complied and forbade such games at that time; Jur. Pen. A2: 157 (June 16, 1561).

41. AEG, R.Consist. 14: 122v.

42. AEG, R.Consist. 16: 212v–13. The hospital functioned not only as an infirmary but also as a poorhouse and a place for disciplining delinquents. On the hospital, see Léon Gautier, *L'Hôpital général de Genève de 1535 à 1545* (Geneva: A. Kündig, 1914); *Sauver l'âme, nourrir le corps, de l'hôpital général à l'hospice général de Genève 1535–1985*, ed. Bernard Lescaze (Geneva: Hospice Général, 1985).

43. AEG, R.Consist. 16: 225, 230v; Jur. Pen. A2: 65 (December 11, 1559).

44. AEG, R.Consist. 17: 29r–v; Jur. Pen. A2: 83v (March 18, 1560).

45. For example, in January 1562, Jacques Conte was ordered to give his son Michel a whipping; AEG, R.Consist. 18: 196v.

46. AEG, R.Consist. 15: 132; Jur. Pen. A2: 37v (July 24, 1559).

47. AEG, R.Consist. 15: 159v–60; Jur. Pen. A2: 45v, 46 (August 28, 31 1559); PC 1ᵉʳᵉ Sér. 853. A few weeks later *Messieurs* acceded to her request to be allowed again to run a tavern; Jur. Pen. A2: 53 (October 13, 1559).

48. AEG, R.Consist. 17: 152; Jur. Pen. A2: 111v (September 30, 1560).

49. AEG, R.Consist. 18: 17v. Even the son of one of the lookouts who searched for truant youths was found playing when he should have been studying his catechism; 18: 18; Jur. Pén A2: 142 (March 24, 1561).

50. AEG, R.Consist. 19: 134.

51. AEG, R.Consist. 18: 13. See also 18: 104r–v; Jur. Pen. A2: 141 (March 17, 1561).

52. AEG, R.Consist. 19: 50v.

53. AEG, R.Consist. 19: 80v. The Consistory limited itself to admonitions.

54. AEG, R.Consist. 19: 168; Jur. Pen. A3–1562: 77 (November 9, 1561).

55. AEG, R.Consist. 19: 14.

56. AEG, R.Consist. 19: 164; 20: 5v.

57. AEG, R.Consist. 20: 125.

58. AEG, R.Consist. 21: 61v. The Council complied; Jur. Pen. A3–1564: 28 (May 15, 1564).

59. Two Genevan girls appeared in court for being truant from catechism in September 1562 and another in January 1563. The Consistory was rather lenient toward all three, limiting itself to admonitions, probably because the girls seemed less culpable than their male counterparts—two of them were servants, and the mistress of one of them had given her chores to do at that time while the mistress of the other was ailing, having just given birth, and needed the girl's services; AEG, R.Consist. 19: 133r–v, 218v.

In dealing with a case in December 1561, however, the Consistory blatantly used two standards in passing sentences against those who were truant from catechism. Three boys and a girl appeared for fooling around (*follatantz*) during catechism. The girl was dismissed with admonitions whereas the three boys, and another who was not present, were to be taken to the hospital to get a whipping; R.Consist. 18: 170. Unless the Consistory concluded that the girl was led astray by the boys—and there is nothing in the record to suggest this—this may imply that Calvin and his colleagues were more concerned about the religious education of males than that of females.

60. Elie-Ami Bétant, "Le Collège de Rive," *Bulletin de l'Institut national genevois* 1 (1853): 523–38.

61. Louis Binz, "Coup d'oeil sur l'histoire du Collège," in *Le Collège de Genève 1559–1959* (Geneva: Alexandre Jullien, 1959), 13–33. In the same volume, see Alain Dufour, "La fondation du Collège de Genève et l'histoire de l'éducation," 35–56. See also Karin Maag, *Seminary or University? The Genevan Academy and Reformed Higher Education, 1560–1620* (Aldershot and Burlington, VT: Scolar Press and Ashgate, 1995); William Naphy, "The Reformation and the Evolution of Geneva's Schools," in *Reformations Old and New: Essays on the Socio-Economic Impact of Religious Change, c. 1470–1630*, ed. Beat Kümin (Aldershot and Burlington, VT: Scolar Press and Ashgate, 1996), 183–94.

62. *R.Consist.* 1: 95, n. 436.

63. Claude Jay, one of the original Jesuits, was an alumnus of La Roche, as was Pierre Favre, a close associate of Francis Xavier; *R.Consist.* 1: 95, n. 437.

64. *R.Consist.* 1: 95.

65. *R.Consist.* 1: 175–76. Bennar's son was back in Geneva by March 29, 1543, when Bennar again appeared before the Consistory. The later appearance gives us reason to believe that Bennar may have been a closet Catholic. A younger son had recently been presented for baptism by a Catholic from La Roche. Though Genevans had been forbidden since 1541 to have Catholics serve as godparents, Bennar pleaded ignorance of that law. Bennar received remonstrances from the Consistory and was further reprimanded by the Small Council; 1: 208n189.

66. AEG, R.Consist. 15: 134v, 152. In December 1563, Nicholas Matringe, originally from Haute Savoie, was admonished because he had sent his child to live with a wet

nurse in a Catholic area. The child had stayed with the wet nurse for four years, though Matringe promptly brought the child back to Geneva after an elder told him to; R.Consist. 20: 182.

67. The funding that supported the Academy to a considerable extent came from property confiscated from the exiled Perrinistes; Naphy, "Reformation and Evolution," 201.

68. On the Academy, see Maag, *Seminary or University?* See also Binz, "Coup d'oeil," 13–33. City leaders apparently paid little attention to vernacular schools, apart from ensuring that teachers were competent. In March 1556, the Small Council ruled that the number of vernacular schools in the city was to be fixed at six and that teachers were to be examined to ensure their suitability; Karin Maag, "The Spectre of Ignorance: The Provision of Education in the Swiss Cities," in *Fear in Early Modern Society*, ed. William G. Naphy and Penny Roberts (Manchester, Manchester University Press, 1997), 143.

69. In 1562, a man from the village of Avully got in trouble for refusing to pay the education tax for the village school; AEG, R.Consist. 19: 104v–5, 123v–24.

70. No secondary education was available for Genevan girls until the nineteenth century; Josiane Ferrari-Clément, "From Household to School, From School to Household," in *Forgotten Women of Geneva*, trans. Rebecca Zorac, ed. Anne-Marie Käppeli (Geneva: Metropolis, 1993), 78–97; Liliane Mottu-Weber, "Les femmes dans la vie économique de Genève, XVIᵉ–XVIIᵉ siècles," *Bulletin de la Société d'histoire et d'archéologie de Genève* 16 (1979): 391.

71. AEG, R.Consist. 21: 51.

72. AEG, R.Consist. 14: 134, 147–8.

73. AEG, RC: 335 (December 24, 1545); Lambert, "Preaching," 337n141.

74. AEG, RC 42: 379, 386 (December 21, 29, 1547); Bétant, "Collège de Rive," 532; John-Barthélemy-Gaïfre Galiffe, *Pages d'histoire exacte soit les procès criminels intentés à Genève, en 1547 contre No. Ami Perrin* (Geneva: Vaney, 1862), 59. Moussard was admitted to the bourgeoisie in 1553; Alfred Covelle, *Le livre des bourgeois de l'ancienne République de Genève* (Geneva: Jullien, 1897), 239.

75. AEG, R.Consist. 14: 153v.

76. AEG, R.Consist. 14: 159.

77. AEG, R.Consist. 15: 5v.

78. AEG, R.Consist. 15: 6.

79. AEG, Jur. Pen. K1: (unnumbered folio; February 16, 1559).

80. AEG, R.Consist. 15: 59.

81. Interestingly, Geneva's Collège de Versonnay, founded in 1389, had prohibited corporal punishment; Naphy, "Reformation and Evolution," 190–91.

82. Elie-Ami Bétant, "Le Collège de Rive," *Bulletin de l'Institut national genevois* 1 (1853): 533–34; *C.O.* 21: 465.

83. AEG, PC 2ᵉ Sér. 936; RC 45: 251v (April 14, 1551).

84. AEG, RC 48: 24v, 25 (March 22, 23, 1554).

85. On this and some other issues, I have a decidedly less sanguine view of the Consistory's efforts to protect the vulnerable than does Manetsch, who writes: "Another

way in which the ministers and elders carried out their pastoral responsibilities was by using corrective discipline to protect the weakest, poorest, and most vulnerable members of Genevan society. The Consistory regularly intervened in cases of child abuse, confronting and often disciplining parents who savagely beat their children or neglected to provide them necessary food, clothing, and shelter." *Calvin's Company*, 215.

86. Henri Heyer, *L'Église de Genève: Esquisse historique de son organisation, suivie de ses diverses constitutions, de la liste de ses pasteurs et professeurs, et d'une table biographique* (Geneva: Jullien, 1909), 457.

87. AEG, RC 58: 91v (August 16, 1563).

88. AEG, PC 1ère Sér. 1147.

89. On the subject of the pervasive discipline, including some actions against abusive teachers, at the *collège* in early modern Geneva, see Louis-J. Thévenaz, *Histoire du Collège de Genève jusqu'à la fin du XVIIIᵉ siècle*, in *Histoire du Collège de Genève* (Geneva: Département de l'instruction publique [de Genève], 1896), 176–96.

90. AEG, R.Consist. 15: 151r–v.

91. AEG, R.Consist. 19: 70.

92. AEG, R.Consist. 20: 62.

93. See, for example, AEG, R.Consist. 20: 7v.

94. For more on the anxieties concerning the behavior of youth and the civilizing role of schools, see Maag, "Spectre of Ignorance," 137–49. She finds that Calvin and other pastors pursued mandatory education more aggressively than did the Small Council.

95. See, for example, Ozment, *When Fathers Ruled*; Heide Wunder, "Construction of Masculinity and Male Identity in Personal Testimonies: Hans von Schweinichen (1552–1616), in His *Memorial*," in *Time, Space, and Women's Lives in Early Modern Europe*, ed. Anne Jacobson Schutte, Thomas Kuehn, and Silvana Seidel Menchi (Kirksville, MO: Truman State University Press, 2001), 305–23.

96. *R.Consist.* 12: 376; AEG, PC 1ère Sér. 694. The *jeu de palets* is a game that somewhat resembles pitching pennies.

97. AEG, PC 1ère Sér. 745.

98. AEG, R.Consist. 18: 111; État Civil, Livres des Morts 6: 144. The Council in fact sentenced Aimé to three days in jail and then to be whipped at the hospital; Jur. Pen. A2: 167 (September 1, 1561).

99 AEG, R.Consist. 20: 78; Jur. Pen. A3–1563: 36 (July 5, 1563).

100. AEG, R.Consist. 17: 108v.

101. AEG, R.Consist. 17: 167; Jur. Pen. A2: 115v (October 25, 1560).

102. AEG, R.Consist. 15: 142. She also physically abused her weak husband, pulling a knife on him on at least one occasion. The Council sent her to jail for three days; Jur. Pen. A2: 40 (August 4, 1559).

103. Admitting that she regularly used excessive force with the girl, Claude was forbidden to take communion and referred to the Small Council, which sentenced her to three days in jail; AEG, R.Consist. 17: 65v; Jur. Pén A2: 90 (April 29, 1560). She had a long history of violent behavior. In March 1548, Claude and her husband were called because

they were separated. The Consistory admonished Claude to be obedient to her husband and scolded her for having beaten him with a shovel; *R.Consist.* 4: 19.

104. AEG, R.Consist. 18: 82, 89v–90. On July 31, 1561, the Consistory forbade Arlod to take communion and sent him to the Small Council, which sentenced him to three days in jail; Jur. Pen. A2: 163v (August 4, 1561).

105. *R.Consist.* 5: 247–48.

106. AEG, R.Consist. 20: 71v–72.

107. AEG, R.Consist. 20: 176r–v.

108 .AEG, R.Consist. 19: 15v, 24v–25; PC 1ère Sér. 1017.

109. AEG, R.Consist. 13: 55v; RC 54: 197 (May 30, 1558).

110. AEG, R.Consist. 20: 18. Camut was also excluded from communion and had been admonished the previous June for truancy from church; 19: 84v, 90v.

111. *R.Consist.* 4: 90, 94, 95, 99–100, 105; AEG, RC 43: 155, 158 (August 6, 9, 1548).

112. AEG, R.Consist. 18: 44, 50.

113. See Karen E. Spierling, "Father, Son, and Pious Christian: Concepts of Masculinity in Reformation Geneva," in *Masculinity in the Reformation Era*, 95–119; Joel F. Harrington, "Bad Parents, the State, and the Early Modern Civilizing Process," *German History* 16 (1998): 16–28.

114. *R.Consist.* 6: 211.

115. AEG, R.Consist. 21: 9.

116. Be that as it may, she was condemned to one day in jail; AEG, Jur. Pen. A3–1564: 7v (March 3, 1564).

117. *R.Consist.* 5: 322.

118. *R.Consist.* 11: 238, and n. 1330. The Council actually sentenced her to one day in jail, after which she had to return to the Council to confess her error and to cry for mercy from God and "la Justice"; AEG, RC 52: 38r–v, 41v–42 (October 12, 13, 1556).

119. AEG, R.Consist. 15: 177.

120. AEG, PC 1ère Sér. 611. For the same infraction, authorities condemned another wet nurse, the widow Nicole Odin, two years later, to spend two hours in the stocks (*carcan*) and to ask for forgiveness on her knees; PC 1ère Sér. 873.

121. AEG, R.Consist. 18: 41. For rollover deaths in early modern Geneva, see Watt, *Choosing Death*, 58–61.

122. AEG, R.Consist. 18: 24v; Jur. Pen. A2: 144 (April 7, 1561). *Jeu du charret* (or *Jeu du moulin*) is a board game known in English as Nine Men's Morris; *Wikipedia*, SV "Jeu du moulin."

123. AEG, R.Consist. 18: 121r–v.

124. AEG, R.Consist. 18: 124r–v; Jur. Pen. A2: 169v (September 15, 1561).

125. *R.Consist.* 6: 231; 7: 48.

126. AEG, R.Consist. 17: 148v.

127. *R.Consist.* 8: 174, 179–80, 181.

128. AEG, R.Consist. 15: 143v, 151.

129. *R.Consist.* 11: 15.

130. AEG, R.Consist. 18: 174v.

131. AEG, R.Consist. 20: 27.

132. AEG, R.Consist. 20: 11.

133. AEG, R.Consist. 19: 151. The minutes do not actually identify Pernette as the Garmejeans' servant. It is possible she was simply a boarder.

134. *R.Consist.* 7: 150–51, 196; 8: 59, 61, 174.

135. *R.Consist.* 2: 311, n. 1181; AEG, R.Consist. 19: 59, 63.

136. "Interrogués si elles luy ont ouy tenu des propos deshonnestes, respondent nompas qu'elles sçachent, sinon que une foys elle leur dict en se riant que quand ce venoyt à concepvoir ung enfant il failloyt aller veoir et penser à ung beau personnage, et luy ont ouy dire que quand elle vouldroit concepvoir des enfans, elle regarderoit ou penseroit en Mons. de Besze ou filz de Mons. Dupont, et que en son pays il y avoit ung peintre qui disoyt qu'il failloyt regarder une belle ymage quand ce venoyt à concepvoir d'enfans." AEG, R.Consist. 19: 59. From a criminal investigation, we read: "bien heureuse seroit la mere qui pourroit avoir ung tel enfant comme Mr. de Beze." Bresson added that when she stressed the importance of wisdom and sound doctrine, Aimée Chauvet suggested that she would accordingly think of Calvin, whereupon her teacher suggested that Beza would be her own choice; PC 1ère Sér. 1036.

137. For a good description of these beliefs, see Merry Wiesner-Hanks, *The Marvelous Hairy Girls: The Gonzales Sisters and Their Worlds* (New Haven, CT: Yale University Press, 2009), 131–38.

138. AEG, R.Consist. 20: 130v–31, 133v; PC 1ère Sér. 1036.

139. Lambert also found that many Genevans continued to follow certain Catholic practices through the 1540s but generally adhered to Reformed practices by the 1550s; "Preaching."

140. AEG, R.Consist. 20: 65v, 66.

141. AEG, R.Consist. 18: 55.

142. Barbara Pitkin rightly points out that Calvin did not view small children as more sinful and depraved than adults. Indeed, according to Calvin, younger children manifest the effects of sin less than adults do; "'Heritage of the Lord,'" 164–68.

143. See Monter, "De l'évêché," 145.

144. Lambert, "Preaching," 417–19, 469–79. There was a real jump in the number of suspensions from the Supper starting in 1557 and an even greater one in 1563, but these were the result of the large influx of refugees into Geneva; Grosse, *Rituels*, 497–98. After Calvin's death, less than 1 percent of the Consistory's cases were aimed at ignorance; Manetsch, *Calvin's Company*, 273.

Chapter 4

1. Doumergue, *Jean Calvin*, 2: 463–64. On Idelette's death, see also McKee, *Pastoral Ministry*, 616–18.

2. *Institutes*, IV.xii.27, 2: 527.

3. Among other works, see Kingdon, *Adultery*; Schilling, *Civic Calvinism*, esp. chap. 2; Lyndal Roper, *The Holy Household: Women and Morals in Reformation Augsburg* (Oxford: Oxford University Press, 1989); Harrington, *Reordering Marriage*, esp. 134–66; Todd, *Culture of Protestantism*.

4. Though he insists that both church courts and secular courts were quite active in regulating sexuality in pre-Reformation England, Martin Ingram nonetheless finds an intensification of prosecution during the reign of Edward VI (1547–1553); *Carnal Knowledge: Regulating Sex in England, 1470–1600* (Cambridge: Cambridge University Press, 2017). See also Merry Wiesner-Hanks, *Christianity and Sexuality in the Early Modern World: Regulating Desire, Reforming Practice* (London: Routledge, 2000).

5. For a good brief examination of the Inquisition and gender, see Poska, "Gender on Trial," 240–9.

6. See, for example, various essays in *Sin and Calvinists*, ed. Mentzer.

7. See Watt, *Making Modern Marriage*, 105–6. For studies that did find a double standard in late medieval or early modern Europe, see Edward Britton, *The Community of the Vill: A Study in the History of the Family and Village Life in Fourteenth-Century England* (Toronto: Macmillan, 1977), 52–54; Beatrice Gottlieb, "The Meaning of Clandestine Marriage," in *Family and Sexuality in French History*, ed. Robert Wheaton and Tamara K. Haveren (Philadelphia: University of Pennsylvania Press, 1980), 57; Martin Ingram, *Church Courts, Sex, and Marriage in England, 1570–1640* (Cambridge: Cambridge University Press, 1987), 260, 262; Roper, *Holy Household*, 125–26.

8. Scott M. Manetsch, "Pastoral Care East of Eden: The Consistory of Geneva, 1569–82," *Church History* 75 (2006): 289. Manetsch found that men comprised a smaller majority (54.2 percent) of those excommunicated for fornication or adultery for the lengthier period of 1542–1609; *Calvin's Company*, 201. By contrast, Raymond Mentzer found that women comprised 60 percent of those convoked for illicit sexuality in Nîmes; "La Réforme calviniste des moeurs à Nîmes," in *La construction de l'identité réformée aux XVIᵉ et XVIIᵉ siècles: Le rôle des consistoires* (Paris: Honoré Champion, 2006), 42.

9. *R.Consist.* 4: 44; quoted in Manetsch, *Calvin's Company*, 215.

10. Interestingly, consistories in southern France took one form of police action exclusively against women, ostensibly to impede illicit sexuality: in the 1580s and 1590s, they convoked a number of women for dressing or coiffing themselves provocatively. In such cases, consistories urged women, at times with the threat of public censure, always to be attired in a modest manner. Such actions can be interpreted to mean that members of consistories believed that women bore primary responsibility for sexual misconduct; Graeme Murdock, "The Elders' Gaze: Women and Consistorial Discipline in Late Sixteenth-Century France," in *John Calvin, Myth and Reality: Images and Impact of Geneva's Reformer*, ed. Amy Nelson Burnett (Eugene, OR: Cascade Books, 2011), 69–90; Mentzer, "Réforme calviniste des moeurs à Nîmes," 43; Suzannah Lipscomb, "Refractory Women: The Limits of Power in the French Reformed Church," in *Dire l'interdit*, 17–19.

11. In a letter from October 1549, Calvin urged the Duke of Somerset, uncle of Edward VI and Lord Protector of England (1547–1549), to punish vice, specifically mentioning the sins of fornication, adultery, blasphemy, and drunkenness; Ingram, *Carnal Knowledge*, 294–95n80; M. L. Bush, *The Government Policy of Protector Somerset* (Montreal: McGill-Queen's University Press, 1975), 110.

12. Only in February 1557 did the Council publish the new *Ordonnances sur la Police de la Ville* in which the punishments and fines for each offense were more clearly specified; AEG, Registres des criées et publications, 2: 119–22 (February 16, 1557); *Sources du droit*, ed. Rivoire and van Berchem, 3: 39–40.

13. *Sources du droit*, ed. Rivoire and van Berchem, 3: 36.

14. *R.Consist.* 11: 289.

15. *R.Consist.* 11: 296. The Consistory sent Nepveu to the Small Council, which immediately ordered him jailed. He remained incarcerated for two weeks and was then tried and condemned to get on his knees and cry for mercy from God, to be denied the right to participate in the General Council for three years, and to pay a fine of ten écus; AEG, RC 52: 144v, 161v (December 7, 18, 1556).

16. *R.Consist.* 11: 60; AEG, RC 51: 84, 90v (April 7, 13, 1556).

17. *R.Consist.* 12: 106; AEG, PC Sér. 1ère 643.

18. AEG, PC 1ère Sér. 635.

19. See Watt, *Making Modern Marriage.*

20. AEG, PC 1ère Sér. 687; *R.Consist.* 12: 339–41.

21. AEG, R.Consist. 15: 183v–84; 16: 189. Their false testimony notwithstanding, they were sentenced to only three days in jail; Jur. Pen. A2: 52 (October 9, 1559).

22. In January 1561, the Consistory also expressed its dismay because a female servant had recently gotten married and had worn a garland of flowers on her head at her wedding. Only virgin brides were allowed to wear such a garland, and this servant was guilty of fornication; AEG, R.Consist. 17: 210v.

23. AEG, R.Consist. 19: 46, 71.

24. On this issue, see Grosse, *Rituels*, 393–94. By contrast, Philibert Berthelier was not allowed to marry as long as he was excluded from the Supper; Grosse, *Excommunication*, 69–71. I believe that these cases were treated strikingly differently because Nicolas and Catherine were guilty only of fornication, whereas Berthelier rejected the authority of the Consistory.

25. Grosse, *Rituels*, 378.

26. AEG, R.Consist. 18: 158, 165v–66, 173.

27. AEG, Jur. Pen. A2: 184 (December 16, 1561).

28. Spierling, *Infant Baptism*, 166–70, 186–87; Karen Spierling, "Putting Order to Disorder: Illegitimate Children, Their Parents, and the Consistory in Reformation Geneva," in *Dire l'interdit*, 43–62; Watt, "Impact of Reformation," 1: 147–50; Watt, *Making Modern Marriage*, 92–105. For comparison, see Matthew Gerber, *Bastards: Politics, Family, and Law in Early Modern France* (Oxford: Oxford University Press, 2012).

29. Tim Fehler, "Victims as Actors: Consistories," in *Judging Faith*, 182–83.

30. Suzannah Lipscomb, "Crossing Boundaries: Women's Gossip, Insults and Violence in Sixteenth-Century France," *French History* 25 (2011): 408–26; Lipscomb, "Refractory Women," 13–28. Laura Gowing found that through sexual slander, women in London arrogated to themselves the responsibility of maintaining local morality and honesty; *Domestic Dangers: Women, Words, and Sex in Early Modern London* (Oxford: Clarendon Press, 1996), esp. 59–138; "Language, Power, and the Law: Women's Slander Litigation in Early Modern London," in *Women, Crime and the Courts in Early Modern England*, ed. Jennifer Kermode and Garthine Walker (Chapel Hill: University of North Carolina Press, 1994), 26–47.

31. Sara Beam, "Female Violence and Women's Role as Moral Arbiters in Early Modern Geneva" (paper presented at the Western Association of Women's Historians, Denver, CO, May 12, 2016).

32. In this regard I am a bit less sanguine than Bob Kingdon on the Consistory's success in this matter: "it was perfectly possible for Genevan authorities to enforce a single approved lifestyle on virtually the entire population, at least with respect to sex and marriage. In fact, not only was it possible, our best evidence shows that it was actually achieved." *Reforming Geneva*, 99.

33. AEG, PC 1ère Sér. 1007; R.Consist. 19: 26v.

34. AEG, R.Consist. 21: 69v–70v.

35. AEG, PC 1ère Sér. 1205, 1206.

36. *R.Consist.* 12: 370–71, 374–76, 378–79, 381, 397.

37. AEG, PC 1ère Sér. 700.

38. AEG, Jur. Pen. A2: 9 (March 7, 1559).

39. AEG, R.Consist. 18: 96v–97, 98; R.Consist. 21: 35; PC 1ère Sér. 1175.

40. AEG, PC 1ère Sér. 915.

41. AEG, PC 1ère Sér. 928; Kingdon, *Adultery*, 119–23.

42. AEG, PC 1ère Sér. 944; Kingdon, *Adultery*, 123–26.

43. AEG, PC 1ère Sér. 945, 946; Kingdon, *Adultery*, 126–28.

44. These polities include Basel, Scotland, Béarn, Friesland, the Palatinate, Bern, Transylvania, Virginia, Massachusetts, and Interregnum England. And it must be noted that a few adulterers were put to death in Catholic and Lutheran territories, but these sentences were rarer still than in Reformed states; Benedict, *Christ's Churches*, 483–84.

45. Sonia Vernhes Rappaz hypothesizes that Genevan magistrates were influenced by Bernese laws and by the *Carolina*, the criminal law code of the Holy Roman Empire issued during the reign of Charles V; "La noyade judiciaire dans la République de Genève (1558–1619)," *Crime, Histoire et Sociétés* 13 (2009): 5–23.

46. The ordinances provided that those guilty of simple *paillardise*, involving someone who had fornicated with one member of the opposite sex, would be sentenced to nine days in jail and a fine of sixty sous. A couple who had sexual relations before marriage were sentenced to only three days in jail but had to recognize their fault in church at the celebration of the wedding. Females who were convicted of fornication a second time were to be banished for life, whereas male recidivists were to be banished just for

one year. A married man who committed adultery was subject to twelve days in jail and three hours in the stocks, while his paramour was sentenced to twelve days in jail and a fine. If she was his servant, she was to be banished for life under pain of death. An unmarried man who committed adultery with a married woman was to be whipped publicly and banished for life whereas she was to be drowned. If he was her servant, they both were to be put to death; *Sources du droit*, ed. Rivoire and van Berchem, 3: 167–70. Ecclesiastical ordinances of 1576 complemented these laws, which essentially remained in effect through the end of the Ancien Régime in Geneva at the end of the eighteenth century. In practice, though, capital punishment for *paillardise* was imposed only three times in the seventeenth century: once for double adultery and twice for female recidivists; Liliane Mottu-Weber, "'Paillardises,' 'anticipation' et mariage de réparation à Genève au XVIIIe siècle: Le point de vue du Consistoire, des pères de famille et des juristes," *Revue suisse d'histoire* 52 (2002): 433.

47. Mottu-Weber, "'Paillardises,'" 430–47.

48. *R.Consist.* 8: 127–28. For similar actions elsewhere, see Roper, *Holy Household*, 64; Watt, *Making Modern Marriage*, 105, 181, 255.

49. Referring to actions against illicit sex in Tudor England, Ingram notes, "ordinary people played an important role in bringing cases to court." *Carnal Knowledge*, 82.

50. AEG, PC 1ère Sér. 661.

51. AEG, PC 1ère Sér. 857.

52. AEG, PC 1ère Sér. 1042.

53. *R.Consist.* 5: 277, 283–84, 294–95; AEG, RC 45: 160 (January 5, 1551).

54. AEG, R.Consist. 15: 102r–v.

55. AEG, R.Consist. 15: 115, 119; Jur. Pen. A2: 27, 31v, 35 (June 5, 26; July 11, 1559). Todd found that in dealing with cases of rape, the Scottish sessions punished both the victim and the perpetrator and usually pressured the victim to marry the man who raped her; *Culture of Protestantism*, 296.

56. Also offensive to our sensibilities is the fact that Calvin, though he insisted on the need for consent in marriage, maintained that victims of sexual assault should marry those who raped them to avoid falling into prostitution; John Witte Jr. and Robert M. Kingdon, *Sex, Marriage and Family in John Calvin's Geneva*, vol. 1: *Courtship, Engagement and Marriage* (Grand Rapids, MI: William B. Eerdmans, 2005), 121; Gordon, *Calvin*, 296.

57. *R.Consist.* 9: xxii, 293.

58. AEG, RC 48: 168v, 169r–v (December 25, 27, 1554); RC Part. 8: 210v–11 (December 27, 1554). An *avis*, signed by Calvin, Abel Poupin, the jurist Germain Colladon, and François Chevallier described the boys' crime as among the "most atrocious and abominable." They recommended against the death penalty, however, because of their youth. Given their legal training and stature, Calvin, whose name appears first, and Colladon were almost surely the principal authors of this opinion, which is found in the dossier of a criminal case against a man, Lambert LeBlanc of Paris, who was condemned to death for sodomy in March 1554; PC 1ère Sér. 502. A translation of this *avis* is reproduced in

William G. Naphy, "Sodomy in Early Modern Geneva," in *Sodomy in Early Modern Europe*, ed. Thomas Betteridge (Manchester: Manchester University Press, 2007), 107–8.

59. There is an extant record of the investigation, dated December 26, of the alleged *bougrerie* between Pattu and Levet; AEG, PC 2ᵉ Sér. 1073. Though he does not mention this specific case, William Monter argues that the significant number of actions taken against sodomy between 1555 and 1570 reflected the religious zeal in Geneva and the connections that authorities perceived between sodomy and heresy; "Sodomy and Heresy in Early Modern Switzerland," *Journal of Homosexuality* 6 (1981): 41–55. See also Naphy, "Sodomy in Geneva," 94–111; William G. Naphy, "Reasonable Doubt: Defences Advanced in Early Modern Sodomy Trials in Geneva," in *Judicial Tribunals in England and Europe, 1200–1700, The Trial in History*, vol. 1, ed. Maureen Mulholland and Brian Pullan (Manchester: Manchester University Press, 2003), 129–46.

60. AEG, R.Consist. 18: 143v; Jur. Pen. A2: 176v (October 27, 1561).

61. See E. William Monter, *Frontiers of Heresy: The Spanish Inquisition from the Basque Lands to Sicily* (Cambridge: Cambridge University Press, 1990), 276–99; Michael Rocke, *Forbidden Friendships: Homosexuality and Male Culture in Renaissance Florence* (Oxford: Oxford University Press, 1996); Guido Ruggiero, *The Boundaries of Eros: Sex, Crime and Sexuality in Renaissance Venice* (Oxford: Oxford University Press, 1985), esp. 109–45. Mary Elizabeth Perry, *Gender and Disorder in Early Modern Seville* (Princeton, NJ: Princeton University Press, 1990), 119, 123–24, wrote, "male homosexuality appeared so dangerous that men accused of it were isolated from others in the Royal Prison of Seville, their deviance regarded as a contagion that could easily infect others." By contrast, Maria R. Boes finds that popular attitudes did not share authorities' abhorrence of sodomy in early modern Frankfurt am Main; "On Trial for Sodomy in Early Modern Germany," in *Sodomy*, ed. Betteridge, 27–45; in the same volume, N. S. Davidson argues that the Venetian government was not willing to prosecute sodomy with the rigor that the Roman Catholic Church desired; "Sodomy in Early Modern Venice," 65–81.

62. *R.Consist.* 12: 343.

63. AEG, RC 420, 422, 424v, 426, 440 (November 22, 23, 24, 25; December 2, 1557); PC 1ᵉʳᵉ Sér. 686. See Jeffrey R. Watt, "Childhood and Youth in the Genevan Consistory Minutes," in *Calvinus Praeceptor Ecclesiae: Papers of the International Congress on Calvin Research*, ed. Herman Selderhuis (Geneva: Droz, 2004), 61–62.

64. In April 1557 the Consistory had annulled her engagement to Thomas Lambert because she was about forty whereas he was only twenty-three; *R.Consist.* 12: 133.

65. AEG, R.Consist. 20: 116v–17.

66. AEG, R.Consist. 20: 119r–v. Since a few weeks earlier Blanche Firmin had testified against Deverneto on suspicions of *paillardise* with another woman, his accusation now could have been construed as a form of retribution on his part; 20: 89v–91. Over the next several months, the Consistory rejected three times Blanche Firmin's petition to be readmitted to communion because it believed that she did not fully recognize her sin. Only on her fourth attempt did the Consistory conclude that she was genuinely repentant and therefore readmitted her to the sacrament; 20:177v, 180; 21: 37v, 61.

67. AEG, PC 1ᵉʳᵉ Sér. 862; Naphy, "Reasonable Doubt," 137–38, 140. For her part, Esther was sentenced to witness the execution of Jacquema, be whipped till she bled, and then banished for life. Even Nicolas was strongly rebuked but then released. Naphy analyzes another case involving lesbianism that resulted in capital punishment. Françoise Morel was indeed executed for that crime, but she violently attacked another woman and was apparently guilty of having sexual relations with multiple women, which together could result in harsher treatment; Naphy, 131, 135; PC 1ᵉʳᵉ Sér. 1465.

68. Sherry M. Velasco found that the Inquisition in Spain appeared rather confused when faced with cases of lesbianism and was inconsistent in how it dealt with the accused; *Lesbians in Early Modern Spain* (Nashville, TN: Vanderbilt University Press, 2011).

69. For the years 1564–1569, Monter found that among those excommunicated for dancing, almost three times as many lived in the countryside as opposed to the city; "Consistory of Geneva," 479–80. See also (for Neuchâtel) Robert, *Que dorénavant*, 336–42; and Graeme Murdock, "The Dancing Calvinists of Montauban: Testing the Boundaries of a Reformed Community in the 1590s in France," in *Emancipating Calvin*, 54–57.

70. *R.Consist.* 6: 127, 137.

71. *R.Consist.* 3: 188.

72. AEG, Manuscrits Historiques 293: 75; Galiffe et al., eds., *Notices généalogiques*, 1: 405; *Recueil généalogique suisse: Première Série*, ed. Albert Choisy, Louis Théophile Dufour-Vernes, and Jacques Augustine Galiffe (Geneva: Jullien, 1902–1918), 1: 57.

73. *R.Consist.* 6: 136. On actions taken against others for allegedly dancing at Blondel's wedding, see 6: 143, 145, 150, 158 159.

74. In July 1553, the Consistory reprimanded one of its own members, the lay assistant Jacques-Nicolas Vulliet, for being in the habit of dancing. Vulliet confessed to having acted inappropriately but insisted that he had danced only with other men, not with women; *R.Consist.* 8: 119. James Blakeley found that in the neighboring Pays de Vaud, people danced whenever they got the chance to do so; "Aspects de la confessionnalisation durant l'introduction de la Réforme en Pays de Vaud," *Revue historique vaudoise* 119 (2011): 135–36.

75. *C.O.* 10: 56.

76. AEG, R.Consist. 13: 20v; PC 1ᵉʳᵉ Sér. 717.

77. AEG, R.Consist. 13: 22v; PC 1ᵉʳᵉ Sér. 718.

78. AEG, R.Consist. 17: 162v, 164v, 173v, 175; PC 1ᵉʳᵉ Sér. 932. Among those receiving such a sentence was François Lullin, himself a former assistant of the Consistory.

79. AEG, R.Consist. 21: 68r–v.

80. Manetsch found that men outnumbered women by more than two to one among those who were suspended from the Supper for the years 1568–1582 (711 to 325), but women outnumbered men (142 to 101) among those excluded for dancing and illicit songs; "Pastoral Care," 289.

81. Philippe Chareyre found that the consistory of Nîmes failed in its attempts to eliminate dancing, the most common infraction it heard, in the late sixteenth and early

seventeenth century; "Jeux interdits, jeux tolérés: L'application de la discipline réformée dans la France méridionale," in *Le plaisir et la transgression en France et en Espagne aux XVIe et XVIIe siècles: Colloque international organisé à l'Université de Pau et des Pays de l'Adour les 12 et 13 mai 2005*, ed. Maurice Daumas, Adrián Blázquez, Olivier Caporossi, and Philippe Chareyre (Orthez: Gascogne, 2007), 405; Chareryre, "Great Difficulties," 88–90. See also Murdock, "Dancing Calvinists," 44–59; Todd, *Culture of Protestantism*, 216.

82. Adhémar Esmein, *Le mariage en droit canonique*, 2 vols., 2d ed. (Paris: Librairie du Recueil Sirey, 1929), 1: 100–101; R. H. Helmholz, *Marriage Litigation in Medieval England* (Cambridge: Cambridge University Press, 1974), 26–27.

83. Paul Viollet, *Histoire du droit civil français* (Paris: Librairie de la société du recueil général des lois et des arrêts, 1905), 445. These ages had been set by Roman law.

84. *C.O.* 10: 33–44, 105–14.

85. Seeger, *Nullité de mariage*, 118–19, 196. In 1545 the Consistory decided "to follow whatever edicts there may be, even if they have not yet been passed." *R.Consist.* 2: 81; Kingdon, *Reforming Geneva*, 84.

86. Watt, *Making Modern Marriage*, 58–59; Thomas Max Safley, *Let No Man Put Asunder: The Control of Marriage in the German Southwest: A Comparative Study, 1550–1600* (Kirksville, MO: Sixteenth Century Journal Publishers, 1984), 170–73; Seeger, *Nullité de mariage*, 305–74.

87. Safley, *Let No Man*, 173; Watt, *Making Modern Marriage*, 98–101.

88. Kingdon, *Reforming Geneva*, 82–83; Harrington, *Reordering Marriage*, 106–13.

89. *R.Consist.* 5: 194–95, 206, 216; AEG, RC 45: 91, 93r–v (September 15, 18, 1550); PC 2e Sér. 881. *Messieurs* ordered him "de prendre et nurrir l'enfant."

90. AEG, PC 1ère Sér. 716; R.Consist. 13: 26v–27, 47. We do not know his exact age.

91. AEG, R.Consist. 17: 90r–v.

92. Bernard Gagnebin, "L'Histoire des manuscrits des sermons de Calvin," in *Sermons sur le Livre d'Esaïe, chapitres 13–29*, ed. Georges A. Barrois, *Supplementa Calviniana, Sermons inédits 2* (Neukirchen Kreis Moers: Neukirchen Verlag der Buchhandlung des Erziehungsvereins, 1961), xiv–xxvii; McKee, *Pastoral Ministry*, 499–502.

93. AEG, R.Consist. 20: 76r–v, 78v.

94. AEG, R.Consist. 18: 156r–v.

95. AEG, R.Consist. 18: 158v.

96. AEG, R.Consist. 18: 164r–v; Jur. Pen. A2: 181 (December 1, 1561).

97. Watt, *Making Modern Marriage*, 71. By the early seventeenth century, many Reformed Protestants were backing away from this stand. In France, the Reformed church decided in 1612 that betrothal was not a binding marriage promise, and in seventeenth-century Reformed Holland, marriage betrothals, even those written and notarized, were not necessarily regarded as contractually binding; magistrates seemed reluctant to enforce them unless the couple had had sexual relations; Raymond A. Mentzer, "The Reformed Churches of France and Medieval Canon Law," in *Canon Law in Protestant Lands*, ed. Richard H. Helmholz (Berlin: Duncker and Humblot, 1992), 176.

98. AEG, R.Consist. 15: 157r–v.

99. AEG, R.Consist. 15: 161v–62, 162v–63.

100. Esmein, *Mariage en droit canonique,* 1: 100–101.

101. AEG, R.Consist. 18: 167.

102. *R.Consist.* 11: 184.

103. AEG, RC 51: 255 (August 10, 1556).

104. AEG, R.Consist. 14: 35.

105. AEG, R.Consist. 14: 41v–42.

106. AEG, RC 54: 273 (September 1, 1558); *C.O.* 21: 702. See also Witte and Kingdon, *Sex, Marriage and Family,* 203–9; Seeger, *Nullité de mariage,* 332–34. On demographic information in Reformation Geneva, including the age at first marriage for males and females, see E. William Monter, "Historical Demography and Religious History in Sixteenth-Century Geneva," *Journal of Interdisciplinary History* 9 (1979): 399–427; Perrenoud, *Population de Genève*; Alfred Perrenoud, "Les comportements démographiques," in *L'économie genevoise de la Réforme à la fin de l'Ancien Régime, XVIᵉ–XVIIIᵉ siècles,* ed. Anne-Marie Piuz and Liliane Mottu-Weber (Geneva: Georg, 1990), 85–93.

107. *R.Consist.* 11: 326.

108. AEG, RC 52: 188v, 192v (January 5, 8, 1557); Juridictions Civiles R1, causes matrimoniales: 45r–v. D'Orsières and de Crouz made other appeals for permission to marry but to no avail; RC 52: 195v, 209v (January 11, 19, 1557); *Registres de la Compagnie* 2: 71. A few days later the Consistory asked the Council to draw up an edict prohibiting "l'inegalité des eages de ceulx qu'ilz se marient." *R.Consist.* 11: 331. The Council discussed the matter and the following week composed a text, which, however, is not extant; RC 52: 219v, 234v–35 (January 25, February 1, 1557).

109. AEG, R.Consist. 17: 14, 19.

110. Gordon, *Calvin,* 281–82; *C.O.* 17: 351–53 (epistle 2966). See also Calvin's letter to Farel; 17: 351–53, 335–36 (epistle 2958).

111. Until the age of forty, a woman could not marry a man more than ten years younger than she was; after forty she could not marry a man more than five years her junior. A man sixty years and older could marry a woman only if she were at least half his age; *Sources du droit,* ed. Rivoire and van Berchem, 3: 336; Seeger, *Nullité de mariage,* 329.

112. *R.Consist.* 5: 178–79; AEG, RC 45: 70 (August 18, 1550).

113. *R.Consist.* 5: 230; François-Alexandre Aubert de La Chesnaye Des Bois, *Dictionnaire de la noblesse,* 15 vols. (Paris: Duchesne, 1770–1786), 10: 544; Pierre de Vaissière, *Charles de Marillac, ambassadeur et homme politique sous les règnes de François Iᵉʳ, Henry II, et François II* (Paris: 1889; repr. Geneva: Slatkine, 1971), 72–73, 420.

114. *R.Consist.* 5: 230; AEG, PC 2ᵉ Sér. 888; RC 45: 206v (February 24, 1551).

115. AEG, RC 55: 32v (April 17, 1559). After a bitter denunciation by Jeanne d'Albret, Queen of Navarre, however, Spifame was executed in Geneva in 1566 for, among other things, having supposedly presented to the Consistory a false marriage contract seven years earlier; see the forthcoming *R.Consist.* 15: 139v and note.

116. AEG, R.Consist. 16: 272v; 18: 77v, 81v.

117. AEG, R.Consist. 18: 167v.

118. Alas, this reconciliation did not last. When the couple again appeared for their conflicts the following year, the Consistory excluded them from the Supper and referred them to the Council with the recommendation that they be banished. Magistrates banished them for life in March 1562, and the Consistory advised against their petition to be readmitted in October of the same year; AEG, R.Consist. 19: 18r–v, 162v; PC 1ère Sér. 1022.

119. *R. Consist.* 4: 115. On the actions of Lausanne's consistory against violence, see Nicole Staremberg Goy, "Contenir la parole et le geste à Lausanne au XVIIIᵉ siècle: Le consistoire de la ville face à la violence," in *Sous l'oeil*, 175–92. For litigation concerning domestic violence in seventeenth-century France, see Julie Hardwick, *Family Business: Litigation and the Political Economies of Daily Life in Early Modern France* (Oxford: Oxford University Press, 2009), 183–221.

120. *R.Consist.* 11: 174–75.

121. AEG, R.Consist. 16: 235.

122. AEG, R.Consist. 16: 237v.

123. AEG, R.Consist. 17: 21.

124. *R.Consist.* 1: 104–5; AEG, R.Consist. 18: 178v.

125. Harrington also found that physical abuse rarely resulted in serious punishment; *Reordering Marriage*, 266–67.

126. *R.Consist.* 7: 91.

127. AEG, PC 1ère Sér. 596; RC 52: 17v (September 22, 1556).

128. AEG, R.Consist. 16: 207v.

129. AEG, PC 1ère Sér. 888.

130. AEG, R.Consist. 19: 99r–v; Jur. Pen. A3–1562: 47 (July 6, 1562).

131. AEG, R.Consist. 18: 172r–v; Jur. Pen. 183v (December 25, 1561).

132. AEG, R.Consist. 18: 193. The Consistory's previous threats against Pradaire clearly had no teeth, and, given this last command to obey her husband, I cannot understand how this case can be cited as a good example of the Consistory's desire to protect the weak and vulnerable; see Manetsch, *Calvin's Company*, 217.

133. Beam, "Female Violence."

134. AEG, R.Consist. 18: 201v–2.

135. AEG, R.Consist. 19: 79v–80; PC 1ère Sér. 1045. See Hardwick, *Family Business*, 183–221; Joy Willtenburg, *Disorderly Women and Female Power in the Street Literature of Early Modern England and Germany* (Charlottesville: University Press of Virginia, 1992).

136. James Brundage, *Law, Sex and Christian Society in Medieval Europe* (Chicago: University of Chicago Press, 1987), 146, 433; Esmein, *Mariage en droit canonique*, 2: 56–57, 106; Roderick Phillips, *Putting Asunder: A History of Divorce in Western Society* (Cambridge: Cambridge University Press, 1988), 13–14.

137. Brundage, *Law, Sex and Society*, 334, 374; Phillips, *Putting Asunder*, 86, 90–94; Watt, "Impact of Reformation," 1: 130–31; Watt, *Making Modern Marriage*, 122–28.

138. On divorce in Geneva, see Seeger, *Nullité de mariage*, 375–434; Kingdon, *Adultery*.

139. Studies have found that if a couple had managed to have sexual relations just once, there could be no divorce on the ground of sexual dysfunction; Watt, *Making Modern Marriage*, 135–36.

140. AEG, RC 53: 381, 385v (November 1, 2, 1557); *R.Consist.* 12: 332–33. De Theys's attempts to bypass the Consistory by going back to the Council were in vain; RC 53: 389r–v, 392v–93 (November 5, 8, 1557).

141. AEG, RC Part. 11: 179v–80 (February 1, 1558); *R.Consist.* 12: 428.

142. AEG, R.Consist. 14: 123v–24, 126v–27v.

143. AEG, R.Consist. 14: 155, 159v; Jur. Pen. K1: (unnumbered folio; February 2, 1559); Jur. Pen. A2: 3v (February 13, 1559); PC 2ᵉ Sér. 1188; RC 54: 86 (February 14, 1558).

144. AEG, R.Consist. 15: 22v–23, 24, 25.

145. AEG, R.Consist. 15: 44, 50v; Jur. Pen. A2: 13 (March 27, 1559).

146. AEG, R.Consist. 15: 132v–33, 137r–v; Jur. Pen. A2: 23, 25v, 36, 37v (May 9, 29; July 17, 24, 1559); Galiffe et al., eds., *Notices généalogiques*, 3: 468–69.

147. See Philip Benedict, *Season of Conspiracy: Calvin, the French Reformed Churches, and Protestant Plotting in the Reign of Francis II (1559–60)* (Philadelphia: American Philosophical Society Press, 2019).

148. Charmarie J. Blaisdell, "Calvin's Letters to Women: The Courting of Ladies in High Places," *Sixteenth Century Journal* 13 (1982): 71.

149. AEG, R.Consist. 19: 41v, 48.

150. AEG, R.Consist. 19: 96v, 100.

151. AEG, R.Consist. 19: 172v, 176v, 186.

152. *R.Consist.* 4: 140–43, 149; AEG, RC 43: 211, 214, 219v (October 5, 11, 16, 1548).

153. AEG, RC 53: 16v (February 15, 1557); PC 1ᵉʳᵉ Sér., 610. For a fuller discussion of this case, see Kingdon, *Adultery*, 71–97.

154. AEG, R.Consist. 17: 172v, 173v–74. In January 1561, authorities handled the case of Pierre Pierre—his first and last names were indeed the same!—and his wife quite differently. His wife, whose name was not mentioned, had committed adultery, but Pierre forgave her and she was neither whipped nor banished. The Consistory obliged her to get on her knees and ask for forgiveness from God, *Messieurs*, and her husband. She was to abstain from the Supper of Easter and before being readmitted at Pentecost, she was to acknowledge publicly her error in Saint-Pierre; 17: 215v.

155. AEG, RC Part. 12: 24 (April 14, 1558); R.Consist. 13: 57v, 60v–61, 63r–v; RC 54: 211v (June 13, 1558).

156. In Reformation Neuchâtel, there were examples of men returning home after abandoning their wives and children without providing any financial support or even news of their whereabouts during very long absences (in one case, twelve years). When they discovered that their wives had committed adultery during their absences, they successfully filed for divorce on the ground of adultery and received custody of their children and all the assets of their wives; Watt, *Making Modern Marriage*, 131–33.

157. There were exceptional cases in which the Consistory of Geneva, in considering cases involving lengthy desertions, awarded divorces quite quickly. In February 1560, the Consistory accorded a divorce to Catherine Passirame in just one session; witnesses testified that her behavior was impeccable and that her husband, Claude Garnier, had left her seven or eight years earlier; AEG, R.Consist. 17: 6r–v. Also notable was the divorce granted in 1564 to Michée Bonivard from Jean Gaudi, absent for twelve years. After hearing witnesses in the second week it considered the case, the Consistory ruled in her favor, provided she made announcements to summon him; 21: 5, 6v, 41.

158. Galiffe et al., eds., *Notices généalogiques*, 5: 134–41. For having left Catholicism, he did not inherit the title, but in Geneva he was nonetheless commonly referred to as the Marquis.

159. AEG, R.Consist. 15: 59, 62v–63, 67v, 149; Jur. Pen. A2: 18, 20, 60 (April 17, 21; November 7, 1559).

160. For a fine analysis of this divorce, see Kingdon, *Adultery*, 143–65; see also Benedetto Croce, "Il Marchese di Vico, Galeazzo Caracciolo," in *Vite di avventure di fede e di passione* (Bari: Laterza, 1936), 179–281.

161. After Calvin's death, Theodore Beza wrote *Tractatio de repudiis et divortiis* to serve as a manual for Reformed Protestants on divorce. He extended the Pauline privilege to cover desertion in general, not just for religious reasons; Kingdon, *Adultery*, 166–74.

162. Watt, *Making Modern Marriage*, 122–33; Walther Köhler, *Zürcher Ehegericht und Genfer Konsistorium*, 2 vols. (Leipzig: M. Heinsius Nachfolger, 1932–1942), 1: 109; E. William Monter, "Women in Calvinist Geneva (1550–1800)," *Signs* 6 (1980): 195; Thérèse Pittard, *Femmes de Genève aux jours d'autrefois* (Geneva: Labor et Fides, 1946), 31–34; Safley, *Let No Man*, 175; Seeger, *Nullité de mariage*, 403–4, 417.

163. *R.Consist.*1: 104–5.

164. AEG, R.Consist. 17: 40v. Concerning her husband, see RC 54: 359, 359v, 360v, 361v, 362v (January 19, 20, 23, 26, 27, 1559).

165. AEG, R.Consist. 20: 165v, 168.

166. AEG, R.Consist. 21: 69; Jur. Pen. A3–1564: 32 (May 29, 1564).

167. *R.Consist.* 8: 111, 115–16; AEG, PC 2ᵉ Sér. 1019; RC Part. 7: 100v, 104r–v, 105v–6, 107r–v (July 10, 14, 17, 18, 20, 21, 1553); *R.Consist.* 10: 271; Watt, "Impact of Reformation," 136. Watt finds that, quite exceptionally, matrimonial courts in Neuchâtel in the eighteenth century awarded judicial separations and later divorces for cruelty and eventually even incompatibility; *Making Modern Marriage*, 146–47, 219–60. In the latter half of the eighteenth century, the Consistory of Lausanne started granting separations for cruelty even though it technically did not have the right to do so (in territory subject to Bern, the right to accord separations was reserved to Bern's Chorgericht); Nicole Staremberg Goy, "'Absolument contraire aux égards d'heus au sexe feminine?' Maltraitance conjugale et pratique consistoriale lausannoise à l'époque des Lumières," *Traverse: Zeitschrift für Geschichte=Revue d'histoire* 2 (2005): 45–63.

168. On separations in seventeenth-century France, see Hardwick, *Family Business*. In her work on Scotland, Margo Todd found that kirk sessions did award some separations and obliged men to provide material support for their wives; *Culture of Protestantism*, 283–84.

169. Based on research on early modern rural Bern, Heinrich Richard Schmidt gives a very optimistic assessment of the support that women received from courts in the area of matrimonial disputes: "Marital discipline was a field in which women could domesticate their men. This alliance, between the values of the women complaining and the values that the Chorgericht had to defend, functioned until the end of the *ancien régime*. The idea of marriage revealed by the Reformed morals courts cannot be described as predominantly patriarchal, but originated from the Christian marriage based on equality, consensus and co-operation"; "Morals Courts in Rural Berne," 173. True, a man from Geneva's countryside complained in the early 1600s that the Consistory had produced a "paradise for women" through its zealous policing of marital relations, but we should probably take his jeremiad with a grain of salt; E. William Monter, "Women in Calvinist Geneva," *Signs* 6 (1980): 191; Benedict, *Christ's Churches*, 480–81.

170. In this regard, I disagree with Manetsch's assessment; *Calvin's Company*, 219. By contrast, there definitely was an alliance between women and the consistories in Neuchâtel in the eighteenth century: "That women outnumbered men as plaintiffs for almost all forms of marital litigation underscores the fact that only in the eighteenth century did the *Justices matrimoniales* of the principality of Neuchâtel and Valangin become essentially women's courts." Watt, *Making Modern Marriage*, 260.

Chapter 5

1. On witchcraft in Geneva, see E. William Monter, *Witchcraft in France and Switzerland: The Borderlands during the Reformation* (Ithaca, NY: Cornell University Press, 1976), esp. 42–66. See also Christian Broye, *Sorcellerie et superstitions à Genève: XVIe–XVIIIe siècle* (Geneva: Le Concept moderne, 1990). Michèle Robert found that in Neuchâtel as well the consistories did not hear many cases of witchcraft; *Que dorénavant*, 315–20.

2. In the revised version (1920) of his essay on the Protestant ethic and capitalism, Max Weber wrote that with Calvinism, the "great historic process in the development of religions, the elimination of magic from the world . . . came . . . to its logical conclusion"; *The Protestant Ethic and the Spirit of Capitalism*, trans. Talcott Parsons (London: George Allen and Unwin, 1948), 105. In another work, Weber expressed the view that the Mass was a form of magic; *The Sociology of Religion*, trans. Ephraim Fischoff (Boston: Beacon Press, 1963), 151–52. For examples of scholarship that emphatically rejects the notion that magic and modernity are incompatible, see various essays in *Magic in the Modern World: Strategies of Repression and Legitimization*, ed. Edward Bever and Randall Styers (University Park: Pennsylvania State University Press, 2017).

3. *R.Consist.* 4: 80–81.

4. *R.Consist.* 4: 94.

5. By contrast, the Reformed consistory of Valangin, a small *seigneurie* within the principality of Neuchâtel, heard only four such cases between 1547 and 1699; Robert, *Que dorénavant*, 309.

6. *R.Consist.* 1: 218–19. The disease was variously called *gorraz* or *gormoz*, apparently variants of *gourme*, which means impetigo. Du Chabloz declared that Buclin was cured by "le lovet," probably a variation in spelling of the old French word "le lovin." This referred to aconite, a plant also known as monkshood or wolfsbane. Though parts of this plant are poisonous, its dried roots have long been used as a sedative and painkiller; Frédéric Godefroy, *Lexique de l'ancien français*, ed. J. Bonnard and A. Salmon (Paris: Honoré Champion, 1990), SV "lovin."

7. The Council records, however, do not indicate that Du Chabloz ever actually appeared there.

8. AEG, R.Consist. 20: 89v. The Council sent him to jail; Jur. Pen. A3–1563: 46v (July 30, 1563).

9. AEG, R.Consist. 20: 185v. The Council agreed to try to arrest him; Jur. Pen. A3–1563: 85v (January 3, 1564).

10. Manetsch found that among those suspended from the Supper for "folk religion," women outnumbered men ninety-nine to sixty-three; *Calvin's Company*, 201.

11. These figures include several people who could not be subpoenaed to appear before the Consistory since they lived in villages that were outside Genevan territory. On several occasions, Genevans were censured simply for encouraging others to consult healers even though no one actually followed this advice. In several such cases, the records do not identify the names of the would-be healers. On four occasions, the registers indicate that people sought the services of "bons hereges" without identifying the sex of these healers. There does not appear to be a gender imbalance, however, among those who tried to consult healers. See also Mentzer, "Réforme calviniste des moeurs à Nîmes," 23.

12. *R.Consist.* 3: 34; 5: 51; 6: 176.

13. *R.Consist.* 8: 90, 100.

14. *R.Consist.* 8: 120.

15. See Léon Gautier, *La médecine à Genève jusqu'à la fin du XVIIIᵉ siècle* (Geneva: Jullien, 1906), 171–214.

16. *R.Consist.* 3: 233–34.

17. *R.Consist.* 3: 233–34. For similar findings in Britain, see Owen Davies, *Cunning-Folk: Popular Magic in English History* (London: Hambledon and London, 2003), 15–16; Todd, *Culture of Protestantism*, 355–59.

18. *R.Consist.* 5: 10, 27, 30–31.

19. *R.Consist.* 5: 13, 23, 33, 54.

20. AEG, R.Consist. 20: 100v–101. Subsequently, the Consistory admonished Pierre Lonnex, the man who advised Coplet, and Lonnex's wife. That couple in turn implicated two other men in bringing an unnamed man to them to tend to Lonnex's wife

during an illness. The Consistory excluded one of these men, Nicod Hanse, from communion because he was viewed as the ultimate source of all this disorder; 20: 128r–v, 133v, 139v. Hanse was the only person who received any punishment beyond a censure, and even he was not referred to the Small Council.

21. AEG, R.Consist. 19: 220.

22. See Henri Meylan, "La Bonne Fontaine de Saint-Cergue," *Revue historique vaudoise* 64 (1956): 99–106.

23. *R.Consist.* 11: 226.

24. AEG, RC 52: 32 (October 5, 1556); *R.Consist.* 11: 246.

25. *R.Consist.* 11: 227; RC 52: 31 (October 5, 1556). Aimé Plonjon later served as a member of the Council of Two Hundred in 1559, and his father, Louis Plonjon, had served as syndic in 1509 and 1519; Galiffe et al., eds., *Notices généalogiques*, 3: 419; *R.Consist.* 2: 252n841.

26. Monter did find that among those excommunicated for "superstitions" for the years 1564–1569, rural residents easily outnumbered their urban counterparts; "Consistory of Geneva," 479–80. Likewise, Manetsch found that the percentage of suspensions from the Supper for "folk religion" was considerably higher in the countryside than in the city; *Calvin's Company*, 206–7.

27. *R.Consist.* 12: 105; AEG, RC 53: 99 (April 12, 1557).

28. AEG, PC 1ère Sér. 621.

29. For the history of holy wells in the British Isles, see Janet Bord and Colin Bord, *Sacred Waters: Holy Wells and Water Lore in Britain and Ireland* (London: Granada, 1985); Francis Jones, *The Holy Wells of Wales* (Cardiff: University of Wales Press, 1954); and Alexandra Walsham, "Reforming the Waters: Holy Wells and Healing Springs in Protestant England," in *Life and Thought in the Northern Church c. 1100–c. 1700: Essays in Honor of Claire Cross*, ed. Diana Wood (Woodbridge: Boydell, 1999), 227–56. In Reformation Scotland, kirk sessions convoked many people for making pilgrimages to holy wells, which numbered in the hundreds and were associated with magical cures; Todd, *Culture of Protestantism*, esp. 205–9.

30. See E. William Monter and John Tedeschi, "Toward a Statistical Profile of the Italian Inquisitions, Sixteenth to Eighteenth Centuries," in *The Inquisition in Early Modern Europe: Studies on Sources and Methods*, ed. Gustav Henningsen and John Tedeschi (Dekalb: Northern Illinois University Press, 1986), 130–57; Giovanni Romeo, *Inquisitori, esorcisti e streghe nell'Italia della Controriforma* (Florence: Sansoni, 1990), 176–77, 201–46; Schutte, *Aspiring Saints*, 28–29.

31. See AEG, PC 2e Sér. 1101.

32. Philip Rieder has written a very good article on Catholic healing practices in the area around Geneva from the outbreak of the Reformation to the mid-eighteenth century; "Miracles and Heretics: Protestants and Catholic Healing Practices in and around Geneva 1530–1750," *Social History of Medicine* 23 (2010): 227–43. He does not distinguish, however, between superstitious and Catholic healings. Post-Tridentine Catholicism aggressively attacked a wide range of superstitions. Moreover, Rieder's claim

that Genevans regularly sought Catholic remedies for ills into the eighteenth century is problematic. We should not accept at face value the claims by Catholic priests, who cultivated reputations for working miracles, that Genevan Protestants had been cured of illnesses by the waters at a fountain in Savoy.

33. *R.Consist.* 7: 9–10, 14, 43. There is no record of any of them actually appearing before the Small Council.

34. *R.Consist.* 10: 179–80, 185, 186, 192–93.

35. *R.Consist.* 10: 192–93.

36. AEG, R.Consist. 20: 971r–v.

37. *R.Consist.* 10: 299–300.

38. AEG, R.Consist. 17: 60v.

39. AEG, R.Consist. 17: 64.

40. AEG, R.Consist. 17: 130v.

41. Manetsch, *Calvin's Company*, 208.

42. Rieder, "Miracles and Heretics," 228.

43. Merry E. Wiesner, *Women and Gender in Early Modern Europe* (Cambridge: Cambridge University Press, 1993), 84, 95.

44. By contrast, English clergymen of the sixteenth and seventeenth century asserted that cunning-folk were in league with the devil, a view apparently not shared by the population at large; Davies, *Cunning-Folk*, 29–65.

45. In a letter written in March 1545, Calvin expressed approval of the aggressive actions taken against men and women who reputedly had made a pact with the devil to destroy the city by spreading the plague; *C.O.* 12: 55–56 (epistle 627); John L. Teall, "Witchcraft and Calvinism in Elizabethan England: Divine Power and Human Agency," *Journal of the History of Ideas* 23 (1962): 28n19. Later that year, Calvin and his fellow pastor, Jacques Bernard, appeared before the Small Council to urge authorities to extirpate "heriges" from the area around Peney in the Genevan countryside; AEG, RC 40: 295v (November 19, 1545); Monter, *Witchcraft in France and Switzerland*, 31n36; William G. Naphy, *Plagues, Poisons, and Potions: Plague-Spreading Conspiracies in the Western Alps c. 1530–1640* (Manchester: Manchester University Press, 2002); Oskar Pfister, *Calvins Eingreifen in die Hexer- und Hexenprozessen von Peney 1545 nach seiner Bedeutung für Geschichte und Gegenwart* (Zurich: Artemis, 1947), 33.

46. *R.Consist.* 7: 96; AEG, RC. Part. 6: 10 (June 27, 1552). In 1560 she petitioned the Consistory for permission to divorce and remarry, which the Consistory recommended that the Council grant; R.Consist. 17: 10v, 21v–22, 28r–v. Her life obviously was not unduly troubled by the suspicions expressed back in 1552.

47. AEG, R.Consist. 19: 120v.

48. AEG, R.Consist. 19: 121v.

49. *Livre des habitants de Genève*, 2 vols., ed. Paul Frédéric Geisendorf (Geneva: Droz, 1957), 1: 5.

50. The accused added that Calvin said things in his sermon that Perrotel himself had said in secret in his room and concluded, "Il ne peult cela sçavoir sinon par revellation de

mauvais esprit." AEG, PC 2ᵉ Sér. 882; RC 45: 109v, 111 (October 14, 17, 1550); *R.Consist.*
5: 244, n. 1683.

51. *R.Consist.* 9: 12–13.

52. AEG, R.Consist. 18: 161.

53. AEG, R.Consist. 17: 165v.

54. AEG, R.Consist. 17: 169v.

55. AEG, R.Consist. 19: 57, 60v–61.

56. AEG, R.Consist. 19: 64v, 69.

57. See the various essays that examine the similarities and differences between consistories and Inquisitions of the early modern world in *Judging Faith*, ed. Parker and Starr-LeBeau.

58. Romano Canosa, *Sessualità e Inquisizione in Italia tra Cinquecento e Seicento* (Rome: Sapere 2000, 1994), 223. On love magic, see Mary O'Neil, "Magical Healing, Love Magic and the Inquisition in Late Sixteenth-Century Modena," in *Inquisition and Society in Early Modern Europe*, ed. Stephen Haliczer (London: Croom Helm, 1987), 88–114; Guido Ruggiero, "That Old Black Magic Called Love," in *Binding Passions: Tales of Magic, Marriage and Power at the End of the Renaissance* (Oxford: Oxford University Press), 88–129; and Jeffrey R. Watt, "Love Magic and the Inquisition: A Case from Seventeenth-Century Italy," *Sixteenth Century Journal* 41 (2010): 675–89.

59. *R.Consist.* 7: 179. For an almost identical case, in which the Consistory declared the promises null but paid no attention to the allegations of love magic, see 7: 210–11.

60. AEG, R.Consist. 15: 110, 117v; PC 1ᵉʳᵉ Sér. 826, 830, 833.

61. Raymond A. Mentzer found one instance in which the Consistory of Nîmes severely rebuked a young man for having consulted a magician in order to find some coins that his late father had reputedly hidden; "*Disciplina nervus ecclesiae*: The Calvinist Reform of Morals at Nîmes," *Sixteenth Century Journal* 18 (1987): 94.

62. AEG, R.Consist. 20: 103.

63. AEG, R.Consist. 20: 110v–111. The Council complied, had Goy jailed, and asked both *châtelains* to investigate; Jur. Pen. A3–1563: 54 (August 30, 1563).

64. Though there is no mention of her in the Consistory registers, lay authorities convicted Antonia Patron in December 1542 of trying to employ magic to find lost objects; she was condemned to walk through the streets of the city carrying the sieve and the fork she had used in her spells; AEG, PC 1ᵉʳᵉ Sér. 365.

65. According to Candido Brognolo, a seventeenth-century authority on exorcism and witchcraft, an unconsecrated host could be a powerful weapon in love magic, a consecrated host even more potent, and burning a consecrated host rendered it a still more powerful tool for winning the love of another; *Alexicacon, Hoc est Opus de Maleficiis ac Morbis Maleficiis*, 2 vols. (Venice: Giovan Battista Catanei, 1668), 1: 264.

66. Nicolau Eymerich and Francisco Peña, *Il manuale dell'Inquisitore*, trans. and ed. Louis Sala-Molins (Rome: Fanucci, 2000), 77–78n21; Robert W. Scribner, "Ritual and Popular Belief in Catholic Germany at the Time of the Reformation," in *Popular*

Culture and Popular Movements in Reformation Germany (London: Hambledon Press, 1987), 36, 39–40; in the same volume see "Sorcery, Superstition and Society: The Witch of Urach," 260–61.

67. Mary Douglas, *Natural Symbols: Explorations in Cosmology* (New York: Routledge, 1970), 1, 3, 7; Peter Burke, "The Repudiation of Ritual in Early Modern Europe," in *The Historical Anthropology of Early Modern Italy: Essays on Perception and Communication* (Cambridge: Cambridge University Press, 1987), 223–38. See Grosse, *Rituels*, 14–16.

68. Karant-Nunn, *Reformation of Ritual*, 107–37.

69. Robert W. Scribner, "Ritual and Reformation," in *Popular Culture*, 103–22.

70. Todd, *Culture of Protestantism*, 21, 22.

71. Grosse, *Rituels*, esp. 13–33; see also Roussel, "Comment faire la cène,?" 195–216; and "'Faire la Cène,'" 99–119.

72. AEG, R.Consist. 17: 99v.

73. AEG, R.Consist. 17: 204.

74. A couple of weeks later, three men appeared before the Consistory concerning the issue of taking communion bread home. These included Pierre Joly, who admitted taking some bread home to his sick wife in the hope that it would cheer her up. Espin Guillonet insisted that he was not motivated to take the bread out of "superstition," and the Consistory limited itself to admonishing all three, especially Joly, to attend the sermons more regularly in order to learn more about religion; AEG, R.Consist. 17: 214v. Among the other rare cases that even hint at the possible magical use of communion bread was that involving Antoine Buard in 1555. Though at first denying the charge, Buard eventually admitted that she took the communion bread home, placed it on her buffet, and ate it later that day. She had drunk the wine of the Eucharist with everyone else in the church of St. Gervais. The Consistory excluded her from communion, though this seemed primarily because she was "silly" and "obstinate" for having at first denied the truth. There was no mention of any motive behind taking the bread. The fact that she ate it the same day would militate against a wish to use it in a magical spell; *R.Consist.* 10: 32, 36–37, 45–46.

75. Monter found that the most common allegation mentioned in Genevan witchcraft trials after 1605 was causing demonic possession; *Witchcraft in France and Switzerland*, 59–60. See also Paul Ladame, *Les Possédés et les démoniaques à Genève au XVIIe siècle* (Geneva: Schira, 1892).

76. *R.Consist.* 9: 115; AEG, RC Part. 8: 75, 79 (June 4, 11, 1554).

77. Keith Thomas, *Religion and the Decline of Magic: Studies in Popular Beliefs in Sixteenth and Seventeenth Century England* (Oxford: Oxford University Press, 1971), 493–501.

78. Prosperi, *Tribunali della coscienza*, 422; Oscar Di Simplicio, *Autunno della stregoneria: Maleficio e magia nell'Italia moderna* (Bologna: Il Mulino, 2005), 275–77; Romeo, *Inquisitori*, 143, 244; Jeffrey R. Watt, "The Demons of Carpi: Exorcism, Witchcraft, and the Inquisition in a Seventeenth-Century Convent," *Archiv für*

Reformationsgeschichte 98 (2007): 107–33; Jeffrey R. Watt, *The Scourge of Demons: Possession, Lust, and Witchcraft in a Seventeenth-Century Italian Convent* (Rochester, NY: University of Rochester Press, 2009), 104–40.

79. Sarah Ferber, *Demonic Possession and Exorcism in Early Modern France* (London: Routledge, 2004), esp. 89–112. Ferber's reference to Huguenots' use of "exorcisms" is problematic. It is quite a stretch to equate with exorcism a Reformed pastor's request that the congregation pray for a woman who was reputedly possessed; Ferber, 32.

80. *R.Consist.* 7: 88.

81. "Maudit soit l'home, il m'a bien cuit"; *R.Consist.* 4: 72.

82. "Il fault qu'il recognoisse la bonne voulunté du Seigneur et sa providence et ne faire come le chien qui mord la pierre qu'on luy envoie contre, car toutes choses nous adviennent par la volunté et providence du Soverain." *R.Consist.* 4: 73. On June 4, 1548, Aubert made his case before the Small Council, which asked the *châtelain* of Genthod to investigate the charges of witchcraft. Claude Venarre was imprisoned but was released on June 26 as the Council concluded that the charges against him could not be proved. In October of the following year, however, Venarre was banished for life from Genthod and Satigny on suspicion of having provoked, through witchcraft, a young man to hang himself; *R.Consist.* 4: 73n405; AEG, RC 44: 132, 133r–v, 142, 183v, 229v, 230v, 231 (June 15, 17, 27; August 8; October 1, 3, 4, 1549); PC 1ᵉʳᵉ Sér. 451

83. Euan Cameron says the following about Protestantism's possible contribution to disenchantment: "The reformers inclined, for the most part, to the extreme providentialist view that evil occurred through an ultimately wise, though deeply hidden and mysterious, decision of God. Consequently, all the resources to resist misfortune that had been zealously cultivated in the old Church were beside the point. More deeply still, the reformers' providentialism cast the role of the devil and evil spirits in general into a very different role. The devil was, at best, an entirely captive instrument of the divine purposes." *Enchanted Europe: Superstition, Reason and Religion, 1250–1750* (Oxford: Oxford University Press, 2010), 23.

84. For the years 1537–1681, Monter found in Geneva traces of 477 witchcraft trials, which resulted in 141 executions, amounting to an execution rate of about 30 percent. These figures are skewed, however, by four panics (in 1545, 1567–1568, 1571, and 1615) in which large numbers of people were accused of spreading the plague through diabolical means. These trials against plague-spreaders produced execution rates of over 40 percent, whereas the 68 executions for the remaining 318 trials equate to an execution rate of only 21 percent. Most of those not sentenced to death were banished; *Witchcraft in France and Switzerland,* 45–49. See also Naphy, *Plagues, Poisons, and Potions.*

85. In regard to Geneva's low execution rate of accused witches, Monter persuasively argues, "Calvinism may be a partial explanation for Geneva's remarkably low rate of convictions: given any reasonable grounds for doubt, Genevan judges preferred to leave suspected witches to the judgment of God by expelling them, since they knew that human justice is always imperfect." *Witchcraft in France and Switzerland,* 66.

86. Teall, "Witchcraft and Calvinism," 31.

87. On the issue of reconciliation for Calvin and for Huguenots, see articles in *Conciliation and Confession: The Struggle for Unity in the Age of Reform, 1415–1648*, ed. Howard P. Louthan and Randall C. Zachman (Notre Dame, IN: University of Notre Dame Press, 2004).

88. John Calvin, *Institutes of the Christian Religion, 1536 Edition*, trans. Ford Battles (Grand Rapids, MI: William B. Eerdmans, 1986), 73; quoted in Ezra L. Plank, "Domesticating God: Reformed Homes and the Relocation of Sacred Space," in *Emancipating Calvin*, 214.

89. John Calvin, Commentary on Genesis 26:25, in *Commentaries on the First Book of Moses Called Genesis*, trans. John King, 2 vols. (Grand Rapids, MI: Baker Book House, 1996), 2: 71; quoted in Plank, "Domesticating God," 214.

90. Robert K. Merton, *Science, Technology, and Society in Seventeenth-Century England* (New York: Harper and Row, 1970).

91. Thomas, *Religion and Decline of Magic*.

92. Robert W. Scribner, "The Reformation, Popular Magic, and the 'Disenchantment of the World,'" *Journal of Interdisciplinary History* 23 (1993): 475–94; "Reformation and Desacralisation: From Sacramental World to Moralised Universe," in *Problems in the Historical Anthropology of Early Modern Europe*, ed. R. Po-Chia Hsia and Robert W. Scribner (Wiesbaden: Harrassowitz, 1997), 75–92. By contrast, Michael Bailey has argued that by insisting that all magic stems from diabolical power and that popular spells, rituals, and charms were in and of themselves utterly inefficacious, late medieval demonologists such as Jacob Kramer were actually contributing to a certain disenchantment; "The Disenchantment of Magic: Spells, Charms, and Superstitions in Early European Witchcraft Literature," *American Historical Review* 111 (2006): 383–404.

93. For England, see Alexandra Walsham, "The Reformation and 'The Disenchantment of the World' Reassessed," *Historical Journal* 51 (2008): 497–528.

94. Jitse M. van der Meer, "European Calvinists and the Study of Nature: Some Historical Patterns and Problems," in *Calvinism and the Making of the European Mind*, ed. Gijsbert van den Brink and Harro M. Höpfl (Leiden: Brill, 2014), 103–30. For other reactions to Merton's arguments, see *Puritanism and the Rise of Modern Science: The Merton Thesis*, ed. I. Bernard Cohen (New Brunswick, NJ: Rutgers University Press, 1990).

95. Cameron, *Enchanted Europe*, esp. 156–57, 212–16. Cameron writes, "The only appropriate recourse of the faithful believer was to pray to God, in conscious awareness that God might have decreed that the misfortune should not be removed in this life." Cameron, 215.

96. AEG, RC 51: 255v–56 (August 10, 1556).

97. Roget, *Histoire du peuple*, 5: 28–29. On Calvin's refusal to interpret this incident as a natural phenomenon, see Max Engammare, "Tonnerre de Dieu et 'Courses d'exhalations encloses es nuées': Controverses autour de la foudre et du tonnerre au soir de la Renaissance," in *Sciences et religions: De Copernic à Galilée (1540–1610). Actes du colloque international, École française de Rome* (Rome: École française de Rome, 1999), 161–81, esp. 162.

98. *R.Consist.* 11: xxii, 256–57, 265. Reformed leaders also disapproved of images, including stained-glass windows, though they were slow to eliminate them in Geneva, and many were removed or painted over only in the seventeenth century; Grosse, *Rituels*, 258–60; Lambert, "Preaching," 204–5.

99. The altars were removed from all the churches early in the Reformation and were recycled in some unexpected manners. Three of them, for example, were put together to form the executioner's chopping block, and reputedly the first person to have his head chopped off on this block was a former priest, Jean Soutier; Lambert, "Preaching," 206; Antoine Froment, *Les actes et gestes merveilleux de la Cité de Genève*, ed. Gustrave Revilliod (Geneva: Fick, 1854), 231; AEG, RC 31: 3, 5, 156v, 160 (June 15, 19, 1537; January 11, 14, 1538).

100. See Benedict, *Christ's Churches*, esp. 529.

101. Susan Karant-Nunn's findings on ritualistic changes in Lutheran and Reformed Germany lend themselves to a similar conclusion; *Reformation of Ritual*, 191.

102. AEG, PC 1ᵉʳᵉ Sér. 12420. The Small Council condemned Morié to be censured, to ask forgiveness publicly on his knees for his wrongs, to return the money he received from the victim, and to spend five months in prison beyond the time he had already been incarcerated; RC 274: 221–22 (numeration is by page, not folio; March 20, 1773).

Chapter 6

1. A few European consistories, such as Amsterdam's Kerkeraad, regularly convoked people for bankruptcy, a reflection of the central role that commerce played in that city; Benedict, *Christ's Churches*, 473.

2. *C.O.* 45: 542 (Commentary on Matthew 19:23); William J. Bouwsma, *Calvin: A Sixteenth Century Portrait* (Oxford: Oxford University Press, 1988), 196. Bouwsma provided an excellent brief description of Calvin's ideas on wealth and industry, based primarily on the reformer's biblical commentaries. The translations of this and the following quotations from the *C.O.* are Bouwsma's. On Calvin's economic thought, André Biéler's study is still quite valuable; *La pensée économique et sociale de Calvin* (Geneva: Librairie de l'université, 1959).

3. *C.O.* 50: 102 (Commentary on 2 Corinthians 8:15); Bouwsma, *Calvin*, 199–200.

4. *C.O.* 24: 131 (Commentary on Exodus 11:2), Bouwsma, *Calvin*, 196–97.

5. Bouwsma, *Calvin*, 197; *C.O.* 38: 387 (Commentary on Jeremiah 22:16).

6. *C.O.* 24: 682–83 (Commentary on Exodus 22:25); Bouwsma, *Calvin*, 197–98.

7. *C.O.* 23: 363 (Commentary on Genesis 26:16); Bouwsma, *Calvin*, 198.

8. *C.O.* 26: 296 (Sermon 35 on Deuteronomy [5:13–15]); Bouwsma, *Calvin*, 199; McKee, *Pastoral Ministry*, 186.

9. *C.O.* 47: 219 (Commentary on John 9:4); Bouwsma, *Calvin*, 199.

10. *C.O.* 52: 164 (Commentary on 1 Thessalonians 4:11); Bouwsma, *Calvin*, 199.

11. Theodore Beza, *Quaestionum & responsionum Christianorum libellus*; quoted in Manetsch, *Calvin's Company*, 253.

12. Weber, *Protestant Ethic*, trans. and ed. Baehr and Gordon Wells, 77–78.

13. Weber, *Protestant Ethic*. For an excellent discussion of the scholarship inspired by the Weber Thesis, see Baehr and Wells's introduction to their translation.

14. See, for example, R. H. Tawney, *Religion and the Rise of Capitalism* (New York: New American Library, 1926). For a look at the work on the European continent, see Philip Benedict, "The Historiography of Continental Calvinism," in *Weber's "Protestant Ethic": Origins, Evidence, Context*, ed. Hartmut Lehmann and Kenneth F. Ledford (Cambridge: Cambridge University Press, 1993), 305–25. See also Ulrich H. J. Körtner, "Calvinism and Capitalism," in *Calvin's Impact*, ed. Hirzel and Sallmann, 159–74; Janine Garrisson-Estèbe, *L'homme protestant* (Paris: Hachette, 1980), esp. 63–67, 115–19. For recent critiques of Weber, see Johan J. Graafland, "Weber Revisited: Critical Perspectives from Calvinism on Capitalism in Economic Crisis"; and Philip Benedict, "Calvinism and the Making of the Modern European Economic Mind: A Comment and Call for More Research"; both in *Calvinism and European Mind*, ed. van den Brink and Höpfl, 177–98 and 199–209.

15. H. C. Erik Midelfort, "The Reformation and the Early Social Sciences (Marx, Weber, Durkheim, Freud): Toward a Cultural Epidemiology," in *Witchcraft, Madness, Society, and Religion in Early Modern Germany*, Variorum Collected Studies Series (Farnham and Burlington, VT: Ashgate, 2013), 8: 10; citing Max Weber, *The Protestant Ethic and the Spirit of Capitalism*, trans. Stephen Kalberg (Chicago and London: Fitzroy Dearborn, 2001), 59, and notes 22–23.

16. Karl Holl, "Die Frage des Zinsnehmens und des Wuchers in der reformierten Kirche," in *Gesammelte Aufsätze zur Kirchengeschichte* (Tübingen: Mohr Siebeck, 1928), vol. 3: 385–403.

17. Ernst Troeltsch, *The Social Teaching of the Christian Churches*, trans. Olive Wyon (New York: Macmillan, 1931), vol. 2: 641–50 (quotation from 647). To a degree, Troeltsch saw Calvinism as contributing to a form of Christian socialism, as seen in his brief (and not entirely accurate) reference to the Consistory: "In Geneva . . . [t]he fight against usury and the exploitation of the poor fill the protocols of the Council and of the Consistory, and these Christian-Social elements of Calvinistic doctrine have also left their mark upon ethics." Troeltsch, 648–49.

18. Gordon Marshall, *Presbyteries and Profits: Calvinism and the Development of Capitalism in Scotland, 1560–1707* (Oxford: Clarendon Press, 1980); Stephen Innes, *Creating the Commonwealth: The Economic Culture of Puritan New England* (New York: W. W. Norton, 1995).

19. James A. Henretta, "The Weber Thesis Revisited: The Protestant Ethic and the Reality of Capitalism in Early America," in *The Origins of American Capitalism: Collected Essays* (Boston: Northeastern University Press, 1991), 35–70.

20. Mark Valeri, "Calvin and the Social Order in Early America: Moral Ideals and Transatlantic Empire," in *John Calvin's American Legacy* (Oxford: Oxford University Press, 2010), 19–41. See also Valeri's *Heavenly Merchandise: How Religion Shaped Commerce in Puritan America* (Princeton, NJ: Princeton University Press, 2010).

21. Philip Benedict, "Faith, Fortune and Social Structure in Seventeenth-Century Montpellier," *Past and Present* 152 (1996): 46–78. See also Hartmut Kretzer, "Die Calvinismus-Kapitalismus These Max Webers vor dem Hintergrund französcher Quellen des 17. Jahrhunderts," in Kretzer, *Calvinismus versus Demokratie respective "Geist des Kapitalismus"? Studien zur politischen theorie und zur Sozialphilosophie des französischen Protestantismus im 17. Jahrhundert* (Oldenburg: Bibliothek und Informationssystem der Universität, 1988), 59–71.

22. *Registres du Conseil de Genève à l'époque de Calvin*, vol. 2, *Du 1er janvier au 31 décembre 1537*, ed. Paule Hochuli Dubuis and Sandra Coram-Mekkey (Geneva: Droz, 2004), 208.

23. Olson, *Calvin and Social Welfare*, 117, 176; Timothy G. Fehler, *Poor Relief and Protestantism: The Evolution of Social Welfare in Sixteenth-Century Emden* (Aldershot: Ashgate, 1999), esp. 244–70; Gorski, *Disciplinary Revolution*, 135.

24. Benedict, "Calvin and Transformation of Geneva," 7; citing *Sources du droit*, ed. Rivoire and van Berchem, 2: 526.

25. *R.Consist.* 1: 132.

26. Weber, *Protestant Ethic*, trans. and ed. Baehr and Wells, 105–7. For an excellent study of Genevan Calvinists' impact on punctuality and the perception of time, see Max Engammare, *L'ordre du temps: L'invention de la ponctualité au XVIe siècle* (Geneva: Droz, 2004).

27. *R.Consist.* 1: 174.

28. AEG, R.Consist. 14: 97.

29. AEG, R.Consist. 16: 230v.

30. AEG, R.Consist. 14: 140r–v; RC 54: 357 (January 16, 1559). The Council's relatively harsh sentence no doubt stemmed at least in part from the fact that when the Consistory asked Masson to step out of the chamber while members pondered its decision, he left the building entirely.

31. AEG, R.Consist. 14: 138v–39; 15: 111v; Jur. Pen. A2: 30 (June 19, 1559)

32. AEG, R.Consist. 17: 77v. The Council ordered him jailed; Jur. Pen. A2: 94 (May 27, 1560).

33. In a similar fashion, Reformed churches in France maintained a ban on various *jeux* until the revocation of the Edict of Nantes in 1685; Chareyre, "Jeux interdits," 386.

34. *R.Consist.* 1: 120.

35. *R.Consist.* 1: 152–53, n. 622; AEG, PC 1ère Sér. 366; RC 36: 195a–e, 197–98, 200, 201v, 205, 212r–v (December 20–22, 27, 29, 1542; January 2, 12, 1543).

36. *R.Consist.* 1: 67–68; AEG, PC 1ère Sér. 368; RC Part. 1: 10–11v.

37. Roget, *Histoire du people*, 3: 151.

38. *R.Consist.* 6: 158–59.

39. *R.Consist.* 6: 9.

40. *R.Consist.* 6: 94–95.

41. *R.Consist.* 9: 15; AEG, RC 48: 14v, 116 (February 26; September 10, 1554); *C.O.* 21: 569, 585; Roget, *Histoire du people*, 4: 177.

42. AEG, R.Consist. 19: 20.

43. AEG, R.Consist. 19: 20v–21, 23v, 25, 30, 34v, 35, 38v.

44. AEG, R.Consist. 16: 270r–v.

45. AEG, R.Consist. 16: 194v, 233.

46. Calvin himself enjoyed playing the games of *palet* and *la clef* with friends; Émile Doumergue, *Le caractère de Calvin: L'homme, le système, l'Église, l'État* (Neuilly: La Cause, 1931; repr., Geneva: Slatkine, 1970), 48. The Scots were much stricter than Calvin in forbidding work and forms of recreation on Sundays; Graham, *Uses of Reform*; Parker, "'Kirk By Law Established,'" 184, 188; Todd, *Culture of Protestantism*, 41–42.

47. *R.Consist.* 5: 23.

48. AEG, R.Consist. 16: 211v; Jur. Pen. A2: 58v (November 13, 1559). About three weeks later, authorities permitted him to reside in the village of Petit-Sacconex; Jur. Pen. A2: 64v (December 7, 1559). He was readmitted to the Supper the following August; R.Consist. 17: 142v.

49. AEG, R.Consist. 15: 178v–79; Jur. Pen. A2: 49 (September 18, 1559).

50. AEG, R.Consist. 20: 88; Jur. Pen. A3–1563: 45 (July 26, 1563) At this time, the church of Saint-Gervais seemed to attract people who could not control their bodily functions during the service. On the exact same day that the Consistory reprimanded Claude, Pierre Ferrière asked permission to be readmitted to communion, having been excluded for drunkenness. Under questioning from Calvin and company, Ferrière admitted that he had recently passed gas loudly during the singing of the Psalms in Saint-Gervais. Ferrière also confessed that when another man reproached him as they were leaving church, he said "that it was his ass who was speaking," not himself. Far from readmitting him to communion, the Consistory extended his exclusion and sent him to the Council to be punished; R.Consist. 20: 89.

51. AEG, R.Consist. 19: 164v.

52. AEG, R.Consist. 18: 129v.

53. AEG, R.Consist. 16: 209. The Council agreed and ordered him to stop beating his wife and come live in the city, and appointed a curator for his goods; Jur. Pen. A2: 58v (November 13, 1559).

54. AEG, R.Consist. 17: 31; Jur. Pen. A: 84 (March 25, 1560).

55. AEG, R.Consist. 17: 83v–84.

56. AEG, R.Consist. 18: 38v; 20: 49v.

57. Bernard Lescaze, *Genève: Sa vie et ses monnaies aux siècles passés* (Geneva: Crédit Suisse, 1981), 112. Twelve sous were equivalent to one florin; Lescaze, 110.

58. AEG, R. Consist. 19: 63.

59. AEG, R.Consist. 18: 36. Since it determined that Levet no longer had any assets, the Council limited itself to a reprimand; Jur. Pen. A2: 147v (April 21, 1561).

60. AEG, R.Consist. 17: 35.

61. AEG, R.Consist. 18: 192.

62. AEG, R. Consist. 16: 194v–95. Such disparagement of the clergy was rather rare by this time, four years after the fall of the Perrinistes. Monathon fled Geneva for two years;

he admitted that he attended Mass during this time. The Council ordered him jailed; R.Consist. 18: 140v–41, 150, 157v; Jur. Pen. A2: 175 (October 20, 1561); PC 1ère Sér. 990.

63. AEG, R. Consist. 16: 236v–37.

64. AEG, R.Consist. 17: 86.

65. AEG, R.Consist. 18: 118.

66. AEG, R.Consist. 16: 231.

67. AEG, R.Consist. 17: 52.

68. AEG, R.Consist. 17: 52.

69. AEG, R.Consist. 17: 56v.

70. AEG, R.Consist. 19: 150v.

71. AEG, PC 1ère Sér. 840.

72. AEG, PC 1ère Sér. 1041.

73. In the immense scholarship on poor relief in Reformation Europe, see Robert M. Kingdon, "Social Welfare in Calvin's Geneva," *American Historical Review* 76 (1971): 50–69; Olson, *Calvin and Social Welfare*; Natalie Zemon Davis, "Humanism, Heresy, and Poor Relief in Sixteenth-Century Lyon," in *Society and Culture*, 17–64; Fehler, *Poor Relief*; Maureen Flynn, *Sacred Charity: Confraternities and Social Welfare in Spain, 1400–1700* (Ithaca, NY: Cornell University Press, 1989); Carter Lindberg, *Beyond Charity: Reformation Initiatives for the Poor* (Minneapolis, MN: Fortress Press, 1993); Charles H. Parker, *The Reformation of Community: Social Welfare and Calvinist Charity in Holland, 1572–1620* (Cambridge: Cambridge University Press, 1998); *Health Care and Poor Relief in Protestant Europe*, ed. Ole Peter Grell and Andrew Cunningham (London: Routledge, 1997); Lee Palmer Wandel, *Always Among Us: Images of the Poor in Zwingli's Zurich* (Cambridge: Cambridge University Press, 1991).

74. Jeffrey R. Watt, "Settling Quarrels and Nurturing Repentance: The Consistory in Calvin's Geneva," in *Revisiting Geneva: Robert Kingdon and the Coming of the French Wars of Religion*, ed. Sara K. Barker (St. Andrews: Centre for French History and Culture of the University of St Andrews, 2012), 71–84.

75. Manetsch, "Pastoral Care," 289; Raymond A. Mentzer, "Le consistoire et la pacification du monde rural," in *Construction de l'identité réformée*, 56.

76. Mentzer, "Marking the Taboo," 123–25.

77. See, for example, Jane Kamensky, "Words, Witches, and Woman Trouble: Witchcraft, Disorderly Speech, and Gender Boundaries in Puritan New England," in *New Perspectives on Witchcraft, Magic, and Demonology*, vol. 4, *Gender and Witchcraft*, ed. Brian P. Levack (New York: Routledge, 2001), 196–217.

78. AEG, R.Consist. 16: 248v.

79. AEG, R.Consist. 17: 159r–v, 164, 167v, 172.

80. AEG, R.Consist. 16: 259v. Authorities forbade him to work as a mercenary and jailed him for three days; Jur. Pen. A2: 73v (January 15, 1560).

81. AEG, R.Consist. 14: 119v; RC 54: 350v (December 26, 1558).

82. AEG, R.Consist. 17: 180r–v.

83. AEG, R.Consist. 18: 132, 135v, 140v.

84. AEG, R.Consist. 19: 87v–88; Jur. Pen. A3–1562: 42v (June 22, 1561).

85. AEG, PC 1ère Sér. 999. As we will see below, forced labor on the ramparts was not unusual for males, but it was a very unusual sentence for females.

86. AEG, R.Consist. 21: 33.

87. *R.Consist.* 7: 150–51, 196; 8: 59, 61, 174; RC Part. 7: 161v (October 16, 1553).

88. AEG, R.Consist. 17: 137v.

89. AEG, R.Consist. 17: 21.

90. AEG, R.Consist. 17: 98v–99, 101v–3v.

91. AEG, R.Consist. 19: 167; Jur. Pen. A3–1562: 77 (November 9, 1562).

92. AEG, R.Consist. 20: 79v. The Council jailed Roy and ordered "qu'on face ung rolle [colle?] des aultres vagabonds"; Jur. Pen. A3 1563: 36 (July 5, 1563).

93. See Corinne Walker, "La politique somptuaire à Genève ou les limites de la compétence du Consistoire (XVIe–XVIIIe siècles," in *Sous l'oeil*, ed. Tosato-Rigo and Staremberg Goy, 125–36; Marie-Lucile de Gallatin, "Les ordonnances somptuaires à Genève au XVIe siècle," *Mémoires et documents publiés par la Société d'histoire et d'archéologie de Genève* 36 (1938): 193–272; Herman de Vries, "Les lois somptuaires de la République de Genève au XVIe siècle," *Indicateur de l'histoire suisse* 16 (1918): 229–31. The word *somptuaire* did not actually appear in any of the sixteenth-century ordinances, which became increasingly detailed in the decades following Calvin's death.

94. AEG, RC 37: 61v (April 16, 1543); Gallatin, "Ordonnances somptuaires," 204–7.

95. AEG, RC 42: 115v (May 23, 1547); Roget, *Histoire du people*, 2: 278.

96. AEG, RC 42: 117 (May 24, 1547).

97. AEG, RC 42: 118v–19 (May 25, 1547); Roget, *Histoire du people*, 2: 279–80; *R. Consist.* 2: 158n265. The fact that the Council forbade these breeches seven more times through 1557 palpably shows that many men were flouting this prohibition; Gallatin, "Ordonnances somptuaires," 207.

98. AEG, R.Consist. 20: 144v.

99. AEG, PC 1ère Sér. 1081.

100. AEG, R.Consist. 21: 61v.

101. AEG, RC 59: 51v, 53v (June 2, 6, 1564). See Corinne Walker, "Les lois somptuaires ou le rêve d'un ordre social: Evolution et enjeux de la politique somptuaire à Genève (XVIe–XVIIIe)," *Equinoxe: Revue Romande de Sciences Humaines* 11 (1994): 111–27.

102. AEG, Jur. Pen A2: 18 (April 13, 17, 29, 1559).

103. AEG, R.Consist. 21: 47v.

104. AEG, PC 1ère Sér. 1130.

105. AEG, R.Consist. 19: 205.

106. AEG, R.Consist. 14: 158r–v; Jur. Pen. K1: (unnumbered folios; February 2, 1559).

107. Gallatin, "Ordonnances somptuaires," esp. 240–41, 257. Late in the sixteenth century, Simon Goulart, a French pastor in Geneva, warned, "It is in poverty and in contempt for perishable things that the luster of the Church is seen. When religion gave birth to an abundance of earthly goods, the daughter suffocated the mother." *Seconde partie des discours Chrestiens: Contenant XX. traitez divers, pour l'instruction &*

consolation des fideles (Geneva: Jacob Stoer, 1595), 240–42; quoted in Manetsch, *Calvin's Company*, 240.

108. For attitudes toward usury among medieval scholastics, see John T. Noonan Jr., *The Scholastic Analysis of Usury* (Cambridge, MA: Harvard University Press, 1957).

109. Calvin dismissed the Old Testament prohibitions of usury (e.g., Deuteronomy 23:19) as applying only to the specific political situation of the Israelites, which was radically different from that of contemporary Geneva. Michael Wykes, "Devaluing the Scholastics: Calvin's Ethics of Usury," *Calvin Theological Journal* 38 (2003): 27–51. See also Biéler, *Pensée économique*, 168–69, 453–76; Ludi Schulze, *Calvin and "Social Ethics": His Views on Property, Interest, and Usury* (Pretoria: Kital, 1985), 48–71.

110. *Sources du droit*, ed. Rivoire and van Berchem, 2: 466–67, 504; Robert M. Kingdon, "The Economic Behavior of Ministers in Geneva in the Middle of the Sixteenth Century," *Archiv für Reformationsgeschichte* 50 (1959): 33–39; Mark Valeri, "Religion, Discipline, and the Economy in Calvin's Geneva," *Sixteenth Century Journal* 28 (1997): 131.

111. Valeri should be commended for his fine article on discipline and the economy in Calvin's Geneva, which is based in part on his perusal of the transcription of the Consistory registers. Valeri does, however, give highly inflated numbers when discussing the quantity of consistorial actions against usury, price gouging, and the like. For example, he claimed that the Consistory heard about forty cases of usury in the months January through July 1557 and ten more cases for the rest of that year; "Religion, Discipline, and Economy," 124n4; 128n13. In fact, the Consistory questioned twenty-two individuals for all of 1557, only eleven before the end of July; *R.Consist.* 12. Valeri may have double-or triple-counted cases that were spread out over more than one meeting and may have been counting as suspects people who were merely called as witnesses to alleged cases of usury.

112. AEG, R.Consist. 21: 19v–20; Jur. Pen. A3–1564: 16r–v (March 27, 28, 1564). Peccouz was readmitted to communion two months later; R.Consist. 21: 67.

113. AEG, R. Consist. 19: 75v. The Council fined him 25 écus; Jur. Pen. A3–1562: 34v, 35v (May 26, 29, 1562). Robert Kingdon found that in 1560, the pastor Nicolas des Gallars, a noble from France, apparently lent money with impunity at around 8 percent, slightly above the limit permitted in Geneva; "Economic Behavior," 37–38.

114. AEG, R.Consist. 19: 73v–74.

115. Antoine Roch still had not returned the money to the widow in September of the same year; the Consistory ordered him to do so, again without mentioning the Small Council; AEG, R.Consist. 19: 137.

116. AEG, R.Consist. 21: 24.

117. See Jeffrey R. Watt, "Reconciliation and the Confession of Sins: The Evidence from the Consistory in Calvin's Geneva," in *Martin Luther and John Calvin*, ed. Ward Holder (Grand Rapids, MI: William B. Eerdmans, 2013), 105–20.

118. *R.Consist.* 11: 228.

119. AEG, RC 52: 32v (October 5, 1556).

120. AEG, R.Consist. 17: 98. Magistrates sent Bonivard to jail; Jur. Pen. A2: 98v (June 24, 1560).

121. AEG, R. Consist. 20: 162v; Jur. Pen. A3–1563: 72v (November 22, 1563).

122. AEG, R.Consist. 17: 177. The Council ordered an investigation of such excesses; Jur. Pen. A2: 120 (November 18, 1560).

123. AEG, R.Consist. 19: 68. The Council ordered a new collection; Jur. Pen. 3A 1562: 33r–v (May 18, 1562).

124. AEG, R.Consist. 18: 13. The Council, however, gave her until Pentecost to become "instruitte"; if she failed to do so, she would have to leave the city and would lose the alms she was receiving from the hospital; Jur. Pen. A2: 141 (March 17, 1561).

125. Graafland, "Weber Revisited," 177–98. François Dermange's comments concerning Calvin's attitude toward property are quite apt: Calvin "is less interested in ensuring the safety of property against the envy of others or in showing its social usefulness than in defining the duties of the wealthy in relation to the poor. . . . [E]ach individual is obliged to put the Golden Rule into practice as stated both negatively and positively. Thus, economic ethics is placed under the aegis of justice but also of charity." "Calvin's View of Property: A Duty Rather Than a Right," in *John Calvin Rediscovered: The Impact of His Social and Economic Thought*, ed. Edward Dommen and James D. Bratt (Louisville, KY: Westminster John Knox Press, 2007), 48–49. See also Wykes, "Devaluing the Scholastics."

126. Kingdon, "Economic Behavior," 38–39.

127. See Siegfried Wenzel, *The Sin of Sloth: Acedia in Medieval Thought and Literature* (Chapel Hill: University of North Carolina Press, 1967).

128. AEG, R.Consist. 20: 135v. The Council gave him three days to find work in his profession; failing to do so, he would be sent to work on the fortifications; Jur. Pen. A3–1563: 59v (September 20, 1563).

129. AEG, R.Consist. 20: 57. He was sentenced to three days in jail; Jur. Pen. A3–1563: 28 (May 31, 1563).

130. Referring to Puritans, Weber affirmed that "a change of occupation is in no way regarded as reprehensible, provided it is not entered into lightly, and the change is to a calling which is more pleasing to God, which means, in general, more useful"; Weber, *Protestant Ethic*, trans. and ed. Baehr and Wells, 110. It is hard to discern the notion of calling in the Consistory's blunt declaration that a man should be made to work "in one way or another."

131. Jean Calvin, *Le catéchisme de Genève* (Paris: Editions "Je sers," 1934).

132. *The Heidelberg Confession, 400th Anniversary Edition*, trans. and ed. Allen O. Miller, M. Eugene Osterhaven, Aladar Komjathy, and James I. McCord (Philadelphia: United Church Press, 1963).

133. Weber, *Protestant Ethic*, trans. and ed. Baehr and Wells, 69–87.

134. See various articles in *Économie genevoise*, ed. Piuz and Mottu-Weber; Liliane Mottu-Weber, *Genève au siècle de la Réforme: Économie et Refuge* (Geneva: Droz; Paris: Champion, 1987). Jennifer Powell McNutt has produced a very interesting study of the

Genevan clergy during the era of the Enlightenment. She argues that eighteenth-century clergy embraced "Reasonable Calvinism," affirming that their faith was in accord with reason while continuing to support broadly the piety and theology of Calvin. They approved of the pursuit of happiness but were quite concerned about people's attachments to luxuries, a growing danger because of Geneva's expanding wealth through the production of watches, jewelry, and other luxuries; *Calvin Meets Voltaire: The Clergy of Geneva in the Age of Enlightenment, 1685–1798* (Farnham: Ashgate, 2013), 223–29. Based on his work on Saint Andrews' kirk sessions, Geoffrey Parker argues that the Scots' "godly discipline . . . played a crucial part in grooming the kingdom for its future role as a major industrial power. By accustoming the workforce to social discipline, and by stressing the value of order, restraint, and hard work, the Reformed Kirk unwittingly became the handmaiden of nascent capitalism." "'Kirk By Law Established,'" 192.

Chapter 7

1. The ordinances passed in 1547 concerning the administration of churches in the Genevan countryside mentioned the role of the Consistory in such matters: "if there is hatred or quarrels between people, the minister, taking with him the guards, will do his duty to reconcile them." If he did not succeed then the matter was to be brought before the Consistory, language that shows that the Consistory's role as mediator was essentially an outgrowth of that of the pastors; *Registres de la Compagnie* 1: 8; Christian Grosse, "Les consistoires réformés et le pluralisme des instances de régulation des conflits (Genève, XVIe siècle)," in *Entre justice et justiciables: Les auxiliaires de la justice du Moyen Âge au XXe siècle*, ed. Claire Dolan (Quebec: Les Presses de l'Université de Laval, 2005), 630.

2. Statistics derived from Grosse, *Rituels*, 513, table 11. Conflicts comprised about 6 percent of the causes for suspension from the Supper for the years 1542–1548 but about 20 percent for 1550–1563; Grosse, 536–67. Monter lists quarrels, domestic or otherwise, as the most common reason for exclusion from the Supper for the years 1564–1569, representing more than a third of all excommunications; "Consistory of Geneva," 479. Manetsch found that quarrels and *mauvais ménage* combined made up a fourth of all excommunications for the years 1542–1609; *Calvin's Company*, 201.

I believe that it is important to distinguish domestic discord from other quarrels. The former was part of efforts to control matrimony, and the rate of recidivism for married couples was far greater than that for other people who quarreled. See Chareyre, "Programs of Moral and Religious Reform," 164; Kingdon, *Reforming Geneva*, 101–29.

3. Edwin Bezzina, "The Practice of Ecclesiastical Discipline in the Huguenot Refugee Church of Amsterdam, 1650–1700," in *Emancipating Calvin*, ed. Spierling, de Boer, and Holder, 147–74; Philippe Chareyre, "Great Difficulties,'" 63–96; Christian Grosse, "'Pour bien de paix': La regulation des conflits par les consistoires en Suisse

romande (XVIe–XVIIe siècles)," in *Figure de la médiation et lien social*, ed. Jean-Luc Chabot, Stéphane Gal, and Christophe Tournu (Paris: L'Harmattan, 2006), 85–107; Grosse, "Consistoires réformés," 630; Charlotte Littleton, "Ecclesiastical Discipline in the French Church of London and the Creation of Community, 1560–1600," *Archiv für Reformationsgeschichte* 92 (2000): 239; Raymond A. Mentzer, "Consistoire et pacification" and "Sociabilité et culpabilité: Les conventions de médiation et réconciliation dans la communauté huguenote au XVIe siècle," both in *Construction d'identité réformée*, 49–69, 205–17; Charles H. Parker, "The Rituals of Reconciliation: Admonition, Confession, and Community in the Dutch Reformed Church," in *Penitence in the Age of Reformations*, ed. Katharine Jackson Lualdi and Anne T. Thayer (Aldershot: Ashgate, 2000), 101–15; Spierling, "Negotiating Penance: Consistories," in *Judging Faith*, ed. Parker and Starr-LeBeau, 212; Todd, *Culture of Protestantism*, 183–226.

4. In Scotland, many women successfully petitioned kirk sessions for redress of grievances for defamation involving their sexual honor or accusations of witchcraft; Todd, *Culture of Protestantism*, 244–49.

5. *R.Consist.*, 5: 12, 22.

6. AEG, R.Consist. 18: 134v–35, 150.

7. AEG, R.Consist. 15: 164v. Evidently that encounter did not materialize because two days later, Parent appeared before the Consistory on an unrelated matter (marital discord), but the peddler was told to meet with Mouton after the sermon on Saturday to try to reconcile; 15: 168.

8. *R.Consist.* 4: 32.

9. *R.Consist.* 11: 46

10. *R.Consist.* 7: 94.

11. *R.Consist.* 9: 60, 75.

12. Grosse, "Consistoires réformés," 643; Spierling, "Negotiating Penance," 211.

13. An incident in 1539 showed Calvin's absolute refusal to reconcile even though he admitted that his failure to control his own temper was unchristian. He became furious with Farel, Bucer, and others in their attempts to reconcile Calvin with Pierre Caroli, who deemed it acceptable for Christians to pray for the dead. Calvin was embarrassed by his own conduct but never accepted that he was in any way wrong; Gordon, *Calvin*, 90–91.

14. *R.Consist.* 2: 155–57; AEG, RC 40: 359 (January 27, 1556); 41: 33v–34, 35–36, 37–40, 52v–53, 68 (March 2–6, 16–17; April 8, 1556). See also Kingdon, *Adultery*, 31–32, 63–67; Naphy, *Calvin and Consolidation*, 94–96.

15. *R.Consist.* 6: 63. For an interesting look at Calvin's anger and pride—the latter evaluated on the basis of his changing signature!—see Max Engammare, "John Calvin's Seven Capital Sins," in *Calvin: Saint or Sinner?*, ed. Herman J. Selderhuis (Tübingen: Mohr Siebeck, 2010), 22–39.

16. Mentzer, "Réforme calviniste des moeurs à Nîmes," 32.

17. Schmidt, "Morals Courts in Rural Berne," 163.

18. *R.Consist.* 4: 31.

19. On examining one's conscience in preparation for the Supper, see Grosse, *Rituels,* esp. 503–65.

20. Schmidt, "Morals Courts in Rural Berne," 177. See also Spierling, "Negotiating Penance," 207.

21. *R.Consist.* 12: 281.

22. Bourdet and Lefebvre along with their wives and Duverney were all to meet after the five o'clock service at Saint-Pierre the next morning to reconcile; AEG, R.Consist. 20: 21.

23. AEG, R.Consist. 19: 17r–v.

24. See Chareyre, "Programs of Moral and Religious Reform," 164; Grosse, "Consistoires réformés," 642. The Reformed in Scotland had some rituals of repentance and reconciliation that were far more elaborate than those in Geneva; Todd, *Culture of Protestantism,* 127–82, 227–64.

25. Kingdon, *Reforming Geneva*, 43, 115–21. On rituals of reconciliation, see Grosse, *Rituels,* 544–62.

26. *R.Consist.* 10: 199, 203.

27. AEG, R.Consist. 18: 125r–v.

28. The historian Alfred Soman found that in France as well, Reformed consistories put special emphasis on and enjoyed considerable success in settling differences and assuaging anger; "Deviance and Criminal Justice in Western Europe, 1300–1800, *Criminal Justice History* 1 (1980): 3–28; Grosse, "Inquisition and Consistory Records," 137. Referring to consistories in the south of France, Janine Garrisson argues, "Dans ces villes ou villages occitans, les anciens vont jouer un rôle extrêmement efficace d'arbitres ou même juges de paix." *Protestants du Midi, 1559–1598* (Toulouse: Privat, 1980), 107–8; Lambert, "Preaching," 272n 114.

29. *R.Consist.* 2: 339–40.

30. AEG, PC 1ère Sér. 437; *R.Consist.* 2: 356, n. 1444.

31. AEG, PC 1ère Sér. 437; RC 41: 270v, 273, 275v, 279v, 283v–84, 288, 290v, 291v, 292v, 294v, 296 (December 27, 30, 1546; January 3, 6, 13, 20, 24, 25, 27, 31; February 1, 1547).

32. AEG, R.Consist. 17: 56v.

33. AEG, R.Consist. 20: 12v–13.

34. *R.Consist.* 12: 424–25.

35. A century and a half later, a criminal investigation in Geneva provides palpable evidence of the persistent belief in the need for people to forgive those who had done them wrong, even when this involved a senseless and fatal crime. In October 1707, three men and two women who worked together as domestic servants for a certain Marie Genet were ready for a late afternoon snack. When one of them brought some cheese in the form of a tomme, Françoise (also known as Fanchon) Cartier and François Royer grabbed it at the same time and pulled the tomme apart.

Cartier had served the Genet household for a year and a half, whereas Royer had been working there for just a few weeks. Interrogated after the fact, the other servants all agreed that there had been no sign of bad feelings between the two, but at that moment

Cartier was upset that, given her seniority, Royer had not deferred to her in distributing the cheese. She picked up a knife with the intention of rapping Royer's fingers with the handle. When he pulled back his hand and avoided the blow, Cartier, in a rage, threw the knife at Royer, striking him in the abdomen. Crying out, "Oh my God, I'm dying. I surrender my soul to God," Royer pulled the knife out of his wound and dropped it on the table. Fearing for her life, Cartier fled the scene while the other servants sent for a surgeon, who sewed up Royer's wound.

He died two days later, but the day before he expired he told his fellow servant Isaac Grand, "I hope that Fanchon has run away. I forgive her with as good a heart as [that with which] I beg God to forgive me [for my sins]." The celebration of the Supper was not an issue in this case, but one can plausibly posit that this dying man's desire to forgive his assailant for her act of passion might stem from the repeated pronouncements of Calvin and subsequent Reformed leaders that feelings of rancor were incompatible with genuine piety. Originally from Vevey in neighboring Vaud, Royer clearly took his Reformed faith seriously, including the need to forgive those who had wronged him, even fatally and senselessly. Cartier was found guilty and condemned to be hanged, a sentence that was carried out in effigy since she had fled Geneva and could not be apprehended; AEG, PC 1ère Sér. 5816.

36. AEG, RC 54: 85v (February 14, 1558).

37. Christian Grosse, "Aux origines des pratiques consistoriales de pacification des conflits: Le 'Conseil de paix,' (1527–1529)," in *Les registres du Conseil de la République de Genève sous l'Ancien Régime: Nouvelles approches, nouvelles perspectives*, ed. Sandra Coram-Mekkey (Geneva: Archives d'Etat de Genève and Fondation de l'Encyclopédie de Genève, 2009), 29–63; Grosse, "Consistoires réformés," 627–44.

38. David Warren Sabean, *Power in the Blood: Popular Culture and Village Discourse in Early Modern Germany* (Cambridge: Cambridge University Press, 1984), 37–60. In contrast to the evidence from the Genevan Consistory, Sabean argues that guilt was "an external fact for the villagers" and that conscience was "not an internalized mechanism of control," as witnessed by the fact that settlements in court of legal disputes represented the reconciliation of the parties; Sabean, 50, 51. See also Hans-Christoph Rublack, "Lutherische Beichte und Sozialdisziplinierung," *Archiv für Reformationsgeschichte* 84 (1993): 143–44; Karant-Nunn, *Reformation of Ritual*, 106–7.

39. John Bossy, "The Social History of Confession in the Age of the Reformation," *Transactions of the Royal Historical Society* 25 (1975): 21–38.

40. Reinburg, "Liturgy and Laity," 532.

41. See Grosse, "'Pour bien de paix,'" 104.

42. *R. Consist.* 12: 262.

43. *R. Consist.* 12: 269.

44. AEG, R.Consist. 13: 48v–49.

45. AEG, R.Consist. 15: 119v.

46. AEG, R.Consist. 15: 101r–v.

47. AEG, RC 40: 243 (September 24, 1545).

48. *R.Consist.* 11: 228.

49. AEG, R.Consist. 16: 213v.

50. AEG, R.Consist. 16: 209v, 213v, 215.

51. AEG, R.Consist. 21: 46v–47, 51.

52. AEG, R.Consist. 20: 124.

53. Gordon, *Calvin*, 189–97.

54. *R.Consist.* 10: 110.

55. *R.Consist.* 10: 113, 184.

56. AEG, RC 54: 272v–273 (September 1, 1558); *C.O.* 21: 701–2.

57. William Monter, *Judging the French Reformation: Heresy Trials by Sixteenth-Century Parlements* (Cambridge, MA: Harvard University Press, 1999), 184–92; Grosse, *Rituels*, 464–65.

58. Grosse, *Rituels*, 460.

59. AEG, R.Consist. 17: 20r–v; Jur. Pen. A2: 82v (March 11, 1560). In seventeenth-century Geneva, such acts of *réparation* regularly took place in the Consistory rather than in church. To avoid antagonizing France after the revocation of the Edict of Nantes in 1685, they were performed in private to a pastor; Grosse, *Rituels*, 574–75.

60. AEG, R.Consist. 17: 198v.

61. AEG, R.Consist. 17: 82.

62. AEG, R.Consist. 17: 80v.

63. Philip Benedict has written an excellent study, which shows that Amboise was part of broader Protestant attempts to counter the influence of the Guise during the brief reign of Francis. Benedict persuasively argues that while Calvin was not involved and did not condone the Conspiracy of Amboise, he almost certainly knew about it and, more important, played an active role, along with Beza, in the Maligny affair later that year. Aborted at the last minute, this plot aimed to seize Lyon to pressure calling the Estates General to impeach the Guise; *Season of Conspiracy*. See also Mack P. Holt, *The French Wars of Religion, 1562–1629* (Cambridge: Cambridge University Press, 1995), 44–45.

64. AEG, R.Consist. 17: 82.

65. For the discussion of Anduze and the other Genevan conspirators, see Benedict, *Season of Conspiracy*, 147–66. In December 1562, Genevan authorities were severe in their treatment of the pinmaker Pierre Jacon, who not only attended Mass in France but appeared to support the Catholics in the early phase of the French Wars of Religion. Five men testified that they saw him freely participate in the Mass, and he even reportedly declared that the Catholics were going to win the war and would cut the throats of all the Huguenots. Jacon was excluded from the Supper and sent to *Messieurs*. The Council ordered that Jacon be whipped till he bled, branded on his forehead, and banished under pain of death; AEG, R.Consist. 19: 191v–92, 195; PC 1ère Sér. 1092.

66. AEG, R.Consist. 17: 82v. Geneva experienced a huge increase in such abjurations in the late 1560s with a large influx of refugees arriving during the Wars of Religion in France; Manetsch, *Calvin's Company*, 204.

67. AEG, R.Consist. 20: 13.

68. AEG, R.Consist. 17: 202v.

69. AEG, R.Consist. 17: 207.

70. In August 1561 the Consistory treated another case in the same way even though there was no duress in that apostasy. The Consistory considered the case of Francesco De Luca, who, after converting to Reformed Protestantism, went to Moravia where he lived among and embraced the faith of Anabaptists, a decision he now greatly regretted. The Consistory referred him to the Council and ordered that he do *réparation* either in front of the entire church in Geneva—presumably in Saint-Pierre—or at least in front of the Italian congregation; AEG, R.Consist. 18: 95v. De Luca was almost certainly under no pressure and likely went to Moravia specifically to convert to Anabaptism.

71. The punishment was a far cry from that meted out in Scotland, where adulterers and apostates might have to sit on the stool of repentance during both the morning and afternoon services for six months or even a year. At the last such service, the penitent had to recite an individual confession to the congregation; Todd, *Culture of Protestantism*, 138.

72. AEG, R.Consist. 18: 178.

73. AEG, R.Consist. 18: 178.

74. AEG, R.Consist. 17: 105v, 108.

75. AEG, R.Consist. 18: 77. When she returned on September 2, 1561, she still refused to confess to the theft; 18: 116.

76. AEG, R.Consist. 18: 116v–17.

77. AEG, R.Consist. 17: 79: Jur. Pen. A2: 93v (May 24, 1560). This is one of the few sentences that in any way resembled full excommunication. It does not explicitly mention ostracism, which almost certainly could not have been enforced.

78. AEG, R.Consist. 17: 140; Jur. Pen. A2: 109 (September 5, 1560)

79. AEG, R.Consist. 18: 181v.

80. AEG, R.Consist. 20: 114, 120r–v.

81. AEG, R.Consist. 21: 36v.

82. AEG, R.Consist. 19: 23v.

83. AEG, RC 53: 458v–59 (December 10, 1557); Doumergue, *Jean Calvin*, 3: 329.

84. Doumergue, *Jean Calvin*, 3: 329.

85. AEG, RC 54: 106 (March 2, 1558). Doumergue continues, "Et le 26 février 1561, je trouve ces lignes, où le secrétaire finit par prendre lui-même la parole, comme s'il était ému du spectacle auquel il vient d'assister: 'Le nom de Dieu invoqué, l'on a procédé par ordre aux censures devers chascun des conseillers selon que l'on a congneu respectivement estre requis de remonstrer. Quoy estant fait l'on a rendu grâces à Dieu, lequel je prie augmenter ses bénédictions sur ceste assemblée.'" Doumergue, *Jean Calvin*, 3: 329; RC 56: 152v (February 26, 1561). We find examples of *le grabeau*, sometimes referred to as *censures*, about every three months in the Council minutes; 54: 201, 290v (June 1, September 21, 1558).

86. AEG, R.Consist. 20: 181.

87. Rather than seeing a top-down process, Karen Spierling has stressed in her work on Reformation Geneva the process of negotiation between religious and secular authorities on the one hand and the rank and file on the other in matters pertaining to morality and religious practices; "Negotiating Penance," 204–14; *Infant Baptism*.

88. AEG, R.Consist. 20: 111, 174. A criminal investigation led authorities to determine that Berthod was not in her right mind when this incident occurred. As a result, they sentenced her only to recognize her error, to ask forgiveness from God and justice before the *châtelain* of Céligny with a torch in her hand; her husband was told to take care of her; PC 1ère Sér. 1146.

89. *R.Consist.* 6: 66.

90. AEG, R.Consist. 17: 192v.

91. AEG, R.Consist. 14: 142.

92. For his rebellion in taking communion in spite of the prohibition and for his violence against his wife on the day of the Supper, the Council condemned Berthet to three days in jail on bread and water; AEG, RC 54: 357 (January 16, 1559).

93. AEG, R.Consist. 17: 98.

94. This contrasts with the findings of Bernard Roussel, who asserts that consistorial records indicate that there were relatively few Reformed in France who abstained from communion after examining their own consciences; "Comment faire la cène?," 208.

95. *R.Consist.* 6: 51.

96. *R.Consist.* 4: 70–71.

97. *R.Consist.* 2: 267–68; Kingdon, "Catechesis," 307; Lambert, "Preaching," 453–54.

98. Gerald Strauss avowed that the Reformation was a failure in part because of the reliance on teaching by rote: "nearly everywhere children tended to drone in vacant and mindless automation." The teaching of the catechism "could coerce people to memorize words and reproduce them mechanically when called on to do so. But it was not a technique likely to arouse curiosity and promote comprehension." *Luther's House*, 173–74; Lambert, "Preaching," 447.

99. *R.Consist.* 12: 134.

100. See Philippe Denis, "Remplacer la confession: Absolutions collectives et disciplines ecclésiastiques dans les Églises de la Réforme au XVIᵉ siècle," in *Pratiques de la confession des Pères du désert à Vatican II, Quinze etudes d'histoire*, ed. Groupe de la Bussière (Paris: Éditions du Cerf, 1983), 165–76.

101. Grosse, *Rituels*, 187–89.

102. Grosse, *Rituels*, 145–47.

103. Barbara Pitkin, "Redefining Repentance: Calvin and Melanchthon," in *Calvinus Praeceptor Ecclesiae*, ed. Selderhuis, 275–85.

104. Ronald K. Rittgers, *The Reformation of the Keys: Confession, Conscience, and Authority in Sixteenth-Century Germany* (Cambridge, MA: Harvard University Press, 2004).

105. See Grosse, *Rituels*, 211–13.

106. Benedict, *Christ's Churches*, 485, 643n48; Kingdon, *Reforming Geneva*, 127. Robert Muchembled maintains that a similar trend was taking place in France as early as

the late fifteenth century, before the outbreak of the Reformation. To defuse potentially violent situations, magistrates imposed fines for crimes that impugned someone's honor; *Le temps des supplices: De l'obéissance sous les rois absolus, XVe–XVIIIe siècle* (Paris: A. Colin, 1992), 22–37.

107. Research has shown a homicide rate of 16.1 per 100,000 people for the years 1616–1650 and 14 per 100,000 for the years 1781–1798; Jeffrey R. Watt, *Choosing Death: Suicide and Calvinism in Early Modern Geneva* (Kirksville, MO: Truman State University Press, 2001), 55. By comparison, the homicide rate for the United States for 2017 was 5.3 per 100,000; United States Department of Justice, Federal Bureau of Investigation, *Crime in the United States, 2017*, Table 1.

108. *R.Consist.* 10: 195.

109. *R.Consist.* 12: 293; AEG, RC 53: 337 (September 20, 1557). This banishment was undoubtedly based not just on his misbehavior but also on the fact that Barbarin had not been admitted as a resident in the city.

110. See Grosse, *Rituels*, 326–28

111. AEG, R.Consist. 20: 185, 185v.

112. AEG, R.Consist. 18: 192v.

113. *R.Consist.* 10: 270.

114. True, Calvin discussed "temporary faith," whereby the reprobate could appear to have all the signs of being among the elect but then fall away from faith, indicating that they never were actually part of the elect; *Institutes*, III.ii.11, 1: 608. In the case at hand, Calvin's understanding of "temporary faith" would mean Favre would be damned because he did not truly have the gift of faith, not because he took communion unworthily.

115. Grosse, *Rituels*, 508. See also 207, 211; Manetsch, "Pastoral Care," 283–84; McKee, *Pastoral Ministry*, 250–57.

116. In the *Institutes*, III.xxiii.12–14, 2: 212–16, Calvin dealt with related issues when he answered critics who averred that the doctrine of predestination obviated attempting to avoid sin and rendered meaningless exhortations to do so; *C.O.* 2: 708–11; and 3: 499–504. I am very grateful to John Thompson for bringing this passage to my attention.

117. See Grosse, *Excommunication*, 41–44; *Rituels*, 503–11. Interestingly, on the basis of the *Livre d'excommuniez*, Grosse also found that for the years 1561–1564, 37 percent of those who had been suspended from the sacrament were actually reintegrated without missing a single Supper; Grosse, 392. The key was to be in the proper spiritual state.

118. *R.Consist.* 9: 100.

119. *R.Consist.* 12: 294–95.

120. *R.Consist.* 12: 424.

121. AEG, R.Consist. 13: 36.

122. AEG, R.Consist. 15: 157v. The Council expressed its intention to banish this "maulvaise femme" and her children who were "larrons"; Jur. Pen. A2: 45, 46v (August 28, September 4, 1559).

123. Grosse, *Excommunication*, 40; *Rituels*, 371, 523–24.

124. *Sources du droit*, ed. Rivoire and van Berchem, 3: 101; Grosse, *Rituels*, 375. This ostracism contrasts with Calvin's warnings against severity in implementing discipline; *Institutes*, IV.xii.8, 10, 2: 510, 512.

125. AEG, R.Consist. 15: 173.

126. See Grosse, *Rituels*, 390–96.

127. Karant-Nunn, *Reformation of Ritual*, 98.

128. Robert Christman, "The Pulpit and the Pew: Shaping Popular Piety in Late Reformation Germany," in *Lutheran Ecclesiastical Culture, 1550–1675*, ed. Robert Kolb (Leiden: Brill, 2008), 259–304; Karant-Nunn, *Reformation of Ritual*, 94–107; Ronald K. Rittgers, "Private Confession and the Lutheranization of Sixteenth-Century Nördlingen," *Sixteenth Century Journal* 36 (2005): 1063–85; Rittgers, *Reformation of Keys*. See also various essays in *A New History of Penance*, ed. Abigail Firey (Leiden: Brill, 2008), including a piece by Rittgers, "Embracing the 'True Relic' of Christ: Suffering, Penance, and Private Confession in the Thought of Martin Luther," 377–93.

129. Denis, "Remplacer la confession," 170–71.

130. Karant-Nunn, *Reformation of Ritual*, 128–29; Heinz Schilling, "'History of Crime' or 'History of Sin'? Some Reflections on the Social History of Early Modern Church Discipline," in *Politics and Society in Reformation Europe: Essays for Sir Geoffrey Elton on His Sixty-Fifth Birthday*, ed. Tom Scott and E. I. Kouri (New York: St. Martin's Press, 1987), 289–310. Concentrating on late seventeenth-and early eighteenth-century Germany, however, Hans-Christoph Rublack has found that the Lutheran laity came to view confession as a ritual that did not require serious introspection; it did not appear to be a viable means of effecting social discipline, unlike the actions of Calvin's Consistory; Rublack, "Lutherische Beichte," 127–55.

131. Christman, "Pulpit and Pew," 289–90.

132. See especially Karant-Nunn, *Reformation of Ritual*, 100–4. For an excellent study of Martin Bucer's evolving thought on penance and attempts to implement social discipline in Strasbourg, see Burnett, *Yoke of Christ*.

Conclusion

1. See, for example, Kingdon, *Reforming Geneva*, 101–29; Mentzer, "Sociabilité et culpabilité," 205–17.

2. Kingdon, *Reforming Geneva*, 21.

3. In noting differences between inquisitions and consistories, Christopher F. Black mentioned a number of areas that were *not* under the purview of inquisitions: "morality, social conflict, violence, and misbehavior (prime concerns for consistories) were in the Catholic countries the target for others: parish priests, religious orders, or confraternities. Parish clergy were meant to check on the seriously immoral, unfaithful, and faithless at least through the mandatory annual confession and communion." "Local Contexts and Regional Variations: Inquisitions," 36. In the same edited volume, Sara

Beam rightly observes, "Genevan residents during the 1550s and 1560s probably experienced far higher levels of fear that they would be punished for a wide range of sins than did most Spanish residents during the height of the Inquisition." "Consistories and Civil Authorities," in *Judging Faith*, ed. Parker and Starr-LeBeau, 71.

4. *Institutes* IV.xii.1, 2: 503; Denis, "Remplacer la confession," 174–75.

5. Thomas N. Tentler, *Sin and Confession on the Eve of the Reformation* (Princeton, NJ: Princeton University Press, 1977). In his work on late medieval France, Hervé Martin finds much to support Tentler's arguments; "Confession et contrôle social à la fin du Moyen Age," in *Pratiques de la confession*, 117–34. For changes in confession in Counter-Reformation Germany, see W. David Myers, *"Poor, Sinning Folk": Confession and Conscience in Counter-Reformation Germany* (Ithaca, NY: Cornell University Press, 1996). For an examination of normative sources on confession, see Jean Delumeau, *L'aveu et le pardon: Les difficultés de la confession XIIIe-XVIIIe siècle* (Paris: Fayard, 1990).

6. Lawrence G. Duggan, "Fear and Confession on the Eve of the Reformation," *Archiv für Reformationsgeschichte* 84 (1984): 153–75; Wietse de Boer, *The Conquest of the Soul: Confession, Discipline, and Public Order in Counter-Reformation Milan* (Leiden: Brill, 2001), 84–124.

7. As has been shown, petitions for readmission to the Supper were a very important exception to this rule.

8. See Kingdon, *Reforming Geneva*, 136.

9. Manetsch, *Calvin's Company*, 220.

10. Consistory registers provide far fewer examples than Inquisition records of women who tried to circumvent or rebel against the gendered restrictions placed upon them. If we look at the era of the French Revolution, there were only a few incidents in Revolutionary Geneva that bore even the slightest trace of feminism. In 1794 a Genevan Jacobin complained about the presence of women at the Great Fraternal Club, provoking the wrath of a host of female members who came close to beating him up; in 1797 a group of women proposed a new liturgy for marriage which "would better respect the rights of *homesses* [*sic*]"; Monter, "Women in Calvinist Geneva," 207n76. One can argue that the worst form of oppression is when subjugated groups accept the prevailing customs that relegate them to a subordinate status.

11. Ronnie Po-Chia Hsia, *Social Discipline in the Reformation* (New York: Routledge, 1989), 124.

12. Benedict, *Christ's Churches*, 489. See also Monter, conclusion to *Judging Faith*, ed. Parker and Starr-LeBeau, 335.

13. The following brief discussion owes much to the fruitful exchange of ideas with Amy Burnett, Mack Holt, John Thompson, and Tom Lambert.

14. See Burnett, *Yoke of Christ*.

15. Martin Luther, *The Small Catechism*, http://bookofconcord.org/smallcatechism.php#qanda.

16. John Calvin, *Catechism of the Church of Geneva*, https://reformed.org/documents/calvin/geneva_catachism/geneva_catachism.html.

17. Amy Nelson Burnett, *Debating the Sacraments: Print and Authority in the Early Reformation* (Oxford: Oxford University Press, 2019), esp. 56–70, 310–13.

18. Bernd Moeller, *Imperial Cities and the Reformation: Three Essays*, trans. and ed. H. C. Erik Midelfort and Mark U. Edwards Jr. (Durham, NC: Labyrinth Press, 1982), 46.

19. Moeller, *Imperial Cities*, 114.

20. Robert M. Kingdon, "Control of Morals," 12.

21. Kingdon, *Reforming Geneva*, 101. In his conclusion, he further wrote, "Despite some of the negative stereotypes of Calvin's Geneva when the power of the Consistory was at its peak, it would be fair to say that the pastors relied more on persuasion than on persecution." Kingdon, 137. Manetsch, however, asserts: "As a general rule the consistory served more as a church court than as a counseling service, but there were instances when the ministers offered consolation or encouragement to victims of abuse and misfortune." "Pastoral Care," 311.

22. The registers show that some people found being summoned before the Consistory a most intimidating prospect. A minister reported in February 1564 that the Consistory had been "calumniated" by unidentified individuals who blamed it for the recent suicide of Julienne Bocarde, who had drowned herself in the Rhône River, allegedly because she was distraught about having been summoned by the Consistory; AEG, R.Consist. 21: 3v.

23. John Knox, Letter to Anna Locke, December 9, 1556, in *The Works of John Knox*, ed. David Laing (Edinburgh: Bannatyne Club, 1855), vol. 4: 240; Benedict, "Calvin and the Transformation of Geneva," 11.

24. These findings lend some support to Gorski's claims that Calvinism's special emphasis on discipline contributed to the rise of the modern state; *Disciplinary Revolution*.

25. See Benedict, *Christ's Churches*, esp. 544–46.

26. Monter plausibly asserts, "One could easily argue that the spiritual weapon of excommunication had been strained to the point of diminishing returns by 1570. . . . Excommunicating over three hundred city people each year . . . yields a provisional average of at least one adult in 25 excommunicated every year, and perhaps one adult in fifteen summoned before the consistory every year. . . . [S]o many people were being excommunicated that the process must have lost a bit of its stigma and therefore a bit of its efficacy." "Consistory of Geneva," 484.

27. See Christian Grosse, "'Trop grande rigueur,'" 55–68; *Rituels*, 593–629; Bernard Lescaze, "'Funus Consistori, o miserere!': L'égalité de traitement devant le Consistoire de Genève autour de 1600," in *Sous l'œil*, ed. Tosato-Rigo and Staremberg Goy, 41–55; Manetsch, *Calvin's Company*, 211–14.

28. Benedict, *Christ's Churches*, 484–89. Benedict adds, "quantitative breakdowns of offenses computed from the archives of repression always contain a fundamental ambiguity. Do the levels of the offenses revealed testify to the actual frequency of the behavior in question? or to the degree to which it troubled those doing the repressing?" If there was a tenfold decrease in the number of cases of fornication, "is one to conclude that the church members became ten times more chaste? that the church's elders grew ten times

less vigilant about watching for this offense? or that the scribe of the consistory became ten times more solicitous of his neighbors' reputations?" Benedict, 461.

29. AEG, R.Consist. 35: 62v; quoted in Manetsch, *Calvin's Company*, 211. A greater portion of the Consistory's activities also concerned dancing, singing illicit songs, gambling, and excessive drinking.

30. Pinelli claimed, however, that this absence of swearing was actually a ruse by the devil to "deceive simple-minded people" with the "appearance of a reformed life." "Alcune cose più notabili e pericoli accaduti a me Luca Pinelli della Compagnia di Giesù" (1596), quoted in Manetsch, *Calvin's Company*, 182.

31. Valentin Andreae, *Respublica Christianopolitana* in Philip Schaff, *The Creeds of Christendom*, vol. 1 (repr. Grand Rapids, MI: Baker Books, 1985), 460; quoted in Manetsch, *Calvin's Company*, 185.

32. By contrast, Geoffrey Parker makes a persuasive argument that the dramatic decline in the number of prosecutions of illicit sexuality in Saint Andrews, Scotland, in the 1590s reflected a real drop in such activity. The draconian penalties apparently deterred people from having sex outside of marriage; "'Kirk By Law Established,'" 188–91. Other studies on Scottish and Dutch Reformed communities lend support to this argument, but the findings for Neuchâtel did not follow this trend; Benedict, *Christ's Churches*, 485; Watt, *Making Modern Marriage*, 99–101.

33. By the eighteenth century, the Consistory of Geneva was undeniably weaker than in the sixteenth century and concentrated on crimes of illicit sexuality; Grosse, "Inquisition and Consistory Records," 137–38.

34. William Monter has persuasively argued that the administrative history of Geneva probably would have pursued the exact same course if Calvin had never set foot in the Republic, "[e]xcept—and it is . . . an enormous 'except'—for the functioning of Calvin's Consistory and his Corps of Pastors. The Church of Geneva, embodied in these two peculiar institutions, was Calvin's creation and the locus of his vocation, the task which held him despite his will in a city which he personally disliked"; *Studies in Genevan Government*, 120.

35. Mentzer, "Local Contexts: Consistories," 26.

36. Benedict, *Christ's Churches*, 488–89. The greatest success of the Reformed discipline on a national level occurred in Scotland. On the basis of her perusal of the minutes of the kirk sessions, which she claimed were the greatest single means of nurturing a culture of Protestantism, Margo Todd insists that the Reformation introduced a revolutionary cultural change and enjoyed a rapid and profound success in Scotland. Rejecting the notion that Calvinism was merely an "abstract, intellectual religion of the elite" (Hsia, *Social Discipline*, 154), she claims that in Scotland it became "genuinely a religion of the people" and that within a couple of generations, Scotland was not just Protestant but also puritan; *Culture of Protestantism*, 83, 402–12.

Only works that are cited repeatedly in the notes or that contain information that is crucial to the argument or narrative are listed in this bibliography.

Archival Sources

Archives d'État de Genève, Geneva, Switzerland
État Civil: Livres des Baptêmes, Mariages et Morts
Juridictions Civiles R, causes matrimoniales, 1542–1582, 1783–1794
Juridictions Pénales A1: "Livre des informations prises contre ceulx de la faction de Perrin, Vandel et complices"
Juridictions Pénales A2: "Livre des Criminelz," i.e., sentences du Conseil, 1559–1561
Juridictions Pénales A3–1562, 1563, 1564: "Livre des Criminelz," i.e., sentences du Conseil, 1562–1564
Juridictions Pénales K1: "Rapports et Renvois du Consistoire, 1559–1797"
Manuscrits Historiques
Procès Criminels, 1ère et 2e Séries
Registres du Conseil
Registres du Conseil pour les affaires des Particuliers
Registres du Consistoire de Genève
Registres des criées et publications

Published Works

Benedict, Philip. *Christ's Churches Purely Reformed: A Social History of Calvinism*. New Haven, CT: Yale University Press, 2002.
———. *Season of Conspiracy: Calvin, the French Reformed Churches, and Protestant Plotting in the Reign of Francis II (1559–60)*. Philadelphia: American Philosophical Society Press, 2019.
Betteridge, Thomas, ed. *Sodomy in Early Modern Europe*. Manchester: Manchester University Press, 2007.
Binz, Louis. *Vie religieuse et réforme ecclésiastique dans le diocèse de Genève pendant le Grand Schisme*. Geneva: Jullien, 1973.
Bouwsma, William J. *Calvin: A Sixteenth Century Portrait*. Oxford: Oxford University Press, 1988.

Brodbeck, Thomas. "'Christliche Zucht' durch di Chorgerichte: Die Alltagspraxis der Sittenzucht." In *Berns mächtige Zeit: Das 16. und 17. Jahrhundert neu entdeckt*, 241–48. Edited by André Holenstein. Bern: Stämpfli Verlag, 2006.

Buisson, Ferdinand. *Sébastien Castellion: Sa vie et son oeuvre (1515–1563)*. Edited by Max Engammare. Geneva: Droz, 2010.

Burnett, Amy Nelson. *Debating the Sacraments: Print and Authority in the Early Reformation*. Oxford: Oxford University Press, 2019.

———. *The Yoke of Christ: Martin Bucer and Christian Discipline*. Kirksville, MO: Sixteenth Century Journal Publishers, 1994.

———, and Emidio Campi, eds. *A Companion to the Swiss Reformation*. Leiden: Brill, 2016.

Calvin, John. *Institutes of the Christian Religion*. 7th ed., 2 vols. Translated by John Allen. Philadelphia: Presbyterian Board of Christian Education, 1936.

———. *Ioannis Calvini Opera Quae Supersunt Omnia*. Edited by Gulielmus Baum, Eduardus Cunitz, and Eduardus Reus. Brunswick: C.A. Schwetschke and Sons, 1834–1968.

Cameron, Ewan. *Enchanted Europe: Superstition, Reason and Religion, 1250–1750*. Oxford: Oxford University Press, 2010.

Chareyre, Philippe. "Jeux interdits, jeux tolérés: L'application de la discipline réformée dans la France méridionale." In *Le plaisir et la transgression en France et en Espagne aux XVIᵉ et XVIIᵉ siècles: Colloque international organisé à l'Université de Pau et des Pays de l'Adour les 12 et 13 mai 2005*, 385–417. Edited by Maurice Daumas, Adrián Blázquez, Olivier Caporossi, and Philippe Chareyre. Orthez: Gascogne, 2007.

Le Collège de Genève 1559–1959: Mélanges historiques et littéraires. Geneva: Jullien, 1959.

Coram-Mekkey, Sandra, Christophe Chazalon, Catherine Santschi, Gilles-Olivier Bron, Paule Hochuli Dubuis, Amélie Isoz, Salomon Rizzo, François Longchamps, Sonia Vernhes Rappaz, eds. *Registres du Conseil de Genève à l'époque de Calvin, 1536–1542*. 7 vols. Geneva: Droz, 2003–2018.

Cressy, David. *Birth, Marriage, and Death: Ritual, Religion, and the Life-Cycle in Tudor and Stuart England*. Oxford: Oxford University Press, 1999.

Davis, Natalie Zemon. *Society and Culture in Early Modern France*. Stanford: Stanford University Press, 1975.

Del Col, Andrea. *L'Inquisizione in Italia: Dal XII al XXI secolo*. Milan: Mondadori, 2010.

———. "I processi dell'Inquisizione come fonte: Considerazioni diplomatiche e storiche." *Annuario dell'Istituto storico italiano per l'età moderna e contemporanea* 35/36 (1983–1984): 33–49.

Dentière, Marie. *Epistle to Marguerite de Navarre and Preface to a Sermon by John Calvin*. Translated and edited by Mary B. McKinley. Chicago: University of Chicago Press, 2004.

Doumergue, Émile. *Jean Calvin, les hommes et les choses de son temps*. 7 vols. Lausanne: G. Bridel, 1899–1927.

Elias, Norbert. *The History of Manners.* Translated by Edmund Jephcott. New York: Pantheon Books, 1982.

Engammare, Max. *L'ordre du temps: L'invention de la ponctualité au XVIe siècle.* Geneva: Droz, 2004.

Esmein, Adhémar. *Le mariage en droit canonique.* 2d ed., 2 vols. Paris: Librairie du Recueil Sirey, 1929.

Fazy, Henry, ed. *Procédures et documents du XVIe siècle (1546–1547).* Geneva and Basel: H. Georg, 1886.

Foucault, Michel. *Discipline and Punish: The Birth of the Prison.* Translated by Alan Sheridan. New York: Pantheon Books, 1977.

Fragonard, Marie-Madeleine, and Michel Perronet, eds. *Actes du VIIIe Colloque Jean Boisset: Catéchismes et Confessions de foi.* Montpellier: Université Paul Valéry, 1995.

Galiffe, Jacques Auguste, John-Barthélemy-Gaifre Galiffe, Eugène Ritter, and Louis Dufour-Vernes, eds. *Notices généalogiques sur les familles genevoises, depuis les premiers temps, jusqu'à nos jours.* 7 vols. Geneva: J. Barbezat, 1829–1895.

Gallatin, Marie-Lucile de. "Les ordonnances somptuaires à Genève au XVIe siècle." *Mémoires et documents publiés par la Société d'histoire et d'archéologie de Genève* 36 (1938): 193–272.

Gautier, Jean-Antoine. *Histoire de Genève, des origines à l'année 1691.* 7 vols. Geneva: Rey et Malavallon, 1896–1914.

Ginzburg, Carlo. "The Inquisitor as Anthropologist." In *Clues, Myths, and the Historical Method*, 141–48. Translated by John and Anne C. Tedeschi. Baltimore: Johns Hopkins University Press, 1989.

Gordon, Bruce. *Calvin.* New Haven, CT: Yale University Press, 2009.

Gorski, Philip S. *The Disciplinary Revolution: Calvinism and the Rise of the State in Early Modern Europe.* Chicago: University of Chicago Press, 2003.

Graham, Michael F. *The Uses of Reform: "Godly Discipline" and Popular Behavior in Scotland and Beyond, 1560–1610.* Leiden: Brill, 1996.

Grosse, Christian. "Les consistoires réformés et le pluralisme des instances de régulation des conflits (Genève, XVIe siècle)." In *Entre justice et justiciables: Les auxiliaires de la justice du Moyen Âge au XXe siècle*, 627–44. Edited by Claire Dolan. Quebec: Les Presses de l'Université de Laval, 2005.

———. *L'excommunication de Philibert Berthelier: Histoire d'un conflit d'identité aux premiers temps de la Réforme genevoise (1547–1555).* Geneva: Société d'Histoire et d'Archéologie de Genève, 1995.

———. "Aux origines des pratiques consistoriales de pacification des conflits: Le 'Conseil de paix,' (1527–1529)." In *Les registres du Conseil de la République de Genève sous l'Ancien Régime: Nouvelles approches, nouvelles perspectives*, 29–63. Edited by Sandra Coram-Mekkey. Geneva: Archives d'Etat de Genève and Fondation de l'Encyclopédie de Genève, 2009.

———. *Les rituels de la cène: Le culte eucharistique réformé à Genève (XVIe–XVIIe siècles).* Geneva: Droz, 2008.

Guggisberg, Hans R. *Sebastian Castellio, 1515–1563: Humanist and Defender of Religious Toleration in a Confessional Age*. Translated and edited by Bruce Gordon. Aldershot, England and Burlington, VT: Ashgate, 2002.

Haag, Eugène, and Emile Haag, eds. *La France protestante ou vies des protestants français*. 2d ed., 6 vols. Paris: Sandoz and Fischbacher, 1877–1888.

Haas, Louis. *The Renaissance Man and His Children: Childbirth and Early Childhood in Florence 1300–1600*. New York: Palgrave Macmillan, 1998.

Harrington, Joel F. *Reordering Marriage and Society in Reformation Germany*. Cambridge: Cambridge University Press, 1995.

Hardwick, Julie. *Family Business: Litigation and the Political Economies of Daily Life in Early Modern France*. Oxford: Oxford University Press, 2009.

Hendrix, Scott H., and Susan C. Karant-Nunn, eds. *Masculinity in the Reformation Era*. Kirksville, MO: Truman State University Press, 2008.

Hirzel, Martin Ernst, and Martin Sallmann, eds. *John Calvin's Impact on Church and Society, 1509–2009*. Grand Rapids, MI: William B. Eerdmans, 2009.

Hsia, Ronnie Po-Chia. *Social Discipline in the Reformation*. New York: Routledge, 1989.

Ingram, Martin. *Carnal Knowledge: Regulating Sex in England, 1470–1600*. Cambridge: Cambridge University Press, 2017.

Kamen, Henry. *The Spanish Inquisition: A Historical Revision*. 4th ed. New Haven, CT: Yale University Press, 2014.

Karant-Nunn, Susan. *Reformation of Ritual: An Interpretation of Early Modern Germany*. London: Routledge, 1997.

Kingdon, Robert M. *Adultery and Divorce in Calvin's Geneva*. Cambridge, MA: Harvard University Press, 1995.

———. "Catechesis in Calvin's Geneva." In *Educating People of Faith: Exploring the History of Jewish and Christian Communities*, 294–313. Edited by John van Engen. Grand Rapids, MI: William B. Eerdmans, 2007.

———. "The Control of Morals in Calvin's Geneva." In *The Social History of the Reformation*, 3–16. Edited by Lawrence P. Buck and Jonathan W. Zophy. Columbus: Ohio State University Press, 1972.

———. "La discipline ecclésiastique vue de Zurich et Genève au temps de la réformation: l'usage de Matthieu 18, 15–17 par les réformateurs." *Revue de théologie et de philosophie* 51 (2001): 343–55.

———. "The Genevan Revolution in Public Worship." *Princeton Seminary Bulletin* 20 (1999): 264–80.

———, (with Thomas M. Lambert). *Reforming Geneva: Discipline, Faith, and Anger in Calvin's Geneva*. Geneva: Droz, 2012.

———, and Jean-François Bergier, eds. *Registres de la Compagnie des Pasteurs de Genève au temps de Calvin, 1546–1553*. 2 vols. Geneva: Droz, 1962–1964.

———. "Social Welfare in Calvin's Geneva." *American Historical Review* 76 (1971): 50–69.

Köhler, Walther. *Zürcher Ehegericht und Genfer Konsistorium*. 2 vols. Leipzig: M. Heinsius Nachfolger, 1932–1942.

Lambert, Thomas A. "Cette loi ne durera guère: Inertie religieuse et espoirs catholiques à Genève au temps de la Réforme." *Bulletin de la Société d'Histoire et d'Archéologie de Genève* 23/24 (1993–1994): 5–24.

———. "Preaching, Praying and Policing the Reform in Sixteenth-Century Geneva." Ph.D. diss., University of Wisconsin-Madison, 1998.

Lipscomb, Suzannah. "Crossing Boundaries: Women's Gossip, Insults and Violence in Sixteenth-Century France." *French History* 25 (2011): 408–26

Maag, Karin. "The Spectre of Ignorance: The Provision of Education in the Swiss Cities." In *Fear in Early Modern Society*, 137–49. Edited by William G. Naphy and Penny Roberts. Manchester: Manchester University Press, 1997.

Manetsch, Scott M. *Calvin's Company of Pastors: Pastoral Care and the Emerging Reformed Church, 1536–1609*. Oxford: Oxford University Press, 2013.

———. "Pastoral Care East of Eden: The Consistory of Geneva, 1569–82," *Church History* 75 (2006): 274–313.

McKee, Elsie Anne. *The Pastoral Ministry and Worship in Calvin's Geneva*. Geneva: Droz, 2016.

Mentzer, Raymond A. *La construction de l'identité réformée aux XVIᵉ et XVIIᵉ siècles: Le rôle des consistoires*. Paris: Honoré Champion, 2006.

———, ed. *Sin and the Calvinists: Morals Control and the Consistory in the Reformed Tradition*. Kirksville, MO: Sixteenth Century Journal Publishers, 1994.

———, Françoise Moreil, and Philippe Chareyre, eds. *Dire l'interdit: The Vocabulary of Censure and Exclusion in the Early Modern Reformed Tradition*. Leiden: Brill, 2010.

Moeller, Bernd. *Imperial Cities and the Reformation: Three Essays*. Translated and edited by H. C. Erik Midelfort and Mark U. Edwards Jr. Durham, NC: Labyrinth Press, 1982.

Monter, E. William. "The Consistory of Geneva, 1559–1569." *Bibliothèque d'Humanisme et Renaissance* 38 (1976): 467–84.

———. "Sodomy and Heresy in Early Modern Switzerland." *Journal of Homosexuality* 6 (1981): 41–55.

———. *Studies in Genevan Government (1536–1605)*. Geneva: Droz, 1964.

———. *Witchcraft in France and Switzerland: The Borderlands during the Reformation*. Ithaca, NY: Cornell University Press, 1976.

———. "Women in Calvinist Geneva (1550–1800)." *Signs* 6 (1980): 189–209.

Mottu-Weber, Liliane. *Économie et Refuge à Genève au siècle de la Réforme: La draperie et la soierie (1540–1630)*. Geneva: Société d'histoire et d'archéologie de Genève, 1987.

———, Anne-Marie Piuz, and Bernard Lescaze. *Vivre à Genève autour de 1600*. 2 vols. Geneva: Slatkine, 2006.

Muir, Edward. *Ritual in Early Modern Europe*. Cambridge: Cambridge University Press, 1997.

Naef, Henri. *Les origines de la Réforme à Genève.* 2 vols. Geneva: Droz, 1968.

Naphy, William G. "Baptisms, Church Riots and Social Unrest in Calvin's Geneva." *Sixteenth Century Journal* 26 (1995): 87–97.

———. *Calvinism and the Consolidation of the Genevan Reformation.* Manchester: Manchester University Press, 1994.

———. "The Reformation and the Evolution of Geneva's Schools." In *Reformations Old and New: Essays on the Socio-Economic Impact of Religious Change, c. 1470–1630,* 185–202. Edited by Beat Kümin. Aldershot, England and Burlington, VT: Scolar Press and Ashgate, 1996.

Oestreich, Gerhard. *Neostoicism and the Early Modern State.* Translated by David McLintock. Edited by Brigitta Oestreich and H. G. Koenigsberger. Cambridge: Cambridge University Press, 1982.

Olson, Jeannine E. *Calvin and Social Welfare: Deacons and the "Bourse française."* Selinsgrove, PA: Susquehanna University Press, 1989.

Ozment, Steven. *When Fathers Ruled: Family Life in Reformation Europe.* Cambridge, MA: Harvard University Press, 1983.

Parker, Charles H. *The Reformation of Community: Social Welfare and Calvinist Charity in Holland, 1572–1620.* Cambridge: Cambridge University Press, 1998.

———, and Gretchen Starr-LeBeau, eds. *Judging Faith, Punishing Sin: Inquisitions and Consistories in the Early Modern World.* Cambridge: Cambridge University Press, 2017.

Perrenoud, Alfred. *La population de Genève du seizième au début du dix-neuvième siècle: Étude démographique.* Geneva: Société d'histoire et d'archéologie de Genève, 1979.

Phillips, Roderick. *Putting Asunder: A History of Divorce in Western Society.* Cambridge: Cambridge University Press, 1988.

Pitkin, Barbara. "'The Heritage of the Lord': Children in the Theology of John Calvin." In *The Child in Christian Thought,* 160–93. Edited by Marcia J. Bunge. Grand Rapids: William B. Eerdmans, 2000.

Piuz, Anne-Marie, and Liliane Mottu-Weber, eds. *L'économie genevoise de la Réforme à la fin de l'Ancien Régime, XVIᵉ–XVIIIᵉ siècles.* Geneva: Georg, 1990.

Pollmann, Judith. "Off the Record: Problems in the Quantification of Calvinist Church Discipline." *Sixteenth Century Journal* 33 (2002): 423–38.

Prosperi, Adriano. *Tribunali della coscienza: Inquisitori, confessori, missionari.* Turin: Giulio Einaudi, 1996.

Reinburg, Virginia. "Liturgy and Laity in Late Medieval and Reformation France." *Sixteenth Century Journal* 23 (1992): 526–46.

Rieder, Philip. "Miracles and Heretics: Protestants and Catholic Healing Practices in and around Geneva 1530–1750." *Social History of Medicine* 23 (2010): 227–43.

Reinhard, Wolfgang. "Pressures towards Confessionalization? Prolegomena to a Theory of the Confessional Age." In *The German Reformation,* 172–92. Edited by C. Scott Dixon. Oxford: Blackwell, 1999.

Rittgers, Ronald K. *The Reformation of the Keys: Confession, Conscience, and Authority in Sixteenth-Century Germany.* Cambridge, MA: Harvard University Press, 2004.

Rivoire, Émile, and Victor van Berchem, eds. *Les sources du droit du canton de Genève.* 4 vols. Aarau: H.R. Sauerländer, 1927–1935.

Robert, Michèle. *"Que dorénavant chacun fuie paillardise, oisiveté, gourmandize…": Réforme et contrôle des moeurs: La justice consistoriale dans le Pays de Neuchâtel (1547–1848).* Neuchâtel: Alphil-Presses universitaires suisses, 2016.

Roget, Amédée. *Histoire du peuple de Genève depuis la Réforme jusqu'à l'Escalade.* 7 vols. Geneva: Jullien, 1870–1883 [repr. Nieuwkoop: B. de Graaf, 1976].

Roper, Lyndal. *The Holy Household: Women and Morals in Reformation Augsburg.* Oxford: Oxford University Press, 1989.

Roussel, Bernard. "'Faire la Cène' dans les Eglises réformées du Royaume de France au seizième siècle (ca. 1550–ca. 1575)." *Archives de sciences sociales des religions* 85 (1994): 99–119.

Ruggiero, Guido. *The Boundaries of Eros: Sex, Crime and Sexuality in Renaissance Venice.* Oxford: Oxford University Press, 1985.

Safley, Thomas Max. *Let No Man Put Asunder: The Control of Marriage in the German Southwest: A Comparative Study, 1550–1600.* Kirksville, MO: Sixteenth Century Journal Publishers, 1984.

Schilling, Heinz. *Civic Calvinism in Northwestern Germany and the Netherlands: Sixteenth to Nineteenth Centuries.* Kirksville, MO: Sixteenth Century Journal Publishers, 1991.

Schmidt, Heinrich Richard. *Dorf und Religion: Reformierte Sittenzucht in Berner Landgemeinden der frühen Neuzeit.* Stuttgart: G. Fischer, 1995.

———. "Morals Courts in Rural Berne during the Early Modern Period." In *The Reformation in Eastern and Central Europe,* 155–81. Edited by Karin Maag. Aldershot and Burlington, VT: Scolar Press and Ashgate, 1997.

Schutte, Anne Jacobson. *Aspiring Saints: Pretense of Holiness, Inquisition, and Gender in the Republic of Venice, 1618–1750.* Baltimore: Johns Hopkins University Press, 2001.

Scribner, Robert W. *Popular Culture and Popular Movements in Reformation Germany.* London: Hambledon Press, 1987.

Seeger, Cornelia. *Nullité de mariage, divorce et séparation de corps à Genève au temps de Calvin: Fondements doctrinaux, loi et jurisprudence.* Lausanne: Société d'histoire de la Suisse romande, 1989.

Spierling, Karen E. *Infant Baptism in Reformation Geneva: The Shaping of Community, 1536–1564.* Aldershot and Burlington, VT: Ashgate, 2005.

———, Erik de Boer, and R. Ward Holder, eds. *Emancipating Calvin: Culture and Confessional Identity in Francophone Reformed Communities. Essays in Honor of Raymond A. Mentzer.* Leiden: Brill, 2018.

Strauss, Gerald. *Luther's House of Learning: Indoctrination of the Young in the German Reformation.* Baltimore: Johns Hopkins University Press, 1978.

Tentler, Thomas N. *Sin and Confession on the Eve of the Reformation*. Princeton, NJ: Princeton University Press, 1977.

Todd, Margo. *Culture of Protestantism in Early Modern Scotland*. New Haven, CT: Yale University Press, 2002.

Tosato-Rigo, Danièle, and Nicole Staremberg Goy, eds. *Sous l'oeil du consistoire: Sources consistoriales et histoire du contrôle sous l'Ancien Régime*. Lausanne: Études de Lettres, 2004.

Valeri, Mark. "Religion, Discipline, and the Economy in Calvin's Geneva." *Sixteenth Century Journal* 28 (1997): 123–42.

van den Brink, Gijsbert, and Harro M. Höpfl, eds. *Calvinism and the Making of the European Mind*. Leiden: Brill, 2014.

Wandel, Lee Palmer. *The Eucharist in the Reformation: Incarnation and Liturgy*. Cambridge: Cambridge University Press, 2006.

Watt, Isabella M., Thomas A. Lambert (vols. 1–5), Jeffrey R. Watt (vols. 6–14), and M. Wallace McDonald (vols. 2, 9), eds. *Registres du Consistoire de Genève au temps de Calvin, 1542–1557*. With the collaboration of Jeffrey R. Watt (vol. 1), M. Wallace McDonald (vols. 3–8), and James S. Coons (vol. 9). Under the supervision of Robert M. Kingdon (vols. 1–6) and Lee Palmer Wandel (vols. 8–9). 14 vols. Geneva: Droz, 1996–2020.

Watt, Jeffrey R. *Choosing Death: Suicide and Calvinism in Early Modern Geneva*. Kirksville, MO: Truman State University Press, 2001.

———. *The Making of Modern Marriage: Matrimonial Control and the Rise of Sentiment in Neuchâtel, 1550–1800*. Ithaca, NY: Cornell University Press, 1992.

———. *The Scourge of Demons: Possession, Lust, and Witchcraft in a Seventeenth-Century Italian Convent*. Rochester, NY: University of Rochester Press, 2009.

———. "Women and the Consistory in Calvin's Geneva." *Sixteenth Century Journal* 24 (1993): 429–39.

Weber, Max. *The Protestant Ethic and the "Spirit" of Capitalism and Other Writings*. Translated and edited by Peter Baehr and Gordon C. Wells. New York: Penguin, 2002. First published 1905 by Unwin Hyman (London).

Wiesner, Merry E. *Women and Gender in Early Modern Europe*. Cambridge: Cambridge University Press, 1993.

INDEX

Page numbers in italics indicate illustrations.

Printed and bound by CPI Group (UK) Ltd, Croydon, CR0 4YY

07/07/2026

14916224-0003